Money and the Real Economy

Money and the Real Economy

Sheen Liu
Washington State University, USA

World Scientific

NEW JERSEY • LONDON • SINGAPORE • BEIJING • SHANGHAI • TAIPEI • CHENNAI

Published by

World Scientific Publishing Co. Pte. Ltd.

5 Toh Tuck Link, Singapore 596224

USA office: 27 Warren Street, Suite 401-402, Hackensack, NJ 07601

UK office: 57 Shelton Street, Covent Garden, London WC2H 9HE

Library of Congress Cataloging-in-Publication Data
Names: Liu, Sheen author http://id.loc.gov/authorities/names/n2025014120
http://id.loc.gov/rwo/agents/n2025014120
Title: Money and the real economy / Sheen Liu, Washington State University, USA.
Description: New Jersey : World Scientific, [2027] | Includes bibliographical references and index.
Identifiers: LCCN 2025013924 | ISBN 9789819814992 hardcover |
ISBN 9789819815005 ebook | ISBN 9789819815012 ebook other
Subjects: LCSH: Money http://id.loc.gov/authorities/subjects/sh85086790 |
Finance, Personal http://id.loc.gov/authorities/subjects/sh85048263 |
Economics http://id.loc.gov/authorities/subjects/sh85040850
Classification: LCC HG220.A2 .L587 2027 | DDC 332.4--dc23/eng/20250626
LC record available at https://lccn.loc.gov/2025013924

British Library Cataloguing-in-Publication Data
A catalogue record for this book is available from the British Library.

For any available supplementary material, please visit
https://www.worldscientific.com/worldscibooks/10.1142/14361#t=suppl

Desk Editors: Soundararajan Raghuraman/Geysilla Jean

Typeset by Stallion Press
Email: enquiries@stallionpress.com

For my wife,
Jingling,
softly mingling
with my keyboard clinking.

Preface

I have been teaching finance—teaching money—for over twenty years. Yet I have consistently found that finance textbooks often assume that money is so familiar that it needs no explanation. When I ask my undergraduate and graduate students this very question, their answers vary widely. While addressing this question without delving into economics is challenging, economics itself, particularly in models such as IS-LM, often treats money as self-explanatory. Despite various theories of money, old and new, economists remain divided. This unsettled question is what inspired the exploration within this book.

Money is everywhere in the economy, but its true nature is often hidden, like salt dissolved in water. This book aims to uncover it. It first considers the real economy independently of money, then reintroduces money step by step to evaluate its effects. Because the real economy is about physical processes and money today, is a social invention, the book explores both natural and social domains that lie beyond the usual scope of finance and economics.

This book begins by tackling a simple question: How does the real economy function autonomously, devoid of money and interference from governments or central banks? Though laissez-faire capitalism remains a subject of economic debate, Chapter 1 presents a negative answer through system stability analysis. This chapter introduces the Hamiltonian, a concept that may be the most challenging material in this book; however, its mathematics is kept at an undergraduate level, limited to calculus and linear algebra. Rather than relegating the math to an appendix, it is integrated into the main text to keep the discussion accessible.

The math in the book prioritizes intuition over rigorous proof. To make the math easy to follow for less mathematically inclined readers, it is kept as simple as possible, with certain tedious steps retained—a deliberate choice in line with Ludwig Boltzmann's advice: "Matters of elegance ought to be left to the tailor and to the cobbler." This philosophy underpins the writing throughout; grasping the core ideas of Chapter 1 will make the rest of the book, built upon the Hamiltonian, much more accessible.

Chapter 2 identifies three forms of money: commodity money (e.g., gold and silver), currency, and credit/debt. While governments create *currencies*, banks create *credit/debt*, which dominates today's economy. This chapter compares the theories of influential economists and philosophers regarding these forms of money, demonstrating the role of credit/debt with a simple example. Readers with a liberal arts background may find this chapter an ideal starting point.

Chapter 3 reintroduces money into the economy. For an above-normal money supply to exert a real effect, the real economy must possess available inventory. Within these limits, more money can *directly* influence the real economy. Conversely, once inventory is exhausted, additional money affects the economy solely through *indirect* means.

Financial and real asset markets are the playground of money. Money generates assets, creating *wealth*, and its continuous flow sustains these markets. Beyond the *primary* market, where individuals directly provide funds to firms for the purchase of *working* assets, idle assets are traded in other markets. The money flow has only *indirect effects* on the real economy through the *wealth effect* on asset holders. Chapter 4 defines the working and idle assets and provides a brief discussion of financial and selected trading strategies.

Governments create currency and profit from seigniorage. They also redistribute money within the economy through taxation and government programs. Chapter 5 examines how taxes—such as income, corporate, sales, and capital gains taxes—together with government programs impact the real economy.

Imbalances in real economies create importing and exporting countries, with currencies playing a central role in international trade. Countries often manipulate their currencies to gain advantages. Chapter 6 reviews free trade theory and examines the currency games between nations, which carry the risk from trade disputes to full-scale trade wars.

While the real economy produces limited tangible goods, money is limitless. Thus, money measures exchange value, but not economic value. Chapter 7 introduces the work theory of value, identifying work—a form of energy—as the driving force of the real economy and grounding economic progress in thermodynamics. The work theory of value addresses the central question raised in Chapter 1: how to measure aggregate real goods and the real economy. It also explores the implications of energy shortages and artificial intelligence in an economy increasingly dominated by the service sector.

Readers with a science or engineering background may prefer to start with Chapters 1 and 7. Those with a math background might focus on the mathematical models that form the book's skeleton and then explore specific sections to put flesh on the math. For readers pressed for time, skipping the math won't detract from understanding, as the material is intuitive, and math simply offers a more precise language.

This book offers a broad overview of money and economy, revisiting older, seemingly "outdated" ideas rather than focusing on recent theories. While its scope precludes a deep dive into specific developments, references are provided for further reading. Given that modern tools such as the Internet and AI can supply detailed information at any time, an outline suffices to communicate the central concepts. For this reason, the material in this book is brief, ensuring it does not become overly long. The discussion draws chiefly on anecdotal and historical evidence rather than extensive statistical analyses of "big data."

The book's aim is to reach beyond professionals, because the compartmentalization of knowledge limits a comprehensive grasp of money and the economy. By integrating insights from other disciplines, it encourages readers to connect the ideas to their own experiences and develop answers to contemporary financial and economic challenges, identifying the hidden rules behind the observations and linking the micro to the macro world (see Appendix to Chapter 1, A.3.3). Everyone must manage their own finances, and money creation and tax policies affect people from all walks of life. It is therefore vital that citizens understand these issues and use their collective power to influence economic decisions.

Sheen Liu

About the Author

Sheen Liu is Professor Emeritus at Washington State University. He earned a PhD in finance, an MBA and a master's degree in computer science from Syracuse University, as well as a PhD in mechanical engineering from MIT. His research in finance focuses on asset pricing and taxation, and he has published more than 30 journal articles, including in the *Journal of Financial Economics*, *Management Science*, and the *Journal of Heat Transfer*. His scholarship has been recognized with several honors, including the Peter L. Bernstein Award for Best Paper of the *Institutional Investor Journals* and the Best Paper Award from the *American Society of Mechanical Engineers, Heat Transfer Division.*

Contents

List of Figures

List of Tables

Chapter 1

The Real Economy

The economy is a physical system that exists to meet human physiological needs. Economics remains a frontier of knowledge because millions of people still suffer from malnutrition, and homelessness continues to plague our streets. While various projects are at the forefront of science and technology—such as quantum supercomputing, gene editing, advanced medical technologies, space exploration, artificial intelligence (AI), and climate research—they do little to address these critical issues. The space program searches for planets that might serve as a new Earth, yet large-scale human migration to other planets is improbable. If another biblical flood were to occur, building an economy on the ocean would be more feasible than colonizing Mars.[1]

As AI continues to advance, a prominent concern is its potential to displace human workers, leading to anxieties about large-scale job

[1]Archaeologists discovered a 7th century B.C. tablet written in cuneiform, the writing system used in Mesopotamia. The tablet contained a record of the Ark, which is a round-shaped boat used by the Babylonians, referred to as a "gopher" in Arabic (Genesis 6:14). The boat measured 3,600 m^2 in area and stood seven meters high, with animals housed beneath the deck and a small house on top of the gopher (Smith (1880); *The Ark Before Noah, Decoding the Story of the Flood* by Dr. Irving Finkel, Megalithomania UK, retrieved on December 19, 2024). Additionally, in the Epic of Gilgamesh, written as early as 2100 B.C., Utnapishtim constructed a vessel, the "ark," to protect life from a devastating flood (George, 1999). The early Chinese encyclopedia *Huainanzi*, written in 136 B.C., also contains a legend about the flood. According to the legend, the heavens were once shattered, causing a disastrous flood. The goddess Nüwa repaired the sky.

losses. But we should also ask: Why is it not a benefit for robots to take over human labor? We address these questions head-on.

Governments and central banks have long tried to solve economic problems with money. Money is deeply embedded in people's lives: Individuals strive to earn it, businesses produce goods for profit, and governments levy taxes upon it. The idea of separating money from the economy—which supports essential needs like food and housing—may seem impossible, but like untangling a knot, the right approach can gradually loosen it, while the wrong one can make it more entangled. Finding the right starting point is crucial.

This book adopts René Descartes' method of organizing thoughts: "starting with the simplest and easiest to know, ascending little by little, and, step by step, to more complex knowledge." If this approach proves insufficient, economics and finance might turn to other philosophical insights. As Noam Chomsky observed, "The greatest progress is in the sciences that study the simplest systems. Physics has an advantage in that if something gets too complicated, they hand it to someone else."

1.1 Real Economy

All living organisms have biological requirements for survival. The economy is how humans differentiate themselves from other life forms by coordinating activities to meet these biological needs. According to Maslow's hierarchy of needs,[2] physiological needs are at the base of the pyramid. Only after these basic needs for food, clothing, and shelter are met can people pursue safety needs, such as job security and national security. After these come the needs for love and belonging and finally, esteem and self-actualization. Without sufficient production of essentials—food, clothing, and shelter—Maslow's pyramid collapses, leading to instability in the entire structure of human society.

---

[2]Maslow's hierarchy of needs is not a scientific principle but rather a conceptual framework describing how individuals prioritize their motivations. According to this framework, the first four levels of needs - *Deficiency Motivation* - must be met before an individual experiences the *Metaneeds* (and the later addition *Transcendence Need*). These higher-level needs are largely psychological (Maslow, 1971).

The economy functions as a system to provide for people's physiological needs and, to some extent, their psychological desires, such as through the availability of luxury goods. The term "real economy," as used here, diverges from its conventional definition. The real economy encompasses essential sectors that provide food, housing, and necessary industrial goods, serving as the backbone of the entire economic system. Importantly, it is crucial to measure the real economy without the influence of money, which acts like a liquid pH meter that alters the very solution it seeks to assess. Money has the potential to distort economic realities.

1.1.1 *The controversy of real output*

The concept of an aggregate of real goods, or real output, is controversial. John Maynard Keynes strongly opposed this concept: "But the proper place for such things as net real output and the general level of prices lies within the field of historical and statistical description, and their purpose should be to satisfy historical or social curiosity, a purpose for which perfect precision—such as our causal analysis requires, whether or not our knowledge of the actual values of the relevant quantities is complete or exact—is neither usual nor necessary (Keynes, 1936)." Keynes provided the reasons for his opposition:

(1) "...it is a grave objection to this definition for such a purpose that the community's output of goods and services is a non-homogeneous complex which cannot be measured, ...
(2) The difficulty is even greater when, in order to calculate net output, we try to measure the net addition to capital equipment, for we have to find some basis for a quantitative comparison between the new items of equipment produced during the period and the old items which have perished by wastage. But, until a satisfactory system of units has been adopted, its precise definition is an impossible task..."—Keynes (1936).

Keynes even ridiculed attempts to compare real outputs across time, likening them to claims such as, "Queen Victoria was a better queen but not a happier woman than Queen Elizabeth." He argued that relying on such vague concepts as the basis of quantitative analysis would lead to "mock precision." Despite this, Keynes himself occasionally aggregated real goods, when necessary, such as when he measured "real balances": "In my *Tract on Monetary Reform* [*JMK,* vol. IV] (Chapter III, §I) I measured real balances by what I called 'consumption units,' namely units 'made up of a collection of specified quantities of their (the public's) standard articles of consumption or other objects of expenditure';..." (Keynes, 1930).[3]

Keynes' reluctance to accept aggregates of real goods was parallel to operationalism, a doctrine that defines scientific concepts in terms of measurable operations. Percy Williams Bridgman, a physicist who coined operationalism: "We mean by any concept nothing more than a set of operations; the concept is synonymous with the corresponding set of operations" (Bridgman *et al.*, 1927).[4] He rejected any concept that could not be measured as a *scientific* concept.

Various real goods must share a common property to be measurable as a bundle. However, weight and volume do not serve as economic measures of real goods. As Karl Marx noted, this common property "cannot be either a geometrical, a chemical, or any other natural property of commodities" (Marx, 2005). The search for an economic measure of real goods has been a central quest for economists.

1.1.1.1 *Economic holy grail*

The early classical economists sought the economic "holy grail"—the determinants of wealth. Marx's first sentence in *Capital, Volume I* reads as follows: "The wealth of societies in which the capitalist mode of production prevails appears as 'an immense accumulation of commodities,' its unit being a single commodity," which underlying value is labor time. The classical economists did not stop at the common belief that wealth is simply money; they delved deeper into what determines the value of a commodity. Despite their efforts,

[3]Keynes himself had a lengthy discussion on various methods: direct, indirect, "highest common factor" methods, the method of limits, the "crossing of formulae," the chain method to estimate aggregates of real goods, the composite commodity, consumption standard, wholesale standard, international standard, index numbers, currency standard, and the purchasing power of money based on the aggregates (Keynes, 1930). The key difference is that he still measured aggregates with money and fixed the percentages of the goods in the aggregates.

[4]Percy Williams Bridgman was a physicist at Harvard University whose pioneering work in the physics of high pressures earned him the Nobel Prize in 1946.

their investigation encountered an obstacle stemming from lack of the concept of *economic* value (see Chapter 7).

Adam Smith was the first to contend that in a primitive economy, where capital stock (such as equipment and machines) is minimal, the number of labor hours is the primary economic measure of goods. As economies advanced and capital stock became an essential part of production, Smith recognized that laborers had to share the fruits of their labor with the owners of the capital stock that employed them: "The whole produce of labour does not always belong to the labourer. He must in most cases share it with the owner of the stock which employs him" (Whitaker, 1904).

In more advanced economies, David Ricardo expanded on this idea by considering not only the labor hours embedded in a commodity's production but also the labor required to produce the capital stock and raw materials. He argued, "In fixing on the quantity of labour realized in commodities as the rule which governs their relative value, we are in the right course" (Sraffa and Dobb, 1951).

However, Ricardo faced challenges with the variability in commodity prices and acknowledged, "Perhaps I should find the difficulties nearly as great in this view of the subject as in that which I have adopted" (Sraffa and Dobb, 1951).[5]

Marx's labor theory of value represents the culmination of this incomplete search for the determinant of value. He argued that money represents the quantity of congealed labor time and that the price of a commodity reflects the labor required to produce it. Keynes expressed sympathy for Marx's labor theory, agreeing with the pre-classical view that "everything is produced by labour." Both Marx and Keynes recognized the constant fluctuation of prices, attributing the deviations to the law of supply and demand.

Since Léon Walras introduced general equilibrium theory in the late 19th century, fewer economists have adhered to the labor theory

[5]Ricardo viewed labor as an "invariable measure of value" in commodities but struggled with relative measures: "The relative value of commodities was regulated by two causes instead of one, namely, by the relative quantity of labour necessary to produce the commodities in question, and by the rate of profit for the time that the capital remained dormant, and until the commodities were brought to market" (also see the work of Sinha, 2010).

of value. General equilibrium seemingly resolved the issue of commodity prices by demonstrating how prices are determined simultaneously through the complex interdependence of supply and demand across all markets.

Nonetheless, Keynes was erroneous in asserting that one cannot discuss an exact quantity of goods without money. Even without a unique measure for different real goods, "the aggregate of real goods" remains a valid scientific concept. In fact, the principle of operationalism has since been abandoned by the scientific community. Physics, for example, uses concepts such as mass and gravitational force, which lack direct operational procedures for measurement (Lindsay, 1937). Even Bridgman later acknowledged the limitations of operationalism, stating: "The scientific method, as far as it is a method, is nothing more than doing one's damnedest with one's mind, no holds barred" (Bridgman, 1953).

We adopt the concepts of "aggregates of real goods" and "real output" as scientific concepts and examine the real economy as the starting point to untangle the knot intertwined with money. Chapter 7 will present a theory of *economic* value, establishing it as the key metric for measuring both individual and aggregate goods and the overall performance of an economy.

1.1.2 *The identity of real economy*

Core economic questions are often framed in monetary terms. Keynes, for example, illustrated the problem of over-saving with a parable about banana plantations (Keynes, 1930).[6] In this section, we identify the key components of a real economy in the absence of money, using an isolated farm as the simplest model of a closed real economy. The farm grows a single crop, keeping a portion of the output as seeds (its investment) while consuming the remainder.

The term "investment in seeds" fits intuitively in this setting. In this simplified economy with only one good, the capital stock and the consumption good are the same: the crop. The farm can either consume its crop or save part of it as seeds for the next season's planting. In a more complex, industrialized economy, capital goods

[6]Keynes' distinction between monetary consumption and monetary investment led to different conclusions, as the consumption and investment measured by money can differ from real consumption and investment.

and consumption goods are distinct, but they can be exchanged for one another.

Seeds are a unique form of capital stock due to their short lifespan of just one season, whereas machines, equipment, and factories have multi-year lifespans. Economically speaking, seeds have a 100% depreciation rate per season. Capital stock—machines, equipment, and production facilities—gradually wears out, ages, or becomes obsolete. The resulting reduction in capital stock due to this process is defined as depreciation.[7] For an annual crop, the depreciation rate $\delta = 1$.

The relationship between consumption (C), investment (I), and output (Y) in this farming economy is straightforward:

$$C + I \leq Y. \tag{1.1}$$

Here, total consumption represents the aggregate demand of all households, total savings represent the aggregate investment in seeds, and total output is the aggregate production of the farm. The $\leq$ sign indicates that the sum of consumption and investment may be less than or equal to output, as waste reduces the amount of output available for either use. Waste is a constant factor in any economy, taking forms physical material byproducts and operational inefficiencies.

Normal economic theories often ignore waste, and supply is assumed to equal demand: Supply (output) is automatically matched by demand (consumption and investment).[8] As David Ricardo asserted in his critique of Malthus, "Demand depends only on supply." Keynes described this as Say's Law: "supply creates its own demand."[9] Say's Law assumes that supply inherently generates

[7]Depreciation generally only applies to durable assets. Durable assets are designed to last for an extended period, though there is no universal definition of how long. Consumer durables, a subset of durable goods, typically last at least three years. The Bureau of Economic Analysis defines durable goods as products purchased by households for nonbusiness use, with a life expectancy of at least three years. For private business and government, equipment is defined as goods with a life expectancy of at least one year. The EPA also defines durable goods as items with a lifespan of three years or more, though some exceptions apply.

[8]Supply and demand determine the price of a specific good. Walrasian equilibrium simultaneously determines prices of multiple goods, and the market clears.

[9]Jean-Baptiste Say introduced the law in his *Traité d'économie politique* in 1803, but he also accepted the possibility of a "general glut" of unsold goods. Keynesian economists do not accept Say's Law because money has no role in the law itself.

demand, Ricardo assumed that nobody wastes labor producing something nobody wants. People have purified water because of pollution and have made safe drinking water a commodity. Ricardo's supply includes both consumption and capital goods.

If we replace the $\leq$ sign with an equal sign, Eq. (1.1) becomes:

$$I = Y - C, \tag{1.2}$$

which is the macroeconomic identity. However, this identity is subject to interpretation. In conventional macroeconomics, it is interpreted as a balance of monetary flows, as Keynes did. In this book, we use the following notation for monetary balance as:

$$P_I I = P_Y Y - P_C C, \tag{1.3}$$

where I, Y, and C are real investment, real output, and real consumption, and P_i is the price of good i.

If output, consumption, and investment all share the same price P, then the price P_i cancels out in Eq. (1.3), reducing Eq. (1.3) to Eq. (1.2). This illustrates the concept known as the "classical dichotomy," which posits that real economic variables govern the behavior of the economy, while money only influences the price level (Beenstock and Ilek, 2010).

The classical dichotomy can be likened to measuring a box with various units of length, such as meters or feet. Regardless of whether the units are long or short, the choice of measurement does not affect the outcome. The French Academy of Science once used a platinum–iridium bar to define the meter. Today, the meter is tied to the speed of light, making it a universally consistent standard. Measuring a box with either SI units or Imperial units yields the same size.

However, money is not such a measure. It once served as a "gold ruler," anchoring the value of goods. After the gold standard was abandoned, however, this ruler became more elastic—like a rubber band—stretching or shrinking as the money supply changes or currency exchange rates fluctuates.

In addition, central banks and governments have no control over the relative prices of output, consumption goods, and investment goods. Different goods have different prices and their "rubber bands" stretch and shrink at different rates.

When we interpret I, Y, and C as real goods, the macroeconomic identity Eq. (1.2) reflects the conservation of physical goods: The farm allocates its output Y between consumption C and investment I. Equation (1.2) represents a *partial* conservation law. It is "partial" because it applies only to finished goods. The production process that produces Y, on the other hand, takes inputs like seeds and multiply them, capturing the "magic" of the economy.

1.2 Trade-off between Consumption and Investment

Given the conservation of the physical goods produced, the farming economy confronts a fundamental economic decision each season: how to allocate its total crop output, Y, between consumption, C, and seeds for future planting, which serve as investment, I. Increasing current consumption reduces the seeds available for the next season, while increasing seed investment limits current consumption. This trade-off between consumption and investment is crucial for the economy's growth.

Consider a simple scenario where the seed-to-output ratio is 1:2.5, a ratio common in parts of Europe during the 9th century (Bornewasser, 1977).[10] For instance, a farm that produces 2.5 million bushels of crops might save 1 million bushels as seeds and consume the remaining 1.5 million bushels. If the farm continues this pattern season after season, it achieves what is known as an *equilibrium* in economics.

Equilibrium has been a central concept in economics since Léon Walras introduced general equilibrium theory. Walras demonstrated that in a perfectly competitive market, goods and prices automatically adjust to reach a stable point where supply equals demand. Former Finance Minister of German Austria and economist Joseph Schumpeter highly praised this intellectual achievement and called Walras the "greatest of all economists." Walrasian equilibrium theory has since become a cornerstone of modern economics, further developed by scholars, such as Irving Fisher, Kenneth Arrow, and Gérard Debreu.

Here is a simple example: a market has beef (b) and chicken (c) only. Beef costs \$3 per pound and chicken \$1 per pound. Suppose

---

[10]During the 14th century in the Low Countries of Europe, the innovative technology—a system of crop rotation—increased the seed-output ratio to 1:14.

people prefer white meat (chicken) to red meat (beef), and that chicken provides twice the satisfaction of beef; that is, $\ln(c) = \ln(2b)$, where $\ln(.)$ measures people's satisfaction (see Section 1.2.2.1 for utility function). A family spends \$300 on meat, so its budget constraint is \$3b+\$1c=\$300. The family maximizes its utility $\ln(c)+\ln(b) = \ln[2(300-3b)]+\ln(b)$. Upon solving for the first-order condition, we find that $b = 50$ and $c = 150$. The result implies that, at equilibrium, the family consumes chicken at a rate three times greater than that of beef.

While supply and demand may momentarily balance, the economy is constantly in motion—similar to how passengers feel balanced inside a train that is steadily accelerating or decelerating. The monetary balance captures the market equilibrium, but the real economy—the farming economy—evolves season after season, continually changing. In this dynamic context, the real economy can be either stable or unstable.[11]

The difference between stable and unstable equilibrium can be illustrated by the analogy of parking a car. A car parked at the bottom of a valley is in a stable equilibrium—if pushed slightly, it will naturally roll back to its original position (Figure 1.1). On the other hand, a car parked on top of a hill is in an unstable equilibrium—any small push will cause it to roll further away from its original position (Figure 1.2). There is also a neutral equilibrium, where a car on a flat surface will remain steady regardless of the direction it is pushed.

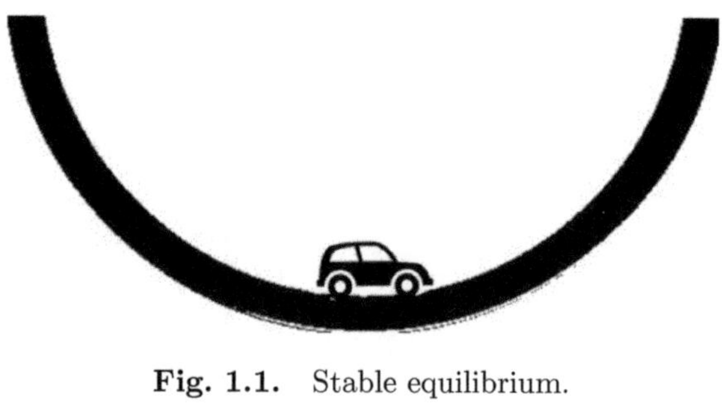

Fig. 1.1. Stable equilibrium.

[11]Economists use the term "instability" differently from dynamic system analysts. For example, economists may use "instability" as in "... the recession caused instability ..." (Morrissey *et al.*, 2020).

Fig. 1.2. Unstable equilibrium.

To determine whether an equilibrium is stable, one can introduce small disturbances to the system. If the system returns to equilibrium, it is stable; if it moves away, it is unstable. Unfortunately, the equilibrium of the farming economy is not stable. Even a slight deviation from equilibrium—whether by consuming a little more or saving a little more—can drive the economy further away from balance.

For example, suppose a "lavish" farm increases its consumption by just 1% of output, from the equilibrium level of 1.5 million bushels to 1.525 million bushels. This slight increase disrupts the economy, leading to a cumulative decline in output. As shown in Table 1.1, this 1% overconsumption causes the farm's output to be cut in half within just five seasons.[12] For simplicity, we assume the farm maintains no crop reserves. However, throughout history, humans have developed various methods to preserve food. For example, sun-drying has been utilized since as early as 12,000 B.C. to extend the shelf life of food (Nummer and Brian, 2002).

This overconsumption has significant long-term consequences. The reduction in seed investment causes output to drop at a faster rate. The longer this underinvestment persists, the more difficult it becomes to restore the economy to equilibrium. In the second season, cutting consumption by just 0.025 million bushels would restore

---

[12]Frank Ramsey used the terms "improvident" and "thrift" to describe two classes of people in his model of economic behavior (Ramsey, 1928). This text uses "lavish" and "frugal" to describe two types of economies, avoiding monetary implications in the terminology.

Table 1.1. Declining farm.

Season	Δ seeds (million/ season)	Seeds (million/ season)	Output (million/ season)	Consumption (million/ season)
1		1	2.5	1.525
2	−0.025	0.975	2.438	1.525
3	−0.0625	0.913	2.281	1.525
4	−0.1563	0.756	1.891	1.525
5	−0.3906	0.366	0.914	1.525

equilibrium. However, by the fifth season, restoring balance requires a drastic reduction in consumption—16 times the initial cut.

Keynes made a similar point on the overconsumption problem: "The only radical cure for the crises of confidence which afflict the economic life of the modern world would be to allow the individual no choice between consuming his income and ordering the production of the specific capital-asset which, even though it be on precarious evidence, impresses him as the most promising investment available to him" (Keynes, 1936). Once again, Keynes spoke of money, but the lesson one can learn is one of common sense—a small dose of medicine taken early can prevent the need for painful treatment later.

Conversely, a "frugal" farm that invests slightly more than the equilibrium amount can experience significant growth. If this farm reduces consumption to 1.475 million bushels, investing the extra 0.025 million bushels, the output will steadily increase. Over five seasons, a 1% cut in consumption leads to more than 60% increase in output (Table 1.2). Aristotle's observation, "Patience is bitter, but its fruit is sweet," captures this idea nicely well.[13]

However, continuous growth without corresponding increases in consumption can also lead to problems, particularly in agricultural economies with perishable goods. Historical periods of overproduction, such as during the 1920s when technological advances in farming led to excess supply, resulted in wasted produce. Farmers, particularly dairy farmers, faced devastating losses as they were

[13]Galor and Özak (2016) state the following: "It advances the hypothesis and establishes empirically, that geographical variations in natural land productivity and their impact on the return to agricultural investment have had a persistent effect on the distribution of long-term orientation across societies."

Table 1.2. Growing farm.

Season	Δ seeds (million/ season)	Seeds (million/ season)	Output (million/ season)	Consumption (million/ season)
1		1	2.5	1.475
2	0.025	1.025	2.563	1.475
3	0.0625	1.088	2.719	1.475
4	0.1563	1.244	3.109	1.475
5	0.3906	1.634	4.086	1.475

forced to dump milk and destroy crops. During the Great Depression, Latin American countries, especially Brazil, burned large quantities of coffee due to a lack of demand. Similar overproduction issues arose during the coronavirus pandemic, when disruptions in supply chains caused fresh produce to be wasted.[14]

The example in Table 1.2 represents a *closed* economy. In an *open* economy, farms can export their surplus crops in exchange for other goods or assets, making overproduction a prerequisite for exports. In a similar vein, "lavish" farms may import crops from abroad, paying for them with their own assets. Chapter 6 discusses the implications of these interactions.

Both "lavish" and "frugal" farms illustrate that equilibrium in the real macroeconomy is often unstable. While a Walrasian equilibrium balances supply and demand through market prices, it does not account for the imbalances that occur in the real economy beneath this apparent balance. Consider a hypothetical scenario where farms rely on genetically modified seeds to cultivate their crops and are required to purchase these seeds from a specific producer. While the supply of the seeds may not match the exact number of seeds needed to keep the farm stable, the price of the seeds brings the market to Walrasian equilibrium by clearing the market. Although the price mechanism can restore balance in markets, the underlying real economy remains unstable.

[14]Karl Marx attributed overproduction problems to the underconsumption of the working class, while John Maynard Keynes described economies facing overproduction in a "liquidity trap," where excessive savings meet insufficient consumption.

1.2.1 *Economic principles*

The farming economy example may be criticized for being simplistic and lacking in realism. However, this simplicity is beneficial because it offers crucial insights into fundamental economic decisions. "The intuitive mind is a sacred gift, and the rational mind is a faithful servant" (attributed to Albert Einstein or Anonymous). Economists often attribute the difficulty of their discipline to the sheer number of variables involved. Alfred Marshall's perspective exemplifies this notion:

> The element of time is a chief cause of those difficulties in economic investigations which make it necessary for man with his limited powers to go step by step; breaking up a complex question, studying one bit at a time, and at last combining his partial solutions into a more or less complete solution of the whole riddle. In breaking it up, he segregates those disturbing causes, whose wanderings happen to be inconvenient, for the time in a pound called Ceteris Paribus. The study of some group of tendencies is isolated by the assumption other things being equal: the existence of other tendencies is not denied, but their disturbing effect is neglected for a time. The more the issue is thus narrowed, the more exactly can it be handled: but also the less closely does it correspond to real life... Each exact and firm handling of a narrow issue, however, helps towards treating broader issues, in which that narrow issue is contained, more exactly than would otherwise have been possible. With each step more things can be let out of the pound; exact discussions can be made less abstract, realistic discussions can be made less inexact than was possible at an earlier stage.—Marshall (2009)

Before Isaac Newton, the belief that God communicated through the stars was deeply embedded in the traditions of ancient civilizations. As early as 3000 B.C. in Mesopotamia, people began interpreting celestial observations as divine messages and used them to predict the future. This concept eventually spread to India, but it found its most significant development in Greek civilization during the Hellenistic period. Astrology later entered Islamic culture as part of this Greek legacy, and it was reintroduced to Europe through Arabic scholarship during the Middle Ages.[15]

In ancient China, during an eclipse, people beat gongs and pans, believing that noise could scare away a giant celestial dog trying to eat the moon. In contrast, today's Chinese often continue their daily routines and sleep through the night. The philosopher Ludwig Wittgenstein once remarked, "Man has to awaken to wonder—and so perhaps do peoples. Science is a way of sending him to sleep again" (Wittgenstein, 1984). In this case, it was Newton who lulled people back to slumber.

The universe is filled with an immense variety of objects, ranging from distant stars to everyday apples. One might wonder: How many variables are in God's mind? Newton and his contemporaries dared to think of themselves as readers of God's mind. Newton decoded these divine messages into three simple laws, leaving his peers and future scientists in awe. "The most incomprehensible thing about the Universe is that it is comprehensible" (Albert Einstein or Anonymous). Compared to the economic system built by humans, could God's mind be simpler and more comprehensible?[16]

The success of physics, particularly after physicists understood that pressure, temperature, and volume measured the macro equilibrium of countless gas particles in collision, inspired early

---

[15]The most prominent theory is that the constellations represented a "gospel in the stars," which was thought to be a primal message from God interpreted by early humans through star patterns; this idea gained particular attention in the 19th century when Frances Rolleston published her work "Mazzaroth," which proposed this theory extensively (Rolleston, 2008).

[16]"The fact that it is comprehensible is a miracle" (Einstein or Anonymous). But it is no accident that natural sciences, computer science, and mathematics are positive. The reason that the world is comprehensible is that human beings are a part of nature. Our bodies and brains follow the laws of nature. Consciously or unconsciously, our brains follow the logos of the universe. Therefore, the man-made mathematics and computers we create have no other way but to obey the only laws our brains follow. This can respond to what Eugene Wigner said about the unreasonable efficiency of mathematics: "a wonderful gift which we neither understand nor deserve." It is a gift built in when we were born.

economics. James Clerk Maxwell developed the velocity distribution of gas particles, while Ludwig Boltzmann analyzed molecular motion (Mirowski, 1991; Sornette, 2014). Their successes influenced economic theories such as Francis Ysidro Edgeworth's limit theorem,[17] and Alfred Marshall's equilibrium analysis.

Although some economists have drawn inspiration from physics, economics has followed a distinct trajectory. While physics seeks a single unifying principle, modern economists push for more "realistic" models, utilizing computational power to capture nonlinear dynamics and complex interactions. In his 1974 Nobel Prize acceptance speech, Friedrich von Hayek warned against imitating physical sciences too closely. He argued: "It seems to me that this failure of the economists to guide policy more successfully is closely connected with their propensity to imitate as closely as possible the procedures of the brilliantly successful physical sciences—an attempt which in our field may lead to outright error. It is an approach which has come to be described as the 'scientistic' attitude—an attitude which, as I defined it some thirty years ago, is decidedly unscientific in the true sense of the word, since it involves a mechanical and uncritical application of habits of thought to fields different from those in which they have been formed" (Von Hayek, 1989).

In economics, "unrealistic" often is a basis for criticism and a justification for dismissing a theory altogether. As John Maynard Keynes stated:

> It is a great fault of symbolic pseudo-mathematical methods of formalizing a system of economic analysis...that they expressly assume strict independence between the factors involved and lose all their cogency and authority if this hypothesis is disallowed...Too large a proportion of recent 'mathematical' economics are merely concoctions, as imprecise as the initial assumptions they rest on, which allow the author to lose sight of the complexities and interdependencies of the real world in a maze of pretentious and unhelpful symbols.—Keynes (1936)

[17]As the number of agents increases without bound, an economy approaches Walrasian equilibrium.

Econometrics (see Appendix A.3) has become a key tool for analyzing economic complexity and interdependence, but the phrase ceteris paribus has fallen out of favor. Ironically, Newton's laws would not pass today's "ceteris paribus" or "realistic" tests. His first law states that an object will remain at rest or move in a straight line at constant speed if no net external forces act on it. Yet, no object in the universe is free from external forces. Newton's first law describes something that does not exist. For Newton, his laws were not mere hypotheses, 'I do not make hypotheses," he said.[18] Even so, other physicists viewed them as hypotheses. These "unrealistic" laws became the foundation of physics, the very knowledge of the universe!

Newton's law of gravity, which ignores shapes, wind, and friction, might seem "unrealistic." Consider dropping a piece of paper from the Pisa Tower—Newton's law won't tell you when or where it will land. Yet this law underpins aerodynamics, from the flight of birds to supersonic aircraft. Statistical analysis can identify many factors that influence when and where a paper lands, but isolating the principal factor—the underlying law—requires the development of a paradigm (see Section A.3.3).

Could statistical analysis of data alone reveal Newton's law by eliminating endogeneity? Astrologers began observing stars and collecting data as early as Mesopotamia (3000 B.C.). Tycho Brahe (1546–1601) compiled vast datasets over his lifetime, which he passed on to Johannes Kepler (1571–1630). Kepler used these observations to develop his three laws of planetary motion. His third law inspired Newton. Data and statistical correlations offer valuable insights, but scientists must abstract from them to discover fundamental laws. Without the leap from real data to an "unrealistic" world, we would still be listening to astrologers interpreting the stars.

In *War and Peace*, Lev Tolstoy uses an analogy to describe history's constant movement: "A locomotive is moving. Someone asks: 'What moves it?' A peasant says the devil moves it. Another man says the locomotive moves because its wheels go round. A third asserts that the cause of its movement lies in the smoke which the wind carries away." If people lacked engineering knowledge, they could collect data and use Judea Pearl's intervention framework (see

[18] *Hypotheses non fingo.*

Section A.3.3), identify many potential "causes" across the locomotive's subsystems—engine, electrical, cooling, and so on. But can the framework alone discover the underlying laws that guide engineering design? Pearl argues that machine learning is ultimately "curve fitting" and only causal reasoning can attain genuine intelligence.

Occam's razor, the principle of parsimony, favors simpler theories that are easier to test. In an unfinished note on "the greatest possible simplification of the hypothesis," Nietzsche, who was not fond of science, explained this principle:

> The hypothesis that explains the existing world with the fewest assumptions and means should be preferred, for in such a hypothesis, there is the least amount of arbitrariness, and free play with possibilities is prohibited. If there are two hypotheses that both explain the world, a strict test must be applied to determine which better satisfies the demand for economy. The one who can explain the world with simpler and more familiar forces, especially mechanical ones, who deduces the existing edifice of the world from the smallest possible number of forces, will always be preferred over the one who allows more complicated and less familiar forces, in greater number, to carry on the world-creating play.—Nietzsche (1997)

The most popular version of Occam's razor states, "Entities are not to be multiplied without necessity."[19] Nicolaus Copernicus placed the sun at the center of the universe in his heliocentric model. Mathematically, the center can be anywhere in space via a transformation, such as in the geocentric Ptolemaic model, but the geocentric model only complicates matters.

The real world plays mathematical games with humans. A linear equation such as $1 + x = 3$ has a single solution: $x = 2$. A nonlinear equation such as $x^2 = 4$ offers two opposite answers. Proving the existence and uniqueness of solutions in complex models with multiple nonlinear equations is challenging. Numerical solutions can become entangled in multiple answers. Keynes' response to multiple answers was to leave all possibilities on the back burner. No wonder President

[19]Formulated by Irish Franciscan philosopher John Punch in 1639, Wikipedia, accessed on August 30, 2024.

Harry Truman pleaded, "Give me a one-handed economist. All my economists say, "'on the one hand...,' then 'but on the other....'"[20]

1.2.2 *Economic models*

The macroeconomic identity in Eq. (1.2) applies to economies in general, whether free-market or centrally planned. In a planned economy, there is no competition among producers. Governments set output targets and distribute goods according to central plans.

In contrast, much of the world today lives under capitalist systems, where private businesses own the means of production. In the purest form of capitalism, known as a laissez-faire economy, the market operates with minimal government regulation or interference. However, throughout capitalist history, economies have experienced periodic crises, leading to debates about the role of government intervention. In practice, most governments intervene in their economies, implementing fiscal policies, legislatures passing laws on economic spending, and central banks implementing monetary policies aimed at maintaining employment and price stability. As a result, modern capitalist economies are often a far cry from the laissez-faire ideal.

Laissez-faire economists assumed that market economies could function autonomously—effectively on "autopilot"—and naturally stabilize themselves, with any instability attributed to external factors. However, the Great Depression shook that belief, and economists such as John Maynard Keynes advocated for government intervention to maintain stability and ensure a quasi-optimal equilibrium in the economy (Skidelsky, 2010). Despite these interventions, crises continue to arise, and the debate endures.[21]

---

[20] American economist Edgar Russell Fiedler said, "Ask five economists and you'll get five different answers—six if one went to Harvard."

[21] The economic policy for a laissez-faire economy is to adopt no policy, but the proponents of a managed economy must answer what government can control and what policies can achieve a specific economic outcome. For example, Roy Harrod and others introduced uncertainties, examined local and global equilibria and stabilities, and designed various policies to achieve specific economic outcomes (Domar, 1989).

In the debate between the laissez-faire school and Keynesian economics, Henry Hazlitt and Ludwig von Mises stood as staunch defenders of minimal government intervention. Hazlitt provided a detailed critique of Keynesian economics, challenging it line by line. Despite the efforts of governments and central banks, they have not prevented economic crises entirely, and ongoing criticism of the government's role in economic instability has reignited this long-standing debate. Friedrich Hayek helped revive this discussion after being awarded the 1974 Nobel Memorial Prize in Economic Sciences.

On the other hand, throughout economic history, there have been periods when governments adopted a hands-off approach, allowing economies to flourish—yet crises often followed these prosperous times. This history raises the question: Can a laissez-faire economy stabilize itself and ensure prosperity, or do governments need to play an active role in managing the economy? This debate centers on the stability of a laissez-faire economy versus the interventionist approach of modern capitalism.

Traditional stability analyses of economic systems have limitations, primarily because they often represent the economy in monetary terms rather than focusing on the real economy. However, it is not necessary to reinvent the wheel. Instead, some existing models can be reshaped for new applications, while others may need to be replaced altogether.

The Ramsey model, for example, is a dynamic model expressed in monetary terms. Under Keynes' influence, Ramsey also adopted the monetary measure of the economy. By stripping away this monetary "coating," we can reveal the underlying structure of the real economy. This section reinterprets the Ramsey model as a model of the real economy, reformulating it with new initial and terminal conditions to reflect the dynamics of the real economy.

The Ramsey model operates in continuous time, which allows for the development of closed-form solutions. Households continuously invest, first to offset depreciation, as machines, equipment, and production facilities gradually wear out, age, or become obsolete, and then expand to the capital stock (K), represented as $\dot{K} = dK/dt$, where the dot denotes differentiation with respect to time. After accounting for depreciation, denoted as δK, where δ is the depreciation rate, the change of the capital stock can be positive, negative, or zero. Thus, investment is a dynamic process, expressed as:

$$I = \dot{K} + \delta K.$$

And Eq. (1.2) in continuous time becomes:

$$\dot{K} = Y - C - \delta K, \tag{1.4}$$

which is a dynamic version of the real-economy macroeconomic identity in Eq. (1.2). As the discussion of a moving train on p. 11, prices make supply equal demand and maintain an equilibrium inside the train, while the train itself continues to move. Equation (1.4) specifies whether the economic train is moving or has stopped and, if it is moving, whether it is accelerating or decelerating.

Figure 1.3 illustrates the real economy, which takes capital stock and labor as inputs to produce output. Over time, all capital stock depreciates and requires new investment to maintain its condition. If investment—output minus consumption—is insufficient to cover depreciation, the capital stock will decline and the annual change of capital stock, ΔK, will be negative, reducing production capacity. Conversely, if investment exceeds depreciation, the surplus goes toward expanding the capital stock and the annual change of capital stock, ΔK, will be positive, increasing the economy's productive potential.

Figures 1.4–1.6 illustrate the farming economy as a special case of the real economy, as shown in Figure 1.3. The farming economy is assumed not to be constrained by labor L, and the changes in output depend solely on the capital stock—seeds (K). In Figure 1.4, the farming economy is in equilibrium. The farm has a capital stock of one million bushels of seeds, producing an output of 2.5 million bushels. The farm consumes 1.5 million bushels of this output and saves 1 million bushels for the next season as investment. This investment covers exactly one million bushels of depreciation—the foregone seeds—resulting in no net change in capital stock ($\Delta K = 0$).

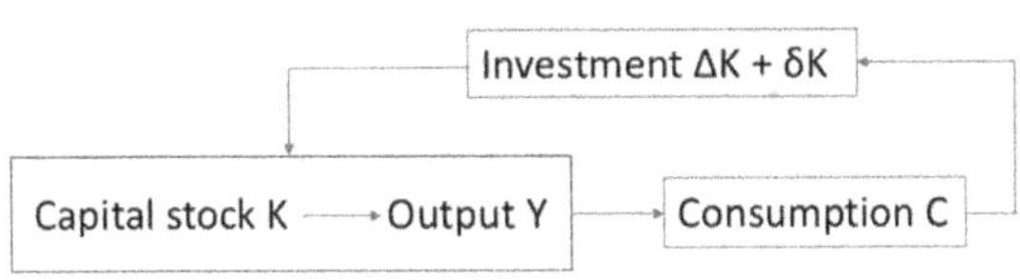

Fig. 1.3. The real economy.

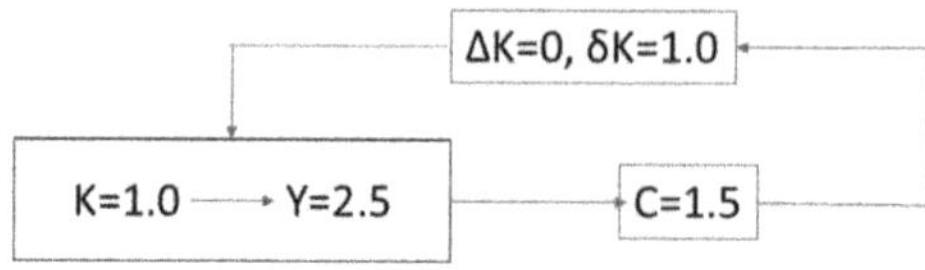

Fig. 1.4. The farm in equilibrium.

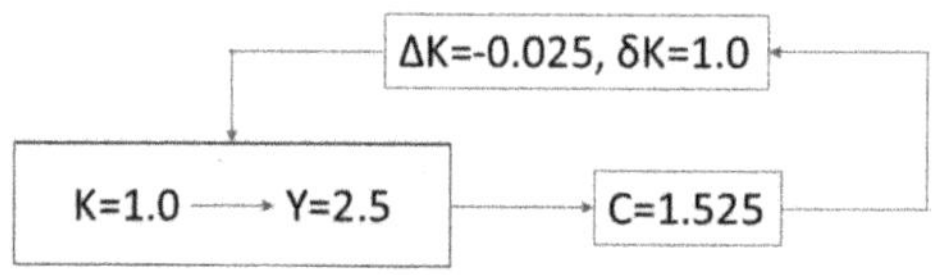

Fig. 1.5. Declining farm.

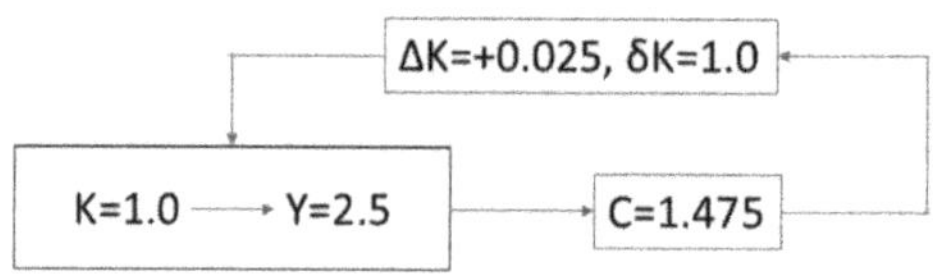

Fig. 1.6. Growing farm.

Figure 1.5 depicts a declining farming economy. In the first year, the farm consumes 1.525 million bushels and leaves 0.975 million bushels for investment. Since this investment is insufficient to replace the 1 million bushels of foregone seeds, next year's capital stock decreases by 0.025 million bushels ($\Delta K = -0.025$).

Conversely, Figure 1.6 shows a growing farming economy. In the first year, the farm consumed 1.475 million bushels and used 1.025 million bushels for investment. This investment not only replaces the 1 million bushels of foregone seeds but also adds 0.025 million bushels to the seeds for the next year ($\Delta K = +0.025$).

These examples highlight the importance of real investment in sustaining long-term economic health. Without adequate investment, a farm—or any economy—cannot survive in the long run. In addition to machines, equipment, and factories, modern economies rely heavily on infrastructure such as highways, railroads, airports, and telecommunications. No matter how wealthy a country may be, its real economy will decline without sufficient investment to offset depreciation.

In the above examples, the output of the farming economy is 2.5 times the capital stock (the seeds), expressed as $Y = AK$, where

$A = 2.5$. This relationship is known as the *AK model*, where doubling the capital stock doubles output. In this model, the gross return on capital stock, $dY/dK = A$, remains constant, which is realistic only over a short term. For a farming economy with abundant factors of production such as land and labor, the crop output depends primarily on the number of seeds. Thus, the macroeconomic identity of this farming economy is simpler:

$$\begin{aligned} \dot{K} &= AK - C - \delta K, \\ &= 1.5K - C, \end{aligned} \tag{1.5}$$

where consumption C is constant. At the equilibrium point of the economy, investment is zero, $\dot{K}^* = 0$:

$$\dot{K}^* = 1.5K^* - C = 0. \tag{1.6}$$

To analyze the stability of this system, we check whether a small disturbance around the equilibrium point causes the system to return to equilibrium or move away from it. If it returns, the equilibrium is stable; if it moves away, the equilibrium is unstable.

Mathematically, the farming economy's stability can be examined by taking the difference between Eqs. (1.5) and (1.6), which gives the deviation of the economy from the equilibrium point:

$$\frac{d}{dt}(K - K^*) = 1.5(K - K^*). \tag{1.7}$$

The coefficient 1.5 in Eq. (1.7) represents the slope of the system near equilibrium—a critical indicator of stability. A negative slope indicates stability, as illustrated in Figure 1.1, and a positive slope indicates an unstable system, which is illustrated in Figure 1.2. The farming economy has a positive slope—1.5—and is unstable, and the capital stock follows an explicit solution:

$$K_t = K^* + (K_0 - K^*)e^{1.5t}, \tag{1.8}$$

where K_0 represents the initial capital stock (seeds). Depending on the initial capital stock, the system either declines to zero or grows infinitely. If K_0 is below the threshold $K^* = C/1.5$, the capital stock (the seeds) eventually runs out. If K_0 exceeds this threshold, the capital stock accumulates without bound. This example demonstrates a technique for analyzing stability by examining the system's behavior near its equilibrium point.

The example also illustrates that *capital accumulation* is not a myth. Adam Smith described this process as peaceful when capitalists accumulated "previous or original" capital. In contrast, Karl Marx depicted the "primitive" capital accumulation as a violent and exploitative process, often involving colonialism.

Historical examples, such as the Soviet Union's transition from an agrarian to an industrialized nation, underscore this point. During Stalin's first Five-Year Plan, the Soviet Union reallocated 80% of its investment to the industrial sector, cutting programs deemed unnecessary for heavy industry. This drastic investment in industrial capital led to a 50% increase in total industrial output before World War II, contributing to the Soviet Union's economic independence and military strength.[22] The Soviet Union sustained heavy losses between 1941 and 1945 and eventually defeated fascism (Keefe, 2009). Meanwhile, the people suffered from the scarcity of basic consumption goods, including food. Stalin traded people's consumption for industrial investment.

However, capital accumulation does not necessarily destabilize an economy in all cases. If accumulation is not balanced by growth in consumption, a closed economy must open to trade and export its output (see Chapter 6). Another scenario involves war (see Chapter 5). In Stalin's case, the war absorbed the production of tanks, aircraft, and artillery, effectively "consuming" the excess goods.

1.2.2.1 *Discounted utility function*

In a capitalist economy, households play a crucial role by making consumption and investment decisions that collectively influence broader economic outcomes. Economists build microeconomic theory from the ground up, focusing on how economic agents make decisions among multiple alternatives. Drawing on the work of moral philosopher Jeremy Bentham (1747–1832), economists use utility functions—derived from Bentham's *felicific* calculus—to codify how

[22] *First five-year plan, Industrialization in the Soviet Union*, Wikipedia; accessed on May 5, 2024.

people compare and rank the happiness associated with different choices.

Economists investigate human preferences in detail. Individuals order the same set of alternatives differently, and their preferences change with personal circumstances, economic conditions, and other factors (Robinson and Dow, 2021).[23]

The utility function, $u(x)$, captures human preferences concerning the selection of x. Popular utility functions reflect common preferences, such as the tendency to prefer more consumption over less. For instance, in most models, utility $u(C)$ is an increasing function of consumption C, implying that more consumption leads to greater satisfaction. This relationship is characterized by a positive marginal utility, $u'(C) = du(C)/dC > 0$. However, the law of diminishing marginal utility also applies: The first bite of food provides more satisfaction than the last bite, so the utility function increases at a decreasing rate, meaning $u''(C) < 0$.

This diminishing marginal utility aligns with the sufficient condition for utility maximization.[24] In analytical geometry, the peak and valley in Figures 1.1 and 1.2 can be linked to an equation $h = f(x)$, where h represents elevation and x the horizontal location. In classical economic models, utility maximization is analogous to finding the peak of a curve in analytical geometry. To locate the peak, we take the first derivative and set it equal to zero ($f'(x) = 0$). However, this only identifies a stationary point, which could be either a peak (maximum) or a valley (minimum). The second derivative, $f''(x)$, provides the criterion for distinguishing between the two: If $f''(x) < 0$, the point lies on a concave curve, indicating a local maximum; if $f''(x) > 0$, it lies on a convex curve, signifying a local minimum. In the context of utility maximization, it is essential for the utility

[23] In specific economic models, utility functions can include various factors. For example, the popular Sidrauski model puts money into the utility function (Bénassy, 2011), and in the real estate literature, the utility function includes sociodemographic characteristics and benefits from housing, the "services" provided by housing (Hanushek and Quigley, 1979).

[24] An alternative to the utility maximization of classical economic models is loss minimization. Schwartenbeck *et al.* (2015) provide evidence that the minimization of surprise losses minimization explains people's choices better than the utility maximization alone.

function to be concave. A concave utility function ensures that the first-order condition leads to maximal satisfaction.

Not all needs contribute equally to utility. According to Maslow's hierarchy of needs, basic physiological necessities—such as food, clothing, and shelter—must be met before individuals can pursue higher-order desires. In economic terms, utilities are initially more physiological than psychological. Historical evidence shows that people were content during periods of economic prosperity and peace, even without modern luxuries such as cell phones or movies. Basic needs such as food and shelter hold the highest value in utility functions and are more stable than higher-level desires.

People also save for the future, balancing current consumption against future needs. Those who value future consumption more than present consumption will save and invest more. Paul Samuelson reframed interest as a discount factor in 1937 to quantify the trade-off between present and future consumption (Frederick *et al.*, 2002). The discount factor, ρ, encapsulates time preferences—how much individuals value future consumption relative to current consumption.

For example, if a household is willing to forgo 1 pound of bread now for 1.1 pounds a year later, the discount factor can be determined as follows:

$$1 \text{ lb} = \frac{1.1 \text{ lb}}{1 + \rho\tau} \approx 1.1e^{-\rho\tau}\text{lb}.$$

This gives a discount factor of $\rho = 0.1$, where $\tau = 1$ for a year, and $e^{-\rho\tau}$ is a simpler discount formula in continuous time. The discount rate ρ reflects how patient a household is—lower discount rates indicate a greater willingness to wait for future gains. Different individuals have different time preferences, and at the macroeconomic level, the discount factor reflects the collective time preference of all households in the economy.

By combining the discount factor with the utility function, economists can sum up total utility over a given period:

$$\int_0^T e^{-\rho t} u(C_t) dt. \tag{1.9}$$

This expression represents the satisfaction derived from a consumption plan C_t over a period T. By comparing different consumption plans, individuals choose the one that maximizes their satisfaction.

In a capitalist economy, individuals' microeconomic decisions combine to shape macroeconomic patterns of consumption and investment. However, these decisions are influenced by a variety of factors, including differing utility functions, discount rates, and budget constraints. The poor, the rich, and the middle class all make distinct trade-offs influenced by their unique circumstances (see Chapter 3). The wealth distribution contributes to the overall statistics, affecting patterns of consumption and investment at the macroeconomic level.

Individuals in an economy can be compared to gas particles in a contained space. While each particle behaves differently at the microscopic level, their collective dynamics generate observable macroscopic properties, such as pressure and temperature. Similarly, diverse economic behaviors, shaped by individuals' circumstances, contribute to the broader dynamics observed in the economy.

1.2.2.2 *Production function*

The real economy produces essential goods for human survival, so production is the vital organ of the economy. The factors of production include land, labor, raw materials, capital stock, energy, and technology.

To improve production processes, Frederick Winslow Taylor (1856–1915) pioneered the principle of scientific management in his book, *The Principles of Scientific Management* (1911). Taylor applied scientific principles to improve production processes, advocating for business education and research on physical processes, which influenced the development of both business schools and industrial engineering (Grant, 1996).[25]

Later, Taylor's scientific management split into two parts: the scientific component, which evolved into industrial engineering, and the management component, which business schools adopted. This division, however, diluted the synergy between science and management

[25]Critics, such as Stewart (2009), have argued that Taylor exaggerated or even fabricated aspects of his career.

that was central to Taylor's ideas. Industrial engineering focuses on physical processes using physical measures (the International System of Units (SI)), while management primarily uses monetary metrics to evaluate production. To restore that synergy, *knowledge integration* holds merit in reconnecting engineering and management.

In addition to technology, standard production functions in textbooks typically focus on capital stock and labor. In modern industries, except for agriculture, production no longer depends heavily on land. When energy and raw materials are plentiful and affordable, they do not limit economic production.

In Figure 1.3, the production combines capital stock and labor to produce output. Thus, the production function, $Y = f(K, L)$, links capital stock K and labor L to output. By substituting Y with the production function, Eq. (1.4) becomes:

$$\dot{K} = f(K, L) - C - \delta K. \tag{1.10}$$

This equation expresses the dynamics of capital accumulation, defined as output ($f(K, L)$), produced by capital stock K and labor L, minus consumption (C) and depreciation (δK).

1.2.2.3 *The Cobb–Douglas production function*

Economists have developed various forms of production functions to model the relationship between inputs and outputs in production processes (Shephard, 2015; Griffin *et al.*, 1987). One of the most widely used is the Cobb–Douglas production function[26]:

$$Y = f(K, L) = AK^a L^{1-a}. \tag{1.11}$$

In this equation, a represents the output elasticity of capital stock, measuring how responsive output is to changes in capital stock. Its value ranges between 0 and 1.

[26]Knut Wicksell introduced his production function as $f(K, L) = AK^a L^{1-a}$ in 1916, similar to the Cobb–Douglas production function (Mishra, 2007).

In economic models, advancements in production processes are often encapsulated in a single technological factor, A, within the production function. This technology coefficient abstracts away the complexities of real-world production processes, reducing them to a simple multiplier. While the production function captures the effects of technological progress, it is important to recognize that it is a highly abstract construct rather than a representation derived from scientific principles. Consequently, it streamlines the rich and detailed improvements that methodologies such as Taylorism bring to production in practice.

To further simplify the macroeconomic identity in Eq. (1.10), we express the economy on a per capita basis by dividing by the labor input L. Economic models typically treat labor input as exogenous, remaining either constant or changing at constant rates (see Blanchard and Fisher, 1989; Barro, 2003; Acemoglu, 2008). It is important to clarify the definition of L, as referring to it simply as "population" can lead to confusion.

Consumption (C) represents the total consumption of the population, while L refers specifically to the number of employed workers, excluding those who are not part of the labor force. Each of these workers shares the goods they produce with their dependents, including children and the elderly (see Chapter 7). Conversely, if L is defined as the number of households, then each household supports its dependents—children and the elderly—through an average number of employed individuals within the household.

This distinction is critical for accurately understanding the production function:

$$y = \frac{Y}{L} = f\left(\frac{K}{L}, 1\right) = A\left(\frac{K}{L}\right)^a = Ak^a = f(k). \tag{1.12}$$

Dividing both sides of Eq. (1.10) by L gives:

$$\frac{d}{dt}\left(\frac{K}{L}\right) = A\left(\frac{K}{L}\right)^a - \frac{C}{L} - \delta\frac{K}{L}. \tag{1.13}$$

This transformation allows us to express the production function in terms of capital per worker, $k = K/L$, and $c = C/L$, simplifying the macroeconomic identity:

$$\dot{k} = f(k) - c - \delta k. \tag{1.14}$$

Taking the derivative of Eq. (1.13) with respect to capital, K, gives us the *gross return* or *marginal product* of capital stock:

$$\begin{aligned} f_K(K,L) &= \frac{\partial}{\partial K} f(K,L) = aA\left(\frac{L}{K}\right)^{1-a} \\ &= a\left(\frac{f(K,L)}{K}\right) = f'(k) > 0, \end{aligned} \tag{1.15}$$

where the subscript K indicates the partial derivative with respect to K. The positive marginal product of capital implies that increasing capital stock raises output. However, due to limited production resources, each additional unit of capital yields progressively smaller output gains. For example, as arable land becomes scarce, adding more seeds produces smaller increases in crop yield. This phenomenon of diminishing returns is reflected in the second derivative of the production function:

$$f_{KK}(K,L) = -a(1-a)A\left(\frac{L^{1-a}}{K^{2-a}}\right) < 0, \tag{1.16}$$

where the negative second-order derivative $f_{KK}(K,L) < 0$ indicates the concavity of the production function with respect to capital, a necessary condition for maximization.

Similarly, the *marginal product of labor* measures the change in output when an additional worker is employed:

$$\begin{aligned} f_L(K,L) &= \frac{\partial}{\partial L} f(K,L) = (1-a)A\left(\frac{K}{L}\right)^{a} \\ &= (1-a)f(k) = f(k) - kf'(k) > 0, \end{aligned} \tag{1.17}$$

As with capital, the marginal product of labor is positive, meaning that hiring additional workers increases output. Table 1.3 summarizes commonly used formulas derived from the general production function and the Cobb–Douglas production function.

An economy consists of firms across various industries and at different stages of their life cycles. Alfred Marshall introduced the

Table 1.3. Production functions: General vs. the Cobb–Douglas.

		General	**Cobb–Douglas**
Original	Production Function	$f(K,L)$	AK^aL^{1-a}
	Gross return	$f_K(K,L)$	$af(K,L)/K$
	Net return	$f_K(K,L)-\delta$	$af(K,L)/K-\delta$
	Real wage w/P	$f_L(K,L)$	$(1-a)f(K,L)/L$
Per capita	Production Function	$f(K/L)=f(k)$	Ak^a
	Gross return	$f'(k)$	$af(k)/k$
	Net return	$r=f'(k)-\delta$	$af(k)/k-\delta$
	Real wage w/P	$f(k)-kf'(k)$	$(1-a)f(k)$

concept of the *representative firm* to capture this diversity (Marshall, 2009). He likened the aggregate of firms to a forest, with individual trees at different stages of growth. Just as the forest is more stable than any single tree, the representative firm serves as a stabler benchmark for aggregate production. Over time, economists have revived and refined Marshall's ideas, using the concepts of the representative firm and household to simplify macroeconomic analysis.

By using the Cobb–Douglas production function, this book makes the implications of models more explicit. Despite its simplicity, this function illustrates how key factors such as capital, labor, and technology affect economic output. Table 1.3 presents the main economic factors—gross returns, net returns, and wages—as they relate to the production function. These factors are used throughout the book.

1.3 Ramsey Model

The previous example of a farming economy demonstrates that consumption deviating from equilibrium leads to either growth or decline. However, it assumes constant consumption, C, ignoring households' consumption-investment decisions in response to economic conditions. By introducing a discount factor and a utility function, the Ramsey model considers how the representative household trades off between consumption and investment.

Frank P. Ramsey (1903–1930) developed his model to answer the following question: "How much of its income should a nation save?" (Ramsey, 1928). Ramsey was an exceptional thinker who significantly influenced economics, mathematics, and analytic philosophy. Despite his untimely death at 26, his work left a lasting legacy. British philosopher George Edward Moore (1873–1958)[27] doubted whether Ludwig Wittgenstein's *Tractatus Logico-Philosophicus* could be translated into English, but Ramsey did so at the age of 19 and influenced Wittgenstein intellectually (Misak, 2020).[28] Although Paul Samuelson acknowledged Ramsey's contributions in 1970, economics historian Pedro Garcia Duarte argued that Ramsey was recognized in economics well before 1950 (Duarte, 2009). Today, the Ramsey model remains a workhorse of economic theory (Bénassy, 2011).

The representative household maximizes its utility of consumption:

$$\max_{c}\left(\int_{t}^{T} e^{-\rho s}u(c_s)ds + e^{-\rho(T-t)}S(k_T)\right), \tag{1.18}$$

where the current maximization is over a finite time horizon T, rather than infinity as in Ramsey's original model. Consequently, Eq. (1.18) introduces $S(k_T)$, which represents the production capacity at time T. The goal is to maximize discounted utility by optimally adjusting the consumption path, while ensuring that a specified capital stock is saved for the future. In control theory, $S(.)$ is known as a *scrap value function*. In the current context, it reflects the economic resources saved, which contribute to future productive capacity.

In a laissez-faire economy, the absence of a central planner implies no predefined scrap value function, leaving the terminal value unconstrained in the utility maximization problem:

$$\max_{c}\int_{t}^{T} e^{-\rho s}u(c_s)ds, \tag{1.19}$$

where c, the consumption per capita, is the *control variable* in dynamic control theory.

The capital stock k in the Ramsey model is the *state variable* in this dynamic system. The objective of optimal control in this context is to determine the optimal path of the state equation (1.14)

[27]Moore disliked his first name, and his wife called him "Bill."

[28]In 1929, Ramsey became Wittgenstein's Ph.D. supervisor at Cambridge.

that maximizes discounted utility. The state variable—capital stock k constrains the control variable—consumption c through the state equation, (1.14). The initial conditions are the capital stock k_{IC} and consumption c_{IC} at the initial time t:

$$k_t = k_{IC}, \tag{1.20}$$

$$c_t = c_{IC}, \tag{1.21}$$

$$\dot{c} < \infty. \tag{1.22}$$

The current Ramsey model solves Eq. (1.19) subject to the constraint Eq. (1.14), and the conditions in (1.20), (1.21), and (1.22). The main differences between the current version and the textbook versions of the Ramsey model are: The time horizon is finite from t to T; consumption c_t has an initial condition c_{IC} and cannot jump, $\dot{c} < \infty$, whereas in the textbook versions, including the original Ramsey model, the time horizon is infinity, with no initial condition for c_t.

Economic textbooks such as those by Acemoglu (2008), Bénassy (2011), Weber (2011), and Sydsæter *et al.* (2008) provide detailed coverage of the mathematical background and solution methods. This book, however, takes a more heuristic approach to the maximum principle (Sydsæter *et al.*, 2008; Obstfeld, 1992), using intuitive shortcuts rather than rigorous proofs to introduce the Hamiltonian method for readers who are less interested in the formal mathematics underlying the maximum principle.

A period from t to T can be divided into two subperiods: from t to τ and from τ to T. At time τ, the decision-maker faces the same optimization problem, with the initial condition being the terminal outcome from the previous subperiod. If the solution to the optimization problem Eq. (1.19) at time t is represented by $J(k_t)$, then the solution at time τ becomes $J(k_\tau)$, with the only change being the initial condition. At time τ, the optimization in the previous period changes the capital stock from k_t to k_τ and the consumption from c_t to c_τ, while the decision rules remain unchanged. This is the essence of Bellman's principle of optimality: Any segment of an optimal solution path is, in itself, optimal when considered as a new problem beginning from the preceding period's terminal conditions.

Therefore, $J(k_t)$ can be rewritten as

$$J(k_t) = \max_c \left\{ \int_t^\tau e^{-\rho(s-t)} u(c_s) ds + e^{-\rho(\tau - t)} J(k_\tau) \right\}. \tag{1.23}$$

Recall that the derivative with respect to the upper bound of an integration gives:

$$\frac{d}{dx}\int_t^x f(s)ds = f(x),$$

and following the chain rule in calculus to take derivatives of Eq. (1.23) with respect to τ yields

$$0 = \max_c \left\{ e^{-\rho(\tau-t)} u(c_\tau) - e^{-\rho(\tau-t)} \left[\rho J(k_\tau) - J'(k_\tau)\dot{k_\tau} \right] \right\}. \quad (1.24)$$

The derivative is zero because $J(k_t)$ is maximized. As $\tau \to t$, Eq. (1.24) simplifies to

$$0 = \max_c [u(c_t) - \rho J(k_t) + J'(k_t)\dot{k_t}]. \quad (1.25)$$

Equation (1.25) involves only time t, which can be omitted for simplicity if there is no confusion. Bellman's principle implies that present optimization by governments or planners also applies to the future economy. However, short-term terminal conditions must be consistent with the long-term ones, which are ensured via backward induction. Thus, short-term optimizations embed the consequences of long-term optimization.

In physics, the Hamiltonian represents the conservation of energy, while in economics it is employed to solve optimization problems subject to constraints, like Eq. (1.14). In the current maximization problem, the Hamiltonian, $\mathcal{H}(c, k, \theta, t)$, is defined as

$$\mathcal{H}(c, k, \theta, t) = \rho J(k). \quad (1.26)$$

Defining the co-state variable, $\theta = J'(k)$, which is analogous to the Lagrange multiplier in constrained optimization problems. Equations (1.25) and (1.26) give the Hamiltonian:

$$\mathcal{H}(k, c, \theta, t) = u(c) + \theta\dot{k}, \quad (1.27)$$

which combines the utility maximization problem Eq. (1.19) and the state variable dynamics Eq. (1.14) into a single equation through the co-state variable θ (Dorfman, 1969) and transforms the maximization problem in (1.25) into the maximization of Hamiltonian. In economics, the co-state variable represents *the shadow price* of the corresponding state variable. In Eq. (1.27), θ is often interpreted in textbooks as the shadow price of $\dot{k}$, since capital stock investment is measured by money. Energy underlies the production process described by the state Eq. (1.4), which takes specific forms of energy—work—and outputs products (see Chapter 7). Thus, θ should be understood as the "energy" required per unit of capital stock investment.

The derivative of Eq. (1.25) with respect to k gives:

$$0 = -\rho J'(k) + J''(k)\dot{k} + J'(k)\frac{\partial}{\partial k}\dot{k}. \tag{1.28}$$

Using $J'(k) = \theta$ and $J''(k)\dot{k} = \dot{\theta}$, we rewrite Eq. (1.28) as

$$\theta\frac{\partial}{\partial k}\dot{k} = \rho\theta - \dot{\theta}. \tag{1.29}$$

Taking the partial derivative of Eq. (1.27) with respect to k establishes the relationship between the Hamiltonian and the co-state variable:[29,30]

$$\frac{\partial}{\partial k}\mathcal{H}(k, c, \theta, t) = \theta\frac{\partial}{\partial k}\dot{k} = \rho\theta - \dot{\theta}, \tag{1.30}$$

which is a differential equation for θ, and θ must satisfy either an initial condition k_{IC} or a terminal condition k_{TC}. The latter

[29] It is a heuristic jump from Eq. (1.27) to Eq. (1.30) to treat θ as equivalent to a Lagrange multiplier, even though θ is a function, not a constant. Refer to the references for rigorous proofs for the necessary and sufficient conditions for the maximum principle.

[30] The Hamiltonian $\mathcal{H}$ in (1.30) is the *current-value* formulation. Equation (1.30) can also be written as follows:

$$-e^{-\rho t}\frac{\partial}{\partial k}\mathcal{H}(k, c, \theta, t) = \frac{d}{dt}(e^{-\rho t}\theta),$$

which is the *standard* formulation with Hamiltonian $\tilde{\mathcal{H}}$ and $\tilde{\theta}$:

$$\frac{\partial}{\partial k}\tilde{\mathcal{H}}(k, c, \theta, t) = e^{-\rho t}\frac{\partial}{\partial k}\mathcal{H}(k, c, \theta, t),$$

$$\tilde{\theta} = \frac{d}{dt}(e^{-\rho t}\theta),$$

$$\frac{\partial}{\partial k}\tilde{\mathcal{H}}(k, c, \theta, t) = -\tilde{\theta}.$$

is the *transversality condition* at time T:

$$\theta_T = \begin{cases} \text{no constraint} & \quad (1.31) \\ \geq 0 \qquad k_T = k_{TC} & \quad (1.32) \\ = 0 \qquad k_T > k_{TC} & \quad (1.33) \\ = 0 \qquad k_T \ \text{ is free.} & \quad (1.34) \end{cases}$$

The transversality condition is crucial for understanding the Hamiltonian optimal solution and, in the current context, for understanding the stability of the Ramsey economy. While modern interpretations of Ramsey models suggest that the Ramsey economy is stable, the current, reformulated Ramsey model reaches the opposite conclusion, largely due to the implications of the transversality condition (see Section 1.3.3 for a more detailed discussion). The transversality condition on the terminal capital stock plays a key role in how we interpret the Ramsey economy. Unlike optimal control problems in engineering, where terminal conditions on state variables are often clearly defined, households in a laissez-faire economy make decisions between consumption and investment without a predefined terminal condition for capital stock. As a result, conditions 1.32 and 1.33 are not applicable since no terminal value is imposed.

Condition 1.34 stipulates that the co-state variable is zero at the terminal time, implying that the shadow price—the marginal utility of additional capital stock—is zero. Such a condition is not relevant in the current context. If any capital stock did persist, it could have been utilized to enhance utility through consumption. Therefore, condition 1.34 specifies an end of the world and is consequently ruled out.

When a solution does not involve co-state conditions (as in condition 1.31), the amount of capital stock at the terminal time T is *not explicitly considered.* This may lead to a solution that only partially accounts for the trade-offs between consumption and investment. Through its control variable (consumption), the economy may become focused on short-term trajectories, thereby neglecting long-term optimality criteria. In a laissez-faire economy, households, when making consumption decisions, do not collectively account for the full impact on economy. Consequently, the state variable remains unconstrained at the terminal time T, as there is no coordinated mechanism to enforce optimal economic growth. This dynamic is characteristic of a laissez-faire economy. For a detailed mathematical background on transversality conditions, readers can refer to Acemoglu (2008), Sydsæter *et al.* (2008), and Weber (2011).

Taking the derivative of Eq. (1.14) with respect to k gives

$$\frac{\partial}{\partial k}\dot{k} = f'(k) - \delta, \tag{1.35}$$

and substituting into Eq. (1.29) to have the differential equation for θ:

$$\dot{\theta} = [\rho - f'(k) + \delta]\theta, \tag{1.36}$$

with the solution

$$\theta_T = \theta_t e^{\int_t^T [\rho - f'(k_s) + \delta] ds}. \tag{1.37}$$

1.3.1 *A laissez-faire economy: The free Ramsey model*

Using a concrete utility function can help grasp the idea of this model. Economists propose various utility functions concerning different human behaviors. Just like production functions, utility functions are constructs. Gérard Debreu proved that completeness and transitivity are the conditions required for a preference ordering of a finite set of alternatives to be expressible by utility functions. Edmund Eisenberg (1961) proved that if individuals' utility functions are homogeneous plus the regularity conditions, a representative utility function aggregates the individual's utility function.

This book uses a logarithmic utility function, $u(c) = \ln c$, a simple case of a family of utility functions.[31] The logarithmic utility $u(c) = \ln c$ increases with consumption ($u'(c) = 1/c > 0$), but each

[31]The logarithmic utility function is a member of the constant relative risk aversion (CRRA) class of utility functions in the context of uncertainty. In the 18th century, Daniel Bernoulli sought to resolve the St. Petersburg Paradox by introducing the logarithmic utility function. Fischer (1979) shows that superneutrality does not hold along transition paths except in the case of logarithmic utility. For the models in this book, superneutrality does not hold even in the case of logarithmic utility.

additional unit of consumption adds less utility ($u''(c) = -1/c^2 < 0$), satisfying the sufficient condition required for maximization.

Substituting $u(c) = \ln c$ into Eq. (1.27) gives the Hamiltonian of the Ramsey model:

$$\mathcal{H}(k, c, \theta, t) = \ln c + \theta \dot{k}. \tag{1.38}$$

Using Eq. (1.14) and taking the partial derivative of Eq. (1.38) with respect to c gives the first-order condition for consumption:

$$\frac{\partial}{\partial c}\mathcal{H}(k, c, \theta, t) = \frac{1}{c} - \theta = 0, \tag{1.39}$$

which gives θ:

$$\theta = \frac{1}{c}. \tag{1.40}$$

Thus, θ is a function of consumption. The second-order derivative of Eq. (1.39) with respect to c is negative, satisfying the second-order condition.

Substituting Eq. (1.40) into Eq. (1.36) gives the differential equation of consumption:

$$\dot{c} = [f'(k) - \delta - \rho]c, \tag{1.41}$$

which can also be derived from the *principle of least action* in physics (see Euler equation in Appendix A.1). Integrating Eq. (1.41) with the initial condition for consumption, $c_t = c_{IC}$, gives the optimal consumption path:

$$c_T = c_{IC} e^{\int_t^T [f'(k_s) - \delta - \rho] ds}. \tag{1.42}$$

Equation (1.41) or (1.42) represents the Ramsey rule, which provides the solution to the optimal consumption-investment problem. According to the Ramsey rule, households will opt to increase their consumption today if the net return on capital, $r = f'(k) - \delta$, exceeds the discount factor ρ. Conversely, if the net return is lower than or equal to the discount factor, households will either maintain their current level of consumption or reduce it.[32]

[32]The Ramsey rule is known as the Keynes–Ramsey rule. Keynes made suggestions to Ramsey who acknowledged them in his paper, and Keynes promoted the paper, but the Ramsey model is in opposite spirit and method to Keynesian economics. This book calls it the Ramsey rule.

The research of Martin and Hill (2015) emphasizes that saving behavior significantly enhances economic well-being. Their findings align with Collins (2009), which highlight that under conditions of severe poverty, savings play a significant role in improving the well-being of the world's poorest people. The study of Epper *et al.* (2020) on the relationship between individuals' time discounting and the wealth distribution using Danish administrative data finds a stable correlation. Their findings suggest that savings behavior drives the observed association between patience and wealth inequality, as predicted by the Ramsey rule.

A key distinction between the current interpretation of the Ramsey economy and the traditional perspective is economic stability. While both frameworks adhere to classical stability analysis of dynamic systems, the current model highlights the nuanced implications of stability within the Ramsey framework.

1.3.1.1 *Stability of the Ramsey model*

The method used to determine the stability of a farming economy (see Eq. (1.7)) can also be applied to the Ramsey model. To identify the stability of a system, we first need to find the equilibrium points of the dynamic system. At equilibrium points, both consumption and capital stock remain constant, i.e., $\dot{c}^* = \dot{k}^* = 0$, where the superscript $*$ denotes equilibrium values. Setting $\dot{k}^*$ in Eq. (1.14) and $\dot{c}^*$ in Eq. (1.41) to zero yields the following equilibrium conditions:

$$\dot{c}^* = F_1(c^*, k^*) = \left[f'(k^*) - \delta - \rho\right] c^* = 0, \tag{1.43}$$

$$\dot{k}^* = F_2(c^*, k^*) = f(k^*) - c^* - \delta k^* = 0. \tag{1.44}$$

A system can have multiple equilibrium points (Laurent and Sghari, 2009). The type of stability is specific to each point; some points may be stable, while others are unstable. The Ramsey model, for instance, includes an equilibrium point where both $c^* = k^* = 0$, indicating a dead economy—a scenario of limited interest to economists.

Small deviations of c and k from an equilibrium point cause changes in F_1 and F_2, moving the system away from equilibrium. The signs of $\frac{d(c-c^*)}{dt}$ and $\frac{d(k-k^*)}{dt}$ indicate whether the system moves toward or away from equilibrium. In the Ramsey model, consumption

c and capital stock k exhibit a nonlinear relationship. Near the equilibrium point, we apply the Taylor expansion to $F_1(c,k)$ and $F_2(c,k)$, resulting in linear approximations. For instance, the Taylor expansion of $F_1(c-c^*, k-k^*)$ is:

$$\begin{aligned}\frac{d(c-c^*)}{dt} &= F_1(c,k) = \frac{\partial F_1}{\partial c^*}(c-c^*) + \frac{\partial F_1}{\partial k^*}(k-k^*) + \cdots \\ &\approx \begin{bmatrix} \frac{\partial F_1}{\partial c^*} & \frac{\partial F_1}{\partial k^*} \end{bmatrix} \begin{bmatrix} c-c^* \\ k-k^* \end{bmatrix} \cdots .\end{aligned}$$

This system involves two equations and four partial derivatives. To simplify the notations and facilitate the analysis, we collect the partial derivatives in a Jacobian matrix, $\mathcal{M}$, which provides a systematic way to analyze the local stability of the system near the equilibrium point, offering insights into how the system responds to small perturbations. The matrix is constructed from the first-order partial derivatives of the functions F_1 and F_2 with respect to the variables c and k. Specifically, $\mathcal{M}$ is given by:

$$\frac{d}{dt}\begin{bmatrix} c-c^* \\ k-k^* \end{bmatrix} = \mathcal{M}\begin{bmatrix} c-c^* \\ k-k^* \end{bmatrix}, \tag{1.45}$$

$$\mathcal{M} = \begin{bmatrix} \frac{\partial F_1}{\partial c^*} & \frac{\partial F_1}{\partial k^*} \\ \frac{\partial F_2}{\partial c^*} & \frac{\partial F_2}{\partial k^*} \end{bmatrix} = \begin{bmatrix} f'(k^*)-\delta-\rho & f''(k^*)c^* \\ -1 & f'(k^*)-\delta \end{bmatrix}. \tag{1.46}$$

Using Eq. (1.43), $f'(k^*)-\delta = \rho$, simplify the matrix to

$$\mathcal{M} = \begin{bmatrix} 0 & f''(k^*)c^* \\ -1 & \rho \end{bmatrix} \tag{1.47}$$

which has two eigenvalues:

$$\frac{1}{2}\left(\rho \pm \sqrt{\rho^2 - 4c^* f''(k^*)}\right). \tag{1.48}$$

Given the diminishing marginal returns, the second-order derivative of the production function $f''(k^*)$ is negative, ensuring that the square root term is always greater than the first term in the brackets. As a result, the two eigenvalues of the system have opposite signs.

At an equilibrium point, the signs of the two eigenvalues determine the type of stability, with three outcomes. An equilibrium point

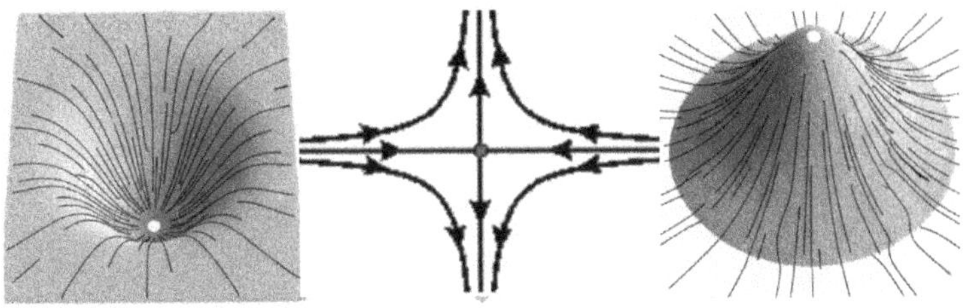

Fig. 1.7. Types of stability (The figures on the left and right were generated using Gemini AI).

with two negative eigenvalues is stable. As shown on the left of Figure 1.7, all paths around a stable equilibrium point converge toward it, like water being sucked into a sink (valley). Conversely, an equilibrium point with two positive eigenvalues is unstable, as depicted on the right of the figure, where all paths diverge from the equilibrium point, resembling water flowing out of a source (peak). An equilibrium point with one negative and one positive eigenvalue exhibits *saddle-point stability*. In the middle of the figure, horizontal arrows converge on the equilibrium point, while vertical arrows move away from it, and no other paths reach the equilibrium point.

To illustrate saddle-point stability, picture a horse saddle. The ridge of the saddle features a low point where a ball can rest, symbolizing the equilibrium point. However, if the ball strays slightly from this ridge, it will roll down the slope on either side, leading to instability. This picture captures the essence of saddle-point stability: only specific trajectories converge to the equilibrium point, and slight deviations place the system onto the unstable paths, diverging away from it (Greiner and Semmler, 1996).

Figure 1.8 presents the trajectories within the Ramsey model. The horizontal axis denotes capital stock k, while the vertical axis denotes consumption c. This phase portrait features arrows that illustrate both the direction and the rate of change of k and c.

The four main lines in the figure intersect at the equilibrium point. Lines I and III feature arrows moving toward the equilibrium, while lines II and IV feature arrows moving away. The system can only reach equilibrium along lines I and III, known as *stable paths* or *stable arms*.

Four prominent curved lines in the figure represent sample paths, each beginning from a tiny circle. These curves show that even though

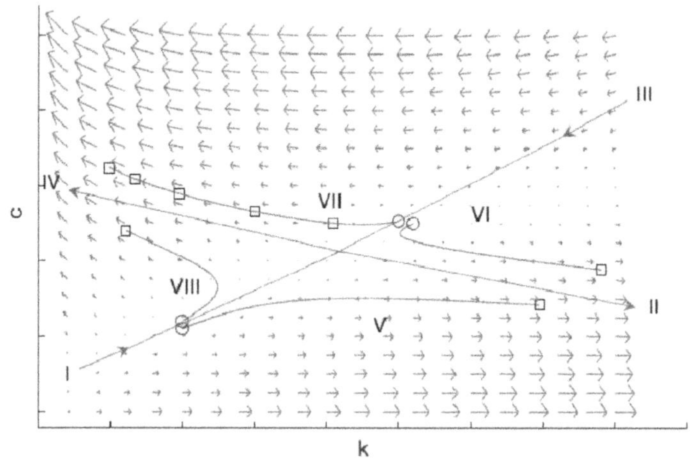

Fig. 1.8. Phase plot of the Ramsey model.

some starting points are close to the stable paths; they diverge over time if not precisely on the stable paths. The divergence highlights the fragility of saddle-path stability, where any slight deviation leads the economy away from the stable path. Staying on the stable path is like walking on a rope. An acrobat can fall off the rope with a tiny slip. Any slight deviation from the stable path is the point of no return, without intervention from outside the laissez-faire economy.

Lines II and IV partition the economies near paths I and III into two types: "frugal" and "lavish" economies. In a "frugal" economy, consumption decreases, while in a "lavish" economy, it increases. Meanwhile, lines I and III divide the economy into "shrinking" and "expanding" categories. A "shrinking" economy experiences declining capital stock, while an "expanding" economy sees increasing capital stock. Figure 1.9 divides the economy into four quadrants: "expanding, frugal," "shrinking, frugal," "expanding, lavish," and "shrinking, lavish" economies.

Keep in mind that "lavish" and "frugal" refer to increasing and decreasing consumption in economies situated near the stable paths I and III. In a "shrinking, lavish" economy, consumption rises, but capital stock declines.

Conversely, a "shrinking, frugal" economy experiences decrease in both consumption and capital stock. Consumption decreases, but the increase in investment is not enough to cover depreciation, and the economy is still losing capital stock. It should be stressed that the

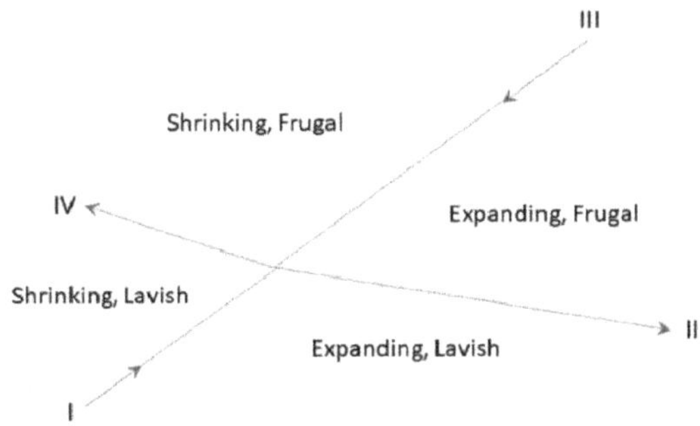

Fig. 1.9. Instability quadrants.

categories "frugal" and "lavish" are meaningful only for economies not too distant from the stable paths. Once economies move far away, unusual behavior may arise. Figure 1.8 shows that consumption can still go up as capital stock approaches zero. This occurs because, as capital stock diminishes, the economy consumes the remaining capital stock, treating it as consumption goods. Examples of such seemingly "suicidal" economic behavior are not lacking. Most capital goods are different from consumption goods in an industrialized economy, but the economy can exchange capital goods for consumption goods.

A "shrinking" economy with multiple sectors does not mean all sectors are shrinking evenly or simultaneously. Some sectors can even grow at the expense of others. A war economy is a prime example. While the overall economy may shrink due to destruction or other factors, sectors such as defense can expand by diverting production capacity and resources from non-defense sectors. For instance, Great Britain's economy was on the path to bankruptcy during World War II, yet it still managed to sustain a growing defense sector. Wartime net losses of British national wealth totaled 18.6% (£4.595 billion) of pre-war wealth (£24.68 billion) at 1938 prices. The proportion of GDP devoted to the war effort rose from 15.3% in 1939, peaking at 55.3% in 1943.[33]

An "expanding" economy increases its capital stock. In an "expanding, frugal" economy, capital stock grows, but consumption

[33] *United Kingdom home front during World War II*, Wikipedia, accessed on August 30, 2024.

decreases. In an "expanding, lavish" economy, both consumption and capital stock increase. The increase in consumption reduces investment, but the investment is more than depreciation and the capital stock still increases. However, an economy cannot continually accumulate capital and produce more than it consumes. Closed economies cannot sustain either the "expanding, lavish" or "expanding, frugal" types; they must either raise consumption to absorb the excess output or open to external trade for exports.

For example, in the late 1980s, Japan could no longer rely on export-driven growth as it had in previous decades. To sustain growth, Japan shifted its focus to boosting domestic demand. Policies were introduced to improve the standard of living, promote high-tech products, and enhance healthcare, housing, and entertainment. Japanese consumers responded with increased spending, driving growth in domestic high-tech industries. As a result, Japan's imports began to outpace exports after 1986. However, despite these efforts, the bubble eventually burst in 1991, highlighting the challenges of managing an unstable expanding economy.

1.3.2 *The managed Ramsey model*

When social planners or governments establish specific goals, such as consumption or capital stock $S(k_T)$ targets at the end of the time horizon, effectively setting additional, terminal conditions (Benassy, 2011; Barro, 2003).[34] Then the Ramsey model solution needs to satisfy both initial and terminal conditions.

The system comprising the Ramsey rule, Eq. (1.41), and the state equation, Eq. (1.14), fully describes the real economy. Both are the first-order differential equations; each requires either an initial condition or a terminal condition for a unique solution but not both. Equation (1.20) and Eq. (1.21) set two initial conditions for the Ramsey model free from terminal constraints.

The co-state variable, θ, represents the reciprocal of consumption ($\theta = 1/c$), and the Ramsey rule, Eq. (1.41), serves as an alternative representation of the co-state equation, Eq. (1.36).

[34]Readers who are not interested in the technical details of the transversality conditions may wish to skip Section 1.3.2.

To fulfill an additional terminal condition, we differentiate either the co-state equation (1.36) (or the Ramsey rule Eq. (1.41)) to have a second-order differential equation that can satisfy both initial and terminal conditions:

$$\frac{d^2}{dt^2}\theta = (\rho - r)\dot{\theta} = (\rho - r)^2\theta, \tag{1.49}$$

which assumes $r = f'(k) - \delta$ is constant for simplicity. The approximation holds in the short term; however, over the long horizon, diminishing returns require r to fall.

The solution to a first-order differential equation will also satisfy the corresponding second-order equation obtained through differentiation. For instance, in classical mechanics, the position s with respect to time has the first-order derivative representing velocity $\dot{s} = v = at$, and the integration gives:

$$s_t = b_1 + \int_0^t v_s ds,$$

which has one constant b_1 and can only satisfy either an initial or a terminal condition. The second-order derivative representing acceleration:

$$\frac{d^2}{dt^2}s = \dot{v} = a.$$

The solution for the first-order differential equation automatically satisfies the second-order differential equation. Integrating the second-order differential gives the position $s = b_2 + b_1 t + \frac{1}{2}at^2$, showing that the second-order equation includes two constants (here, b_1 and b_2) and thus can satisfy both initial and terminal conditions.

The general principle is that while the solution of a first-order equation will satisfy the corresponding second-order equation, the reverse is not always true. For example, a harmonic-oscillator equation $\frac{d^2}{dt^2}x + \omega^2 x = 0$ has a sinusoidal solution $x(t) = A\cos\omega t + B\sin\omega t$, where A and B are constants, but a related first-order equation can have an exponentially decaying solution, $x(t) = Ce^{(-\omega t)}$, where C is a constant, highlighting that the two systems describe two different dynamics.

Therefore, Eq. (1.49) satisfies the Ramsey rule and can accommodate additional conditions. This section presents two examples that use second-order differential equations to specify system dynamics under a terminal condition set by a central planner. The next two sections present two simple examples of the Ramsey model with terminal conditions.

1.3.2.1 *The minimum consumption constraint*

A central planner or a government wants to control minimum consumption at the end of the planning period. Under this constraint, the transversality condition for θ is

$$\theta_T = \begin{cases} > 0 & c_T = c_{\min} \\ = 0 & c_T > c_{\min}, \end{cases} \tag{1.50}$$

where θ cannot be zero because θ is equal to $1/c$. Thus, we have

$$\theta_T = \frac{1}{c_T} = \frac{1}{c_{\min}} > 0. \tag{1.51}$$

Assuming short-term constancy of $r = f'(k) - \delta$, we can find a closed-form solution for Eq. (1.49) that satisfies both the initial and terminal conditions. The general solution for $0 \le \tau \le T$ is

$$\theta_\tau = \frac{1}{c_\tau} = B_1 e^{(\rho - r)\tau} + B_2 e^{-(\rho - r)\tau}, \tag{1.52}$$

with the initial condition at time $t = 0$ and the terminal condition:

$$\begin{aligned} \theta_0 &= \frac{1}{c_{IC}}, \\ \theta_T &= \frac{1}{c_{\min}}. \end{aligned} \tag{1.53}$$

Then we establish the following relationships:

$$\begin{aligned} \theta_0 &= B_1 + B_2, \\ \theta_T &= B_1 e^{(\rho - r)T} + B_2 e^{-(\rho - r)T}. \end{aligned} \tag{1.54}$$

Solving B_1 and B_2 yields,

$$\begin{aligned} B_1 &= \frac{\theta_T - \theta_0 e^{-(\rho - r)T}}{e^{(\rho - r)T} - e^{-(\rho - r)T}}, \\ B_2 &= \frac{\theta_0 e^{(\rho - r)T} - \theta_T}{e^{(\rho - r)T} - e^{-(\rho - r)T}}. \end{aligned} \tag{1.55}$$

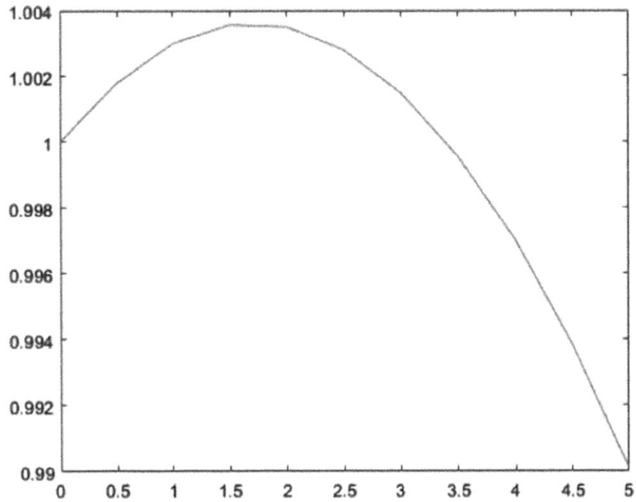

Fig. 1.10. Consumption with terminal value at $T = 5$.

Figure 1.10 illustrates the consumption path with a terminal constraint at $T = 5$. Consumption initially rises before declining to the terminal level. This behavior exemplifies systems with fixed terminal values, where consumption reaches a peak between the initial and terminal times but must revert to specified values at the terminal time T.

The solutions of optimal control problems over finite horizons exhibit a turnpike property. This property suggests that optimal solutions typically comprise three stages: In the first, the system moves from the initial condition to the optimal state, and in the last stage, the system moves into the terminal state. Figure 1.11 compares the effects of discount factors on the turnpike arcs over a longer horizon $T = 50$. The top curve has $r = 0.03$ and the bottom curve has $r = 0.02$. Although the difference between net returns is only 0.01, the effect on consumption is significant.

1.3.2.2 *The scrap value constraint*

When an economy aims to maintain a certain capital stock at terminal time, the scrap value $S(k_T)$ in Eq. (1.18) is positive. In this scenario, the terminal co-state variable is given by $\theta_T = S'(k_T)$ (Chang,

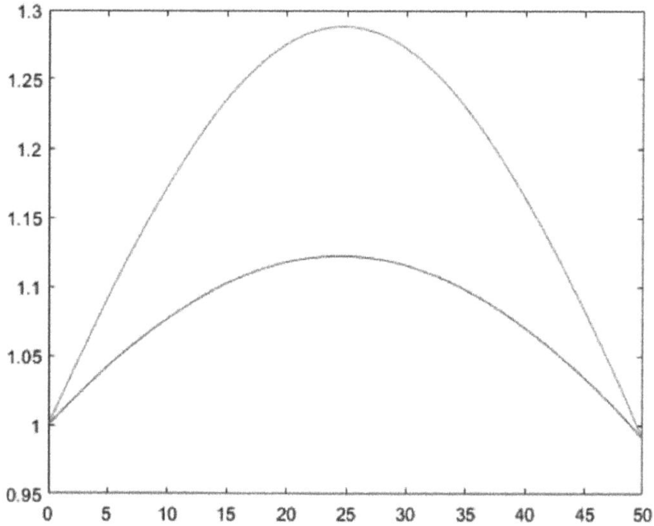

Fig. 1.11. Consumption with terminal value at $T = 50$.

2016). If the economy's goal is to leave capital stock at time T, for example,

$$\theta_T = S'(k_T) = 1/(Ak_T),$$

where the scrap function S is not arbitrary and must be consistent with the unit of $\theta = 1/c$, where c is a flow variable (see p. 171). For instance, $S = \ln(k_T)/\alpha$ and $S'(k_T) = \theta_T = 1/(\alpha k_T)$, where α is a constant and αk_T has the unit of output flow. Thus, the co-state θ must satisfy the initial condition $\theta_t = 1/c_{IC}$ and the terminal condition $\theta_T = 1/(\alpha k_T)$, which is also consistent with Eq. (1.32), $\theta_T \geq 0$. Replacing θ_T with $1/(\alpha k_T)$ in Eq. (1.55) yields the corresponding solution for an economy with the scrap value constraint.

The examples thus far have operated under the assumption of direct control over *real* variables by a central planner. The practical question is how to realistically control them but still giving people choices. Controlling real variables contrasts with the reality of most managed economies, where governments primarily influence the economy through *monetary* variables. The practice raises the critical question of whether such monetary tools can effectively regulate real economic activity, a topic explored in later chapters. We now return to the analysis of the laissez-faire economy.

1.3.3 *Justify the divergent conclusions*

1.3.3.1 *Initial and terminal conditions*

Ramsey's original paper did not discuss its stability implications. Later, David Cass and Tjalling Koopmans extended it into what became known as the Ramsey–Cass–Koopmans model. Spear and Young (2014) proposed that the neoclassical growth model might be more accurately named the Ramsey–Malinvaud–Cass model. The *modern* versions of the Ramsey model claim that the only path for the economy is the stable saddle path, eliminating all other paths. This claim relies on two key assumptions: perfect foresight and consumption jumps. The *current* Ramsey model excludes perfect foresight and requires a continuous consumption path without jumps.

Perfect foresight assumes that households know the trajectory of the economy and can project it into the future, thereby enabling them to follow the stable path to the equilibrium point. This assumption allows the modern Ramsey model to specify the terminal condition at infinity.

For the two first-order differential equations, Eqs. (1.14) and (1.41), which govern the system's dynamics, the current Ramsey model specifies two initial conditions, whereas the modern Ramsey model chooses one initial condition and one terminal condition. The terminal condition, the transversality condition, ensures no Ponzi schemes and that no wealth is left behind at infinity (Cass, 1965; Koopmans, 1965).

A Ponzi scheme pays earlier investors with money taken from new investors—borrowing from the new investors to pay the existing investors. The no-Ponzi-scheme condition ensures that no debt remains at the terminal time. One version of the transversality condition is expressed as (Malinvaud, 1953),

$$\lim_{t\to\infty} k_t^* \theta_t e^{-\rho t} \geq 0, \tag{1.56}$$

where k_t^* is measured by money. In a Ponzi scheme, perpetrators could accumulate debt and sustain negative wealth indefinitely, thereby violating Eq. (1.56).

With perfect foresight, rational individuals would spend all their money if they knew for sure that tomorrow was the end of the world. In this case, Eq. (1.56) becomes an equality:

$$\lim_{t\to\infty} k_t^* \theta_t e^{-\rho t} = 0. \tag{1.57}$$

The interpretation of the modern Ramsey model with the transversality condition can be summarized as follows: An infinitely lived household that overconsumes experiences infinite utility loss, while under-consumption yields infinite utility gain—both outcomes violate the transversality condition Eq. (1.57). In other words, should the household detect any deviation of the economy from the path implied by Eq. (1.57), it would swiftly adjust its consumption upward or downward, effectively steering the economy back toward stability.

This transversality condition makes the Ramsey model mathematically elegant.[35] However, the assumption of perfect foresight has been heavily criticized (Gandolfo, 1997).

First, economic history—with its boom-and-bust cycles—demonstrates that perfect foresight does not align with reality. Furthermore, the transversality condition at infinity is paradoxical. Infinity has no end, and even if we accept infinity as an approximation of a long time in the future, the transversality condition requires knowledge of the exact time the world will end. Without this knowledge, individuals may either leave wealth behind or exhaust all resources prematurely, leading to a self-fulfilling prophecy of economic collapse. Keynes famously remarked, "In the long-run we are all dead," and "...this long run is a misleading guide to current affairs" (Keynes, 1923). Perfect foresight constitutes a profoundly unrealistic assumption; households lack perfect foresight and do not plan for the infinite time horizon.

The claim that the economy always follows a stable saddle-path assumes that households coordinate their consumption. If the economy deviates from the stable path, households are expected to adjust

[35] "I adhered scrupulously to the precept of that brilliant theoretical physicist L. Boltzmann, according to whom matters of elegance ought to be left to the tailor and to the cobbler" (Hawking, 2009).

their consumption to bring the economy back on track. The adjustment requires households to know where the economy stands and where the stable path is, and to coordinate their actions precisely. In a capitalist system, however, consumption is an individual choice, and the collective effect of individuals' free choices is more likely to push the economy off track than to keep it on the stable path. As Solow observed, perfect foresight is implausible, and exact coordination is impossible in a decentralized economy (Solow and Diamond, 1990):

> The problem is not just that perfect foresight into the indefinite future is so implausible away from steady states. The deeper problem is that in practice—if there is any practice—miscalculations about the equilibrium path may not reveal themselves for a long time. ... In a decentralized economy it will not be clear who knows what, or where the true converging arm is, or, for that matter, exactly where we are now, given that some agents (speculators) will already have perceived the need for a mid-course correction while others have not. This thought makes it hard even to imagine what a long-run path would look like. It strikes me as more or less devastating for the interpretation of quarterly data as the solution to an infinite time optimization problem.—Solow and Diamond (1990)

The modern Ramsey model also claims that when households realize the economy is off the stable path, their optimal response is to immediately adjust consumption to the corresponding point on the stable path. However, this assumption is both mathematically inconsistent and unrealistic in practice.

First, from a mathematical perspective, allowing consumption to "jump" violates the continuous nature of the state equation Eq. (1.14), which governs the evolution of capital stock. In this equation, investment $\dot{k}$ is continuous, and output $f(k)$ must also be continuous. A discontinuous jump in consumption would disrupt this balance because it would necessitate an instantaneous jump in capital stock, which is inconsistent with the continuous structure of the differential equation governing output, investment, and consumption.[36]

[36]Incorporating jumps in Eq. (1.14) requires a different model (Getz and Martin, 1980). Moreover, the total capital stock in an economy cannot be increased instantaneously, although it can be destroyed in an instant.

In the real economy, physical constraints limit how quickly the economy can change. Firms take time to expand production capacity, although they can quickly cut output by idling production.[37] Similarly, consumption can increase within the limits of firms' inventories, but increasing inventory production diverts resources from investment in capital stock, altering the economy's trajectory (see Chapter 3).

In the Ramsey model, consumption is the control variable. In general, system control models do not require control variables to be continuous. With a known optimal solution, the system starts at the optimal point and then follows the optimal path continuously. However, economic models cannot assume all economies begin on the stable path.

Additionally, a control variable jump does not necessarily cause a system to jump. For example, turning a heater on or off changes the room temperature gradually, not instantly. Likewise, sudden changes in government or central bank policy, such as a jump in tax rates or interest rates, do not lead to immediate jumps in the real economy. The real economy has inertia, much like a heavy truck that speeds up gradually even after the gas pedal is pressed to the floor. This is one of the key differences between money and the real economy—money can jump, but the real economy grows only gradually.

The current model reformulates the modern Ramsey model by introducing two important adjustments. First, it maximizes utility over a finite time horizon rather than an infinite one. This reflects the fact that households make consumption decisions over finite time horizons. Decision-makers, such as governments and central banks, operate within finite terms. For example, people elect the U.S. president every four years, and a four-year term can be viewed as a reasonable time horizon for the government policy. Similarly, Federal Reserve officials serve four-year terms, which can be renewed, making four years a realistic policy horizon for the Fed.

---

[37] *Ibid.*

Second, the current model replaces the transversality condition with the initial condition in Eq. (1.21) and enforces a no-jump condition on consumption $\dot{c} < \infty$ in Eq. (1.22).[38] Under the initial and no-jump conditions for consumption, any economy that starts off the stable path cannot jump back to the stable path and must move along the trajectory dictated by the system dynamics. With these reformulated conditions, the Ramsey model reveals that the real economy exhibits inherent instability.

1.4 Measure and Control Instability of the Real Economy

An economy can gauge its deviation from the stable path by comparing the trajectory's slope to the stable path's slope near the equilibrium point in the phase plot. The stable path's slope, denoted as Π^*, represents the direction of the stable paths near the equilibrium point on the phase portrait in Figure 1.8:

$$\Pi^* = \lim_{k \to k^*, c \to c^*} \frac{c - c^*}{k - k^*} \text{ for } \{k, c\} \text{ on paths I and III.} \tag{1.58}$$

The eigenvalues provided in Eq. (1.48) determine the slope of the stable path.[39]

By comparing the realized slope to the slope of the stable paths in Eq. (1.58), we obtain a measure of the economy's instability, denoted as Δ slope:

$$\Delta \text{ slope} \approx \left| \frac{\Delta c}{\Delta k} - \Pi^* \right|. \tag{1.59}$$

where Δc and Δk are the changes in consumption and capital stock in a time interval.

---

[38]If consumption c lies in a convex set and the Hamiltonian $\mathcal{H}$ is strictly concave in c, then an optimal control c must be continuous.

[39]See Benjamin Moll's lecture notes, *Analysis of optimal trajectories, transition dynamics in growth model*, by Benjamin Moll, for the details on the eigenvalues as the slope of saddle path of the Ramsey model (benjaminmoll.com/lectures).

In Figure 1.8, an unstable economy at a point $\{c, k\}$ moves in the direction indicated by the small arrow. The directions of these small arrows differ significantly from the direction of the stable-path direction. An economy can detect this difference even without precise data. When close to the stable path, the difference decreases. As it approaches the equilibrium point, the difference in Eq. (1.59) eventually approaches zero.

1.4.1 *Control of the real economy*

In the Ramsey model, the instability of the economy is *intrinsic*, rooted within the system. In early agrarian economies, farmers, often as serfs, exhibited a high degree of self-sufficiency after paying rent to the landowner, typically in the form of a share of their harvest or through labor on the lord's demesne (the reserved land). This arrangement blurred the line between producers and consumers, as farmers were both cultivating their own food and consuming it.

Capitalist economies create a clear separation between these roles: firms are dedicated to producing goods while consumers engage exclusively in consumption. Households make individual consumption choices independently, lacking any coordinated effort, while firms make individual production decisions based on demand forecasts, and they compete intensely. Decentralized production and consumption do not naturally achieve balance, and the laissez-faire economy is devoid of an intrinsic mechanism for ensuring stability.

In modern economics and finance, *external disturbances* are often introduced as sources of economic instability. Stochastic economic models incorporate Brownian motion or jump processes to represent these disturbances. These external shocks are akin to gusts of wind affecting a parked car. A car parked at the top of a hill can be easily blown off by a strong gust of wind, while a car in a valley, although affected by the wind, gravity pulls it back to stability. The car's intrinsic stability, whether on a hill or in a valley, is not altered by wind, unless subjected to the blast or shock waves of nuclear explosions. Robert Merton introduced Brownian motion into models,[40] but Brownian motion does not fundamentally alter consumption and investment behaviors, although his model is not a reflection of the

[40] Appendix A.4 provides a model that incorporates uncertainty.

real economy, nor does it examine economic stability (Merton and Samuelson, 1992). External shocks primarily knock an economy off its path, making the Ramsey economy less stable and more prone to deviations from the stable path.

A stable system can withstand disturbances within certain ranges and return to equilibrium. When an unstable system faces an unexpected shock, optimal control can be designed to counteract its effects. Various industries, such as aerospace, have long used the Kalman filter—a Bayesian approach—to control disturbances in systems like rockets. In principle, economics can adopt similar system control techniques to stabilize economies in response to external disturbances.

However, controlling an economy also means influencing human behavior. While the challenges of influencing human behavior are often emphasized, the ease with which humans can be motivated is sometimes overlooked. Humans tend to be more readily influenced toward desired outcomes compared to machines. Straightforward instruction or a source of motivation can effectively inspire people to put in effort, while programming machines to achieve comparable results requires a far higher level of complexity and never evokes the same level of creativity found in human effort. A capitalist economy serves as an excellent illustration of these principles. On a smaller scale, practices such as intra-sourcing and crowdsourcing among employees can lead to improved problem-solving and outcomes. Toyota's reward system significantly enhanced the quality of its vehicles. The key issue is designing the right system, not controlling humans like machines. The unique strength of capitalism is its ability to motivate individuals to maximize their utility. A system that benefits individuals can motivate broad participation, enhancing the efficiency of the economy without constraining the advantages of capitalism.

Governments have been managing economies long before the capitalist system emerged. The word "economy" comes from the Greek word[41] meaning "household management." The earliest detailed discussions on economics date back to ancient Greece. Critobulus defined an economist as someone who manages "his own house or

[41] *oikonomia.*

estate well" (Xenophon, 1890). Socrates, known for his probing questions, asked Critobulus if an economist should be paid for managing a house, just as one might be paid for building one. An economist, as suggested in Socrates' question, was like a manager (Atanelishvili and Silagadze, 2018). Then their conversations moved from managing soil, sowing, to war. Socrates suggested that a ruler must manage the economy and war: "I hope, to imitate the kings of Persia? That monarch, it is said, regards amongst the noblest and most necessary pursuits two, which are the arts of husbandry and war, and in these two he takes the strongest interest." The success of Persia's monarchs suggested that effective leadership derives from integrating economic management with military strategy, in contrast to Plato's ideal of philosopher-kings.

Managing the economy was not optional for rulers; it was a necessity for feeding the population and supporting war efforts. Henry Kissinger famously said, "Control the food, control the people. Control the energy, control the continents, control the money, control the world." In modern times, international politics is deeply intertwined with money and the economy. Regardless of political philosophy, governments intervene in their economies to varying degrees, leading to a spectrum of economic systems. At one end of the spectrum is the planned economy, while at the other is pure laissez-faire. The recent economic and financial crises continue to pose the unresolved challenge of stabilizing the economy and fostering prosperity.

Managing an agrarian economy, as discussed earlier, represents the simplest case. The farm in Eq. (1.5) follows the AK production model, given in per capita form as:

$$\dot{k} = (A - \delta)k - c. \tag{1.60}$$

Subtracting $(A-\delta)k$ on both sides and multiplying by $e^{-(A-\delta)t}$, then integrating gives:

$$k_T = e^{(A-\delta)t}\left[k_{IC} - \frac{c}{A-\delta}\right] + \frac{c}{A-\delta}.$$

In an economy that follows the AK model, growth at rate g requires consumption and investment to increase at the same rate. Balanced growth can be demonstrated by dividing the terms in

Table 1.4. Steadily growing farm.

Year	Seed	Yield	Consumption
	48% of Yield		52% of Yield
1	1	2.5	1.3
2	1.2	3.00	1.56
3	1.44	3.60	1.872
4	1.728	4.32	2.246
5	2.074	5.184	2.700

Eq. (1.60) by k. When the capital stock grows at rate $g = \dot{k}/k$ on the left-hand side, the ratio c/k must remain constant at $A-\delta-g$. This balanced-growth property is specific to the AK framework. Readers may derive for themselves the general condition under which balanced growth holds.

If a farm wants to increase output by 20% annually, it must ensure that consumption and investment also increase by 20%. This is the steady growth shown in Table 1.4.

In a farming economy, a fraction $(1-s)$ of the output is consumed:

$$c = (1-s)y = (1-s)Ak,$$

where s is a constant and $0 < s < 1$. The remaining fraction is saved as seeds. The capital stock follows the AK production model:

$$\dot{k} = Ak - (1-s)Ak - \delta k = (sA-\delta)k, \tag{1.61}$$

which has the solution:

$$k_t = k_{IC}e^{[sA-\delta]t}. \tag{1.62}$$

In Table 1.4, the seed-output ratio is $A = 2.5$, and the depreciation rate of seeds is 100%, or $\delta = 1$. For a growth rate of 20%, we have

$$sA - \delta = 0.2, \tag{1.63}$$

which yields an investment (saving) rate of $s = 0.48$. Thus, the farming economy saves 48% of output as seeds, consumes 52% of output, and $c/k = A - \delta - g = 1.3$.

Robert Merton Solow developed the Solow growth model, also known as the Solow–Swan model (Solow, 1956, 1985; Barro and Sala-i-Martin, 2003; Acemoglu, 2008). The Solow model replaces Ak with $f(k)$ in Eq. (1.61) and assumes a fixed ratio of consumption to output, $(1 - s)$. In the Solow model, the gross investment, the investment before depreciation, is a fixed fraction of output, $sf(k)$, with no consideration of households' time preferences or utility functions. Consumption moves in lockstep with output. Consequently, the Solow model simplifies to a single equation for capital stock k:

$$\begin{aligned} \dot{k} &= sf(k) - \delta k, \\ k_0 &= k_{IC}. \end{aligned} \tag{1.64}$$

With the Cobb–Douglas production function, Eq. (1.64) becomes an explicit equation:

$$\dot{k} = sAk^a - \delta k, \tag{1.65}$$

which has a closed-form solution. By multiplying both sides by $(1 - a)k^{-a}$ and substituting $x = k^{1-a}$, we can transform Eq. (1.65) into a linear first-order differential equation:

$$\dot{x} + (1 - a)\delta x = (1 - a)sA. \tag{1.66}$$

Multiplying both sides by $e^{(1-a)\delta t}$ and substituting $z = xe^{(1-a)\delta t}$ simplifies Eq. (1.66) to:

$$\dot{z} = (1 - a)sAe^{(1-a)\delta t}. \tag{1.67}$$

Integrating Eq. (1.67) yields:

$$k_t^{1-a} = \frac{sA}{\delta}\left[1 - e^{-(1-a)\delta t}\right] + k_{IC}^{1-a}e^{-(1-a)\delta t}. \tag{1.68}$$

In the Solow model, the economy grows steadily and reaches the equilibrium, which is implied by Eq. (1.68):

$$k_t^{1-a} = \frac{sA}{\delta} \tag{1.69}$$

In Figure 1.12, the horizontal axis denotes capital stock k (cumulative investments), while the curve at the top represents output. Output

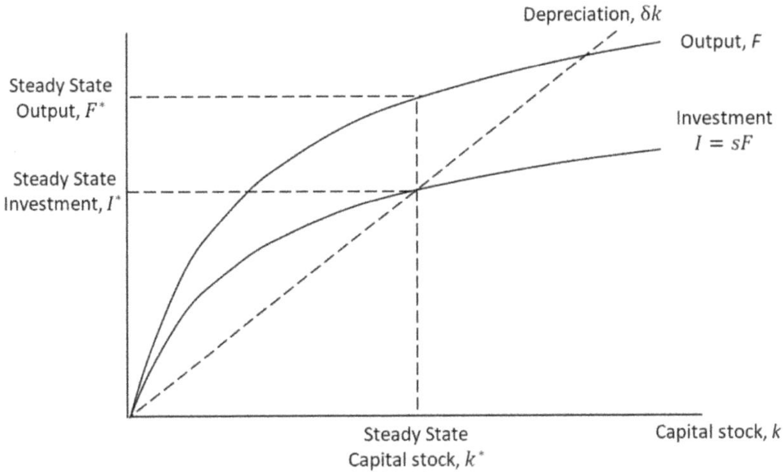

Fig. 1.12. Solow growth model.

increases with capital stock, but the curve bends downward due to diminishing marginal returns on capital stock, characterized by a negative second-order derivative, $f''(k) < 0$. The diminishing returns in the Solow model account for resource constraints, making it more realistic than the AK model in the long term.

In Figure 1.12, the investment as a fraction of the production output also curves downward. In contrast, depreciation, δk, grows with capital stock at a constant rate, δ. The investment curve intersects the depreciation line at the equilibrium point, where investment is just enough to cover depreciation:

$$\dot{k}^* = F(k^*) = sf(k^*) - \delta k^* = 0. \tag{1.70}$$

The Solow model has a single variable, k, and the slope near the equilibrium point is given by:

$$\frac{d(k - k^*)}{dt} = [sf'(k^*) - \delta](k - k^*), \tag{1.71}$$

where the slope of the investment curve is less than the slope of depreciation, $sf'(k) - \delta < 0$, indicating that the equilibrium point is stable. For $k > k^*$, the right-hand side of Eq. (1.71) is negative and $d(k - k^*)/dt < 0$, driving k back toward the equilibrium point k^*. For $k < k^*$, the right-hand side of Eq. (1.71) is positive and

$d(k - k^*)/dt > 0$, pushing k upward toward the equilibrium point k^*. This dynamic is analogous to a car at the bottom of a valley in Figure 1.1, which returns to the bottom when pushed to either side.

Figure 1.12 divides the Solow model into two regions. In the region where $sf(k) < \delta k$, investment (savings) is insufficient to cover depreciation, causing capital stock to fall and pulling the economy back to equilibrium. In the region where $sf(k) > \delta k$, investment exceeds depreciation, causing capital stock to grow and pushing the economy up to equilibrium. Thus, the equilibrium point is stable.

The Solow model implies that, at the equilibrium point, the level of capital stock k depends on the saving rate s:

$$k^*(s) = \left(\frac{sA}{\delta}\right)^{1/(1-a)}.$$

Thus, the consumption at the equilibrium point is also a function of s:

$$c^*(s) = f[k^*(s)] - \delta k^*(s). \tag{1.72}$$

By optimizing the saving rate s, households maximize consumption, which is referred to as the "golden rule" of consumption (Acemoglu, 2008). Taking the derivative of Eq. (1.72) with respect to s yields:

$$\frac{\partial c^*(s)}{\partial s} = \frac{\partial}{\partial s}[f(k^*(s)) - \delta k^*(s)] = [f'(k^*(s)) - \delta]\frac{\partial k^*(s)}{\partial s} = 0, \tag{1.73}$$

which implies the golden rule:

$$f'(k^*(s_{\text{gold}})) = \delta. \tag{1.74}$$

Using the Cobb–Douglas production function,

$$f'(k^*) = aAk^{*.a-1} = \delta, \tag{1.75}$$

in which the second equality results directly from Eq. (1.69). Using Eq. (1.75), we have the golden rule saving rate:

$$s_{\text{gold}} = a. \tag{1.76}$$

Equation (1.76) shows that the optimal fraction s of output to invest back into capital stock is equal to the output elasticity of capital, a.

Production output can be divided into two parts:

$$f(K, L) = af(K, L) + (1 - a)f(K, L),$$

where $af(K, L)$ represents gross return and $(1-a)f(K, L)$ represents wages. A firm chooses labor to maximize profit:

$$\max_L Pf(K, L) - wL - P\delta K, \tag{1.77}$$

where w is the nominal wage and P is the price of production output. The first-order condition for profit maximization is

$$\frac{\partial}{\partial L}[Pf(K, L) - wL] = 0. \tag{1.78}$$

Taking the derivative with respect to L of $f(K, L)$ gives the *marginal product of labor*, which measures a firm's output increase when it adds one more unit of labor. Solving Eq. (1.78) for wage gives:

$$w = P\frac{\partial}{\partial L}f(K, L) = P(1 - a)A\left(\frac{K}{L}\right)^a = P(1 - a)f(k). \tag{1.79}$$

Thus, the real wage is given by:

$$\frac{w}{P} = (1 - a)f(k). \tag{1.80}$$

The golden rule of the Solow model, Eq. (1.76) implies that the optimal investment, $sf(k) = af(k)$, is the gross return on capital, while the optimal consumption is equal to the real wage, $(1 - s)f(k) = (1 - a)f(k) = w/P$ (Eq. (1.80)). If households spend all their wages on consumption and invest their net returns on capital stock back to the economy, this consumption-investment trade-off maximizes consumption at the equilibrium point. The elegance of this result lies in its simplicity: spending all wages on consumption—a practical means of maximizing consumption without the need for intricate measurement. However, for this to work, households must have savings for children and the elderly, making it feasible only in an economy dominated by the middle class. In a dichotomous economy characterized by a significant wealth disparity, where the poor have limited investment and the affluent tend to consume only a small fraction of their income, such a strategy would be impractical and unlikely to yield effective results (see Chapter 3).

While the Solow model ensures that the economy gradually converges to an equilibrium, it faces practical limitations. Solow himself criticized the implausibility of required coordination among households to remain on the saddle-path of the Ramsey model. However, the Solow model requires a similar level of coordination: households must be fully informed about total production and consistently consume a fixed fraction of output. In effect, the Solow model assumes an inherent control mechanism where households behave uniformly in their consumption decisions.

The Solow model suggests that an economy with a built-in mechanism, akin to "gravity" in the natural world, can adjust itself based on the difference between savings and depreciation. This "gravitational pull" ensures that the economy returns to equilibrium whenever it deviates. Why doesn't the Ramsey economy display this kind of "gravity?" Because it operates as a laissez-faire system without control. If a system lacks "gravity," system control techniques can introduce one into the system.

In certain cases, system control techniques can even leverage unstable systems. Various industries, such as the aerospace, have successfully exploited unstable systems for their benefits, like how aircraft control designs use instability to increase the maneuverability of fighter jets. Similarly, economics can adopt such techniques to maximize human benefits.

System control techniques can be applied to the real economy. For readers interested in system control design, Appendix A.2.1 provides an illustrative example of controlling the AK economy in Eq. (1.62). The intuition is simple: The farming economy seeks to maintain specific levels of consumption c_τ and capital k_τ, ensuring $(A-\delta)k_\tau - c_\tau = 0$. Deviations in capital stock are monitored, and if capital stock k_τ exceeds its expected value—indicating lower-than-expected consumption—corrective actions increase consumption. Conversely, if k_t falls below its expected value—signaling higher-than-expected consumption—corrective actions reduce consumption. Appendix A.2.1 shows how a feedback loop can implement this control, with penalties (gain factors) large enough to counter any imbalances caused by overconsumption or underconsumption.

Governments and central banks effectively impose control over the economy, whether intentionally or unintentionally, by adopting system control techniques. Central banks implement such techniques, often formalized in economic models like Dynamic Stochastic General Equilibrium (DSGE) models, to determine the optimal path for setting the policy rate (the control variable) to stabilize inflation and output (the state variables).

Firms use dynamic optimization models to set production levels (the control variable) to meet forecasted demand while minimizing costs associated with holding inventory (the state variable) and backorders (see Chapter 3).

A special case of the Ramsey model further illustrates the application of system control techniques. In his original model (Ramsey, 1928), Ramsey set $\rho = 0$ and emphasized the subjective nature of the discount factor:

> One point should perhaps be emphasized more particularly; it is assumed that we do not discount later enjoyments in comparison with earlier ones, a practice which is ethically indefensible and arises merely from the weakness of the imagination;....

For $\rho = 0$, the stability matrix in Eq. (1.47) reduces to:

$$\mathcal{M} = \begin{bmatrix} 0 & f''(k^*)c^* \\ -1 & 0 \end{bmatrix}, \tag{1.81}$$

which yields a special case: two real eigenvalues of equal magnitude but opposite sign:

$$\pm\sqrt{-c^* f''(k^*)}. \tag{1.82}$$

The opposite signs indicate that the stable arms (I and III) approach the equilibrium point at the same rate that the unstable arms (II and IV) diverge from it. A feedback controller (see Appendix A.2.2) can be designed to stabilize the system. The system control techniques hold promise for application in the real economy.

Ramsey's arguments for a zero discount factor are defensible, particularly for an economy in equilibrium where production and consumption remain constant, and the net return on investment is zero ($r = f'(k) - \delta = 0$). Besides discount factor, in the above examples, individuals' choices in consumption are under control. So does the Solow model, households' preferences—utility and discount factor—no longer influence the economy. By contrast, households' choices play a crucial role in the capitalist economy (see Chapter 7).

In addition, when money is introduced into the economy, and when governments and central banks attempt to manage economic conditions through fiscal and monetary policies, the dynamics of the real economic system shift dramatically. This prompts critical questions: How is money related to the real economy, and can money be used to effectively control economic outcomes? These issues are explored in detail in a later section of this book.

Appendix A

A.1 The Euler-Lagrange Equation Applied to the Ramsey Model

The economic objective is to maximize $e^{-\rho t} \ln c$, and Eq. (1.14) links consumption c to k and $\dot{k}$:

$$c = f(k) - \delta k - \dot{k},$$

which shows that capital growth raises consumption through output but reduces it through depreciation and investment. Rewrite the objective as functions k and $\dot{k}$:

$$F(t, k, \dot{k}) = e^{-\rho t} \ln c = e^{-\rho t} \ln[f(k) - \delta k - \dot{k}],$$

then

$$\frac{\partial}{\partial k} F(t, k, \dot{k}) = e^{-\rho t} \frac{1}{c} [f'(k) - \delta], \tag{A.1}$$

$$\frac{\partial}{\partial \dot{k}} F(t, k, \dot{k}) = -e^{-\rho t} \frac{1}{c}, \tag{A.2}$$

$$\frac{d}{dt} \left(\frac{\partial}{\partial \dot{k}} F(t, k, \dot{k}) \right) = e^{-\rho t} \left(\rho \frac{1}{c} + \frac{\dot{c}}{c^2} \right). \tag{A.3}$$

The Euler equation for the Ramsey model is:

$$\frac{\partial}{\partial k} F(t, k, \dot{k}) - \frac{d}{dt} \left(\frac{\partial}{\partial \dot{k}} F(t, k, \dot{k}) \right) \tag{A.4}$$

$$= \frac{1}{c} e^{-\rho t} \left([f'(k) - \delta - \rho] - \frac{\dot{c}}{c} \right) = 0, \tag{A.5}$$

which yields the Ramsey rule Eq. (1.41).

A.2 Stabilizing Economy

A.2.1 *Stabilizing the AK economy*

To stabilize the economy that follows Eq. (1.60), $\dot{k}(t) = Ak(t) - c(t) - \delta k(t)$, at the equilibrium point $(A-\delta)k(0) - c(0) = 0$, first apply the Laplace transform to Eq. (1.60) to obtain an algebraic equation:

$$sk(s) = (A - \delta)k(s) - c(s),$$

where s is the standard symbol that replaces t after the Laplace transform. Then solve for $k(s)$ to give the transfer function G:

$$G = \frac{k(s)}{c(s)} = \frac{-1}{s - \alpha},$$

where $\alpha = A - \delta$. This open system is unstable because its pole $s = \alpha > 0$ resides in the right half of the s-plane. The poles in the right half of the s-plane correspond to the positive eigenvalues in the dynamic system. Proportional Feedback Control feeds back the deviation from the equilibrium point back to the input, closing the loop and turning the system into a closed-loop system. After feeding back the deviation, the system produces a new $k^*(s)$:

$$k^*(s) = G[c(s) + \kappa k(s)],$$

where κ is the gain factor which multiplies the deviation to generate the desired correcting signal. In the square brackets, the input $c(s)$ is combined with feedback. The feedback system has the closed-loop transfer function T (see Fig. A.1):

$$T = \frac{G}{1 - \kappa G} = \frac{1}{s - (\alpha - \kappa)}.$$

Choosing $\kappa > \alpha$ moves the pole from the right-half s-plane to the left-half plane. Take the inverse Laplace transform $1/[s - (\alpha - \kappa)]$ to give:

$$\mathcal{L}^{-1}\left[\frac{1}{s - (\alpha - \kappa)}\right] = e^{(\alpha - \kappa)t},$$

which has $\alpha - \kappa < 0$, and the closed-loop stabilizes the system.

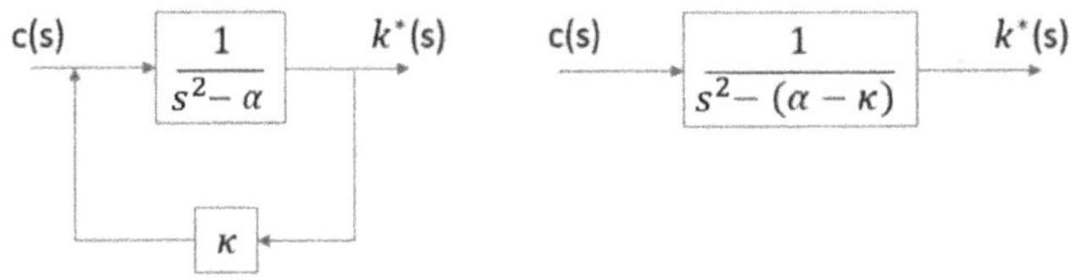

Fig. A.1. The AK model control.

A.2.2 *Stabilizing the Ramsey economy with zero discount factor*

The transfer function for Eq. (1.82) is

$$G = \frac{1}{s^2 - \alpha}, \tag{A.6}$$

where $\alpha = -f''(k^*)c^* > 0$. This open system is unstable because it has a positive pole at $+\sqrt{\alpha}$. Proportional-Derivative Control can cure the problem with the transfer function G^*:

$$G^* = \frac{1}{s^2 + \beta_d s + (\beta_p - \alpha)}. \tag{A.7}$$

Now, the poles are:

$$\frac{1}{2}\left[-\beta_d \pm \sqrt{\beta_d^2 - 4(\beta_p - \alpha)}\right]. \tag{A.8}$$

To move both poles to the negative plane, we use the Routh-Hurwitz Criterion, which requires both β_d and $(\beta_p - \alpha)$ to be positive.

A.3 Appendix: Economics and Images of Science

While natural sciences focus on the natural world, social sciences seek to understand human experience. Scientists wonder: do the human world and the natural world share the same principles? Philosophers have debated this since the dawn of human history. Many social scientists agree that both natural and social sciences aim to identify correlations between variables and make predictions based on those correlations. Thomas Kuhn, in his book *The Structure of Science Revolution* (Kuhn, 1970), examines the natural sciences from a new perspective. His insights bring the natural sciences closer to the common perceptions of economics but not the other way around. Kuhn discusses the natural sciences exclusively and mentions the social sciences only occasionally.

Kuhn introduces the concept of *paradigm* in the preface of his book:

> Particularly, I was struck by the number and extent of the overt disagreements between social scientists about the nature of legitimate scientific problems and methods. Both history and acquaintance made me doubt that practitioners of the natural sciences possess firmer or more permanent answers to such questions than their colleagues in social science. Yet, somehow, the practice of astronomy, physics, chemistry, or biology normally fails to evoke the controversies over fundamentals that today often seem endemic among, say psychologists or sociologists. Attempting to discover the source of that difference led me to recognize the role in scientific research of what I have since called "paradigm."

A paradigm behaves like Willard Van Orman Quine's "web of belief": it can be adjusted at the periphery to protect the integrity of its core. Kuhn suggests that, in terms of developing a paradigm, the social sciences fall behind the natural sciences: "In parts of biology—the study of heredity, for example—the first universally received paradigms are still more recent; and it remains an open question what parts of social science have yet acquired such paradigms at all." When science goes from the pre-paradigm to the paradigm stages, scientific research reports also shift from books to the form of professional journals. Kuhn says, "In parts of the social sciences they may well be occurring today." Economics has completed this transition. Today, professional research reports are published exclusively in professional journals. The theories used by economic researchers are not accessible to layman anymore. However, it is not clear whether economics has recognized Keynesian or neoclassical theories as the paradigm of economics. Today, every social science discipline has its own journals, and their number has exploded, much like information in general.

In Kuhn's book, "science" refers to the natural sciences. Economists debate whether economics measures up to the standards of the natural sciences. This debate raises broader questions about the differences between social sciences and natural sciences. Historically, natural sciences were regarded as instruments for approaching final truth. However, under Kuhn's analysis, natural sciences are shown not to possess such characteristics.

A.3.1 *The invariants*

Many social scientists believe that natural sciences are falsifiable, but economics may not be. According to Popperians, the true theories must be falsifiable to meet scientific standards. However, since falsifiability does not apply to the natural sciences either, they are, in this regard, no different from economic theories.

Due to the subject matter of economics, economists are less committed to the concepts of uniformity of nature, deductive methodology, but more committed to empirical adequacy. Freed from mirroring the real world, economics is dominated by a pragmatic, Friedmanite instrumentalism that judges a theory solely by its predictive utility. In fact, natural sciences grapple with all the same controversial issues that economists debate. Therefore, the question is not whether economics measures up to the natural sciences, but rather what sciences truly do.

A.3.2 *Economic assumptions*

Kuhn rejects the concept of the universal law of nature. The "thing-in-itself" is not knowable. There is no sense in talking about the nature of "thing-in-itself." Kuhn regards the so-called "laws" as the beliefs of a science community, held to be true, much like Newton's law of gravity in Newtonian physics.

Econometrics got under way at the end of the 1930s and the 1940s and was conducted at the Cowles Commission for Research in Economics in Chicago. The key ideas rested on four elements:

1. simultaneous equations,
2. equations containing both "random" terms and "systematic" ones,

3. time-series data, and
4. data defined at the aggregate rather than individual level.

The equations are the fundamental part of the method: "... there would not be much purpose in devising a model... if we did not have some hope that at least some features of our model would be invariant with respect to some changes in the circumstances... If all the model is good for is to describe a particular set of data... then we might as well forego the effort of devising the model" (Duncan, 1980). The equations must remain unchanged under the changing conditions. Econometricians nowadays talk about targets, manipulation, and forecasting. The challenge is whether the parameters estimated under past conditions will continue to hold under new innovations. If the parameters do not hold, the method does not help forecast what would occur when the proposed economic policies or conditions change. The well-known Lucas critique questions whether the parameters are estimated from past observations are reliable when the policymaker hopes to set the exogenous variable at some level and expects that the equations predict the resulting state of the economy. But that will not work.

Lucas argues that the parameters are not independent of the policy level—the exogenous variables. The structure of the fundamental equations is influenced by the agents' expectations of policy shifts, which undermines the stability of the macroscopic parameters across policy changes. While macroscopic parameters are set by the micro-level factors, these factors themselves react to expectations about the macroscopic variables the policy aims to control. Lucas says (Lucas Jr., 1976), "Without this extreme assumption, the kinds of policy simulations called for by the theory of economic policy are meaningless."

Physics explores everything from the smallest quarks and quantum particles to the largest stars. Many large-scale phenomena—such as aerodynamics, fluid mechanics, and thermodynamics—are the outcome of countless microscopic interactions. It is a misconception to assume that micro-entities in physics are invariant. In fact, quantum particles and subatomic entities display complex and often enigmatic behaviors that are only partially understood. Furthermore, the field of physics tackles the micro-macro relationship in a fundamentally different manner than econometrics does.

A.3.3 *Paradigm*

John Stuart Mill argued that while controlled experimentation is possible in physics, it is impractical in economics, where outcomes are shaped by the multiplicity and interdependence of variables. His solution was the deductive method (Mill, 1836, 2012): first establish micro-level principles—such as "people seek more wealth"—and then derive macroeconomic implications (Stewart, 1979; Hausman, 1989). In this deductionist framework, reinforced by Carnap's logical positivism, the macro level possesses no independent reality. It is merely a "summary" of micro properties, *verifiable* either through logic (a priori) or empirical observation.

W. V. O. Quine challenged the Verification Principle, contending that language constitutes a "seamless web" (Quine, 1951). Just as gravity, mass, and force are interdependent in mechanics and relativistic physics, altering a definition inevitably reshapes one's conceptual framework. Yet, Quine also acknowledged a bottom-up continuity: namely, the logical and physical progression from atoms to macro-objects.

By contrast, the top-down view of complex systems holds that the macro level is irreducible to micro mechanisms, functioning instead as an autonomous layer of reality governed by its own laws. From this top-down perspective, macro structures guide inquiry at the micro level. Kuhn argued that scientific practice is not verification but puzzle-solving within a paradigm, with contradictions deferred until crises precipitate a scientific revolution. Consider the Gas Law: Boyle (1662), Charles (1787), and Clapeyron (1834) articulated its "macro" form, $PV = nRT$, long before its microscopic rationale was understood. Only with Maxwell (1859) and Boltzmann (1872–1877) did the law acquire a micro foundation, revealing how the macro notion of entropy emerges from the hidden dance of atoms (see Chapter 7).

Both particle motion in physics and household consumption and investment in economics satisfy the Euler–Lagrange equation (see Section A.1). Yet, while the equation yields the Ramsey rule in economics, its teleology appears inverted: the principle of least action in physics is mirrored by a principle of maximum intertemporal allocation in economics. Nature is frugal with energy, whereas households are insatiable for pleasure. Both frameworks, however, converge on the logic of optimization.

Economists such as Hayek argued that the subjective behavior of economic agents renders the atomistic method unsuitable for economics. Yet even in physics, micro-entities are far from simple. Gases consist of diverse particles—oxygen, carbon dioxide, water vapor, metals, and pollen—that, under varying atmospheric conditions, can generate complex phenomena such as rain, snow, or hail. The intricate behavior of these "super particles" remains a central challenge for physicists today.

The Euler-Lagrange equation (see Section A.1) embodies the principle of least action, whereby physical objects "choose" the path requiring minimal action between initial and final points. A falling stone, for example, appears to "choose" the shortest trajectory—a metaphor Schopenhauer (1966) compared to free will. Gas particles with varying speeds and positions likewise follow straight-line after collisions. In economics, households with differing wealth and income "choose" consumption and investment paths to maximize utility. At the macro level, these micro choices aggregate into a collective trajectory that follows the optimal path.

When macro conditions change, micro-entities respond. For instance, when the external temperature or pressure around a balloon shifts, the speeds of the molecules inside adjust until their distribution stabilizes. Likewise, households react to changes in fiscal or monetary policy. At equilibrium, macro conditions align with the underlying micro-states.

For Kuhn, the macro-paradigm serves as both the "map" and the "directions" guiding micro-level inquiry. Human knowledge can be seen as a tension between the Micro (hidden rules) and the Macro (observable world). Hilbert's sixth problem in his 1900 list of Grand Challenges sought a mathematical link between the micro world of atoms and the macro world of fluids. Similar connections arise in economics, where individual household choices aggregate into national patterns of consumption and production, and in Bitcoin, where individual transactions aggregate into a synchronized ledger (see Section 2.5). Each thinker engages a distinct "battleground" in explaining how the macro and micro levels relate. Summarized, the relation between micro and macro may be expressed as a "Master Formula": Micro-Mechanism to Macro-Pattern through Group Theory Action.

For example, Newtonian macro laws of conservation are implied by the continuous space-time group symmetries.

Noether's theorem (1918) states that for every continuous symmetry of a system's action corresponds to a specific conservation law. Quantum mechanical particles satisfy continuous symmetries and obey Noether's theorem. In economics, however, households differ in wealth, income, and preferences. To construct a Master Formula linking Micro to Macro without requiring symmetry, one turns to the Principle of Stationary Action (the Hamilton–Jacobi equation or the Hamilton–Jacobi–Bellman (HJB) equation (see Section A.4)).

The Master Formula must satisfy four conditions:

Ergodicity—requiring a probability distribution that yields statistical predictability in the aggregate.

Integral of Action—summing over microscopic temporal increments and utilizing the calculus of variations to identify the path where the first variation of the action is zero.

Time-Scale Separation—ensuring that micro-systems relax to equilibrium rapidly enough for stable macro-laws to emerge.

The Bridge–Hamiltonian—transmitting feedback from the micro-level optimization to the macro-level distribution, and vice versa.

Instead of building a "Bridge," econometric models developed in the 1930s relied primarily on statistics to uncover causal relationships. David Hume argued that causality entails no necessary connection between events, and that constant conjunction, like induction, can never achieve logical certainty. Confronting this challenge, David Lewis and Judea Pearl reframed causality in formal terms. For Lewis, "A caused B" means that if A had not occurred, B would not have occurred—an analysis grounded in counterfactual worlds. Pearl, by contrast, warned that artificial intelligence can be misled by mere correlations—for example, inferring that roosters cause the sunrise. Genuine intelligence requires understanding the consequences of interventions, expressed formally as $P(Y|do(X))$: the probability of an outcome given the intervention operator $do(X)$ (Pearl and Mackenzie, 2018). By assigning a "treatment" to half of a randomized group, one breaks the "micro-symmetry," effectively eliminating all incoming "causal" arrows to the treatment variable. In social sciences, the difference-in-differences method, which compares temporal changes between treated and untreated groups, has become a prevalent tool for causal inference. Yet, this approach collides with Pearl's vision of deep causality, sparking a Kuhnian paradigm war.

Consider the experiment of dropping objects from a skyscraper: if interventions are imposed without reference to Newtonian physics, countless causal relationships emerge—height, shape, weather factors, and more. By contrast, the Newtonian paradigm distills this complexity into a simple formula that links the key factors governing an object's motion. After Einstein's revolution, Newtonian gravity was no longer strictly required within the framework of relativity. Can causal inference lead to Kuhnian paradigms and paradigm shifts? Pearl's framework assumes "neutral observation," where Directed Acyclic Graph establish causal relationships that make the world intelligible. Kuhn, however, denies any "God's eye view" of data: perception is paradigm dependent. When paradigms shift, the scientist "is like a man wearing inverting lenses." Thus, Newton discerned independent space and time, while Einstein perceived a warped four-dimensional continuum. Likewise, Classical, Austrian, Keynesian, and Neoclassical economists interpret evidence differently, shaped by their theoretical commitments. Interventions may uncover causal links in data, but shifting in a Kuhnian paradigm requires a leap—demanding creativity and, at times, revolutionary minds.

A.3.4 *Contact point between theory and nature*

In the late 19th century, in the so-called *Marginal Revolution* economists like William Stanley Jevons, Carl Menger, and Léon Walras sought to formalize economics by grounding their analysis in the concept of marginal utility. These theories characterized rational economic agents as those who maximize utility under a budget constraint, rejecting the labor theory of value associated with classical economists such as Adam Smith, David Ricardo, and Karl Marx. The concept of individual "utility" became the foundation of microeconomics because it offers a systematic framework to explain how individuals make economic choices.

Lionel Robbins (2007) defended John Stuart Mill's view with an influential but debatable argument:

> The propositions of economic theory, like all scientific theory, are obviously deductions from a series of postulates. ... The main postulate of the theory of value is the fact that individuals can arrange their preferences in an order, and in fact do so. The main postulate of the theory of production is the fact that there are more than one factor of production. The main postulate of the theory of dynamics is the fact that we are not certain regarding future scarcities. These are not postulates the existence of whose counterpart in reality admits of extensive dispute once their nature is fully realized. We do not need controlled experiments to establish their validity: they are so much the stuff of our everyday experience that they have only to be stated to be recognized as obvious.

Not all economists agreed with him. Economists Richard Lester tested the propositions of the neoclassical theory of the firm (Lester, 1946, 1947). Lester's tests consisted of imperfectly designed business surveys, but the tests prompted economists to scrutinize economics' postulates more seriously. Since economists have increasingly accepted the value of empirical testing. However, critics like Fritz Machlup fiercely attacked both Lester's methods and his results (Machlup, 1956): "But we would certainly not find that all of the businessmen do so all of the time. Hence, the assumption of consistently profit-maximizing conduct is contrary to fact."

Today, the so-called behavioral economics theory is increasingly popular. It challenges the rational choice theory and incorporates psychological research into economics and finance. However, Macro theories do not rely on the behavior of individual micro-objects to establish laws; instead, they guide micro theory in uncovering the underlying rules that give rise to those laws.

In physics, statistical mechanics neither requires all gas particles to behave identically nor depends on "true" micro-level assumptions. Moreover, assumptions in the natural sciences are not amenable to direct empirical testing. Natural sciences rely on reduction to reach the contact point between theory and nature. Empirical tests then serve to support or reject the validity of both the assumption and the theory itself.

For example, Newton's law and Einstein's general relativity are neither absolutely true nor can they be tested directly. The deduction based on these theories provides the points of contact between theories and nature. Developing points of contact is immensely difficult. It is a classic example of how the predictions of Newton's law and Einstein's general relativity were tested against nature, a topic we will revisit in a later section.

A.3.5 *Inexact science*

Social scientists may think that natural sciences are exact. However, Kuhn, Van Fraassen, and others have pointed out that this view of the natural sciences is mistaken. Kuhn states:

> All historically significant theories have agreed with the facts, but only more or less. There is no more precise answer to the question whether or how well an individual theory fits the facts. But questions much like that can be asked when theories are taken collectively or even in pairs. It makes a great deal of sense to ask which of two actual and competing theories fits the facts better.

Van Fraassen (2000) specifically explains using Newton's laws as an example:

> This is the precise point where we notice a very deep assumption at work, which was again highlighted by Reichenbach. In this "fitting in" a certain assumption is made. I'll give it a special name: Approximation Principle: if certain conditions follow from the ideal case then approximately those conditions will follow from an approximation to the ideal case. Newton demonstrates that from a very idealized, simplified description of the solar system, something approximating the known phenomena follows.... But is this Principle true? Newtonian mechanics does not imply that it is. It was well known long before the advent of Chaos theory that classical physics allows for cases in which that is just not so. Therefore the basic science cannot justify use of the Principle. But the special sciences, conceived of as extensions of basic science, are established under the assumption of that Principle-indeed, that Principle is the only and the crucial link between the special sciences and their more basic parent sciences. Therefore the special sciences cannot justify this principle for us without circularity.

Experiments play important role in verifying or rejecting the results of deductions, and in checking whether significant factors have been left out. Nonetheless, nature imposes constraints on the accuracy of experiments.

First, an experiment intends to establish the relation between the measurements of a pair of factors by keeping all other factors constant. The ceteris paribus clause includes any other factor except the factors the experiments intend to measure. Scientists have limited control over those conditions. Each measure inevitably carries some effect from disturbances. The errors are inseparable parts of any experiment.

Second, nature sets a limit on any measurement accuracy. Before quantum mechanics, scientists thought that measurement errors could be reduced to zero. After quantum mechanics, the Heisenberg uncertainty principle explicitly established the limit.

Third, chaotic behaviors exist between variables in certain systems. For a function $y = f(x)$, a change Δy responds to a change Δx, that is, $y + \Delta y = f(x + \Delta x)$. Whether Δy approaches zero in response to $\Delta x \to 0$ depends on the function $f(x)$. For certain nonlinear systems, Δy does not approach zero and may lead to bifurcation or chaos.

Scientists and engineers have been striving to increase accuracy in experiments and predictions. They developed widely used methods for controlling disturbances. Various disturbances can cause a rocket to stray off track to the target. Rudolf Emil Kálmán (1930–2016), a Hungarian American electrical engineer, developed the Kalman filter, which helps in experiments by effectively handling noisy measurements and filtering out measurement errors. It excels in sensor fusion, where data from multiple sensors are combined.

A.3.6 *Pragmatic virtue*

Kuhn asks: "which of two actual and competing theories fits the facts better," economics relies on the hypothetico-deductive method to arbitrate these disputes and falls back on pragmatic virtue and predictive success over descriptive accuracy. Newton's law and Einstein's general relativity predict the deflection of light near the Sun and the two predictions differ by 0.875 arc-second, or 0.875/3600 of 1°. British astronomer Arthur Eddington's 1919 solar-eclipse experiment confirmed Einstein's prediction.

Economics and finance often leave different answers behind and just move on to other questions, accumulating more and more "answers" and more and more sophisticated conflicting "results," like the basket of apples in Descartes' analogy. Fresh apples are mixed with rotten apples. To prevent the rot from spoiling the whole basket, someone must throw out the rotten apple as early as possible[42]:

> ...They then attempt to separate the false beliefs from the others, so as to prevent their contaminating the rest and making the whole lot uncertain. Now the best way they can accomplish this is to reject all their beliefs together in one go, as if they were all uncertain and false. They can then go over each belief in turn and re-adopt only those which they recognize to be true and indubitable.—Descartes (2013)

Philosophy faces the problem that philosophers disagree on which apples are good and which are rotten in the first place. Economics, as an empirical science, has a touchstone—experiments—to check and discard the rotten ones.

A part of the reason that natural sciences have more accurate models than social sciences do is not the subject matter but their methodologies. Before Newton, people used astrology, which was based on the positions of stars, to predict seasonal shifts and social events in their lives. The difference between astrology and physics lies in how they generate predictions.

It is a common belief that the natural sciences have realistic assumptions, whereas economics does not. Milton Friedman offered a solution to the difficulties raised by Lester and others in his essay, *The Methodology of Positive Economics* (Friedman, 1953). Friedman showed that economics satisfies positivist standards by providing useful predictions, even if not explanations. This view was contentious until philosophers like Kuhn provided the philosophical support for Friedman's perspective (Van Fraassen, 1980):

> Theory acceptance has a pragmatic dimension. While the only belief involved in acceptance, as I see it, is the belief that the theory is empirically adequate, more than belief is involved. To accept a theory is to make a commitment, a commitment to the

[42]Some journals, including so-called top journals, discourage debates. An eminent author advised young authors on publication: "do not think you are smarter than others," an implicit warning—"do not criticize, do not debate." Such advice may reduce overt conflict and create the appearance of steady progress; however, it can also inhibit intellectual engagement and leave research trajectories poorly specified.

> further confrontation of new phenomena within the framework of that theory, a commitment to a research program, and a wager that all relevant phenomena can be accounted for without giving up that theory. That is why someone who has accepted a certain theory, will henceforth answer questions ex cathedra, or at least feel called upon to do so.

Friedman may not be aware of the Duhem–Quine thesis, which claims that it is not possible to falsify a single hypothesis because it is a conjunction of hypotheses that is assessed. Natural sciences are indispensable to Platonic entities, such as real numbers and electrons. Thus, it is hopeless to try to eliminate them. As we can see, the natural sciences face the same challenges as economics regarding the impossibility of falsifying a single hypothesis. The distinction between economics and physics lies in physicists' willingness to embrace "unrealistic" assumptions as starting points for theoretical development. In contrast, economists generally reject them. Strikingly, theoretical physics seeks to unify gravity and quantum mechanics by formulating hypotheses such as string theory, in which the fundamental components—one-dimensional vibrating strings—are purely mathematical constructs that lack experimental evidence.

Friedman's pragmatic program, on one hand, rightly embraces "unrealistic" assumptions as a useful starting point; however, on the other hand, Friedman went too far in accepting assumptions that are obviously false or grossly imprecise.

A scientific assumption does not mean that anything goes, nor must it be "realistic." Just like points or the lines in geometry: points have zero size, and the lines have zero width, and they are "unrealistic" and do not exist. Einstein's thought experiments exemplify the process of developing assumptions and theories: imagine an object moving in a straight line through space-time, whose four-dimensional geometry is distorted by the masses of stars.

A.3.7 *Beyond physics: positive feedback*

One notable difference between physics and other sciences lies in the role of feedback. In fields such as chemistry, biology, and the social sciences, feedback is much more prevalent. Engineering, including mechanical engineering, a direct offshoot of physics, has developed various feedback controls for practical applications.

Physics developed conservation laws, from the conservation of momentum (Rene Descartes and Gottfried Leibniz) to Emmy Noether's invariance theorem (Noether, 1983), which provide a framework for understanding the physical world. These principles are universal and unify diverse physical phenomena, offering predictive power in physical systems, with notable exceptions such as nuclear fission and the Big Bang. In nuclear fission, a chain reaction occurs when a neutron strikes a heavy nucleus, causing it to split and release more neutrons. This positive feedback does not violate energy conservation according to Einstein's famous equation, $E = mc^2$, as mass is converted into energy.

Positive feedback occurs in "open" systems—such as those found in organic chemistry, biological systems, and the social sciences—energy flows in and out, and feedback can cause systems to grow or decay. For example, genes are self-replicating entities that program their own transmission, occasionally leading to "selfish genetic elements" that enhance their own replication at the expense of the rest of the genome. Richard Dawkins popularized this gene-centric view of evolution in his landmark book, *The Selfish Gene* (Dawkins, 2016b).

Over time, self-consciousness emerges, and feedback processes reach a new stage. Though the exact mechanism remains a mystery, the "hard problem" of consciousness seeks to explain how subjective experience emerges from material processes. Self-conscious humans intentionally intensify and sustain positive feedback loops, creating *cosmo-bias* and *time-bias*.

Humans interact with their families, and their workplaces in everyday life. As a result, humans naturally exhibit a preference for the microcosm. This bias shapes human research, which tends to focus on the immediate and familiar. In the microcosm, a self-aware entity feels that its actions are freely chosen and makes choices to take advantage of positive feedback—such as profits on money.

As the division of labor in scientific research breaks down the cosmos into smaller, more manageable domains, it inadvertently reinforces the bias toward free will, making the larger, more distant macrocosm seem increasingly remote.

For example, a person may feel free to play games. In a small group, such as friends or relatives playing cards, the stakes might involve insignificant amounts of money with negligible impact beyond the group. In contrast, when people gamble in a casino—whether on Indian land or in Las Vegas—the economic effects extend to local communities. Similarly, betting on asset markets can have significant impacts on both domestic and, at times, global economies.

If we view the macrocosm and microcosm as relative concepts, we can imagine an onion-like structure in which each cosmos is enveloped by a larger cosmos. A tiny variation in an inner layer can result in a substantial change in the macrocosm, according to some. However, large physical changes in macro scales require significant energy. "If a butterfly flutters its wings in Brazil, could it cause a tornado in Texas?" The answer lies in understanding the source of energy, which prevents exaggerating the influence of microcosmic phenomena on macro-scale dynamics. Any positive feedback mechanism is inherently unstable and cannot persist indefinitely, as doing so would ultimately violate the laws of physics; a snowball grows downhill but eventually breaks under its weight.

Humans have a finite lifespan. Fernand Braudel's division of time into three levels—la longue durée (the long duration), conjuncture (the medium term), and événements (short-term human events)—challenges social scientists to think beyond individual events and consider the deeper forces that influence historical change (Braudel, 1969). Borrowing from Alvin Toffler's term, *time-bias*, individuals tend to place more emphasis on short-term events rather than long-term consequences.

Anthropologists and historians, by contrast, tend to analyze long-term developments, which makes them more attuned to the inevitable consequences of historical processes. Marx's theory of historical materialism sought to uncover the underlying economic processes that shape historical development (see Section 2.1.3.1). However, governments and central banks often prioritize short-term goals, reflecting a broader societal tendency to emphasize immediate concerns. This is what people call "kicking the can down the road."

In the short term, humans often perceive themselves as having more control over nature. Rulers may even believe they control the fate of their states or even the world, failing to recognize the inevitable forces that shape their outcomes. These forces typically become clear only after their downfall. Even the greatest conquerors, who once seemed to control vast empires, history eventually eroded their legacies. Their great accomplishments turned out to be mere roadblocks, slowing down human progress. In the long term, humanity cannot escape the constraints of the physical world. Ultimately, on a collective scale, the free will exercised in the microcosm gives way to larger, unavoidable necessities.

Social sciences aim to create a significant impact on society, yet questions of temporal and cosmic perspectives frequently remain unaddressed, leading to time bias and cosmic bias being overlooked. For individuals and firms, the focus often lies on immediate outcomes—such as how to accumulate wealth or maximize profits—while nations concentrate on strategies for achieving victory in conflicts. On one hand, people have built economic and financial systems and believe they control these systems. On the other hand, the economy has long been understood as operating within the constraints of nature—specifically, resource limitations. However, cosmo-bias and time-bias often lead individuals to underestimate or overlook the fact that the economy is part of the natural world.

A.4 Appendix: Economy with Uncertainty

Many economic studies incorporate uncertainty in their models (Flaschel *et al.*, 1997; Bagliano and Bertola, 2004; Nymoen, 2005; Gong and Semmler, 2006; Sargent, 2009; Alogoskoufis, 2019). The instability of the economy in the Ramsey model is *intrinsic*. An example of external shocks is given here to show how Brownian motion affects the stability of an economy.

$$\sup_c E_r \int_0^T -e^{-\gamma c} ds, \tag{A.9}$$

$$\dot{k_t} = rk_t - c_t - \sigma dW_t, \tag{A.10}$$

where W_t is a standard Brownian motion with zero mean and unit standard deviation. We employ the Hamilton–Jacobi–Bellman (HJB) equation to formulate and solve the optimal control problem of the economy:

$$\sup_c \left[-e^{-\gamma c} + J_k(k)(rk - c) + J_{kk}(k)\frac{\sigma^2}{2} - J(k)\rho \right] = 0.$$

We have the solution:

$$J(k) = -e^{-r\gamma(k+G)}.$$

The first-order condition for the HJB equation implies:

$$c = r(k+G) - \frac{\ln r}{\gamma},$$

where G is:

$$G = \frac{1}{r}\left(\frac{\ln r}{\gamma} - \frac{\sigma^2}{2}r\gamma + \frac{\rho - r}{r\gamma}\right).$$

By setting σ to zero, we have the system without uncertainty:

$$c = rk + \frac{\rho - r}{r\gamma}.$$

The difference between the systems with and without uncertainty is that the optimal consumption is reduced in proportion to the variance of the Brownian motion.[43]

---

[43]Bertsekas, Dimitri P. (2012). Dynamic Programming and Optimal Control: Volume I, (Belmont MA: Athena Scientific).

Chapter 2

Money

It might be surprising, but even today, there are still communities that do not use money at all. Luke Korns visited the Solomon Islands, a remote and isolated place, where he observed a community that functions as a large family, sharing food and resources without any monetary transactions.[1] The Solomon Islands offer a glimpse into a true economy that operates without money.

The communities that do not use money are few and exceptional. In most parts of the world, money has been the official measure of things from individual goods to the whole economy. Economists accept money as the measure of an aggregate of goods and Keynes believes it is a good measure: "'It is my belief that much unnecessary perplexity can be avoided if we limit ourselves strictly to the two units, money and labour, when we are dealing with the behavior of the economic system as a whole..." (Keynes, 1936).

Talking about size, we cannot avoid the unit of meter or foot; talking about economy and finance, we cannot avoid money. Money is self-evident for most people because it is the daily object with which they are most familiar. "The commonest way in which we deceive either ourselves or others about understanding is by assuming something as familiar; ..." (Hegel, 2018). People believe that money is so powerful and magical that, in the Chinese saying, "money can

[1] *I Visited the Island that Capitalism Never Reached (no money used here)*, Luke Korns on YouTube, accessed on March 9, 2024.

make a ghost pull a roller mill."[2] Governments believe in the power of money, trying to exercise control with money. But what money truly does still spark debate.

Surveys indicate that the public lacks financial knowledge, yet few surveys ask the question: What is money? In August 2009, the Cobden Centre commissioned a group of students at the French business school ESCP[3] to survey 2,000 people about their understanding of money (Baxendale, 2010). The results showed widespread misconceptions. For instance, 74% of respondents believed they were the legal owners of the money deposited in their bank accounts. When asked what their bank does with their money, 66% of respondents answered, "do not know," and 33% disagreed that banks lend out their deposited money, believing they hadn't given their bank permission to do so. Once a depositor puts money in a bank, they become a creditor of the bank, and the bank owns the funds, which it can then lend out as it chooses. This process allows the money deposited in banks to continue circulating, with banks' lending out principal and collecting back both principal and interest. But where does the extra money—the interest—come from? Such questions often lead to confusion.

Keynes categorized money into four types: commodity money, managed money, fiat money, and bank money. Commodity money encompasses both physical goods, such as gold, and representative certificates, such as gold certificates; fiat money is created and issued by the state; managed money is like fiat money but is tied to an objective standard, such as gold or other currencies. "Commodity money and managed money are alike in that they are related to an objective standard of value" (Keynes, 1930).

Irving Fisher listed 13 types of money Fisher (1936): (1) gold, (2) gold certificates, (3) silver dollars, (4) silver certificates, (5) U.S. notes or greenbacks, (6) currency certificates, (7) Treasury notes, (8) National Bank notes, (9) Federal Reserve notes,

[2]The idea behind this idiom is stated by Euripides in the fifth century B.C. (dictionary.com).

[3]Students at École Supérieure de Commerce de Paris worked under Dr. Anthony Evans, and the market research company ICM was responsible for fieldwork and data collection.

(10) Federal Reserve Bank notes, (11) subsidiary silver, (12) minor coins, and (13) deposits subject to check. Today, we could add two more: cryptocurrency and digital currency. Official economic classifications of money, such as M0, M1, M2, M3, and M4,[4] can make the concept of money even more confusing.

To clarify what money is, we need to answer two key questions: Where does money come from, and how does it interact with the real economy? This chapter addresses the first question, while the remaining chapters of this book address the second.

2.1 The Origin of the Commodity Money

As early as 330 BC, Aristotle provided an account of the origin of money, arguing that as isolated households expanded into larger communities, they naturally began exchanging surplus goods for necessities. To overcome the logistical inefficiencies of direct barter, these societies eventually agreed upon a universally transportable commodity to serve as money (Aristotle, 2006). Aristotle also reflected on the differences between money and real goods:

> ... for money is the first principle and the end of trade; nor are there any bounds to be set to what is thereby acquired.... We have now considered that art of money-getting which is not necessary, and have seen in what manner we became in want of it; and also that which is necessary, which is different from it; for that economy which is natural, and whose object is to provide food, is not like this unlimited in its extent, but has its bounds.—(Aristotle, 2006)

Aristotle distinguishes between necessary, natural wealth (for basic needs) and unnecessary, unnatural wealth (for the sake of accumulation). In particular, he identified a critical challenge whose relevance would only become fully apparent centuries later: real goods

---

[4]M0 refers to the monetary base, which includes coin currency, physical currency, and central bank reserves. M1 includes M0 plus demand deposits and traveler's checks. M2 covers M1 along with savings deposits and money market shares. M3 constitutes M2 plus money market funds such as mutual funds, repurchase agreements, and commercial paper. M4 encompasses M3 and other less-liquid assets, typically outside commercial banks.

are finite, but money is not. In today's global monetary system, controlling the amount of money created by banks and governments is becoming increasingly challenging.

2.1.1 *Adam Smith*

It was Aristotle's sharp sense of observation that made him take notice of the division of labor. During the Industrial Revolution, the division of labor reshaped the economic landscape, driving the transition from craft production to factory-based systems. Both Adam Smith (1723–1790) and Immanuel Kant (1724–1804) noted the advantages of the division of labor:

> All crafts, trades, and arts have profited from the division of labour; for when each worker sticks to one particular kind of work that needs to be handled differently from all the others, he can do it better and more easily than when one person does everything. Where work is not thus differentiated and divided, where everyone is a jack-of-all-trades, the crafts remain at an utterly primitive level.—Kant (2016)

Aristotle's theory of the origin of money survived through the Middle Ages and eventually reached Adam Smith, who developed it into classical economic theory. According to Smith, the division of labor created markets, and people specializing in specific goods relied on the market to obtain other goods. In markets, goods became commodities, produced not for personal consumption but for other commodities. Without money, barter might prevent people from getting what they need:

> The butcher has more meat in his shop than he himself can consume, and the brewer and the baker would each of them be willing to purchase a part of it. But they have nothing to offer in exchange, except the different productions of their respective trades, and the butcher is already provided with all the bread and beer which he has immediate occasion for. No exchange can, in this case, be made between them.—Smith (2010)

Craftsmen in skilled trades had to find buyers for their products. In today's economic jargon, the time and effort spent finding trading partners are known as search costs. Commodities that became widely accepted in trade evolved into money, a medium of exchange.

For example, a butcher could exchange his meat for money and then use that money to buy the commodities he needed. Money facilitated trade by reducing search costs.

From a different perspective, money increases the utility of a specific product. A craftsman creates items for others, and these products hold no use-value for the craftsman himself. If they go unsold, their utility to the craftsman is zero. However, once sold, the craftsman can use the money to buy useful commodities. Furthermore, as the saying goes, "Beauty is in the eye of the beholder." Money enables individuals to purchase goods in the market that offer the highest utility values to them. At the base of Maslow's hierarchy, the needs are physiological, yet preferences still vary. For example, some people might prefer wheat over rice or renting a house rather than owning one. At higher levels of Maslow's hierarchy, needs become more psychological than physiological, and individual preferences can differ widely. This is why \$100 in cash holds greater utility than a \$100 gift card for a specific merchant. Most importantly, the money spent in markets serves as a vital indicator of people's preferences for various goods and provides essential signals to producers and economic planners.

Archaeologists and historians have discovered various forms of money throughout history. During the Roman Empire, salt was a common medium of exchange due to its use in seasoning food, preserving meat, and disinfecting wounds. Roman soldiers were even paid with salt as part of their salary. The word "salary" comes from the Latin word *salarium*, meaning "money used to buy salt." Salt's value and importance led to the expression "worth one's salt," meaning someone was worthy of their wages. Across the world, various societies used different commodities as money, such as cacao grains, squares of cotton cloth, small nuggets of gold, pieces of tin, and precious feathers. These all served as forms of "commodity money."

One of the most unusual examples of money was yak dung, which was used as currency in Tibet between 9,000 and 6,000 B.C. The yak, native to the Himalayas, was revered in Tibetan culture. Yak dung was used for fuel, building materials, and even medicine, making it a valuable commodity. Yak owners could buy almost anything with dung cakes. Another unique example of commodity money is cigarettes, which were used as currency in POW camps during World War II, as described by Radford (1945).

These forms of money served as mediums of exchange in local markets, but they did not have the same impact on the economy as later forms of money, such as gold or silver. For example, in ancient Tibet, yak dung facilitated trade, but it did not transform the economy because it was perishable like other goods. The property that redefined money's role in the economy was *durability.* If King Midas had ruled Tibet, he would not have wanted to turn everything into yak dung, which would not last forever. When durable money such as gold emerged, it was not only fungible but also remarkably durable.

Adam Smith's observation that money should be "less perishable" captures the characteristic of durability, which makes the physical accumulation of wealth possible. He characterized commodity money as both an instrument of commerce and a measure of "value." Money should be divisible and combinable and easily formed into bars or coins (Smith, 2010).

Today, the International Monetary Fund (IMF) defines money by its functions: as a medium of exchange, a unit of account, and a store of "value." In simple terms, money should be fungible, durable, portable, and divisible.

Gold became a preferred form of money due to its unique properties. Among the elements in the periodic table, gold stands out for being durable, non-toxic, and non-radioactive. It is also portable, dense, valuable in small quantities, and easily divisible, malleable, and ductile. With a melting point of around 2000°F, gold could be formed into coins or bars, making it fungible as people gradually accepted it in trade. Gold fueled the prosperity of the crown, religious and other institutions, as well as individuals.

In a free market, money transforms perishable goods into lasting wealth, serving as an elixir of life when those goods are sold before they spoil. From states to individuals, there is a common desire to accumulate gold as a form of wealth: "Like Midas in the fable, who from his insatiable wish had everything he touched turned into gold" (Aristotle, 2006). This magic power of money is encapsulated in the saying, "Money is wealth across time and space." Gold, as money, can travel through time because of its durability and across space because of its portability.

Money measures "value" and stores "value," which leads to the deeper question: What is value? Without answering this question, the mystery surrounding money will remain. Karl Marx gave his answer to the question.

2.1.2 *Karl Marx*

Marx's theory did not just influence economics; it altered the course of human history and continues to shape economic policies and political thought today. Yet, the clash between capitalism and Marxism plays out mostly in politics, with only a group of economists engaging it directly. The reason may be that the two camps speak entirely different theoretical languages, akin to two strangers trying to argue over who arrived at a parking spot first, only to realize they cannot understand each other. Without an interpreter, they might simply give up. If economics is truly a science, then between two theories that draw opposite conclusions, at least one must be false. The two theories should not coexist unchallenged. Marx spoke the language of dialectics—a convoluted, sometimes opaque language. This chapter attempts to translate Marx's theory into plain language and compare it with mainstream economic theory.

Adam Smith distinguished between "value in use" and "value in exchange," demonstrating that the two do not always align. Air and water, essential for human survival, have immense "value in use" but historically had little or no "value in exchange." Smith's observation holds true even though, in modern times, water has gained exchange value as a result of scarcity caused by pollution.

Marx adopted and expanded on Smith's concepts of "value in use" (which Marx termed "use-value") and "value in exchange" (exchange-value), but he described them through the lens of dialectics. In Marx's theory, commodities of different use-values—such as wheat and beef—are exchanged in the market according to their exchange values. Despite having distinct utility values, they are made equivalent in the process of exchange:

$$10 \text{ bushels of wheat} = 100 \text{ lbs of beef.}$$

There are various commodities, corn, fish, wine, and others. The equation expands to a long chain. Those goods have different utility values. Nonetheless, in the equation of exchange, they are equal. To be equal, they must share something in common. This equivalence is possible only through an abstraction: the concept of exchange value.

Abstraction is the way we group things. John, Nancy, and Tom each have a sheep, which is a concrete object. Ignoring their individuals' characteristics, people group them into specific breeds of sheep, such as Merino Wool, Rambouillet, Suffolk, and other breeds, which are the abstraction of concrete sheep. The order of abstraction forms a taxonomy system, which has major groups, such as species, genus, family, and so forth. As we group more diverse things together, the shared characteristics become fewer, and the group becomes more abstract. Philosophers pondered millennia the relation between concrete objects and abstraction. Two thousand years ago, Chinese philosopher Gongsun Long advanced the paradoxical claim that a white horse is not a horse. What is a "horse?" Obviously, there is no such "horse" that is not white, not black, and has no color at all.

Similarly, wheat and beef have different uses, which make them different goods. They are exchangeable in the market. Equating 10 bushels of wheat to 100 pounds of beef abstracts the use-values and imports them into "exchange-value" by ignoring the differences between the use-values and retaining what is common between them. The concept "exchange-value" just like "horse" is an abstract concept but not a concrete object. But a miracle happens: the abstract—the exchange-value—takes bodily form:

$$\text{10 bushels of wheat} = \text{100 lbs of beef} = \text{1 oz of gold.} \tag{2.1}$$

The abstract exchange-value crystallizes into gold! By analogy, the abstract "horse" suddenly changes into a visible animal—neither black, white, nor any specific hue! Marx argued that, through this market process, commodity fetishism causes the social relationships between human producers to appear as objective relationships between things.[5] Reification converts subjects to objects, a fallacy and a "vicious abstractionism" (James, 1975). Marx's followers use the concept—reification—to explain how people's ideas become real things that are independent of people and beyond their control. Money becomes the incarnation of exchange-value, yet reification does not clarify exchange-value; instead, it mystifies money.

[5] *Verdinglichung* means "reification" (literally, making into a thing) in German.

2.1.2.1 *The labor theory of value*

Adam Smith was among the first to articulate what characteristics are left in the abstract concept of *value in exchange*, noting that all commodities are products of human labor and that *value in exchange* is determined by the labor hours used to produce a specific commodity. Marx propelled the labor theory of value to its peak. Marx stated the following: "As exchange-values, all commodities are merely definite quantities of congealed labour-time" (Marx, 2004), while he emphasized that it was the "socially necessary labor time," that is, the amount of labor-time needed to produce a commodity, as determined by society. The exchange-value of a commodity came from human labor, and then money became "the direct incarnation of all human labour" (Marx, 2004).[6]

David Ricardo (1772–1823) viewed labor as an "invariable measure of value" in commodities but struggled with the variability of the relative values of commodities (see Chapter 1). In the labor theory of value, "value" is neither use-value nor "exchange value." Ricardo and Marx missed this distinction. In Eq. (2.1), 10 bushels of wheat are exchanged for 100 pounds of beef, where the exchange value is influenced by people's preferences and determined by the Walrasian equilibrium. Labor-hours are one type of resource required to produce a certain quantity of a commodity. Thus, the labor theory of value attempted to establish the concept of socially necessary work input (economic value for short), which represents the economic resources congealed in a commodity. Therefore, use-value measures the utility of a commodity, exchange value measures the market value of a commodity in terms of money, and economic value measures the amount of resources required to produce a commodity.

The labor theory of value, as characterized by Ricardo, was "in the right direction" (Sraffa and Dobb, 1951). Developing the labor theory of value as the foundation of exchange value is a misguided effort. In markets, people—whether rich, poor, or middle-class—use

---

[6]In other places, Marx rejected the view that labor is the only source of all values: "Nature is just as much the source of use-values (and what else is material wealth?) as labour, which is itself only the expression of a natural power, human labour power" (Marx, 1972).

money to "vote" for what they need and prefer, and these "votes" send vital signals to the economy. Marx made a critical error by overlooking the difference between exchange value and economic value, leading Marxists to advocate for the abolition of money. Without these market "votes," the economy becomes blind and deaf to people's needs, straying from the goal of improving people's well-being and failing to utilize economic resources efficiently (see Chapter 7).

For Marx, *alienation* is another dialectical concept. Workers are estranged from their essential human nature—the capacity for conscious, creative, and purposeful activity. Instead of engaging in free creation, their labor is compelled merely to sustain physical existence. Alienation thus signifies the worker's loss of control over their own labor and humanity. Engels's writings strongly suggested how workers are reified—reduced to abstract categories like "labor power", while Georg Lukács (1971) formalized the term "reification".

Money for money's sake becomes capital. Marx compared the role of money in the process of commodity exchange with its role of money in the process of surplus value accumulation. In the process of commodity exchange,

$$C_m - M - C'_m, \tag{2.2}$$

a person starts with commodity C_m, turns C_m into money M, and then exchanges M for a different commodity C'_m. The goal of this process is to exchange a commodity for a different one. In the process of surplus value accumulation,

$$M - C_m - M' - \cdots, \tag{2.3}$$

a capitalist starts with money M, uses M to purchase commodities including labor, producing commodity C_m, and then sells C_m for more money M'. M represents the money to purchase the factors of production to produce commodity C_m, and then the commodity C_m is sold for the exchange value M', which is more than M. Capital accumulation as described in Eq. (2.3) hinges on two key conditions. First, the factors of production used to create C_m must embody less labor than the labor embodied in C_m itself. Second, and crucially, the aggregate money supply must expand from M to M' to facilitate this transaction and generate a monetary profit.

In Marx's analysis, capitalist surplus value satisfies the first condition. The capitalist purchases labor power with an initial sum of money, M, and then uses that labor power to produce commodities that can be sold for a larger sum, M'. The exchange value of labor is the wage, determined by the cost of the worker's subsistence. Capitalists keep wages at a minimum, only to prevent the working class from dying out. As Marx's lifelong co-author, Friedrich Engels put it: "the price of labor, or the wage, will, in other words, be the lowest, the minimum, required for the maintenance of life" (Engels, 2020).

However, labor has a unique use-value—it creates more value than its own maintenance costs, generating surplus value for the capitalist. This surplus value represents the difference between the wage paid to labor and the exchange value of the commodities the labor produces. A capitalist pays the exchange value of 7 shirts to purchase a tailor's labor for one day. A skilled tailor makes 10 shirts a day, which is the use-value of the tailor. After selling the shirts, the capitalist converts the shirts into money. The capitalist exploits the tailor for the surplus value—the exchange value of 3 shirts. Marx's surplus value theory resonated with the working class, serving as a rallying cry in their fight against capitalism. Yet the theory itself is not without flaws (see Chapter 7).

In the capitalist production process, the price—the exchange-value—shadows the use-value of labor. In the above example, the skilled tailor's labor disappears when the shirts are sold on the market, and the price disguises the unique use-value of labor as the source of surplus value. Money seems to grow by itself and to deserve more money by its nature.

Marx's capital production requires that $M'>M$—that the capitalist ends up with more money than they started with. However, this accumulation depends on the availability of money in the economy. Money must grow.

Imagine an economy with a fixed supply of gold, where capitalists have exploited labor to the extent that wages are at their minimum—the lowest possible level. In this scenario, the capitalists control all the money, yet the limited amount of gold constrains the total money supply M, leaving no additional money available in the economy.

The exploitation of labor does not fully explain where this additional money would come from, leading to a conundrum: capitalists cannot continually accumulate wealth simply by exploiting labor if the money supply remains constant. This leads us to the *quantity theory of money.*

2.1.2.2 *Quantity theory of money*

The quantity theory of money, one of the oldest surviving theories in economics (Dimand, 2008), was initially introduced by Nicolaus Copernicus in 1517 and subsequently expanded and popularized by Irving Fisher. It has often been debated and critiqued. The theory can be expressed in a simple form:

$$MV = PY, \tag{2.4}$$

where M is the money supply, V is the money velocity, P is the price level, and Y is the real production output. Here, V represents the frequency with which money circulates over a year, often considered constant over certain periods. The real output Y signifies the quantity of goods that money M chases. We refer to Eq. (2.4) as the *money identity*, which parallels the macroeconomic identity.

Keynes criticized this theory for its oversimplification, particularly its failure to account for distinct types of money and the reasons people hold it (Keynes, 1930). He emphasized that people hold cash not only as a medium of exchange for daily transactions but also for precautionary reasons and speculative purposes. Historically, when gold and silver were the dominant forms of money, individuals needed to hold physical money to prepare for emergencies or capitalize on future opportunities. However, in modern economies, gold and silver no longer serve as mediums of exchange. Today, people use credit cards in day-to-day transactions and earn returns on their money if they pay their balances in full each billing cycle. In addition, financial assets and the money market offer both liquidity and returns. Therefore, Keynes' theory of liquidity preference is less applicable today.[7]

David Ricardo made an important distinction between the *quantity* of money and the *rate of change* of money. According to him, the quantity of money, M, has no real effect on an economy in equilibrium. For example, consider two isolated farming economies. In one farming economy, 0.1 million ounces of gold circulate once a year ($V = 1$) alongside the production of one million bushels of wheat.

[7]Today, credit instruments (e.g., credits and debt) prevail in the economy and money transactions are digital. Households therefore have no need to keep cash; the shopping time is effectively zero in the shopping time model (Hueng, 1999).

In this case, each bushel of wheat sells 0.1 ounces of gold. The second farming economy circulates one million ounces of gold, with the same wheat production. Here, each bushel would sell for one ounce of gold. Despite the difference in gold quantity, both economies function identically.

If bakers purchase wheat from farmers once a year, then, in the former case, the bakers pay 0.1 million ounces for one million bushels of wheat at 0.1 ounce per bushel. In the latter case, bakers and farmers trade the same way, except for one million ounces of gold circulating. The people in the two economies have the same standard of living regardless of the amount of money in an economy.

Keynes emphasized the factors that can change the money supply: "If, that is to say, Ricardo had argued that it would make no permanent alteration to the rate of interest whether the quantity of money was fixed by the monetary authority at ten million or at a hundred million, his conclusion would hold. But if by the policy of the monetary authority we mean the terms on which it will increase or decrease the quantity of money, i.e., the rate of interest at which it will, either by a change in the volume of discounts or by open-market operations, increase or decrease its assets. . .then it is not the case either that the policy of the monetary authority is nugatory or that only one policy is compatible with long-period equilibrium; . . . Assuming flexible money-wages, the quantity of money as such is, indeed, nugatory in the long period; but the terms on which the monetary authority will change the quantity of money enters as a real determinant into the economic scheme" (Keynes, 1936). This is a typical Keynesian remark, which intertwines multiple factors in a specific discussion. To avoid distraction, let us focus solely on changes in the money supply.

The discovery of new gold mines, for example, could increase the money supply from 0.1 million to 0.12 million ounces, leading to a 20% inflation in wheat prices, assuming no change in wheat output. Conversely, if wheat production rises to 1.25 million bushels while the gold supply remains constant, wheat prices would fall by 20%. The transition to a new equilibrium, however, may be smooth or turbulent, much like a lake adjusting to an influx of water, depending on how fast, and where the water pours in. The way new money is introduced—who receives it and in what amounts—shapes the redistribution of wealth and the broader economic impact. Without considering these effects, the quantity theory of money cannot fully explain the transition process.

Ricardo's distinction between the quantity and change of money is critical for understanding money's role in the economy. Taking the derivative of Eq. (2.4) with respect to time, we have the relationship between the rate of change of money, output, and prices:

$$\pi = \frac{\dot{P}}{P} = \frac{\dot{M}}{M} - \frac{\dot{Y}}{Y}, \tag{2.5}$$

where π is inflation. In simple terms, price inflation is driven by the difference between the rate of change of money supply and the rate of change in production output. For example, in a closed economy that produces one million cars a year with \$20 billion in circulation in the car market, the average price of a car is \$20,000. If car manufacturers increase output by 10% to 1.1 million cars, and the money supply also increases by 10% to \$22 billion, the average price remains unchanged. However, if the money supply increases by more (or less) than 10%, inflation (or deflation) will occur, affecting the average price of cars.

Although Eq. (2.5) describes the transition as a kind of quasi-equilibrium process, in which price changes uniformly across an economy, it holds locally during transitions. For example, when money moves out of one market and into another, the price in the former market decreases, while the price in the latter market increases, in accordance with Eq. (2.5). Given the importance of money supply change, Eq. (2.5) will also be called the money identity if there is no confusion. As a simplified approximation of how prices adjust across an economy over time, Eq. (2.5) illustrates the core dynamic: Money inflow tends to increase prices, while outflow exerts downward pressure on them.

From 1200 to 1500, there were occasional price spikes, particularly during poor harvests, but inflation remained nearly zero on average.[8] After Columbus discovered the New World in 1492 and as the Spanish began extracting vast amounts of gold and silver from Mexico and South America during the 16th century, the global supply

[8] *What can we learn from medieval prices and wages?* by Mirko Lorenz, Datawrapper, accessed on December 29, 2024.

of precious metals grew substantially over the following centuries.[9] The increase in the global supply of precious metals contributed to rising inflation after 1550. The Industrial Revolution then led to a significant increase in the supply of goods, which, in turn, resulted in a decrease in inflation (Abdujalilov and Sheraliev, 2024). After the "Nixon shock"—the suspension of the direct convertibility of the dollar to gold—in 1971, the money supply became uncontrollable, and inflation began to run wild.

The money identity also implies that capitalists might inadvertently harm themselves by expanding production when the money supply is fixed—higher output could lead to falling prices. Marx's notion that M' (capital with surplus value) is always greater than M (initial capital) does not necessarily hold. If the total money supply declines, $M' < M$, "greed" would not pay off for capitalists. The puzzle is that capitalists cannot make more money just by exploiting workers if no new money is available.

2.1.2.3 *Money and capitalists' profits*

Marx's theory has no concept corresponding to *money neutrality*. Money neutrality is a term used in mainstream economics to describe a situation where changes in the money supply only affect nominal variables, such as prices, and have no *long-term* impact on real economic variables, such as output or consumption (Beenstock and Ilek, 2010). Mainstream economics is divided on this issue: The classical dichotomy, as explained by the classical economists, posits that money only influences the price level, while real variables—like labor and capital—determine the real economy. The monetary sector's role is thus limited to influencing prices, making money neutral in the long run.

Money is considered *superneutral* if changes in the money supply have no impact on real economic activity in both the short and long run. However, if money affects real variables in the long run, it is referred to as non-neutral.

In a simple economic model, the total amount of money M in the goods market helps determine the average price P of goods. The

[9] *World Produces More Gold In A Day Than It Did For An Entire Year During 16th Century* by Steve St. Angelo, Money Metals, accessed on December 29, 2024.

relationship can be represented by the following equation:

$$Pf(K,L) = MV, \tag{2.6}$$

where $Pf(K,L)$ is the production output measured by money. Wage costs, denoted by wL, are the variable costs, while depreciation $P\delta K$ represents fixed costs, such as rents, utilities, and maintenance costs of capital stock (see Table 1.3). Capitalists' net profit is the output net of the variable and fixed costs (see p. 61):

$$Pf(K,L) - wL - P\delta K = PaAK^a L^{1-a} - P\delta K = PrK. \tag{2.7}$$

This equation shows that profits depend on the relationship between output, wages, and fixed costs, and are influenced by the price level and the production process.

For capitalists to maintain nominal profit in line with the real profit rK, prices must remain stable, $\dot{P} = 0$. A drop in prices leads to a corresponding drop in profits. To avoid this, the growth rate of money $\dot{M}/M$ must match the growth rate of production output $\dot{Y}/Y$:

$$\frac{\dot{M}}{M} - \frac{\dot{Y}}{Y} = 0. \tag{2.8}$$

Assuming a fixed labor force L, economic output $Y = f(K,L)$ increases with capital stock $\dot{K}$, the growth rate of output can be expressed as

$$\dot{Y} = f_K(K,L)\dot{K} = af(K,L)\frac{\dot{K}}{K} \tag{2.9}$$

and

$$\frac{\dot{Y}}{Y} = a\frac{\dot{K}}{K}. \tag{2.10}$$

This equation shows that output growth depends on both the growth rate of capital stock and the output elasticity a of that stock.

Before exploring the general effects of money on the real economy, we first establish the conditions under which money has no impact on the real economy, that is, money does not alter the macroeconomic identity in Eq. (1.10).

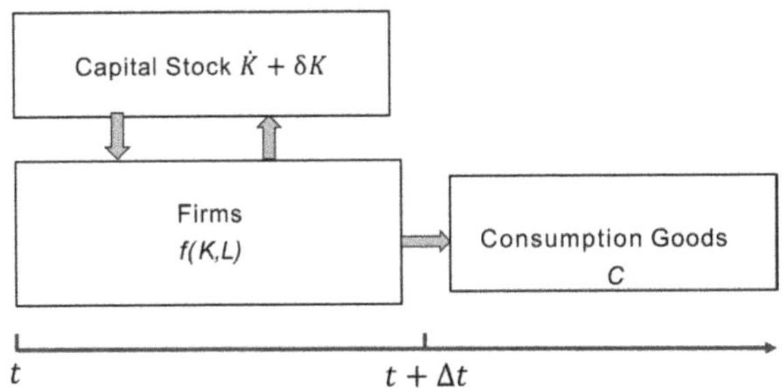

Fig. 2.1. The macroeconomic identity.

To express the macroeconomic identity in monetary terms, we multiply Eq. (1.10) by the price level (see Fig. 2.1). Then using Table 1.3, we rewrite the equation as follows:

$$\begin{aligned} P\dot{K} &= Pf(K,L) - PC - P\delta K \\ &= PrK + wL - PC. \end{aligned} \tag{2.11}$$

Equation (2.11), also known as the *household budget* or *wealth equation*, represents how households allocate their income between consumption and investment in capital stock. On the right-hand side of the equation, the first term (PrK) is the net return on capital stock accruing to households, the second term (wL) represents wages, and the third term (C) corresponds to consumption. The left-hand side captures the surplus (or deficit) that is reinvested in—or deducted from—the capital stock. The real budget per capita, obtained by dividing Eq. (2.11) by PL, is (see Fig. 2.2):

$$\dot{k} = rk + \frac{w}{P} - c. \tag{2.12}$$

Equation (2.12) indicates that if real wages remain constant, changes in the price level will not affect the household budget. Under flexible wage conditions, money does not impact on the real economy. Inflation, therefore, becomes an epiphenomenon—a nominal phenomenon with no real effects on economic fundamentals.

Two cautionary notes are in order. First, the rate of price change (dP/dt) is assumed to be sufficiently slow relative to the price level P, so that the transient effect is small and therefore ignored. If this

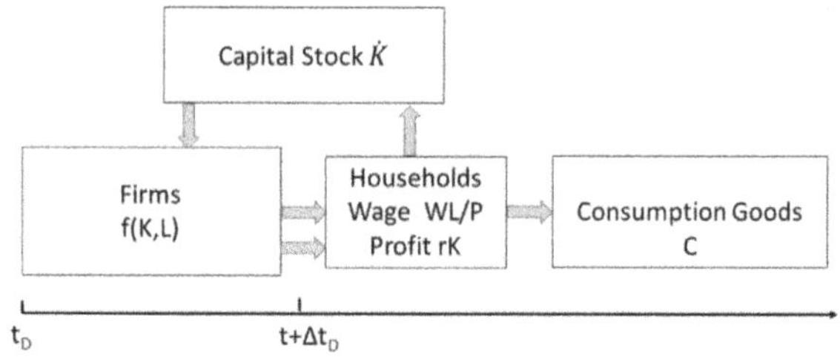

Fig. 2.2. Household budget.

assumption fails, the transient effect creates uneven price inflation, and money neutrality no longer holds. Chapter 4 is devoted to the case of asset inflation.

Second, households' savings are not equivalent to investment in the real economy, primarily due to depreciation. While households receive a net return, rk, after depreciation on their ownership in firms, this measure only accounts for the wear and tear of the firms' capital stock, not public infrastructure. In the real economy, investment must also account for the depreciation of public infrastructure—such as roads, bridges, airports, seaports, powerlines, and communication networks.

If the price change is quasi-equilibrium and public infrastructure depreciation is overlooked, the alignment between the representative household's budget and the macroeconomic identity supports the classical dichotomy, which separates the effects of money on the price level from real economic variables. In this framework, money influences prices but not real variables, such as output or employment. The following conditions must be met for this consistency to hold:

C.1 Wealth is distributed evenly among all households.
C.2 All real output is either consumed or invested in capital stock.
C.3 Prices change sufficiently slowly and uniformly over time.
C.4 Nominal wages are flexible.

The representative household model simplifies the economy by assuming that the behavior of one household can reflect the behavior of all households collectively. However, this model is less restrictive than Condition C.1, which requires an even distribution of wealth. The representative household model allows for unequal wealth distribution while still representing aggregate behavior (see Section 3.1).

Condition C.2 requires that all savings be invested directly in capital stock, ensuring they contribute to production. Thus, using savings to purchase non-productive assets like old houses or antiques would violate the condition. It also requires that supply (output) equals demand (consumption and investment), ensuring the market clears and all output is fully utilized. Condition C.3 dictates that price changes are sufficiently slow and uniform. To keep households' purchasing power constant, the nominal wage in Eq. (2.12) must adjust proportionally to price changes, which, in turn, leads to Condition C.4, requiring flexible nominal wages.

In practice, this classical dichotomy is difficult to sustain. For example, the U.S. Congress, through the Federal Reserve Act of 1977, mandated the Fed to pursue price stability. However, the Fed does not have complete control over the quantity of money created by banks and the government. While the Fed's chair, Jerome Powell, sets a 2% inflation target, he lacks the ability to ensure uniform prices increase. Furthermore, minimum wages set by some states violate Condition C.4.

Although these conditions are restrictive, they are essential for understanding how money affects the real economy. These four conditions may be violated individually or in combination, and money shapes the real economy in diverse ways. Each condition will be reviewed, with the next section focusing on wages (Condition 4). Wages and employment are not the central focus of this book, though they mark a key division between Marxism and mainstream economics. The following cases will illustrate the nuanced relationship between workers' wages and capitalists' profits, highlighting what was missing from Marx's analysis.

2.1.2.4 *Implications of sticky wages*

Keynes challenged the assumption of flexible wages, arguing that wages are often sticky, meaning they do not adjust quickly to changes in prices. If wages remain sticky, capitalists cannot reduce wages in response to falling prices, but they can reduce labor force L (see Table 1.3 and Eq. (1.79)):

$$L = \left[\frac{P(1-a)A}{w'}\right]^{1/a} K, \tag{2.13}$$

where w' is the sticky wage, which limits employment. Consequently, the net profit for capitalists becomes:

$$\begin{aligned} PrK &= Pf(K,L) - w'L - P\delta K \\ &= \left[a(PA)^{1/a}\left(\frac{1-a}{w'}\right)^{(1-a)/a} - P\delta\right] K. \end{aligned} \tag{2.14}$$

At a certain minimum price,

$$P_{\min} = \left(\frac{\delta}{\beta}\right)^{a/(1-a)},$$

where β is:

$$\beta = aA^{1/a}\left(\frac{1-a}{w'}\right)^{(1-a)/a},$$

the capitalists' net profit becomes zero, indicating the lowest price they can accept without incurring losses. Under sticky wages, deflation steadily erodes capitalist profits, which collapse altogether when the price level falls to $P_{\min}$.

2.1.2.5 *Zero money growth scenario*

If there is no money growth $\dot{M} = 0$, that is, $M = M'$ in Marx's formula, prices would decrease at the rate of output growth. In this case,

$$\frac{\dot{P}}{P} = -\frac{\dot{Y}}{Y} = -a\frac{\dot{K}}{K}.$$

The net profit growth is attenuated by a factor $(1-a)$:

$$\frac{d}{dt}(PrK) = r[\dot{P}K + P\dot{K}] = r(-a\dot{K}P + P\dot{K}) = rP\dot{K}(1-a),$$

The greater the output elasticity of capital, a, the more capital stock is required, and the less labor is required, the weaker the deflationary impact on net profit.[10]

2.1.2.6 *Wage and capitalists' profits*

Marx did not anticipate the possibility that workers might acquire common stock, thus assuming ownership stakes in firms. In the economic models of Chapter 1, households own firms. For the sake of comparison with Marx's theory, we still call the people who receive the firms' profits "capitalists." They may be workers too.

In Marxist economics, capitalists are defined as the owners of the means of production. They exploit workers by paying them subsistence wages, while keeping the surplus value—the difference between the value of what workers produce and what they are paid—as profit. Capitalists maximize their wealth by continuously increasing the exploitation of labor, which leads to the worsening of workers' living conditions over time, "Capital is dead labour, which, vampire-like, lives only by sucking living labour, and lives the more, the more labour it sucks," (Marx, 2004).

In contrast, mainstream economics offers a distinct perspective on how firms generate profits. Capitalists optimize production and labor costs by ranking potential projects according to market demand—the "votes" of buyers—which determine expected profitability. They then prioritize the most profitable ventures and hire workers accordingly. The firm ranks the most profitable project as #1 and determines the number of workers for it first. Then the firm moves down to #2, #3, ... #n projects until the marginal product of labor—the additional output produced by one more worker—equals the marginal cost of labor, i.e., the wage paid to that worker.

In practice, this process requires information about future prices. Firms often use *pro forma* accounting statements to forecast profits, adjusting revenues and costs based on past performance while

---

[10]The net return r is assumed to be constant in the short term. The empirical studies on the Cobb–Douglas production function reported different values of the output elasticities of capital stock a. Some reported $a>1$ and others rejected the Cobb–Douglas production function (Shephard, 2015). The modern economy has increasingly depended on capital stock, with a approaching 1. When capital stock is close to 1, net profit does not grow unless the money supply expands.

assuming certain changes in future business conditions. In doing so, this implicitly blends the effects of several factors, including—often unintentionally—the anticipated future money supply.

One key point of intersection between Marxist and mainstream economics is the role of wages. Marx regarded capitalist profit as the result of exploiting workers by continuously lowering their wages and exhausting their labor, thereby sucking workers dry. By contrast, mainstream economics views profit as the residual income from workers' productivity after wages, attributed to productivity gains. Capitalists exploit the gap between the exchange value and the economic value of their products. This exploitation, as discussed in Chapter 7, is presented as the mechanism through which resources are optimally allocated within the economy.

2.1.2.7 *Absolute and relative impoverishment of workers*

Marx argued that workers' living conditions would worsen under capitalism, leading to their absolute impoverishment. However, this claim overlooks the competitive dynamics facing capitalists. A capitalist cannot unilaterally raise prices or lower wages without repercussions. In a competitive market, raising prices alone would result in a loss of market share to competitors. Similarly, capitalists compete for workers, and if the labor pool is not abundant, lowering wages risks losing them.

In Eq. (2.13), replacing the sticky wage with the minimum wage $w_{\min}$ yields the employment $L_{\min}$, constrained by the minimum wage:

$$L_{\min} = \left(\frac{P(1-a)A}{w_{\min}} \right)^{1/a} K. \tag{2.15}$$

In a scenario with a limited labor pool, firms are compelled to offer higher wages to attract and retain employees. In an alternative scenario characterized by abundant labor and wage flexibility, employment expands as workers accept wages below the minimum wage, $w < w_{\min}$, thereby, the number of workers L at wage w provides the employment ratio:

$$\frac{L_{\min}}{L} = \left(\frac{w}{w_{\min}} \right)^{1/a}. \tag{2.16}$$

With respect to the purchasing power of low-wage workers, the imposition of a minimum wage diminishes their aggregate purchasing power:

$$\frac{L_{\min} w_{\min}}{Lw} = \left(\frac{L_{\min}}{L}\right)^{1-a} < 1,$$

which uses Eq. (2.16).

Mainstream economics views competition as a driving force of economic progress, including among workers. As Hayek noted, "Competition is a discovery procedure"—a process of learning and self-improvement. For Marx, however, the pressure on wages stemmed both from the actions of capitalists and the forces of competition. Capitalists aim to purchase labor at the lowest possible cost, treating it as just another production input. Furthermore, workers find themselves in competition with one another—and even with themselves—a manifestation of alienation. The harder workers labor, the less they earn:

> The labourer seeks to maintain the total of his wages for a given time by performing more labour, either by working a great number of hours, or by accomplishing more in the same number of hours. Thus, urged on by want, he himself multiplies the disastrous effects of division of labour. The result is: the more he works, the less wages he receives. And for this simple reason: the more he works, the more he competes against his fellow workmen, the more he compels them to compete against him, and to offer themselves on the same wretched conditions as he does; so that, in the last analysis, he competes against himself as a member of the working class.—(Marx, 1902)

Marx concluded that workers' living standards would deteriorate both relatively and in absolute terms, leading inevitably to a workers' revolution. In Marx's theory, any increase in labor productivity does not benefit the workers:

> To sum up: the more productive capital grows, the more it extends the division of labour and the application of machinery; the more the division of labour and the application of machinery extend, the more does competition extend among the workers, the more do their wages shrink together.—(Marx, 1902)

Marx's observations of the stark disparities between impoverished workers and wealthy capitalists during industrialization were astute, but his projection of widespread, increasing absolute poverty has not materialized, and a global revolution of the working-class has not yet occurred.

2.1.2.8 *Scientific analysis versus moral judgment*

Current critiques of capitalism from Marxists and socialists often focus on ethical issues like capital ownership and wealth distribution. However, these views diverge from Marx's approach, as he rejected ethical critiques, viewing them as unscientific distractions from scientific economic analysis.

> I have dealt more at length with the "equal right" and "fair distribution," on the one hand, to show what a crime it is to attempt, on the one hand, to force on our party again as dogmas ideas which in a certain period had some meaning but have now become obsolete verbal rubbish, while again perverting, on the other, the realistic outlook which it cost so much effort to instill into the party, by means of ideological nonsense about right and other trash so common among the democrats and French socialists.—(Marx, 1972)

For Marx, productivity shaped economic realities, with ethical norms located in the ideological "superstructure" that stood above the economic base. He insisted, "It is not consciousness that determines life, but life that determines consciousness" (Marx and Engels, 1970). In his materialist framework, the superstructure—including morality, religion, and the state—is shaped by the economic base and evolves dialectically. Marx aimed for scientific analysis rather than moral critique.

Although Marx rejected ethical arguments, his critique of capitalism raises ethical questions about the fairness of systems marked by significant wealth disparities, extending the debate beyond economics and into ethics.

The distinction between scientific statements and moral judgments is essential, for understanding science and economics. For instance, the statement "larger wealth gaps worsen economic and social stability" is a scientific claim grounded in historical evidence. Importantly, this assertion is conditional; it may change as new information or circumstances arise.

Statements like "Equal distribution is good" or "Capitalism is evil" are moral judgments which fall outside the bounds of scientific economics. They use absolute terms such as "good" and "evil," suggesting definitive stances that cannot be measured or proven empirically. Such assertions reflect deeper values and aspirations, venturing into moral and philosophical territory rather than empirical evidence. However, the question of what defines the absolute "good" or "evil" cannot be answered, as interpretations of these concepts vary widely across individuals and cultures (see pp. 114–115).

This book avoids absolute moral debates, focusing instead on evaluating economic systems based on efficiency and scientific analysis (see Chapter 1). However, economics intersects with normative considerations in areas like tax laws and business regulations. While laws incorporate ethical principles, they cannot address all ethical dilemmas; actions may be considered unethical despite being legal, and vice versa. Laws aim to provide enforceable and universally applicable rules, while ethics are often more nuanced and subjective, shaped by individual values and circumstances.

Examples such as accounting rules, business laws, and taxes are essential to economics and finance. Regulations, from the Code of Hammurabi (see Section 2.2) to modern accounting standards, often lack scientific rigor. Frequent changes in U.S. tax laws require updates to accounting rules, highlighting how non-scientific factors influence economic realities. The real growth of an economy lies in its investment in productive capacity. This principle holds collectively for firms and cannot be otherwise. Equation (1.3) shows that when economic growth is measured solely by prices—the exchange value—it distorts real growth. Financial accounting that relies exclusively on monetary measures likewise could misrepresent the physical operations of individual firms.

The real growth of a company depends on its tangible investment in production, in discrete time, it be expressed as:

$$\Delta K_0 = f(K_u, L) - \frac{w}{P} - \delta K_u, \tag{2.17}$$

where ΔK_0 denotes real investment at time 0, and ΔK_u is the existing capital stock invested at an earlier time u.

During the following year, the real wage paid by the company increases with production output (see Table 1.3):

$$\frac{w_1}{P_1}L = (1 - a)f(K_u + \Delta K_0, L). \tag{2.18}$$

The gross return pays for depreciation, and whatever is left becomes the company's net return on capital stock:

$$\text{Net return} = af(K_u + \Delta K_0, L) - \delta(K_u + \Delta K_0). \tag{2.19}$$

In accounting, an investment in the income statement is depreciated over time according to predefined rules. The number of years over which an investment is depreciated depends on the type of capital goods—different types of equipment or machinery. For a piece of equipment or a machine depreciated over n_i years, the annual depreciation depends on how much was paid for it:

$$P_i\delta_C(\Delta K_i) = P_i\frac{\Delta K_i}{n_i}, \tag{2.20}$$

where δ_C is the depreciation rate according to accounting rules, and P_i represents the historical price that the firm paid at the time of purchase.

The accounting measure of profit is net income. For year 1 it is:

$$\begin{aligned}\text{net income}_1 &= P_1 af(K_u + \Delta K_0, L)\\ &\quad - P_0\frac{\Delta K_0}{n_0} - P_u\frac{K_u}{n_u}.\end{aligned} \tag{2.21}$$

Equation (2.21) shows two depreciation terms—one for investment in year 0 and another for investment made u years earlier. But in reality, most firms deal with longer list of depreciation schedules because they constantly expand production or replace equipment that has become obsolete or broken. Meanwhile, each year some items drop out of the depreciation list. Equation (2.21) assumes that K_u has not completely depreciated in year 1, otherwise, there is no depreciation of K_u and

$$P_u\frac{K_u}{n_u} = 0. \tag{2.22}$$

Depreciation in the real economy differs markedly from depreciation in accounting. For example, a building may be fully depreciated in accounting terms yet remain operational, whereas the monetary value of a plastic bag is written off immediately after use. Economically, however, the bag depreciates slowly, requiring resources for cleanup (see Section 7.3.2.1).

In the real economy, profit, measured by the net return r is different from the accounting income in Eq. (2.22) for two reasons: First, the accounting depreciation spreads out lump-sum investment over years, making profits artificially smooth. In addition, the accounting framework substitutes investments with a series of depreciation values that are influenced by the price levels P_u, P_0, and P_1. Inflation (where $P_1 > P_0 > P_u$), tends to enhance net income, while deflation adversely affects it. This illustrates how subjectivity can affect the fields of economics and finance.

Karl Marx strongly defended his theory as scientific, distancing himself from potential allies who framed the anti-capitalist movement solely in moral terms. Yet Marx's arguments and methodologies were not entirely devoid of subjectivity. For instance, his dialectical materialism obscured the ethical nature of the justification of private property. The debate between methodologies—dialectics versus formal logic—transcends empiricism yet remains essential for understanding the intricacies of Marxism.

The economic challenges confronting capitalist economies today have fueled growing interest in socialism and communism, especially among younger generations. A March 2023 Fraser Institute survey found that nearly one-third of Britons aged 18–34 view communism as the ideal economic system.[11] Additionally, around 40% of Millennials have a positive perception of Vladimir Lenin, with even higher support among younger cohorts.[12]

The economic problems in capitalist economies today are different, and socialism and Marxism are not a solution. A deeper understanding of Marx's methodology could yield valuable insights that contribute to the ongoing discourse on economic systems.

2.1.3 *Methodology: Dialectic or formal logic*

Marx's theory evolved from three main sources: dialectical materialism, scientific socialism, and classical economics. Of these, dialectical materialism was his primary tool. Modern economics, by contrast,

---

[11] *Britain: communism, the youth, and the fight for revolution*, by Rob Sewell, 19 September 2023, Marxism.com.

[12] *New poll finds strong support for socialism in the U.K.*, by Jason Clemens and Steven Globerman, Fraser Institute, March 24, 2023; *U.S. Attitudes Toward Socialism, Communism, and Collectivism*, Survey by YouGov, October 2020.

relies on mathematics, which uses precise definitions and their relationships to derive implication, free from metaphysical speculation. Logic, too, focuses on the relationship among statements, with Euclidean geometry serving as a prime example of the close connection between mathematics and logic. Natural sciences have harnessed the power of mathematics to solve a variety of problems. Marx, however, chose a different approach: dialectics, drawn from Hegel's philosophy.

Hegel's[13] dialectics was a theory of change driven by contradiction. He revived Zeno's paradoxes,[14] generalized the contradiction in the paradoxes, and made the contradiction a universal principle.

In the paradox of the arrow in flight, Zeno reasoned that for motion to occur, an object must change its position.[15] However, at any given moment, the arrow occupies a single point in space and is neither moving to another point nor having arrived from a previous one. It remains stationary in that instant. Since time is composed of a series of such instants, in which the arrow does not move, Zeno concluded that motion is impossible.

Another of Zeno's paradoxes is his dichotomy paradox. A person walks to a temple. Before he can arrive, he must reach halfway there. He must reach a quarter before he can reach halfway, then one-eighth, one-sixteenth, and so on, requiring an *infinite* number of tasks, which makes completing the trip to the temple impossible. A different version of Zeno's dichotomy paradox—Achilles and the Tortoise—has a similar argument. A popular version changes Achilles and the tortoise to the hare and the tortoise, so that the hare cannot catch up to the tortoise in front.

Hegel admitted that Zeno's paradoxes underpinned his view that reality was inherently contradictory. "Something moves, not because now it is here and there at another now, but because in one and the same now it is here and not here, because in this here, it is and is not at the same time" (Hegel and Wallace, 1975). He famously stated, "Everything is inherently contradictory":

---

[13]Georg Wilhelm Friedrich Hegel (1770–1831) was a German philosopher.
[14]Zeno of Elea (c. 490–430 B.C.) was a Greek philosopher.
[15]*Zeno's arrow paradox*, Philosophy Stack Exchange, accessed on June 28, 2024.

> ... and in the sense that this law in contrast to the others expresses rather the truth and the essential nature of things. ... contradiction is the root of all movement and vitality; it is only in so far as something has a contradiction within it that it moves, has an urge and activity.—Hegel (2014).

He rejected the law of non-contradiction of mathematics, arguing that mathematics dealt with quantity "... but taken uncritically from our generalized image of it, we are liable to exaggerate the range of its validity, ... And that such a danger is real, we see when the title of exact science is restricted to those sciences the objects of which can be submitted to mathematical calculation" (Hegel and Wallace, 1975). Nonetheless, Hegel mischaracterized mathematics and underestimated its flexibility. Modern mathematics has solved Zeno's paradoxes. The mathematical concepts of *infinity* and *infinitesimal* are closely related to the motion in Zero's paradoxes. The concept of infinitesimal seemed paradoxical and took decades for mathematicians to reconcile the contradiction.

Imagine an object moving along a line from point A to point B, taking a certain amount of time. The average speed of the object is calculated by dividing the distance between A and B by the time taken. However, as the two points move closer together and eventually coincide, mathematics encounters the problem of zero distance divided by zero time. Yet mathematics did not stop there; it reinvented itself by introducing the concept of *infinitesimals*. Marx's comrade Engels called it bad infinity: "Here the fixed categories dissolved, mathematics had arrived on a terrain where even such simple relations as that of mere abstract quantity, bad infinity, assumed a completely dialectical shape and forced mathematics, against its will and without knowing it, to become dialectical" (Engels, 1960). Marx called it chimera: "The closely held belief of some rationalizing mathematicians that dy and dx are quantitatively actually only infinitely small, only approaching 0/0, is a chimera, ..." (Marx, 1933). Even philosophers such as Bertrand Russell and Rudolf Carnap called infinitesimal pseudo-concept.

In fact, mathematics solved the problem while preserving mathematical logic. Much like science, as described in Thomas Kuhn's *The Structure of Scientific Revolutions*, the paradigm of mathematics does not easily break. Instead, it adapts by incorporating new concepts, adjusting, and answering new questions. Since Newton and

Leibniz, calculus has become an indispensable tool for scientists and engineers, as well as a foundational subject in colleges and universities. Calculus, along with other advanced branches of mathematics, has transformed infinitesimals into a powerful concept for further development.[16] Mathematics gives a simple answer to Zeno's paradox with the sum of the infinite series,

$$\frac{1}{2} + \frac{1}{4} + \cdots = 1.$$

This sum is finite. Achilles catches and passes the tortoise in a finite time.

Philosophy has also moved on since Hegel and Marx. Analytical philosophy intends to put language and mathematics on the solid ground of formal logic. Analytical philosophers cross out ambiguous metaphysical concepts from the vocabulary of philosophic dictionary:

> The opposition between a philosophy guided by scientific method and a philosophy dominated by religious and ethical ideas may be illustrated by two notions which are very prevalent in the works of philosophers, namely, the notion of the universe, and the notion of good and evil. A philosopher is expected to tell us something about the nature of the universe as a whole, and to give grounds for either optimism or pessimism. Both these expectations seem to me mistaken. I believe the conception of "the universe" to be, as its etymology indicates, a mere relic of pre-Copernican astronomy: and I believe the question of optimism and pessimism to be one which the philosopher will regard as outside his scope, except, possibly, to the extent of maintaining that it is insoluble.—Russell (1914)

Bertrand Russell regarded the grand philosophical systems that seek to weave together all aspects of life as mere "fake philosopher's stones" (Russell, 1914). These systems, like those of Hegel, were relics

[16]Only after 1960 could mathematicians express the properties of infinitesimals in formal mathematical language. That is what mathematics students learn in calculus using the "$\delta \to \epsilon$" language. Mathematicians have also developed other techniques for handling infinitesimals.

of pre-scientific thinking. Analytical philosophers give little attention to such vague notions, instead focusing on clarity and precision.

Both Hegel and Marx built their sweeping theories of the universe on dialectics—the claim that everything is contradictory. Hegel's system of dialectical idealism proposed that the Absolute Mind or Universal Spirit was the basis of ultimate reality. Marx criticized Hegel, claiming that he had turned dialectics upside down: "With him it is standing on its head. It must be turned right side up again, if you would discover the rational kernel within the mystical shell" (Marx, 1992). In Marx's dialectical materialism, matter is the basis of the world, and thought reflects the material world, with dialectical laws governing change in both material conditions and social superstructures.

Hegel's and Marx's contradictions directly challenge formal logic, the system upon which human reasoning and communication rely. Hegel's logic sought to alter the way people understand language and thought, but his grand system was criticized for being too convoluted to make sense. Nietzsche saw that these misguided attempts could only produce the extinct beasts and commented that there was more sense in a page of Hume than in the entire works of Hegel.[17]

No other philosopher than Hegel's contemporary Arthur Schopenhauer rejected Hegel's philosophy outright and criticized Hegel's work as "stringing together senseless and extravagant mazes of words" (Schopenhauer, 1966). Schopenhauer lectured in philosophy at the same time as Hegel did, but nearly all the students went to Hegel's lectures. Hegel was so influential in his time that people had hopes for a new era of human thought and scientists wished that his dialectics were a breakthrough in logic and scientific methodology. The followers of Hegel and Marx built a dialectic logic system that incorporates contradictions, but the results were not successful.[18]

[17] *Nietzsche Philosophy in an Hour*, audiobook, AudiobookVerse (audio ebooks5848).

[18] "Hegel, installed from above, by the powers that be, as the certified Great Philosopher, was a flat-headed, insipid, nauseating, illiterate charlatan who reached the pinnacle of audacity in scribbling together and dishing up the craziest mystifying nonsense. This nonsense has been noisily proclaimed as immortal wisdom by mercenary followers and readily accepted as such by all fools, who

People follow formal logic even without formal training in logic. Humans are born with brains that have the natural ability to reason.[19] Like computers, the memories of human brains are large but limited. The average is about one billion synapses per person based on the research of neuroscientists.[20] With limited memory, humans are born with a system that uses its resources efficiently. A library classification system organizes related information in groups and orders the groups systematically. The simplest yet efficient system uses dichotomous classification or binary classification—classifying objects by recursively splitting them into two groups. The two groups must be mutually exclusive. A fiction book cannot be a non-fiction book, nor can the information have stored in human brains. The brains retrieve and communicate information from the system. Communication must have consistent structure with the system. Formal logic, which underpins mathematics and language, mirrors this neural organization.

Chomsky's linguistic theory also points to the brain's natural ability to process language with limited stimuli, a phenomenon known as the "poverty of the stimulus" problem. He posited that children are born with an innate linguistic ability, which enables them to acquire

---

thus joined into as perfect a chorus of admiration as had ever been heard before. The extensive field of spiritual influence with which Hegel was furnished by those in power has enabled him to achieve the intellectual corruption of a whole generation." "But the height of audacity in serving up pure nonsense, in stringing together senseless and extravagant mazes of words, such as had previously been known only in madhouses, was finally reached in Hegel, and became the instrument of the most barefaced general mystification that has ever taken place, with a result which will appear fabulous to posterity, and will remain as a monument to German stupidity." Schopenhauer and Hegel happened to have philosophy seminars scheduled at the same time at the University of Berlin. Almost everyone went to Hegel's seminar, leaving Schopenhauer's seminar pretty much empty (Schopenhauer, 1966).

[19]Frege's anti-psychologicalism is correct in holding that logic and mathematics are independent of psychology, but they depend on the structure of the human brains. Neuroscience may help clarify links between brain structure and logic, mathematics, and language.

[20]Over 130 years ago, pioneering neuroscientist Santiago Ramón y Cajal first suggested that the brain stores information in neurons, relates any two pieces of information through neural connections, and establishes and rearranges synaptic connections between neurons.

language quickly despite limited exposure. This natural capacity for language mirrors the brain's ability to follow logic. "There does exist what we have called an internalized language and that it is a problem of the natural sciences to discover it." As Chomsky noted, the brain is a device that operates based on certain inherent structures, just as mathematics and computers are built on formal logic systems: "...we understand mental states and representations to be physically encoded in some manner" (Chomsky, 2006). Beyond language ability, child music geniuses or child prodigies are hard to explain without reference to innate brain structures. Mikhail Osipov, a Russian three-year-old chess prodigy, first came to fame when he was on a Russian TV show playing against world champion Anatoly Karpov and the show went viral.[21]

Human brains are logic and language devices: "An engineer faced with the problem of designing a device meeting given input-output conditions would naturally conclude that the basic properties of the output are a consequence of the design of the device" (Chomsky, 2006). It is no wonder that mathematics created by human brains and computers built by humans adopt the formal logic system (Liu and Liu, 1998). However, formal logic itself is not immune to paradoxes. Bertrand Russell showed Gottlob Frege the paradox—the set of all sets that do not contain themselves (Russell, 2009).[22] This era of self-referential paradox inspired Kurt Gödel, leading him to formulate his landmark result, the incompleteness theorem, which sets the limits of provability in formal axiomatic theories. Russell's paradox and Gödel's incompleteness theorem highlight the limitations of the formal logic system. The human brain as a device has finite memory and finite capacity.

In addition to Hegel and Marx, a group of philosophers support the use of various methods to study the most general features of the world. They endorse any method in research, witchcraft, sorcery, astrology, oracle, and others. It is important to recognize that human

[21] *3 Year Old Chess Prodigy Is Absolutely INSANE*, GothamChess, retrieved accessed on June 17, 2024.

[22] It is a slight translation of his original wording. A popular version is the *Barber paradox*: The barber who shaves all those, and those only, who do not shave themselves. The question is whether the barber shaves himself or not. Either answer yields a contradiction.

brains have a definite structure, not a *tabula rasa*—a blank slate as John Locke claimed. Aristotle rejected tabula rasa long before Locke used language as an example:

> Haven't we already disposed of the difficulty about interaction involving a common element, when we said that mind is in a sense potentially whatever is thinkable, though actually it is nothing until it has thought? What it thinks must be in it just as characters may be said to be on a writing tablet on which as yet nothing stands written: this is exactly what happens with mind.—Aristotle (1986)

When searching for existing books, one follows the library system. Authors can write new books, and librarians categorize them and add them to the system. Nevertheless, authors cannot change the classification system, because there is no place for a book that is fiction *and* non-friction.

Hegel and Marx's dialectics violate the system that human brains organize and process thoughts. These debates will continue as a philosophical topic.[23] Nevertheless, economics, being an empirical field, requires careful attention to methods, as it relies on rigorous logical consistency rather than metaphysical speculation.

2.1.3.1 *Quantitative predictions and testability*

Like the ancient Chinese philosophical symbol Yin and Yang, which represents contradictory forces, dialectical theory posits that opposing forces drive change through conflict. In dialectics, contradictions generate a continuous cycle of change, as the forces of Yin and Yang battle each other, causing shifts in their relative strength. The gradual accumulation of these quantitative changes eventually results in a qualitative leap, a transition from mere quantitative shifts to a

[23]Philosophers talk about continental philosophy vs. analytical philosophy. Hegel originated German idealism, a major strand of continental philosophy. The two diverged after Immanuel Kant and developed along separate routes. The remarkable progress made in natural sciences, particularly physics, put huge pressure on philosophers, who wondered whether philosophy had made any progress. Kant showed three directions for philosophy: providing the foundations for natural and social science as a non-empirical academic discipline, giving up as an academic discipline, and joining natural sciences as a member. Analytic philosophy chose the first direction, and some continental philosophers emphasized the second.

profound qualitative transformation. This dynamic process of change is referred to in dialectic terms as the "quantity-quality law," or the idea that "merely quantitative differences, beyond a certain point, pass into qualitative changes" (Marx, 1992).

Hegel distinguishes between two types of qualities: One is static and represents determinateness, while the other undergoes dialectical transitions. However, dialectics stop short of providing a quantitative description of how these qualitative changes occur or at what point they occur. This limitation arises from the fact that dialectical reasoning is incompatible with mathematics, which excels at pinpointing specifics of change. Marx's economic theory, rooted in dialectical materialism, also halts at qualitative explanations, leaving no quantitative insights.

In dealing with the physical world, natural scientists, engineers, and managers cannot afford to rely solely on dialectics or settle for simple yes-or-no conclusions. Instead, they must answer quantitative questions, such as "how much" or "how many." Mathematics identifies qualitative transitions by quantifying change, describing the transition process, and determining the precise point at which the shift in quality occurs. For example, physicists use the van der Waals equation to predict the phase transition between liquid and gas. Johannes Diderik van der Waals (1837–1923), a Dutch physicist, pioneered the equation of state for gases and liquids.[24]

When describing the real world and providing actionable solutions, dialectics pale in comparison to modern mathematics, which is well suited to quantitative analysis. In this regard, Marx's economics cannot compete with mainstream economics.

The testability of a theory is the cornerstone of empirical science. An economic theory must provide testable predictions. Let us take Zeno's paradox of the arrow in flight as an example. Dialectics would claim that the arrow is simultaneously here and not here at any given moment during its flight, but there is no empirical way to test such a claim. It is possible to verify whether the arrow is here *or* is not here, but it is impossible to test whether the arrow is both here *and* not here at the same time. Similarly, for Marx's claim that "reification" transforms "exchange-value" into money, there is no empirical way to

[24]Van der Waals received the Nobel Prize in Physics in 1910.

test whether the abstract concept "exchange-value" somehow turns into a tangible object such as gold. In general, contradictions, as posited in dialectical reasoning, are not testable.

A scientific theory must also provide a method for generating repeatable predictions in the future. Wittgenstein once suggested in a lecture that a theory could be valid even if it contained contradictions. As a founding figure in analytical philosophy, Wittgenstein viewed theory as "a picture of a world," which might not represent the true picture of "the world." He argued, "The facts in logical space are the world," and stated that "it is the business of philosophy, not to resolve a contradiction by means of a mathematical or logico-mathematical discovery, but to make it possible for us to get a clear view of the state of mathematics that troubles us: the state of affairs before the contradiction is resolved" (Wittgenstein, 2013). Yet, it was his student Alan Turing, who later invented the computer and helped crack the German cipher machine during World War II, who challenged Wittgenstein's statement. Turing reasoned that building a mathematical theory based on contradictions was pointless, as it could lead to the collapse of real-world structure, such as bridges, built on those theories. Marxist or Hegelian philosophy may paint a picture of a "world," but not of the real, empirical world that people live in.

The term "theory" is often used loosely, applied to both hypotheses and scientifically established theories. A scientific theory may rest on untestable assumptions, but it must also produce testable statements derived from those assumptions. For instance, Einstein's theory of general relativity is not directly testable, but its predictions have been tested indirectly. On the other hand, dialectical concepts such as "both being and not being at the same time" are inherently untestable. If we regard Marx's dialectic as a hypothesis, the challenge is to extract testable statements from his economic theory and evaluate them against observable facts.

Marx made several significant claims based on his concept of historical materialism, which applies his dialectical analysis to human economic history. As he wrote:

> Freeman and slave, patrician and plebeian, lord and serf, guild-master and journeyman, in a word, oppressor and oppressed, stood in constant opposition to one another, carried on an

> uninterrupted, now hidden, now open fight, a fight that each time ended, either in a revolutionary reconstitution of society at large, or in the common ruin of the contending classes.

Marx traced human history to what he termed "primitive communism"—societies without private property or money. According to Marx, this stage marked the start of the dialectical progression of economic history (Engels and Untermann, 2021). In these societies, low productivity required resource sharing for survival. Anthropological studies of modern hunter-gatherer groups, such as the Kalahari Bushmen,[25] reveal similar communal characteristics. For example, John and Lorna Marshall's study of the Bushmen in the 1960s noted that a knife given to one member of the community had, over time, passed through the hands of nearly everyone in the band (Graeber, 2012). In such societies, money is unnecessary.

The economic reality of these primeval societies fostered public ownership, egalitarianism, and non-hierarchical social structures. However, as productivity rose, contradictions emerged between the forces of production and the superstructure. Marx defined productive forces as labor and the means of labor (similar to capital in modern terms), excluding material inputs (Marx, 2004). The superstructure—encompassing culture, ideology, institutions, and politics—was shaped by economic development.

When societies began producing more than what was necessary for survival, private ownership emerged, leading to class divisions and the exploitation of labor. As communal ownership gave way, class struggles between oppressors (such as slave owners) and the oppressed (slaves) became a central feature of society. Marx described this transition as the result of private properties, where private ownership allowed for more productive use of surplus goods but also led to conflicts between slaves and their owners (Marx and Engels, 1970).

[25]The San (a label applied by colonists: "Bushmen") people of South Africa and neighboring Botswana and Namibia, who live in the Kalahari Desert. They are traditionally organized into small bands, typically numbering up to about a hundred people each.

In feudal societies, peasants freed from slavery contributed to increased productivity. Over time, the major class conflict shifted from slaves and owners to serfs and lords. New technological advancements led to the rise of capitalists, who sought to expand production beyond the limits of the feudal system. Eventually, the contradictions between industrial production and the feudal social structure caused the collapse of feudalism and gave rise to capitalism. Capitalism itself, Marx argued, was marked by the ongoing conflict between capitalists and workers.

Marx and Engels described this cyclical process of social change as a "spiral form of development." This concept, embodied in the dialectical law of the "negation of the negation," suggested that private ownership would eventually be replaced by a higher form of communism—not a return to primitive communism but a more advanced stage with developed productive forces (Engels, 1960). However, Vladimir Lenin and Mao Zedong introduced the non-antagonistic contradictions that might arise in a future communist society. These questions were often politically dangerous to explore, creating an ironic contradiction within Marxist theory of communist society.

Marx's theory of historical development rests on the notion that contradictions drive social and economic changes, from primitive communism to slave society, feudalism, capitalism, and eventually to a higher-level form of communism. Marxists also highlight other contradictions, such as those between productive forces and social superstructures, between use-value and exchange-value, between capital and labor, and between private property and social production. Yet Marx's dialectics and its focus on contradictions have been subject to misinterpretation. For instance, in Chinese philosophy, Yin and Yang are present in all existence and behind all change. Mao Zedong's book *On Contradiction* (Zedong, 1987), grounded in traditional Chinese philosophy, bore only minimal resemblance to the Hegelian dialectics. Marx, too, obscured the mystical aspects of Hegel's dialectics with his materialist focus, leading followers to overlook the inconsistencies between dialectics and the world we live in.

Unlike scientific theories, Marx's theory of economic history cannot be tested using the frameworks of formal logic. While Marx applied his dialectical model to economic history, critics have pointed out that he sometimes forced history to fit the framework. For example, he avoided addressing New World slavery in his analysis of capitalism, as it did not align with his description of capitalist society. Similarly, Hegel was criticized for manipulating historical facts to fit his dialectical model.

Recent economic history diverges from Marx's dialectical materialist framework, and efforts to impose that model on reality have often produced catastrophic outcomes. Pol Pot's regime sought to create a society without private property or money, symbolically destroying the central bank as part of the experiment. The result was the collapse of Cambodia's financial and economic systems. As Elizabeth Prasso notes, even decades later, Cambodians remained distrustful of their national currency and preferred to convert it into gold, jewelry, or U.S. dollars, perpetuating the weaknesses in the country's financial institutions (Prasso, 2001).

Marx's predictions of increasing poverty under capitalism and the inevitable collapse of the capitalist system have not materialized. In contrast, the planned economy of the Soviet Union failed, while capitalism expanded globally.

Mainstream economics sets a humble goal: to manage limited resources efficiently. In contrast, Marx aimed to change the world—an ambitious and transformative goal. He made this objective explicit: "Philosophers have hitherto only interpreted the world in various ways; the point is to change it" (Marx, 2008). However, this grand ambition had detrimental effects on many of his followers.[26] Many of Marx's followers, despite their limited understanding of the complexities of the world, believed they could reshape it according

[26]The desire to change the world is not unique to Marx. Francis Bacon, in *The New Atlantis*, wrote, "Let the human race recover that right over nature which belongs to it by divine bequest" (Bacon, 2021). Schopenhauer, however, saw this ambition as one of the three follies of human nature—ambition, vanity, and pride (Schopenhauer, 1901), viewing the human will as a "striving without aim and without end." Nietzsche, while recognizing ambition's role in human development, noted that it "humanizes man and makes him more sociable, endurable, and indulgent in small things, after ambition has finished rough-hewing him" (Nietzsche, 1908). Yet, the will is ultimately a desire to exert control over both oneself and others.

to their ideals, as Superman Kal-El of Krypton puts it, "If the world is too big, make it small."

As Richard Louv aptly put it, "by bringing nature into our lives, we invite humility."[27] The awe-inspiring cultural relics of ancient civilizations, preserved as world wonders, remind us of their grandeur. Yet they also highlight the immense economic resources expended and wasted by these societies. Acknowledging the power of nature, an ideal economy would prioritize using its resources to benefit its population fully, leaving nothing wasted at the end of its existence. If humanity seeks to leave a legacy for potential future intelligent beings, it should be the knowledge of how its economy maximizes well-being for all members with limited resources.

Marx's ambition was not merely to erect a monument but to create heaven on earth, embodied in the maxim "From each according to his ability, to each according to his needs." Yet his economics was constructed with a wrong tool: not rigorous logic directed at the efficient use of natural resources, but rather a pre-Socratic idea. Without a genuine economic foundation, his vision of the future remains, at best, a utopia.

2.2 Bank Money: Credit and Debt

In addition to economists, anthropologists and historians have developed their own theories on the origins of money, often challenging the idea that it emerged solely from markets. David Graeber, an American anthropologist, suggested in his book, *Debt: The First 5000 Years*, that debt and credit systems existed long before money or exchange-value or markets existed, potentially pushing the origin of money back by 5,000 years (Graeber, 2012). Historians and archaeologists have also found evidence of exchange value and money in ancient legal codes. For instance, medieval Welsh law provided detailed valuations for items such as milk, cows, and timber.

Reconciling these perspectives with Adam Smith's views on the origin of money involves examining different scales of the division of labor. Archaeologists have discovered artifacts such as amulets

[27]By Richard Lous, an American writer and journalist.

and pottery tools, indicating a rudimentary division of labor in ancient societies. Meanwhile, Adam Smith noted that ten people could produce over 48,000 pins a day when working together, compared to far fewer if they worked individually (Smith, 2010). While a division of labor existed in pre-industrial societies, its impact on the broader economy was limited due to the predominance of self-sufficient farming communities. Before the Industrial Revolution, 80–90% of the global population worked in agriculture, markets and trade were less central to economic life.[28]

The Industrial Revolution was an energy revolution (see Chapter 7). Machines powered by fossil fuels were far more powerful than human labor, yet their capacity remained confined to simple, repetitive tasks. The "division of labor" was, in fact, the division of tasks imposed by machinery. Charlie Chaplin's *Modern Times* captures this vividly, showing the worker endlessly tightening screws until he is virtually swallowed by the machine. The remarkable efficiency of the Industrial Revolution owed to the harnessing of energy, the systematic division of tasks, and the deployment of mechanical power. For example, a worker in 1820 using steam-powered spindles could produce 100 times more thread than their pre-industrial counterpart (Stearns, 2020).

Marx also recognized the role of mechanization, particularly in the cotton industry. British factories had an average of 12,600 spindles per factory, far surpassing the 1,500 in France and Prussia, with each English worker managing 74 spindles compared to 37 in Prussia and 14 in France. This mechanization helped propel England to global dominance, becoming "the empire on which the sun never sets."

Agriculture further highlights this trend. Today, less than 2% of the U.S. population is involved in farming, and productivity gains stem more from mechanization and energy use than from the division of labor.

The early debt-credit arrangements documented by historians and anthropologists functioned, in practice, as forms of money because they facilitated trade, exchange, and resource redistribution. The

[28] *The Changing Nature of Work* by Marian L. Tupy and Ronald Bailey, March 1, 2023, accessed on May 22, 2024.

promise of repayment or future labor—a form of debt/credit—served as a tool for economic interaction. Thus, debt was integral to the functioning of these early economies, supporting the argument that debt itself can be considered a form of money.

Ancient legal codes, such as the Code of Hammurabi, recorded debt cancellations, with four major cancellations occurring during Hammurabi's reign from 1792 to 1762 BC.[29] The Austrian School of economics even regards Hesiod, an ancient Greek poet, as the first economist to address concerns about debt in his work (Evelyn-White *et al.*, 1914; Trever, 1924).

Graeber has expanded the concept of credit to include gift exchange, a form of informal credit in early societies. The Old French word for "finance" means "to settle a debt," and "credit" derives from the Latin *creditum*, meaning "trust." Gift-giving and network reciprocity belong to human economies governed by "trust," which fundamentally resist the quantified, top-down logic of state-enforced "debt", taxes.

While barter economies had systems of debt (Baskin *et al.*, 1999), these debts were often repaid in kind using perishable goods rather than durable assets like gold. Consequently, debt payments using perishable goods had a more limited and less significant economic impact than those made in gold.

Adam Smith recognized that much of the money in circulation did not stem from gold or silver but from paper money (debt). In an economy operating under a 20% fractional reserve system, 100 tons of paper money would require only 20 tons of actual gold as reserve to back it. This system allows for the expansion of the money supply beyond the available gold supply. As a result, the money in circulation could expand to the equivalent of 100 tons of gold (gold certificate), even if the actual gold supply remained at 20 tons. However, Smith warned of the risks involved in relying too heavily on paper money to fuel economic growth:

> The commerce and industry of the country, however, it must be acknowledged, though they may be somewhat augmented, cannot be altogether so secure, when they are thus as it were,

[29] *The Long Tradition of Debt Cancellation in Mesopotamia and Egypt from 3000 to 1000 BC* by Eric Toussaint, September 2, 2012, CADTM (cadtm.org).

> suspended upon the Daedalian wings of paper money, as when they travel about upon the solid ground of gold and silver.—Smith (2010)

While the fractional reserve system supports the economy during expansion, it also poses risks during crisis. Marx noted that during economic uncertainty, capitalists often turn to the security of the "money-commodity"—gold—to preserve their wealth.

Marx acknowledged the role of paper money and other forms of non-commodity money, such as credit. In *Capital, Volume III*, edited by Friedrich Engels and published posthumously, Marx referred to these instruments as "fictitious capital." He wrote, "With the development of interest-bearing capital and the credit system, all capital seems to double itself, and sometimes treble itself, by the various modes in which the same capital, or even the same claim on a debt, appears in different forms in different hands. The greater portion of this "money-capital" is purely fictitious. All the deposits, with the exception of the reserve fund, are merely claims on the banker, which, however, never exist as deposits" (Marx, 1992). This "fictitious capital" was not idle. Capitalists could use it to pay workers, who would then spend it on goods, keeping the economy running. Marx also recognized that bank credit functioned as money, stating:

> Credit money is directly derived from the functions of money as a means of payment... Money as a means of payment has acquired various unique forms of existence, and occupies a field of large-scale transactions in these forms, while silver and gold coins are mainly squeezed into the field of retail trade.—Marx (2004).

It is noteworthy that in today's economy, the total value of debt far exceeds the available supply of gold and silver. The use of paper as money evolved over time. Wealthy individuals, such as prominent goldsmiths, discovered that their written promises to pay—pieces of paper—could function as money. These promissory notes became more convenient and safer than transporting physical gold or silver. Soon, goldsmiths and bankers realized they could issue more paper notes than they had in physical reserves, because not all holders would redeem them for actual money at the same time. This practice led to the development of fractional reserve lending.

The Medici family, for example, became one of the most powerful banking dynasties in 15th-century Italy, leveraging these financial innovations.[30] Cosimo de' Medici, the family's patriarch, used paper notes to facilitate trade and payments across Europe, avoiding the need to transport gold coins. An English merchant could order Italian cloth from the Medici for 100 gold florins, promising to pay with a promissory note. Meanwhile, the Medici could owe 100 florins for French wine. Rather than shipping gold, they could simply transfer paper, which was accepted as equivalent to gold.

A bank's banknote—a form of paper money—is essentially a promissory note issued by a bank, payable to the holder on demand. Initially, commercial banks issued them, redeemable for gold or silver at the issuing bank. Today, central banks regulate it by setting minimum reserve requirements. In the U.S., the Federal Reserve mandates a 10% reserve ratio, meaning banks must hold 10% of their deposits as liquid assets. Reserves above this threshold earn interest from the central bank.

Irving Fisher criticized the fractional reserve banking system, describing it as an inverted pyramid: "Such a top-heavy system is dangerous—dangerous to depositors, dangerous to the banks, and above all dangerous to the millions of "innocent bystanders," the public... under the mob rule of thousands of little private mints" (Fisher, 1936). Fisher recognized the "evils of monetary instability"—specifically, how periodic changes in price levels can lead to economic crises and depressions. He emphasized that only through understanding both the principles and the facts of the fractional reserve system could these fluctuations be reduced, along with the losses they cause (Fisher, 2006).

Fisher used an illustrative example to highlight the problems with fractional reserve banking. Imagine a bank holding $10,000 in its vault, which it loans to a customer. The customer deposits this same $10,000 back into his account. Here is the key: The customer has not repaid the loan; he has simply deposited the money into his account. The bank, in turn, loans it again to other customers, who also deposit it back. This process repeats until the bank has lent

[30]The House of Medici founded the Medici Bank in 1397.

Table 2.1. Balance sheet: A bank.

Assets		**Liabilities and Equity**	
Assets		Liabilities	
Reserves	10	Debt	10
Bank loan	100	Deposits	100
		Equity	
		Interest	5
		Dividends	−5
Total	110	Total	110

out \$100,000, despite having only \$10,000 in physical reserves. The process creates "checkbook money," or credit, which far exceeds the actual money held by the bank.[31] Today, a household applying for a \$100,000 loan provides a similar example. Upon approval, the bank creates a credit-debt contract, where credit and debt are two sides of the same transaction. In a 10% reserve system, the bank would need \$10,000 in reserves to create \$100,000 in loans. This new type of *money* differs from the commodity money—gold—discussed in Section 2.1. Credit money has little use-value.

The household receives a \$100,000 loan created from \$10,000 in reserves by the bank and incurs liability for the principal and interest. The accounting principle requires that for every debit in one account, there must be a credit of equal value in another account. Table 2.1 is the balance sheet of the bank, which provides an example of how the money creation is balanced in double-entry accounting (Yamaguchi and Yamaguchi, 2021). In this example, the household pays \$5,000 in interest (5%) on the loan, which the bank distributes as dividends to its shareholders.

The "Father of Accounting," Luca Pacioli (1447–1517), stated, "a person should not go to sleep at night until the debits equal the credits."[32] Following this principle, people would look at the bank

[31] Irving Fisher introduced the term "pocketbook money" to describe tangible and visible money, in contrast to "checkbook money." Pocketbook money includes "commodity money" and cash.

[32] *8 accountants who changed history*, ICAEW, accessed on June 30, 2024.

account in Table (2.1) and, seeing the debits and credit balanced, would sleep soundly. Yet they were unaware that figures had been created from thin air.

We can also illustrate the 10% reserve system from another perspective. Suppose a bank starts with \$100,000 in deposits. After setting aside the required \$10,000 reserve, the bank lends \$90,000 to a customer. The household uses the loan to purchase a house, and the seller of the house deposits the \$90,000 into another bank. This second bank then sets aside \$9,000 as reserves and lends out \$81,000 to another customer. This cycle repeats, leading to a significant multiplication of total credit in the economy:

$$D = 100(1-x) + 100(1-x)^2 + 100(1-x)^3 \ldots = (1-x)\frac{100}{x}, \tag{2.23}$$

where x is the reserve requirement and, in general,

$$D = D_0 \frac{1-x}{x} = \zeta D_0, \tag{2.24}$$

where D_0 is the initial physical money and $\zeta = \frac{1-x}{x}$ is the loan multiplier or *money multiplier*. For example, with a 10% reserve requirement ($x = 0.1$), the multiplier is $\zeta = 9$, meaning an initial \$100,000 deposit can lead to \$900,000 in new money created through lending. This aligns with Fisher's example of checkbook money creation.

The credit creation theory of banking suggests that banks can create money "out of nothing" by extending credit (Werner, 2014, 2015). The accounting principle, which mandates that every debit in one account must have corresponding credit in another. However, debts and credits can be interpreted differently, though the principle that debits equal credits appears to hold.

Central banks around the world operate under the fractional reserve system. In the United Kingdom, the minimum reserve ratio is 12.5%.[33] (Nichols and Gonczy, 1992, Modern Money Mechanics). Since 2009, G-20 countries have enforced the Basel Accords, requiring banks to meet the liquidity coverage ratio, which ensures banks hold

[33]Bank of England, September 16, 2022 (bankofengland.co.uk).

enough high-quality liquid assets to fund cash outflows for 30 days.[34] To comply, the Federal Reserve set leverage ratios of 5% for insured bank holding companies and 6% for systemically important financial institutions (SIFIs).[35]

Fisher argued that the fractional reserve system operates "on a shoestring of the real economy" (Fisher, 1936). He quoted an experienced banker who warned that no prudent business would run with such a balance sheet, and if it did, no bank would lend to it. Fisher pointed out, "What causes the trouble is the fact that the bank lends not money but merely a promise to furnish money on demand—money it does not possess. The banks can build upon their meager cash reserves an inverted pyramid of such credits—that is, check-book money, the volume of which can be inflated and deflated" (Fisher, 1936).

The dangers of this system were evident between 1929 and 1933 when checkbook money shrank from $23 billion to $15 billion, contributing to the Great Depression. In recent decades, massive amounts of debt were created under the fractional reserve system. For example, the UK's debt grew from $2.96 trillion in 1998 to an all-time high of $11.03 trillion by 2008 before decreasing to $8.78 trillion in June 2024.[36] In April 2023, total U.S. loans and leases in bank credit reached $12.15 trillion, while the national debt stood at $31.46 trillion.[37] The values of loans as a share of total assets of commercial banks in the U.S. in Q4 2022 were as follows: Residential real estate 9.35%, commercial real estate 10.07%, commercial and industrial 8.95%, consumer 7.47%, other 8.3%.[38]

2.2.1 *Banks' right to create money*

Today, credit cards and loans are commonplace, but the legitimacy of creating money from nothing has been a contentious issue

[34]Bank for International Settlements, "Basel Committee on Banking Supervision, Basel III: The Liquidity Coverage Ratio and Liquidity Risk Monitoring Tools," p. 7, accessed on September 4, 2021.

[35]Federal Deposit Insurance Corporation, "Risk Management Manual of Examination Policies, Section 2.1, CAPITAL," September 4, 2021.

[36]CEIC Data (ceicdata.com), accessed on August 25, 2024.

[37]U.S. Treasury Fiscal Data; Board of Governors of the Fed System (U.S.).

[38]Statista (statista.com), accessed on February 26, 2024.

historically. In the early United States, debates over whether banks should issue banknotes were intense. President John Adams condemned the issuance of private banknotes as "downright corruption," insisting that only the government should have the authority to issue money if needed (Adams and Adams, 1871). President Andrew Jackson questioned the constitutionality of a central bank printing paper money instead of using gold. He opposed the extension of the charter for the Second Bank of the United States, which expired in 1836. In the United Kingdom, Prime Minister Sir Robert Peel's government passed the Bank Charter Act of 1844, also known as the Peel Banking Act. This Act restricted money creation to the Bank of England, requiring that new money be backed by additional gold reserves. The British Currency School supported this Act on the ground that unrestricted banknote issuance caused inflation.

The most recent challenge to the legitimacy of bank loans took place in a court drama in 1969, the case of First National Bank of Montgomery vs. Jerome Daly. Jerome obtained a $14,000 home mortgage from the First National Bank and bought a house with the mortgage. He fell behind in payments, and the bank took his house and sold it at auction. Jerome was an attorney and defended himself in court. He challenged the bank's foreclosure on his house on the legal ground of "consideration" in a contract, in which two parties exchange certain things of value, or a "bargained-for exchange." Jerome would either pay down the loan or give the house to the bank, but Jerome contended that the bank had nothing to exchange because the bank did not have the real money to back up his loan, that is, the consideration on the part of the bank did not exist.

Justice Mahoney agreed to Jerome's argument and rejected the right of banks to issue loans out of nothing. The judge said in his memorandum, "the money and credit first came into existence when they created it. Mr. Morgan (president of First National Bank of Montgomery) admitted that no United States Law or Statute existed which gave him the right to do this. A lawful consideration must exist and be tendered to support the note. The Jury found that there was no consideration and I agree. Only God can create something of value out of nothing." The court denied the foreclosure of the bank and, surprisingly, declared the following: "That the Fed Act and the National Banking Act, in so far as they are attempted legislation by the United States authorizing Fed and National Banks as Banking Corporations, is unconstitutional and void and not necessary and proper for carrying into execution the powers vested in the United States Gov. by the people"[39] (Brown, 2007; Humphrey, 2012). The bank appealed the next day, and the higher court reversed the decision on the grounds that the justice of the peace did not have the power to make such a ruling.

Who has the power to make such a rule? Article I, Section 8 of the Constitution of the United States says, "The Congress shall have Power ... To coin Money, regulate the Value thereof, and of foreign Coin, and fix the Standard of Weights and Measures;. . . ." Since citizens elect members of Congress, they hold ultimate responsibility for laws governing money and debt. During elections, the issue of money creation is often overshadowed by other political concerns. Yet it remains one of the most important issues, with significant and lasting impacts on the economy and people's lives.

In 2015, following the 2008–2011 Icelandic financial crisis, the government of Iceland explored a groundbreaking monetary reform proposal. This proposal aims to abolish private money creation and end fractional-reserve banking. The reform was inspired by the belief that such changes could help prevent future financial crises and enhance economic stability. Lacking support from both the central bank and the legislature, the proposal commissioned by the Prime Minister was ultimately not adopted or implemented.

Swiss voters had the opportunity on June 10, 2018, to reform the monetary system through the Sovereign Money Initiative, which proposed a 100% reserve requirement for banks. However, 75.7% of voters rejected the initiative, demonstrating the challenges of implementing monetary reforms. The Swiss banking sector, which includes some of the world's largest financial institutions, strongly opposed the initiative. When asked about banking policies, one-third of the public believed that normal bankruptcy regulations would make banks act more cautiously, while another third supported government guarantees and central bank support in the event of a bank run.

More educated voters on the money could take critical economic decisions affecting their lives into their own hands. Elected representatives and government officials who have a deeper understanding of money and the economy could lead to better economic policies.

[39]Minnesota State Law Library, Minnesota.gov (mn.gov).

Together with Article I, Section 8 of the U.S. Constitution, Article I, Section 10, Clause 1 limits states' power to issue paper money beyond gold and silver:

> No State shall enter into any Treaty, Alliance, or Confederation; grant Letters of Marque and Reprisal; coin Money; emit Bills of Credit; make any Thing but gold and silver Coin a Tender in Payment of Debts; pass any Bill of Attainder, ex post facto Law, or Law impairing the Obligation of Contracts, or grant any Title of Nobility.

In 2023, twelve U.S. states recognized gold and silver coins as legal tender,[40] opting for commodity money rather than the paper-currency system adopted by the federal government.

The challenge, however, is that political imperatives often clash with sound economic principles, incentivizing governments to pursue short-term benefits at the expense of long-term stability. The policies of the Kennedy and Bush administrations, which encouraged banks to expand credit to boost homeownership, illustrate this point. The 2008 financial crisis demonstrated the substantial cost of these policies for both the U.S. and the global economy. While economists may propose reforms, without public support and engagement, these ideas often remain theoretical.

2.2.2 *The 100% reserve system*

Irving Fisher was a key proponent of the 100% reserve banking system, which mandates that all loans be backed by 100% cash reserves (Fisher, 1936). Fisher's proposal aimed to eliminate the risks associated with fractional-reserve banking by ensuring that banks could not create money through lending.

The United Kingdom's adoption of a 100% reserve requirement under the Bank Charter Act of 1844. The Act had lasting implications for the British financial system and contributed to the development of the gold standard, which became the foundation for global currency systems in the late 19th and early 20th centuries. After Fisher, more economists and professionals endorsed the idea. In the

[40] *Gold and Silver Legal Tender States 2023*, akleg.gov, accessed on April 14, 2025.

post-war period, Friedman supported the idea of a 100% reserve requirement. In the 1980s, Tobin echoed similar ideas. Following the 2008 financial crisis, economists John Kay, Laurence Kotlikoff, Jaromir Benes, Michael Kumhof, and *Financial Times* columnist Martin Wolf endorsed the 100% reserve system (Stellinga *et al.*, 2021).

John Maynard Keynes opposed both the 100% reserve system and the gold standard, believing that a flexible money supply was essential for investment and employment. Keynes strongly criticized any monetary system that was too rigid to adapt, as it led to instability and unemployment. He stated, "There is no more certain means of disaster than to be endowed with a system of money which is inextensible to the demands of industry and trade" (Keynes, 1923). Keynes rejected the 100% reserve system because it would constrain credit supply by limiting banks to existing deposits. This restriction, he warned, would severely impair the banking system's capacity to expand credit during periods of rising demand or economic recovery. Moreover, he cautioned that the inflexibility of such a system would elevate borrowing costs, resulting in higher and more volatile interest rates. These conditions, in turn, could suppress entrepreneurial "animal spirits" and reduce investment.

Fisher did not think so. Economic prosperity cannot depend on the "money" that banks furnish to do business. "If we are to have a sound and stable dollar, we must "tinker" with it all the time—but in a purposeful way and not in a random way as at present, when so many banks do the tinkering independently. For, even the gold standard is never really automatic, but requires active management by central banks to maintain redemption." The 100% reserve system is the money management system, in which the government, the Currency Commission, controls the amount of "money," the sum of credit and currency, which is circulating in the economy to satisfy the needs of economic activity.

Fisher listed eight advantages of the 100% reserve system and emphasized advantages six and seven as by far the most important: "6. The 100% system would eliminate great inflations and deflations because the system would deprive banks the power to mint check-book money and to destroy it;.... 7. Booms and depressions would be mitigated; because these are largely due to inflation and deflation." Fisher painted a pleasant economic picture under the 100% reserve system—a stable dollar and steady economic growth, freeing from booms and busts. But the system imposes strict restrictions on banks: "...the banks could no longer over lend by manufacturing money out of thin air so as to cause inflation and a boom." "8. Banker-management of industry would almost cease; ...." Fisher had to convince banks to accept the system, but he failed to do so.

2.2.2.1 *Banks do not buy into the 100% system*

Fisher attempted to convince banks that their opposition to the 100% reserve system was delusional: "One reason why bankers in general will oppose the 100% system is that they do not realize the fool's paradise in which they are now living because of the 10% system" (Fisher, 1936):

> ...even if the quantity of money were kept stationary, bank loans could, under the 100% system, expand with savings, to any legitimate extent. Savings, which of course increase with prosperity, would not only not be killed, but would be nurtured into new life and growth, with the growth of prosperity under the 100% system.

Irving Fisher was correct in his assessment that banks were often shortsighted, prioritizing short-term gains over long-term stability. To banks, the idea of a 100% reserve system, where banks could ensure sustainable prosperity by fully backing their loans with deposits, may have seemed unrealistic. This long-term vision of stability appeared to be nothing more than "pie in the sky."

Banks were not entirely irrational or detached from reality. They understood that the fractional reserve system offered them an immensely profitable advantage. Through fractional reserve banking, banks gained the ability to create money "out of thin air" and then charge interest on it. The system endowed banks with power surpassing even the legendary Midas touch—the ability to create money ex nihilo and charge interest upon it. Whereas Midas merely converted existing material into gold, banks produced money from nothing at all.

Under a 100% reserve system, banks would be required to hold all deposits as reserves. In an ideal arrangement, banks could still earn interest on these reserves through mechanisms such as payments from the Currency Commission.[41] However, the ability to issue loans would be constrained by the amount of deposits they hold.

Under the 100% reserve system, a bank receives interest income from the interest rate R_L on the loans and the interest rate R_C paid by the Currency Commission, minus the interest rate R_D paid to the depositors. That is, profit equals $(R_L + R_C - R_D)D$, where D is the amount of deposits.

Under the 10% reserve system, assuming the Currency Commission pays the same interest rate R_C on the reserves, a bank's profit is $(R_C - R_D)D + 10R_L D$. Comparing the profits between a 10% and the 100% reserve system, the difference is:

$$(R_C - R_D)D + 10R_L D - (R_L + R_C - R_D)D = 9R_L.$$

From 10% to 100% reserve systems, banks lose the interest income they once earned loans equal to nine times their deposit base.[42] Fisher's promise of steadily growing savings under a 100% reserve system fell short of compensating for the significant profit loss that banks would experience. The 100% reserve system directly threatens banks' core profit model, making it an unattractive option despite its potential benefits to economic stability. It is no surprise that banks would staunchly oppose any proposal that implements such a system.

2.3 State Money: Fiat Currency

Governments have long recognized the power of money creation, amplifying their control over the economy and expanding their political influence. From ancient law codes to modern fiat currency systems, governments have consistently played a significant role in

[41]Currently, the Fed pays interest on the reserves that banks deposit at the Fed.

[42]Economist T. J. Dunning said, "With adequate profit, capital is very bold. A certain 10 percent will ensure its employment anywhere; 20 percent certain will produce eagerness; 50 percent, positive audacity; 100 percent will make it ready to trample on all human laws; 300 percent, and there is not a crime at which it will scruple, nor a risk it will not run, even to the chance of its owner being hanged." "If turbulence and strife will bring a profit, it will freely encourage both. Smuggling and the slave-trade have amply proved all that is here stated" (Marx, 2004).

defining and controlling money. Historically, they have determined *legal tender*, i.e., what form of payment can be used to pay debt. They have used their power to create legal-tender currency.

German economist Georg Friedrich Knapp, in his *State Theory of Money* (1905), coined the term "chartalism,"[43] emphasizing the state's role in creating money and assigning value to it as legal tender. Under this view, money's value comes not from intrinsic worth but from the authority of the state, enforced by legal mandate. This idea significantly diverges from classical and commodity- or debt-based theories of money, such as Adam Smith's view, which rooted the origin of money in the barter system, or the debt theory of money, which suggests money emerged from debt obligations.

The very term *money* itself has governmental origins. Derived from the Latin *Monēta*, the word refers to the Roman goddess Juno Moneta, near whose temple on the Capitoline Hill the Romans minted their currency. Legend holds, that the goddess assured the Romans they would not lack money during their wars,[44] a symbolic intertwining of divine protection and state control over currency. A government defined the weight and the metal content of its coins and decreed the face value of its currency, profiting from the difference between the face value of currency and its production cost, known as *seigniorage*. The old French word *seigneuriage* means "the right of a lord to mint money" (Click, 1998).

Coinage first appeared around 650 BC. The Greek historian Herodotus quoted the sixth-century poet Xenophanes, who attributed the invention of coins to the Lydians, stating they were "the first to strike and use coins of gold and silver."[45] Archaeological evidence supports the ancient origins of coin minting beyond Lydia, with the discovery of the world's oldest known coin mint in Guanzhuang, China, dating its operation between 640 and 550 BC.[46]

Rulers and states did not mint coins purely for economic reasons. Some kings minted new coins to display their portraits as symbols of power and legitimacy. For instance, the Roman Emperor Quietus, who briefly ruled a portion of the Roman Empire from 260 to 261

[43]The Latin *charta* means "paper."

[44]*Money* (Wikipedia), Etymology section, accessed on June 30, 2024.

[45]Britannica.com.

[46]*The World's Oldest Coin Mint Is Discovered in China*, December 2021, mheducation.com, accessed on June 30, 2024.

AD, issued two coins with his likeness, displaying the use of currency for political purposes rather than just economic necessity.

Governments earn seigniorage by creating their own currencies. David Graeber recounted the currency creations in Madagascar based on his fieldwork. France invaded Madagascar in 1895, dissolved the government of Queen Ranavalona III, and colonized the country. In 1901, French General Gallieni imposed heavy taxes on the population, who had to pay the taxes with the new money that General Gallieni printed. Graeber refuted Adam Smith's theory of the origin of money. The French General created money and imposed the taxes. The people had to exchange their goods for the newly created money because they could only pay the taxes with it. The money created the market, not the other way around. This is the third theory on the origin of money—the state theory of money—alongside Adam Smith's theory, the debt theory of money. Graeber links rise of cash markets to military expansion and state taxation. Before the French invasion, Madagascar had its market. The king between 1810 and 1828, Radama I, signed the treaty, "The Equivalent," with the United Kingdom, under which gold, silver, and military supplies were provided as compensation for Madagascar's lost revenues from the abolition of the slave trade. Queen Rasoherina between 1863 and 1868 prohibited Sunday markets because of Sunday as the Lord's Day. Nonetheless, the French general not only created money but also used money as a weapon to forcibly destroy local self-sufficiency and extract cheap labor.

The cheapest way to create money is to print it. China's use of paper money, starting in the Song dynasty (998–1022) during the reign of Emperor Zhenzong, offers one of the earliest examples of government-issued notes. 16 merchants initially issued them. These notes were redeemable for coin-based money and became popular. When inflation plagued the Chinese economy, the merchants stopped redeeming the paper money and undermined the credibility of the notes. The notes gained credibility and stability only after Emperor Renzong (1022–1063) centralized their issuance through government agencies.[47]

[47]Archaeologists have found printing plates made of brass from that period and have been able to use the plates for recreating the early banknotes that did not survive. The oldest fragmentary banknote was found in a cave and dated to

In 1296, Marco Polo described in his book, *The Travels of Marco Polo*, Chinese salt money with images of the Grand Khan, and made a brief reference to paper money in the Chinese Empire. Europeans thought paper money so unbelievable that they questioned the credibility of Marco Polo's story. Sweden's introduction of paper money in 1661 was met with skepticism, and the government had to guarantee its value by allowing redemption in goods and commodity money, by having each note signed by more than 16 prominent officials to establish trust.

The analogy between currency and debt, particularly in the context of IOUs, further illustrates the complexity of money creation. Like bank loans issued by banks, currencies represent promises by governments. One theory claims that currency is an IOU, just like debt, but the identity of "I" and "you"—or who owes whom—differs between debt and currency.

For example, a bank issues a mortgage loan to a borrower. The loan is a promise: The bank owes the borrower the amount of the mortgage. When the borrower purchases a house, the bank pays the original owner of the house and no longer owes the borrower the mortgage. At this point, the bank and the borrower completely reverse their roles: The borrower now owes the mortgage back to the bank.

The U.S. government, through the Bureau of Engraving and Printing, produces dollar bills, while commercial banks use reserves held with the central bank (see p. 146) to obtain them. Under the gold standard, currencies were backed by gold, meaning the government effectively owed gold to currency holders. Thus, the government acts like a special bank. Although both currency and bank credit initially represent claims on gold, they diverge once spent or used.

When governments use newly issued currency to finance public programs, the recipients incur no repayment obligation. Unlike a bank mortgage loan—which establishes a two-way debt where the borrower must repay the lender—fiat currency functions as a one-way government IOU. Much like a food stamp, the state obligates itself to provide resources to the holder, while the recipient incurs no debt. Ultimately, because the beneficiaries of government programs and

---

between 1165 and 1174 when two Emperors split China: Emperor Xiaozong of Song dynasty and Emperor Shizong of Jin dynasty.

the taxpayers who fund them rarely overlap, this seigniorage-based currency system is far from a perfect quid pro quo. (see Chapter 5).

The U.S. Congress passed the Legal Tender Act of February 25, 1862, to fund the Civil War. The U.S. government printed about $450 million of paper money that earned the nickname "greenbacks." The government did not specify either a specific amount of gold backing the paper money or any specific redemption date for commodity money.

Under the gold standard, governments decided who could redeem currencies for gold. The Fed notes have not been redeemable in gold since President Franklin Delano Roosevelt issued Executive Order 6102 during the Great Depression. On January 30, 1934, Congress amended Section 16 of the Fed Act, making it a criminal offense for U.S. citizens to own or trade gold. The Act prohibited the Treasury and financial institutions from redeeming dollar bills for gold and prohibited U.S. citizens from hoarding gold coins, gold bullion, and gold certificates. President Roosevelt stated, "In the interest of justice allow none to be paid in gold."[48] The Act transferred ownership of gold reserves from the Fed to the U.S. Treasury at a discount. It also authorized the president to establish the gold value of the dollar by decree. Fed notes have not been redeemable in silver since the 1960s. In 1964, President Ford relaxed this prohibition. On December 31, 1974, with Executive Order 11825, President Ford repealed President Roosevelt's Executive Order, rescinded the 40-year ban on ownership of gold coins, gold bars, and gold certificates.

The Bretton Woods Agreement (1944) established a gold *exchange* standard, where the U.S. dollar was fixed to gold at $35 per ounce, and other currencies were pegged to the U.S. dollar. By the 1960s and early 1970s, concerns over the value of the dollar arose due to the Vietnam War and the accumulation of dollar reserves by foreign nations. In 1971, Britain, France, and other countries began to dump their dollar reserves for gold. Paul Volcker and the Department of the Treasury reported to the President on the gold losses: "Dollar dumping accelerated. France sent a battleship to take home French gold from the New York Fed's vaults."[49] In response to foreign

---

[48]In the U.S., recovery began in early 1933 and the gold inflows were partly due to the devaluation of the U.S. dollar.

[49]Alex J. Pollock, *Fifty Years Without Gold*, August 13, 2021.

nations converting dollars for gold, Nixon *temporarily* suspended the dollar's convertibility to gold on August 15, 1971. The suspension of the gold standard demonstrated the shifting nature of money under government control. The move away from gold-backed currency in 1971 effectively freed governments to create money from the constraints of gold reserves, transforming the global monetary system and giving governments unprecedented flexibility in printing money.

Although Nixon's suspension was a temporary measure, it remains in effect to this day. The gold price is now much higher than $35 per ounce. It reached $4,000 per ounce on November 6, 2025, about 114 times $35 per ounce.

After Nixon suspended the gold standard, the U.S. no longer backed the dollar with gold, and the currency as an IOU is not redeemable for gold. It is like a package box whose gold jewelry has disappeared. One can exchange a $100 bill for two $50 bills but not gold. Nixon freed money from the constraint of gold. Money has truly become free from any limit as Aristotle pointed out 2,500 years ago.

The role of the U.S. dollar as the world's primary reserve currency has significant implications for both the U.S. economy and global finance. The U.S. government has earned considerable seigniorage revenues from both domestic and international sources. From 1972 onwards, despite the suspension of the gold standard, foreign countries continued to exchange goods for dollars—often holding those dollars as reserves. This allowed the U.S. to trade "paper" for real goods, one reason other currencies compete for reserve status. After the U.S. abandoned the Bretton Woods Agreement, creating banknotes for international circulation was a profitable form of seigniorage.[50]

As of March 2009, a substantial portion of U.S. currency was held abroad, totaling $313 billion, which represented about 36.7% of U.S. currency in circulation.[51] This extensive international use of the dollar reflects its dominant role in global trade, finance, and as a reserve currency. Feige's calculations indicate that from 1964 to the early 1990s, the cumulative seigniorage earnings from foreign-held

[50] *Seigniorage* (Wikipedia), accessed on July 1, 2024.

[51] *Seigniorage*, Wikipedia, Global Circulation of U.S. Currency, accessed on May 31, 2024.

U.S. currency amounted to between $167 billion and $185 billion. Over the past two decades, the U.S. earned an average of $6–$7 billion per year from foreign holders of U.S. dollars (Feige *et al.*, 1996).

Domestically, seigniorage is also earned from people who collect currency, such as those who keep coins without circulating it. The U.S. Mint's 50 State Quarters series, which began in 1999, is an example of a successful domestic seigniorage program. It cost the Mint five cents to produce a quarter, yet collectors who kept the complete set provided substantial profit to the government. The Treasury estimates it earned about $6.3 billion in seigniorage from this program over a 10-year period (1999–2008).[52] Combining domestic and foreign seigniorage, the U.S. government earned approximately $25 billion in 2000.

The U.S. dollar faces competition from other currencies, such as the euro, particularly in high-denomination banknotes. For example, the €500 note offers advantages in terms of transportability compared to the $100 bills. The ease of carrying copious amounts of euro banknotes can be appealing for various uses, including illicit activities, due to their lighter weight and smaller size compared to U.S. currency. The logistics of transporting large sums of money involve practical considerations. One million dollars in $100 bills weighs about 22 pounds (10 kg), making it cumbersome to transport without significant security measures. In contrast, the same amount in €500 notes weighs less than three pounds (1.4 kg), making it easier to handle discreetly.[53]

The US dollar has dominated most international oil contracts. The energy-production countries receive petrodollars, U.S. dollars, for their oil exports. China has been purchasing oil and gas in Chinese yuan in recent years to promote its yuan as an international currency. The European Union and China are competitors to the U.S. dollar, vying for their currencies to gain more dominance as international reserves.

---

[52] *Seigniorage* (Wikipedia), accessed on April 29, 2024; *The Coin Analyst: The 50 State Quarters Program 20 Years Later* by Louis Golino, August 27, 2018, CoinWeek, accessed on May 30, 2024.

[53] *Seigniorage* (Wikipedia), accessed on May 31, 2024.

For a currency to maintain its value and status, it must be credible. During the Vietnam War, doubts about the value of the U.S. dollar led foreign countries convert their dollar reserves, contributing to the end of the gold standard. Printing money without maintaining credibility, as seen in Argentina during the 1982 war with the United Kingdom and in Venezuela in recent years, only exacerbates economic problems rather than solving them. Without the backing of the gold standard, a currency's credibility depends on the strength of the real economy that supports it (see Chapter 6).

2.3.1 *Seigniorage versus borrowing money*

2.3.1.1 *Currency debasement*

A government creates money by printing its currency to finance its expenditures. Seigniorage ranges from less than $\frac{1}{2}$% of GDP to more than 10%, and 1% to more than 100% of government spending. Taxation, on average, finances $78\frac{1}{2}$% of government spending from just under 50% to more than 100% (Click, 1998), although these figures vary widely across countries.

When a government faces budget deficits, it has four options, two of which are to collect more taxes or cut spending to balance the government budget. The other two options are printing money or borrowing money. Printing offers a convenient way to fill the gap, which corresponds to political economic wisdom that seigniorage is a residual revenue source (Click, 1998). However, this practice inevitably generates inflation: Old coins contain precious metals and governments cannot mint them with the same metal content. As a result, the governments must debase the coins.

Before and after World War I, a person trading one ounce gold for \$20.67, only to repurchase less than an ounce of gold at \$35 after World War II, illustrates the effect of currency debasement. Over time, the dollar lost 41% of its value against gold. If the person lent \$20.67 to the government, the government would repay the same nominal amount, effectively profiting from the loan through currency debasement.

The U.S. penny, with a face value of one cent, costs 2.10 cents to produce in 2021. For the sixteenth year in a row, production costs exceeded the penny's face value.[54] Currently, the penny consists of copper-plated zinc.[55]

Australia adopted the British sterling silver (92.5%) standard for its coinage when it started to mint coins in 1910. Australian silver coinage continued to adhere to the silver standard until 1946, when the government debased the silver content of silver coins to 50%. Today, the Australian government does not mint silver coins because the silver content exceeds the face value of the coin.[56]

Modern Monetary Theory (MMT), a contemporary version of chartalism, claims that countries such as the U.S. or the U.K. can create money at will to finance government projects. Such countries are not constrained by the same limitations as other nations because they can always meet their obligations by issuing more of their own currencies. They do not need to borrow money by selling bonds and the term "borrowing" is a misnomer in this context, since the government is merely accepting its own IOU—effectively owing money to itself. A government borrows money from its right pocket and then puts it into its left pocket. Furthermore, the IOU is the financial wealth of the private sector. Spending more without increasing taxes—and without adding to the deficit—makes a financial contribution to the economy.

Critics, however, see MMT as a setback for economics, especially after more than a century of economic research. They point out that MMT overlooks the key economic principles of controlling inflation and maintaining public confidence in currency. The theory's core idea, that governments can create money without consequence, has its roots in Keynes' "dig holes" solution to unemployment:

> If the Treasury were to fill old bottles with banknotes, bury them at suitable depths in disused coalmines which are then filled up to the surface with town rubbish, and leave it to private enterprise on well-tried principles of laissez-faire to dig the notes up again (the right to do so being obtained, of course, by tendering for leases of the note-bearing territory), there need be no more unemployment and, with the help of the repercussions, the real income of the community, and its capital

[54] *United States Mint 2021 Annual Report.*

[55] *Penny: History and Current Status*, Congressional Research Service, December 20, 2022.

[56] *Florin (Australian coin)* (Wikipedia), accessed on July 1, 2024.

> wealth also, would probably become a good deal greater than it actually is. It would, indeed, be more sensible to build houses and the like; but if there are political and practical difficulties in the way of this, the above would be better than nothing (Keynes, 1936).

The "dig hole" solution can solve the problem only in one type of economy—a "shrinking, frugal" economy—when weak consumption causes shutting down production and piling up inventories. Taking a "dig hole" as a universal medicine for all economic illnesses is a mistake (see Chapter 3).

2.3.1.2 *Government borrowing*

Governments have the option of borrowing money to finance deficits. When the U.S. government needs to borrow money, it does so through the Department of the Treasury, with the Bureau of the Public Debt managing the national debt.[57,58]

The process of borrowing works as follows: When the Treasury requires funds, it does not borrow directly from commercial banks, whether domestic or foreign. Instead, the Fed facilitates the borrowing process. The Department of the Treasury issues Treasury securities, which the Fed exchanges for reserves that it holds. Upon borrowing $100 million, the government would reflect this borrowing on its balance sheet, Table 2.2, showing the increase in liabilities due to the newly issued debt.

The U.S. government finances its expenditures by issuing bond, a $100 million bond at a 5% interest rate. Here is how the process works in more detail. First, the government issues $100 million worth of bonds, and banks underwrite the bond using their reserves held at the Fed. These banks purchase the bond by transferring $100 million from their reserves to the Fed, and the Fed deposits the $100 million from the banks' reserves into the U.S. government's account,

---

[57]The U.S. debt is categorized into two types: intragovernmental holdings and debt held by the public. Intragovernmental holdings arise when the Treasury borrows from government accounts (e.g., Social Security and Medicare) that are funded by public contributions; the government contributions; is then obligated to repay these funds in the future.

[58]The Treasury bills mature in one year or less, the Treasury bonds in more than 10 years, and the Treasury notes in maturity in between.

Table 2.2. Balance sheet: A government.

Assets		**Liabilities and Equity**	
Assets		Liabilities	
Deposits	100	Debt	100
Expenditure	−95		
Interests	−5		
		Equity	
		Expenditure	−95
		Interests	−5
Total	0	Total	0

giving the government the funds it needs for its expenditure. Now, the government has $100 million, but it spends only $95 million on government projects, reserving the remaining $5 million for interest payments to the banks that purchased them. The $5 million represents the 5% interest on the $100 million bond, which the government is obligated to pay annually.

2.3.1.3 *Debt disease and dollar disease*

Irving Fisher identified two major economic problems—what he called the "debt disease" and the "dollar disease." These were central to his analysis of economic cycles and crises, which he believed were primarily driven by over-indebtedness and deflation. When debt levels become excessive, efforts to reduce this debt can lead to distress selling, causing deflation, which further increases the real burden of the remaining debt (Fisher, 1936). Over-indebtedness creates a vicious cycle that he likened to a "dance of the dollar," in which the economy spirals downward due to falling prices and rising real debt burdens.

Irving Fisher, as a leading economist with a deep understanding of the banking system, missed the biggest economic crisis in history, the Great Depression. He forecasted in *The New York Times* that stock prices had climbed to "a new and permanently high plateau" just weeks before the stock market crash of October 1929, making the beginning of the Great Depression. Fisher failed to recognize that the "dance of the dollars" in financial markets helped inflate an asset bubble. He correctly identified "money disease," but his fixation on deflation obscured the inflationary consequences of money creation in asset prices (see Chapter 4).

In Fisher's vision, his 100% reserve system would prevent the buildup of excessive debt and the subsequent deflationary crises that plagued economies. He proposed that the Currency Commission would back loans with U.S. Treasuries or, in practice, with credit created by the Commission itself. The government would stabilize the economy by ensuring that all money in circulation was fully backed by government-issued credit, eliminating the risks associated with bank-created money.

Fisher's advocacy of the 100% reserve system reflects his intent to curtail banks' power over money creation and shift that authority to a centralized entity. When asked, if the 100% system nationalizes money and banking, Fisher's answer was "Of money, yes; of banking, no." "...the 100% system would involve only a nationalization of the *monetary* function (now usurped by banks)—not a general nationalization of *banking*." The 100% reserve system gives the government agency, the Currency Commission, total control of all forms of money, credit, currency, and commodity money, and full responsibility to back up loans. His plan reflected his faith in government intervention and oversight of the monetary system.

He believed that by nationalizing monetary function, the government could prevent the kinds of financial crises that had led to the Great Depression. Yet, Fisher noted, "In practice, this could be mostly 'credit' on the books of the Commission, as very little tangible money would be called for—less even than at present, so long as the Currency Commission stood ready to supply it on request." He added, "The reserves of the member banks of Fed could remain in the form of credit and not become actual money" (Fisher, 1936). By "credit," Fisher meant: "...in addition, there would be the credit of the United States Government" (Fisher, 1936). His system also introduced contradictions—while he criticized banks for creating money through credit, his proposed Currency Commission would create money, albeit under government control.

For Fisher, the government was like Superman who could catch banks if they fell, but "who could catch Superman?" Fisher did not ask: What will happen if the government fails to control the money? Fisher's ideas were shaped by the economic environment of his time, particularly the inter-war period and the aftermath of World War I. Fisher never foresaw the complete decoupling of currency from gold that would come with the Nixon Shock in 1971, which completely changed the global monetary system and gave governments a free hand in creating money. The debt problem that Fisher identified has only grown worse over time. He did not foresee the potential pitfalls of a government-controlled monetary system without the discipline of the gold standard. The U.S. government's growing debt and the inflationary pressures it has created highlight the risks associated with unchecked government money creation.

For example, U.S. federal debt has increased dramatically, from $256 billion in 1947 to over $35 trillion in 2024,[59] more than a 130-fold increase. This increase far outpaces the growth of real GDP, which has only increased tenfold over the same period.[60] The real GDP has increased from $2,183 billion in 1947 to $22,225 billion in 2023.[61] The rapid accumulation of debt, both public and private, remains a key concern in modern economies, echoing Fisher's warnings about the dangers of over-indebtedness.

In 2022, total global debt reached 230% of global GDP, amounting to $235 trillion. This is large compared to the world GDP of $100.56 trillion that year. The Institute of International Finance (IIF) also reported a record $307 trillion in global debt for 2023, confirming the extent to which debt-based money permeates the global economy.

In the U.S., the Federal Reserve Bank of New York's Center for Microeconomic Data reported that household debt reached $17.06 trillion in the second quarter of 2023. Additionally, non-financial corporate debt in the U.S. totaled $19.78 trillion, according to the Bank for International Settlements (BIS).

Meanwhile, traditional forms of money, such as M0 (which excludes credit), were reported at $5.4 trillion globally by the Federal Reserve in January 2023. In the United Kingdom, only 3% of the money supply is in the form of notes and coins, with 97% consisting

[59]U.S. Department of the Treasury, Fiscal Data (fiscaldata.treasury.gov).
[60]U.S. Bureau of Economic Analysis.
[61]U.S. Bureau of Economic Analysis, based in 2017 dollar.

of commercial bank deposits (loans and reserves). Similar figures are seen in Denmark, where 5% of the money supply is in notes and coins, while 95% is in commercial bank deposits (Bjerg *et al.*, 2017).

The U.S. and global debts continue to grow. According to data from the Congressional Budget Office (CBO) and U.S. Treasury, the U.S. national debt is projected to reach approximately US$ 38 trillion in 2025, encompassing both public debt and intragovernmental holdings. Meanwhile, projections from the Bureau of Economic Analysis (BEA) and the IMF estimate U.S. nominal GDP to be about US$ 28.7 trillion in 2025, resulting in a debt-to-GDP ratio of around 132%.

Debt's dominance is also evident in the structure of the money supply in many countries. On a global scale, estimates from the Institute of International Finance (IIF), World Bank, and IMF indicate that global debt is expected to total around US$337.7 trillion in 2025, which includes public, private, and corporate debt. Global GDP is projected to be approximately US$103 trillion, leading to a global debt-to-GDP ratio of about 327%.

These figures underscore the prevalence of debt as a form of money that facilitates economic transactions. An increase in the money supply does not equate to economic improvement; rather, in the contemporary context, credit (debt) has become the source of economic distortion. The following section presents a simple example that illustrates how debt creates problems for a functioning real economy.

2.4 Debt Economy and Debt Cycle

Debt's primary function as part of the asset structure confers significant importance in accounting, especially in assessing bankruptcy conditions. The accounting equation $A = E + D$, which connects assets, equity, and liabilities, reveals the core concept of financial leverage and its associated risks. Here, A represents assets, E represents equity (or net worth), and D represents liabilities (or debt). When a household or firm has zero or negative equity, its liabilities match or exceed its assets, rendering it effectively insolvent or bankrupt.

For example, consider a household with a $200,000 mortgage and a $20,000 car as assets, totaling $220,000. If the household has repaid the car but still owes \$200,000 on the house and carries a \$20,000 credit card balance, their total liabilities also equal \$220,000. In this scenario, the household has zero equity, indicating a state of financial distress or insolvency. Despite owning substantial assets, the household's financial position is precarious because the bank holds a claim on those assets. Debt-based acquisition structures ensure that control over the associated assets remains with the bank until the debt is fully repaid.

In macroeconomic terms, this implies that an economy, despite having an extensive capital stock, can still become insolvent when debt burdens exceed manageable levels. This paradox underscores a reality that productive economies may face bankruptcy due to the dominance of debt-based ownership models. The following hypothetical illustrates a debt-based economy, where debt serves as the sole medium of exchange.

Consider an agrarian economy characterized by a network of interconnected farms, each devoted to crop cultivation or livestock rearing. In this scenario, every farm finds itself in a state of complete financial indebtedness to a single bank, a condition mathematically represented as $A = D$. The economy is in equilibrium, represented by stable prices and $\dot{K} = 0$, where the capital stock remains constant as depicted in Figure 2.3.

The equilibrium point of this economy follows the golden rule of Eq. (1.76):

$$sf(K, L) = af(K, L) = \delta K.$$

As referenced in Table (1.3), this balance is achieved when the discount factor ρ is zero and so is the net return on capital stock r, the

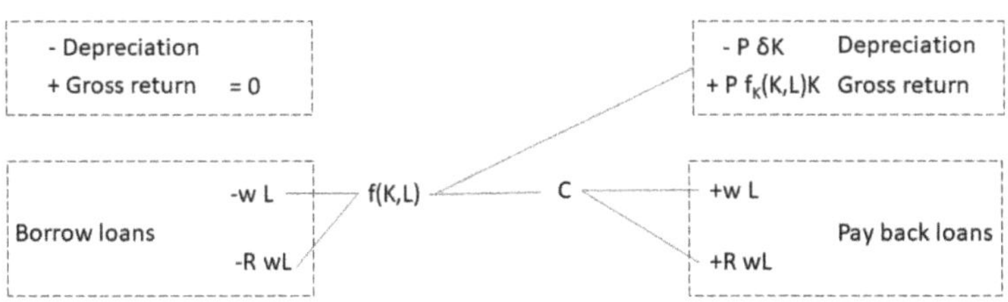

Fig. 2.3. A hypothetical all debt economy.

gross return net depreciation (see Page 63):

$$r = f_K(K, L) - \delta = 0$$

The bank provides liquidity by issuing debt, and farmers borrow from the bank to finance their operations.

At the beginning of the period, the farms borrowed the total amount $wL(1 + R)$ from the bank. The farms take the interest payment RwL into account when determining the wages:

$$\max_L Pf(K, L) - RwL - wL = Pf_L(K, L) - Rw - w = 0,$$

which reduces farmers' wages and their consumption (see Table 1.3):

$$wL = P(1 - s)f(K, L) - RwL = PC - RwL.$$

At the end of a period, the farms produce total output $Y = f(K, L)$. Workers purchase farm products with their wages wL. Meanwhile, the bank receives RwL and pays it to its owner and employees who use RwL to purchase farm products.

Upon selling a portion of their output, valued at wL, to workers and another segment, worth RwL, to the bank owner and employees, farms accrue a total sum of $wL(1+R)$ which is subsequently remitted to the bank, repaying the loan.

To address depreciation expenses, the farms draw upon the gross return $Pf_K(K, L)K$ to cover the depreciation costs $P\delta K$, and the net return $r = f_K(K, L) - \delta$ is zero. The cycle perpetuates, with farms continually roll over their loans to sustain operations, re-borrowing at the commencement of each cycle and repaying at its terminus.

The wage payments in this example are aligned with Marx's criticism of capitalists: Capitalists purchase labor at the beginning of production and, thus, should pay workers upfront. Delaying wages is cheating and part of capitalists' exploitation of workers. In socialist economies, workers are often paid upfront, while in capitalist systems, wages may be paid in arrears. In this example, delaying paychecks forces workers to borrow from the bank to meet their needs before payday. This would not fundamentally change the economy except that the bank receives additional interest from workers and increases the bank's share of consumption and reduces the workers' share of consumption.

In a debt-based economy, credit functions as money, indistinguishable from cash to the workers who receive their paychecks. At the firm level, however, the distinction between credit and traditional money becomes crucial. In this example, while the underlying real economy can continue to function, the farms depend on uninterrupted roll over of debt to survive. If a farm is unable to roll over its loan, it is a death sentence for the farm. When the bank cuts off loans, the entire farming economy collapses. This is why bank crises often lead to broader economic crises. Debt cycles create economic cycles, as evidenced by the 2008 financial crisis.

During the 2008 crisis, the sudden halt in lending brought the economy to a standstill. Even large, well-established companies struggled to pay employees and manage inventories without access to credit. Lehman Brothers, with $768 billion in debt, went bankrupt, and the crisis wiped out $700 billion from the global stock markets.[62] On the other hand, the Royal Bank of Scotland (RBS) narrowly avoided collapse thanks to a government bailout of £45 billion just hours before markets reopened.[63]

Reliance on debt can create "zombie" firms—companies that survive solely on the continuous flow of credit despite being effectively insolvent. The above example illustrates an extreme case in which small liquidity problems lead to bankruptcy of farms because of the heavy debt they have. A farm uses borrowed money to pay bills. If a bill increases slightly and the farm cannot get an additional loan from the bank, the liquidity problem becomes a bankruptcy problem. Japan's economy after the 1990s saw a rise in such firms, contributing to prolonged economic stagnation. Similar phenomena have been observed globally, with governments and banks propping up businesses, thereby evading "bankruptcy" as defined by accounting standards.

Historically, banking crises have often triggered economic depressions. As noted by Richardson and Sablik (2015), crises in 1873 and 1893 led to significant financial turmoil, prompting interventions by financial institutions during the 1901 and 1907 crises. During the

---

[62] *Lehman Brothers—The Bank That Bust the World*, TradingCoachUK, documentary.

[63] *RBS—The Bank That Almost Broke Britain*, TradingCoachUK, documentary.

Panic of 1907, J.P. Morgan's coalition provided liquidity to banks facing runs, preventing depression. The crisis led to the establishment of the Federal Reserve System in 1913, with the government and Fed recognizing that injecting credit is crucial for stabilizing the economy during crises and revitalizing it afterward.

Today, debt is not just a medium of exchange but the lifeblood of the economy. Without continuous access to credit, businesses and entire economies are at risk of collapse, highlighting the inherent dangers of an economy built on debt.

As discussed in Section 2.1.2.8, accounting rules misrepresent the real economy. Consider the above example, in which the farming economy could face bankruptcy if it could not roll over its debt, even if its productivity remains unchanged. We can easily imagine an alternative scenario: bakers granting credit to farmers. In such a system, the economy would continue to function, independent of bank credit. There should be no inherent issue in the real economy—but the banking system creates one by enforcing its own control of credit. The real economy is not at fault; rather, the shrinking availability of credit and the bankruptcy rules impose the crises on economy.

Chinese immigrants once struggled to secure loans because their low credit scores reflected a lack of borrowing, exposing a system that punished financial responsibility. Today, the credit system, accounting standards, and tax laws tilt corporate finance toward borrowing, encouraging firms to rely more on debt (see Chapter 5), with proponents claiming that such leverage stimulates growth. But real growth is limited by natural resources (see Chapter 3), and rapid money expansion merely shifts resources across sectors. Sustainable growth requires patience, like nurturing a plant—forcing it destroys it. A healthy economy is sustained by natural growth rather than debt, which engenders "money disease" and cyclical "money dances."

2.5 Money in the Future

The U.S.'s suspension of the gold standard and the subsequent evolution of global monetary systems mark the profound shift from commodity-backed currency to fiat money and the dominance of credit. When U.S. Representative Ron Paul questioned former Fed

Chair Ben Bernanke about gold being money, Bernanke responded: "It's an asset. To say Treasury bill is money but I don't think it's money either."[64] The former chair of the Fed, a Nobel laureate, pointed out that gold remains an asset and no longer functions as money, while his view of Treasury bills (T-bills)—a debt instrument—was more contentious. Chapter 4 will clarify the concept of assets, though his claim about T-bills conflicts with earlier discussion. The Fed classifies bank deposits as money (M1), which circulates when lent. Confusion arises over loans created under the fractional reserve system. Certificates of deposit (CDs) are counted as M2. Today, the Fed publishes only M1 and M2, having discontinued M3 in 2006. Setting definitional debates aside, our focus is on how these forms of "money" influence the real economy.

After the U.S. suspended the gold standard, the types of money remaining were bank loans and currencies. Today, bank loans also depend on currencies, which hinge on the credibility of governments. A loss of credibility of a currency can trigger inflation, erode the value of money, and destabilize the economy, as seen throughout history. The hyperinflation in China in the 20th century is an example. After the Republic of China overthrew the Qing dynasty, the government switched its currency a few times: from coins on the silver standard to the "fabi"—legal coin in Chinese—to gold yuan certificate before the Chinese Communist Party controlled mainland China in 1949. When the gold yuan certificate was issued, one gold yuan was exchanged for 3 million fabi, which is about a quarter of a U.S. dollar.

The money world is as fragile as the credibility of banks and governments. The advocates of new types of money have high expectations for "cryptocurrencies," which have emerged as a new contender in the monetary landscape. While often perceived as digital gold, their future hinges on broader acceptance by governments and financial institutions. First, cryptocurrencies are not currencies because they are not legal tender, except for Bitcoin in El Salvador. Calling them "currencies" is misleading, and this book uses *crypto* rather than cryptocurrency to avoid misconceptions. If the United States were to recognize a crypto as legal tender, it would thereby attain the status of currency within the U.S. economy.

[64]It is based on the transcript of the testimony.

In addition, for any form of money to function effectively, it must be universally acceptable as a medium of exchange. Bitcoin and other cryptos have, so far, experienced only limited success in convincing banks, merchants, and the broader financial ecosystem to accept them as legitimate payment methods. Currently, only the crypto community and a niche subset of businesses recognize cryptos as a medium of exchange.

Furthermore, cryptos rely on blockchain technology. In a blockchain network, all participating computers (referred to as nodes) typically hold a copy of the entire blockchain. The redundancy ensures that the ledger is fully decentralized and distributed across the network. For instance, in Bitcoin, full nodes download the entire transaction history since its inception. In most public blockchain systems, all full nodes share the same data, ensuring consistency, security, and decentralization.

This decentralized ledger system provides transparency and security but introduces significant challenges. For example, if you were to purchase a cup of coffee from Starbucks using a crypto, the blockchain would record the transaction and would require all full nodes to update their ledgers with the new data. As the number of users and transactions grows, so does the size of the blockchain. Every participant in the network must store an increasingly large volume of transaction data, regardless of how trivial each transaction might seem. The continuous expansion of information presents a scalability issue, as the costs associated with storing and processing vast amounts of data rise over time.

The underlying principle is that information is not free. Physicist James Clerk Maxwell in 1867 proposed a thought experiment

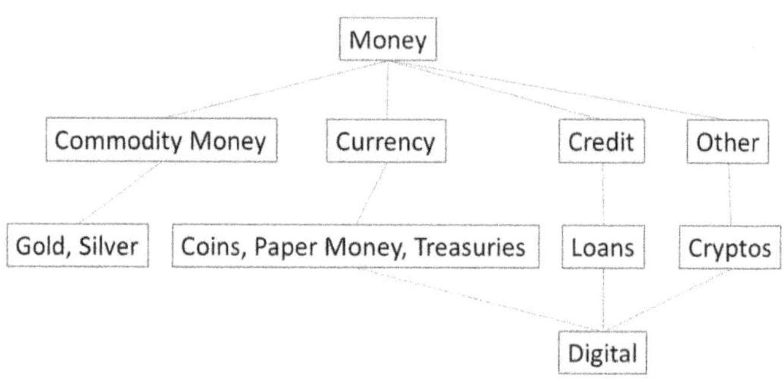

Fig. 2.4. Forms of money.

in which a "Maxwell's demon" could make air-conditioning for free. A demon controls a tiny massless door between two chambers of gas. The demon allows only fast-moving molecules to pass into one chamber and slow-moving molecules into the other, causing one chamber to heat up and the other to cool down (Hemmo and Shenker, 2012). However, it turns out the air-conditioning is not free. The demon must measure the speed of the molecules and record their speeds to determine the cutoff velocity based on the speed distribution of all molecules in the chamber. Eventually, storing information exhausts storage space, and both storing and erasing information require energy. Thanks to the mathematical structures underlying Light Clients (Simplified Payment Verification), individuals can own, send, and receive Bitcoin without storing the entire transaction history that constitutes the full blockchain. However, if every coffee purchase made by 8 billion people were recorded on a single chain, the storage requirements would still become prohibitively large for a decentralized network.

The need to update transactions across billions of nodes in real time, creating the trilemma: decentralization, security, and scalability (Narayanan, 2016). Unlike other blockchain applications, crypto security requires "absolute" decentralization. Centralized systems, like central banks, operate under a single identity that could manipulate the system. Conversely, a loophole in a decentralized system could introduce many unknown threats, potentially destabilizing the network. Thus, achieving both scalability and uncompromising decentralization remains a critical challenge for crypto systems.

The *Group Theory* logic is used today in cryptography to protect data. Évariste Galois used group theory to prove that a general solution to the quintic equation is impossible. Galois wrote his ideas down the night before he was killed in a duel at age 20. He spent his final hours scribbling "I do not have time" in the margins of his papers—solving a 300-year-old mystery. Bitcoin uses groups so large that it would take the age of the universe to "break" the security.

The crypto "paradigm" can be visualized as a tension between the Micro and the Macro (see Section A.3.3), between security (the hidden rules) and transactions. Modern cryptography uses group theory to create "one-way streets," in which it is easy to find a group operation in one direction but almost impossible to reverse unless you have a "secret key."

The most common way this happens today is through Elliptic Curve Cryptography (ECC), which functions like a tiny yet unbreakable lock replacing traditional bulky ones. ECC delivers the same level of security while enabling faster computations and requiring less storage.

The traditional view holds that money must be expensive to produce, as with gold, whose difficulty of extraction ensures its scarcity. However, given today's growing strain on natural resources, it seems irrational to consume vast amounts of energy to produce money that lacks any use-value apart from functioning as a medium of exchange. Furthermore, if the objective is to preserve monetary scarcity and safeguard private ownership, the creation of a second digital "gold" is redundant, as physical gold has long fulfilled that role. Historically, gold certificates and paper money backed by gold provided an economic infrastructure for trade without direct reliance on physical bullion. Thus, the fundamental issue is not the creation of digital gold, but rather the choice between fixed and flexible monetary supplies.

Let us define the total quantity of money—whether measured by the total weight of gold or the total number of Bitcoins—as Q_m, with P_m representing the dollar price. Therefore, the total money in circulation is $M = P_m Q_m / V$ (see Eq. (2.4)). The money identity in Eq. (2.4) implies that, for the money M to purchase economic output Y, it must satisfy:

$$M = \frac{PY}{V},$$

where P denotes the average dollar price of output, and V denotes the velocity of money, which can fluctuate but typically remains within a moderate range. For instance, even assuming a velocity of 5, it's challenging to envision that the total value of Bitcoins would be equivalent to one-fifth of the total value of the annual global economic output per year.[65]

The equation above indicates that the price of a universally accepted money can be expressed as

$$P_m = \frac{PY}{Q_m}$$

[65]Federal Reserve Bank of St. Louis, FRED (fred.stlouisfed.org).

which illustrates that the use value of money, except as a medium of exchange, is irrelevant to its price. Bitcoin's value hinges on its acceptance as a universally recognized medium of exchange. If Bitcoin supplants the dollar as the sole universally accepted medium of exchange, its valuation will hinge entirely on the scale of global economic output, which is denominated in the local currency (dollars) adjusted for both its supply and the speed at which it circulates. Should it fail to achieve this status, it forfeits its key utility, reducing it to an asset just like other idle assets rather than a functioning currency. As with gold, speculation that it could again become a globally accepted medium of exchange sustains much of its price.

The price increases of Bitcoin or gold are driven by two additional factors: First, their price movements are often reinforced by positive feedback. Second, their acceptance as a medium of exchange within specific communities, akin to the use of cigarettes as money in POW camps (see Section 2.1.1) reinforces their value.

Silver serves as another example in this context. Some traders anticipate that the price of silver will rise alongside gold; however, silver is less likely than gold to establish itself as a primary form of money. Additionally, silver has industrial applications, meaning its value is partially influenced by industrial demand. This dual role of silver—as both a precious metal and an essential industrial commodity—contributes to its price dynamics in a way that differs from gold.

As of March 6, 2025, the U.S. government officially designated Bitcoin as a strategic national reserve asset and established a Strategic Bitcoin Reserve. This acceptance of Bitcoin as a reserve asset is different from its use as a medium of exchange. Like gold, Bitcoin would remain an asset rather than a circulating currency. While government endorsement could boost its market value, it would not alter the U.S. dollar's status as the national currency.

Major currencies are competing to be the global reserve, and their governments are reluctant to cede control of their national currencies to other forms of money. Alan Greenspan, former chair of the Federal Reserve, echoed this sentiment when he remarked, "In the absence of the gold standard, there is no way to protect savings from confiscation through inflation. There is no safe store of value. If there were, the government would have to make its holding illegal...." Greenspan made it clear that the government opposes proposals constraining its discretion in money creation—such as Fisher's 100% reserve system—and actively undermines safe stores of value. If future governments adopt Greenspan's stance, Bitcoin is out of luck, especially as governments are exploring and developing their own central bank digital currencies (CBDCs).

Governments globally are exploring CBDCs to enhance monetary policy and financial oversight amid digital transformation. By centralizing monetary control, CBDCs give central banks detailed transaction records and control, raising concerns about potential interference in individual transactions. This system requires strong public trust in government stewardship; without it, individuals may resist sacrificing financial autonomy, unless compelled by the state.

China has advanced further than many nations in CBDC development, shifting from pilot projects to broader deployment and integration. Efforts include expanding domestic coverage, boosting merchant adoption, experimenting with cross-border use, and strengthening infrastructure. Despite this progress, the digital yuan remains marginal, representing only about 0.16% of the broad money supply as of mid-2023. Key debates concern the degree of anonymity, the management of data, and the CBDC's alignment with China's financial-surveillance architecture. Academic work underscores the inherent trade-offs between government oversight, privacy protection, and fostering innovation.

Another approach to achieving stable, solid money is to return to the gold standard. Keynes observed the stability offered by gold due to its limited supply: "Money, that is to say, cannot be readily produced;—labour cannot be turned on at will by entrepreneurs to produce money in increasing quantities as its price rises in terms of the wage-unit" (Keynes, 1936), where the wage-unit is the money wage paid for one man-hour of labor. Gold's limited supply made it an ideal standard of value historically, contributing to long periods of stability.

For instance, under Sir Isaac Newton's oversight as Master of the Mint in England, the gold price was set at £3 17s 10d (approximately £3.89) per ounce in 1717. This price remained stable for nearly two centuries, until World War I. The stability of gold prices was briefly interrupted during the Napoleonic Wars from 1797 to 1821, when the British government imposed a gold embargo. The 1797 Bank Restriction Act prohibited the Bank of England from issuing gold coins or gold bullion in exchange for its paper notes and restricted the export of gold bullion and coins, following a significant run on gold reserves and concerns about domestic gold stocks (Daly, 2007). In the 1800s, the price of gold in the U.S. remained below $19 per ounce for most of the century. Before World War I, the U.S. set the price of gold at $20.67 per ounce, while the British pound was pegged at £4.2474 per ounce.

The classical gold standard, which existed before 1944, required countries to use gold reserves to settle international balance of payments deficits. However, the Bretton Woods Agreement of 1944 introduced a new system—the gold exchange standard—in which the U.S. dollar became the primary international currency. Deficits between countries were settled in dollars, and the price of gold was set at $35 per ounce. This marked a shift from the gold standard to a system more reliant on fiat currency, reflecting the evolving dynamics of global trade and economics.

John Maynard Keynes famously criticized the gold standard for its inelasticity, and his critique rested on arguments parallel to those he used in opposing a 100% reserve system (see p. 134): The fixed supply of gold limited the government's ability to adjust the money supply in response to economic conditions. In times of recession or crisis, governments could not expand the money supply to stimulate demand, often exacerbating economic downturns. Under the gold standard, deflation was a frequent problem during recessions, as hoarding gold reduced the money supply, lowering investment and production (Meltzer and Robinson, 1989). Keynes maintained that if money could be expanded in proportion to economic needs, depression could be avoided or mitigated. As he noted, "...if money could be grown like a crop or manufactured like a motor-car, depressions would be avoided or mitigated because, if the price of other assets was tending to fall in terms of money, more labour would be diverted into the production of money; -as we see to be the case in gold-mining countries, though for the world as a whole the maximum diversion in this way is almost negligible" (Keynes, 1936).

Historical data seems to support the instability of the gold standard. From 1873 to 1896, major economies such as the U.S., U.K., Germany, and France experienced severe deflation, with prices falling over 40%. Conversely, from 1896 to 1913, inflation surged between 39% and 56%. Further inflationary pressures occurred from 1957 to

1970, with inflation ranging from 36% to 88% in these economies (Cooper *et al.*, 1982). These swings in inflation and deflation were attributed to the inherent drawbacks of the gold standard. As Keynes observed, "The Gold Standard, in its palmiest days, was a great convenience, but it has become a barbarous relic" (see p. 134). What was once thought to be stabilizing—the limited supply of gold—ultimately constrained governments in their efforts to stabilize the economy.

However, Fisher's analysis shows that such an argument against the gold standard is false. The fractional reserve banking system and the broader economic context played significant roles in the issues experienced under the gold standard. For example, during the Great Depression, the money supply contracted not only due to a reduction in gold reserves but also because bank-created "checkbook money" fell sharply. Between 1929 and 1933, checkbook money shrank from $23 billion to $15 billion, a 35% decline, severely limiting the money available to the economy. This contraction was not solely due to changes in gold reserves but also reflected the effects of bank policies and the broader economic environment. The gold itself could not by itself cause the 35% reduction in money supply but was implicated due to the constraints it imposed on monetary policy.

The gold standard has periodically resurfaced in debates about monetary policy, though it has received limited support for reintroduction. The U.S. Gold Commission of 1982 considered restoring the gold standard but rejected the idea. Nonetheless, prominent figures, such as Malcolm Stevenson Forbes Jr., who ran for the Republican Party's presidential nomination twice, advocated for a return to a gold-backed monetary system. Forbes held that the gold standard could provide stability and limit the uncontrolled expansion of the money supply.

Interest in the gold standard has resurfaced in recent years. On October 4, 2022, Congressman Alex X. Mooney introduced the "Gold Standard Restoration Act," which would require the U.S. Treasury and Federal Reserve to disclose all gold holdings and transactions within 30 months. After that period, the U.S. dollar would be pegged to a fixed weight of gold at its market price. This proposal reflects ongoing concerns about inflation, currency devaluation, and the need to impose discipline on monetary policy.

However, returning to the gold standard would face significant challenges in today's global economy. Besides the opposition of politicians, the global distribution of gold reserves is uneven. According to the World Gold Council, as of February 2023, about 208,874 tons of gold had been mined throughout history, valued at approximately \$13.2 trillion at a price of \$2,000 per ounce (1 metric ton = 35,274 ounces), less than \$16.9 trillion—the total value of the residential rental real estate in the U.S.[66] This amount pales in comparison to the total value of global financial assets, estimated at \$461.2 trillion, and global real estate, valued at \$379.7 trillion.[67] To sustain a gold standard under the current magnitude of the global economy, the value of gold would need to rise dramatically to accommodate the required monetary base. Even though central banks accumulate gold and affect gold prices, there is a slim chance that the gold standard can return. Countries with large gold reserves would benefit from the comeback of the gold standard, but many others would experience immediate economic disadvantages, making international consensus on this issue unlikely (see Chapter 6 on the Balance of Payments).

Reintroducing the gold standard could also lead to significant price volatility. Given the small value of global gold reserves relative to global financial assets, a sudden surge in demand for gold could destabilize both gold markets and the broader financial system. The transition to a gold standard could cause severe economic disruptions, potentially triggering a financial crisis.

The debate over the gold standard reflects broader discussions about the trade-offs between monetary stability and flexibility. The paramount focus should be on addressing the root causes of economic instability, rather than relying on monetary flexibility to remedy problems after they arise. Once a disease is eradicated, no medicine is needed.

This chapter has only begun to explore the complexities of the monetary system but has already demonstrated that money itself,

[66]World Gold Council, February 8, 2023, retrieved accessed on December 13, 2023.
[67]World Bank website, accessed on December 13, 2023.

particularly under the fractional reserve system as analyzed by Irving Fisher, creates economic risks. "Control the money, control the world." The U.S. dollar became *the* money—the reserve currency in the world—because of its strong real economy and gold reserves. The Nixon shock signaled the beginning of the erosion of the dominant dollar position in the world. In the years ahead, countries continue to compete for their currencies in global trade and for reserve-currency status. Countries compete for position, but the currency stability rests on a strong real economy and maintaining stable purchasing power—controlling money creation—the inflation. The chapters ahead examine money's role in the economy, and Chapter 6 examines the currency games in international trade.

Chapter 3

The Direct Effect of Money on Economy

This chapter, along with the subsequent ones, delves into the ways in which money influences the real economy. At the micro level, households differ in how they consume and invest, and these distributions provide a micro foundation for the macroeconomic identity (see Section A.3.3). In a capitalist economy, money shapes these distributions through income, wealth, and overall financial conditions. Grasping these dynamics is vital for understanding the link between micro and macroeconomics.

3.1 Wealth Distribution

The aggregate consumption C_t of an economy is not merely a function of total wealth but also of the distribution of wealth, as described by the cumulative distribution function $F(\phi_t)$:

$$C_t = \int_0^{\phi_{\max}} c(\phi_t) dF(\phi_t), \tag{3.1}$$

where $c(\phi)$ is individual consumption as a function of an individual's wealth ϕ. The equation captures how the distribution of wealth among households shapes aggregate consumption.

Those living below the minimum acceptable general standard of living $\underline{c}$ will allocate any additional wealth primarily to consumption, as they aim to meet basic needs. The rich, with consumption at the

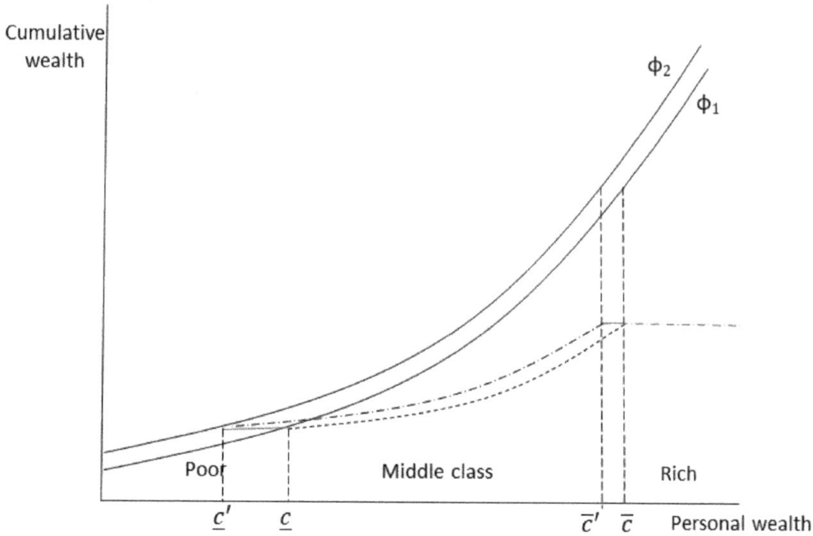

Fig. 3.1. Consumption distribution as a function of wealth.

upper bound $\overline{c}$, are relatively insulated from economic fluctuations. They are more likely to invest in additional wealth rather than spend it on consumption. Only the middle class splits the extra wealth between consumption and investment and adjusts their trade-offs between consumption and investment as macroeconomic conditions change.

Figure 3.1 illustrates people's consumption behavior as the wealth distribution shifts from ϕ_1 to ϕ_2. Economic expansions and contractions can shift the wealth distribution. As wealth increases, some poor households may enter the middle class, while middle-class households may become rich. Conversely, in an economic downturn, wealth distribution shifts in the opposite direction.

The shift in wealth distribution can then affect aggregate consumption. For example, economies in which the middle class is strengthening, and poverty is receding tend to be more sensitive to macroeconomic conditions than economies with a fragile middle class.

Lucas correctly argued that traditional econometric models are unreliable for evaluating economic policy because they rely on historical data, failing to account for how individuals adjust their behavior in response to policy changes. Unlike gas particles in statistical mechanics, whose distribution responds to macro properties like temperature and pressure (see Appendix A.3), econometric models overlook the link between micro and macro economics — the shifts in the distribution of economic agents due to macroeconomic conditions.

Assuming that the only investment is the capital stock, the capital stock per capita (wealth excluding wage per capita) is $\phi = Pk$ and individual workers have the budget constraint:

$$\dot{\phi} = r\phi + w - Pc.$$

For a stable price $\dot{P} = 0$, we have the special case Eq. (2.12):

$$\dot{k} = rk + \frac{w}{P} - c. \tag{3.2}$$

By using $rk = af(k) - \delta k$ and $w/P = (1-a)f(k)$, Eq. (3.2) becomes the same as the macroeconomic identity equation (1.14). Equation (3.2) is the household budget constraint under a different interpretation: It is the budget constraint of the middle-class individual or a representative middle-class household, which will be clear in the following section.

3.1.1 *Becoming rich*

The middle class maximizes its utility from consumption:

$$\max_c \int_0^T e^{\rho t} u(c) dt.$$

As a middle-class household becomes richer, it eventually transitions to the wealthy class, which experiences saturated consumption. To capture the dynamics of the real economy that propel the middle class into the wealthy class, the Hamiltonian adds another variable λ to Eq. (1.38):

$$\mathcal{H}(k, c, \theta, \lambda, t) = \ln c + \theta(f(k) - c - \delta k) + \lambda(\bar{c} - c), \tag{3.3}$$

subject to

$$\lambda = \begin{cases} 0 & c < \bar{c} \\ > 0 & c = \bar{c}, \end{cases} \tag{3.4}$$

where λ functions similarly to a Lagrange multiplier in optimization problems by enforcing the consumption limit $c < \overline{c}$, and the term $\lambda(\overline{c} - c)$ is zero, defined by Eq. (3.4). If $\overline{c} - c$ is not zero, then λ is zero, and the Hamiltonian is the same as Eq. (1.39). If $\overline{c} - c$ is zero, then λ is not zero, and the dynamic of the system must account for the fact that the consumption has reached the limit and cannot increase further.

Like the utility optimization of the Ramsey model in Chapter 1, taking derivatives with respect to k and c gives:

$$\frac{\partial \mathcal{H}(k,c,\theta,t)}{\partial k} = [f'(k) - \delta]\theta = \rho\theta - \dot{\theta}, \tag{3.5}$$

$$\frac{\partial \mathcal{H}(k,c,\theta,t)}{\partial c} = \frac{1}{c} - \theta - \lambda = 0, \tag{3.6}$$

which gives λ:

$$\lambda = \frac{1}{c} - \theta \geq 0. \tag{3.7}$$

If $c < \overline{c}$, the constraint is not binding and $\lambda = 0$ and the solution is the same as Eq. (1.42) of the Ramsey model in Chapter 1:

$$c_t = c_{IC} e^{\int_0^t [f'(k_s) - \delta - \rho] ds} \approx c_{IC} e^{(r-\rho)t}, \tag{3.8}$$

in which the net return on capital stock is $r = f'(k) - \delta$, and, on the right of Eq. (3.8), is an approximation by assuming r is constant.

If $r - \rho < 0$, the middle-class decreases consumption. In the case of $r - \rho > 0$, the middle class starts at c_{IC} and increases consumption. When the middle-class approaches $c \to \overline{c}$, setting $\lambda = 0$ and $\theta = 1/c_t = 1/c_{IC} e^{(\rho - r)t}$ in Eq. (3.7) yields:

$$0 = \frac{1}{\overline{c}} - \frac{1}{c_{IC}} e^{(\rho - r)t}. \tag{3.9}$$

At $t = t_s$, the constraint $c = \overline{c}$ is binding. Solving for t_s gives the switching time at which a middle-class household becomes a member of the rich:

$$t_s = \frac{1}{r-\rho} \ln \frac{\overline{c}}{c_{IC}}. \tag{3.10}$$

In summary,

$$c_t = \begin{cases} c_{IC} e^{(r-\rho)t} & t < t_s \\ \overline{c} & t \geq t_s. \end{cases} \tag{3.11}$$

Once those middle-class households become members of the rich, their consumption becomes insensitive to economic conditions and remains constant:

$$\dot{k} = f(k) - \overline{c} - \delta k. \tag{3.12}$$

A cautionary note is warranted: keep in mind that the principle holds only in an "expanding, lavish" economy (see Fig. 1.8). In contrast, within a "shrinking, lavish" economy, the middle class may emulate the consumption patterns of the rich, yet it experiences erosion of its capital stock and a decline in wealth. To maintain clarity and avoid redundancy, similar cautions will not be restated. The dilemma for a wealthy economy is that, as its wealth increases, the rich do not expand consumption commensurately with their wealth growth. In a closed economy, this results in a mismatch between consumption and investment.

Therefore, a closed economy cannot sustain growth without the active participation of the middle and lower classes. Without their consumption, the economy follows an "expanding" type, which is unstable. In an open economy, achieving growth is possible; however, the expanding production capacity increasingly requires reliance on exports to manage domestic surpluses. Such dependence on external markets constitutes an additional destabilizing factor, leading to trade imbalances and the risk of trade wars, ultimately jeopardizing long-term economic health (see Chapter 6).

3.1.2 *Being poor*

The poor are defined as those who do not have enough income to maintain the lower bound of the general standard of living, denoted as $\underline{c}$. The poor do not have savings (investment), meaning

$\phi = Pk = 0$. If savings were available, they could increase consumption by drawing upon them. The poor are living paycheck-to-paycheck to cover their consumption, and their budget constraint, given by Eq. (3.2), becomes:

$$0 = \frac{w_p}{P} - c_p, \tag{3.13}$$

where the subscript p denotes the poor. The real wage is a function of the capital stock:

$$c_p = \frac{w_p}{P} = (1 - a)f(k) = f(k) - kf'(k), \tag{3.14}$$

which contradicts Keynes's *absolute Income Hypothesis*, which posits that individuals spend a fixed proportion of their current income, as well as Friedman's *Permanent Income Hypothesis* (1957), which instead maintains instead that people save a substantial share of income to smooth consumption over time. Under conditions of extreme wealth disparity—where the population splits between rich and poor and the middle class has vanished—the economy can be represented by combining Eq. (3.12) and Eq. (3.13):

$$\dot{k} = rk + \frac{w_p + w_r}{P} - c_p - \bar{c} - \delta k, \tag{3.15}$$

where w_r is the wage of the rich. Because $c_p = w_p/P$ Eq. (3.15) simplifies to

$$\dot{k} = rk + \frac{w_r}{P} - \bar{c} - \delta k, \tag{3.16}$$

in which the poor become irrelevant to the economy and completely drop out of Eq. (3.16).

In the Ramsey model, consumption is the control variable. However, in Eq. (3.16), which represents an economy without a middle class, consumption no longer functions as a variable. The implication is striking: in an economy without a middle class, the trajectory of the real economy no longer reflects households' consumption–investment trade-offs. Instead, economic expansion is driven exclusively by the rich, who simultaneously consolidate their accumulation of wealth. One of the direct consequences is that a laissez-faire economy without a robust middle class is not only unstable but also exacerbates the wealth gap.

Can money alter the situation, and to what extent can it influence the real economy? The following section integrates money into the real economy and addresses these questions.

3.2 Money Grips Inventory

3.2.1 *Inventory arises out of microeconomy*

The real economy functions within the physical world, requiring direct interaction with physical goods to affect economic change. Money, while not a physical force, acts through economic agents, households, and firms.

Money shapes the real economy through a combination of *direct* and *indirect* effects. For example, when low-income families receive food stamps, these benefits enable them to purchase groceries, resulting in an immediate increase in their actual consumption, representing a *direct* effect on the economy. Conversely, fluctuations in the stock market can influence the economic decisions of stockholders. In this case, money works through the wealth effect: its impact is *indirect.*

For money to have direct effects on the real economy, it must "interact" with real goods. While money can have psychological or indirect effects, such as altering households' expectations about their wealth or prices, no matter how indirect or complex the monetary pathway, the indirect effects of money must eventually manifest as direct effects, materializing as real goods that influence the real economy. This chapter focuses on the *direct effects* of money, postponing discussion of its indirect effects to later chapters.

Inventory represents the available real goods for purchase, acting as a crucial link between money and real economic activity. Without inventory, additional money cannot lead to increased consumption or investment (see Condition C.1 in Section 2.1.2.3). Inventory, therefore, sets a limit on how much money can translate into real goods and thus affect the economy.

Investment, output, and consumption in Eq. (1.2) are *flow variables* measured over time (e.g., per year). By contrast, inventory is a *stock variable*, representing the extra quantity of goods available at a specific point in time. The macroeconomic identity, which balances investment, output, and consumption, is based on these flow variables. In a stable economy, inventory levels remain constant and do not affect the normal flow of goods. However, during periods of economic expansion or contraction, inventory levels decline or accumulate, affecting the flow of goods and firms' production.

If firms and households have *perfect foresight* (Morgenstern *et al.*, 1935), production would exactly match consumption and investment, eliminating the need for inventory. Macroeconomic models often abstract from inventory in the economy. However, in the short term, inventory plays a vital role in absorbing the impacts of changes in economic conditions, allowing the economy to adjust gradually to the new conditions.

The Economic Order Quantity (EOQ) model from supply chain management literature helps explain the factors that determine optimal inventory levels (Snyder and Shen, 2019). Two primary costs are associated with inventory: the ordering cost S (e.g., shipping and handling) and the holding cost H (e.g., storage and insurance). The optimal order quantity involves balancing these two costs to minimize the total cost of maintaining inventory:

$$\frac{D}{\mathrm{EOQ}}S + \frac{\mathrm{EOQ}}{2}H,$$

where D is demand, and EOQ/2 is the average inventory held. Taking the derivative with respect to EOQ, the first-order condition gives

$$\mathrm{EOQ} = \sqrt{\frac{2DS}{H}}.$$

In practice, merchants may set a maximum inventory level Q and a minimum level q. When inventory falls to q, it is replenished to Q (Granger and Lee, 1989). Merchants also use stochastic and Bayesian models for inventory forecasting (Das, 1985; Cobb *et al.*, 2013).

In competitive markets, firms must maintain sufficient inventory to meet customer demand. Whether through physical stores or online platforms such as Amazon, inventory is critical to attracting and retaining customers. Stockouts can drive customers to competitors, resulting in both immediate revenue losses and potential long-term loss of customers.

Holding inventory incurs the *opportunity costs*—such as capital tied up in unsold goods, storage costs, and maintenance. For example, a dealership holding 100 cars, each valued at $30,000, faces a potential opportunity cost of $3 million that could be earning returns elsewhere, in addition to space, maintenance, and security costs. Firms need to weigh the opportunity cost against the cost of lost sales if they fail to have products available when customers demand them.

This section introduces a model that leverages the concept of *financial options* to manage inventory decisions. Financial options, typically discussed in the context of financial markets, are covered in Chapter 4. In contrast to the EOQ model, which balances holding and ordering costs, the inventory model in this section balances the opportunity cost against the cost of lost sales. Viewing inventory decisions through the lens of financial options helps capture demand uncertainty.

The time between production at time t and the moment when products reach the market at $t+\Delta t$ introduces uncertainty into the firm's planning process.[1] Uncertainty tends to grow as the time lag (Δt) between production and delivery lengthens. Inventory turnover, which measures how often a firm sells and replaces its inventory over a year, typically ranges from 5 to 10 times annually. This implies that firms restock their inventory every 36.5 to 73 days, or that $0.1 \leq \Delta t \leq 0.2$ years.

At time t, a firm forecasts its sales at time $t+\Delta t$ to be $E_t S_{t+\Delta t}$, where E_t denotes the expectation operator at time t, and $S_{t+\Delta t}$ is the actual demand or sales at time $t+\Delta t$. The sales forecast is based on past experiences and current information, while future sales $S_{t+\Delta t}$ are inherently uncertain.

As a simplified example, suppose the future demand for a firm's product follows a binomial distribution: high demand S_H or low demand S_L at $t+\Delta t$. The probability of low demand S_L is p_d, and the probability of high demand S_H is $1-p_d$. The expected demand is:

$$E_t S_{t+\Delta t} = (1-p_d)S_H + p_d S_L. \tag{3.17}$$

At time t, the firm optimizes its inventory level Q_t. If demand is high, the firm risks losing sales, quantified as $[S_H-(E_t S_{t+\Delta t}+Q_t)]^+$, where the superscript + denotes:

$$(x-y)^+ = \begin{cases} x-y & \text{if}\, x > y \\ 0 & \text{if}\, x \leq y. \end{cases}$$

Thus, a loss of sales arises only when demand exceeds the forecasted sales plus the inventory on hand. In financial terms, the loss of sales

[1]Time delays in continuous-time models require solving differential-difference equations (Keller, 2010; Ellis and Christofides, 2015), whereas discrete-time models can handle such delays more straightforwardly.

is analogous to a *call option*, where the higher the demand for S_H, the higher value of the call option: similarly, in this model, a higher S_H implies greater potential sales loss. Conversely, if demand is low, the firm incurs an opportunity cost of holding unsold inventory, represented by $r[(E_t S_{\Delta t} + Q_t) - S_L]^+$. This opportunity cost is the lost return r on the unsold goods, similar to a put option in financial terms. The lower the demand for S_L, the more unsold goods the firm holds, and the higher the opportunity cost.

The expected inventory cost $h(S_{t+\Delta t}, Q_t)$, where h(.) is the inventory loss function, is the sum of the cost of potential lost sales and the potential opportunity cost:

$$h(S_{t+\Delta t}, Q_t) = (1 - p_d)[S_H - (E_t S_{t+\Delta t} + Q_t)]^+ + p_d r[(E_t S_{t+\Delta t} + Q_t) - S_L]^+. \tag{3.18}$$

In linear programming, the Fundamental Theorem states that the optimal solution must occur at one of the corners of the feasible region:

$$Q_{\text{opt}} \geq 0. \tag{3.19}$$

Figure 3.2 illustrates the model graphically, showing the potential losses from sales shortfalls and the opportunity cost of holding excess inventory. The horizontal axis denotes inventory, while the left vertical axis represents sales, and the right vertical axis shows inventory losses. The horizontal line in the middle represents expected sales $E_t S_{\Delta t}$. The dashed-double-dot line with a 45° angle shows the total of expected sales and inventory $E_t S_{\Delta t} + Q_t$. The dashed line represents potential lost sales and reaches its maximum at zero inventory. As inventory increases, the cost of lost sales decreases. The dash-dot line represents the potential opportunity cost, which rises as inventory increases.

The solid line depicts the total expected inventory cost, combining the potential lost sales and opportunity costs. The potential lost-sales line slopes downward, while the potential opportunity cost slopes upward. The minimum total expected inventory cost occurs at the "corner" where the slope switches from negative to positive:

$$Q_{\text{opt}} = S_H - E_t S_{t+\Delta t}.$$

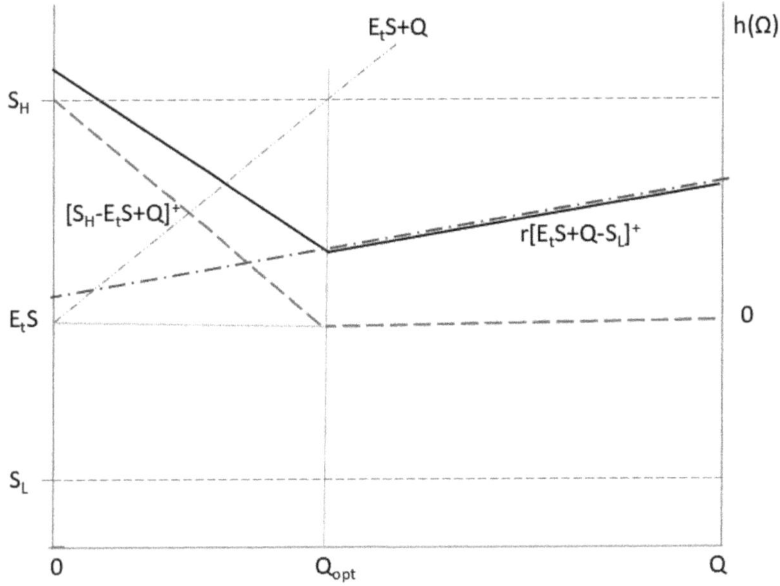

Fig. 3.2. Inventory losses: Binomial model.

The lowest inventory loss at the point that the cost of loss of sales $S_H - (E_t S_{\Delta t} + Q_t)$ is zero. Increasing inventory reduces the cost of loss of sales but increases the opportunity cost, while the marginal cost of loss of sales is always greater than the opportunity cost before the cost of loss of sales drops to zero.

Like a compressed spring, a tight inventory system cannot absorb sudden spikes in demand. But firms with significant market power, such as Toyota and Walmart, can implement lean inventory management more successfully because they can exert influence over their supply chains and maintain stable demand. Walmart's advanced inventory management systems allow it to restore efficiently while keeping inventory levels low.

Toyota, a pioneer of a pull inventory system, developed the *just-in-time* system, designed to streamline operations by minimizing or eliminating inventory. The lead time in a pull inventory system refers to the time it takes to produce and deliver a product after receiving an order. The JIT system emphasizes lean operations, reducing the costs associated with holding inventory. By only producing goods when an order is placed, JIT helps ensure that firms do not overproduce or waste resources on products that may not be sold promptly.

The downside of JIT is its sensitivity to supply chain disruptions. Without a buffer of inventory, any delay in the supply chain can halt production and lead to significant delivery delays. Toyota encountered this challenge during the 2021 global chip shortage, which compelled the firm to temporarily abandon its lean operation principles and secure one to four months of component stocks as a safeguard.

Firms relying heavily on JIT can struggle to meet unexpected increases in demand, which lead to lost sales and customer dissatisfaction. JIT is more viable for firms whose products are highly differentiated and lack close substitutes. In such cases, customers may be willing to wait for the firm to produce and deliver the product, as there are few alternatives available. Widespread adoption of JIT can make the overall economy more vulnerable to disruptions. Firms that produce standardized products with substitutes, or that operate in competitive markets, find JIT riskier and often maintain higher levels of inventory to buffer against fluctuations in demand and supply.

The above example assumes a binomial distribution of future demand, while the option pricing model assumes a continuous distribution. The economic variables, such as sales or stock prices, do not go below zero. Normal distribution does not apply to these variables, but the log-normal distribution does. Combining the log-normal distribution with the continuous-time, the future stock price follows the geometric Brownian motion:[2]

$$dS_t = S_t \exp\left(\mu_S dt + \sigma_S dW\right),$$

where μ_S is the expected growth rate of demand, σ_S is the volatility of demand, and W is the standard Brownian motion with zero mean and unit standard deviation. Assuming μ_S and σ_S are constant, the Black–Scholes option pricing model (Black and Scholes, 1973) gives:

$$\begin{aligned} Q_{t+\Delta t} = \arg\min_{Q_t} \{ & \left[S_t N(d_1) - K e^{-r\Delta t} N(d_2)\right] \\ & + r\left[K e^{r\Delta t} N\left(-d_2\right) - S_t N\left(-d_1\right)\right]\}, \end{aligned} \tag{3.20}$$

[2]Those who have no background in stochastic calculus may skip the option-pricing model without loss of continuity in understanding the rest of this book.

where $N(x)$ is the cumulative distribution from $-\infty$ to x for a standardized normal distribution and $K = E_t(S_{t+\delta t} + Q_t)$ is the strike price in the option and

$$d_1 = \frac{\ln \frac{S_t}{K} + \left(r + \frac{\sigma^2}{2}\right)\Delta t}{\sigma\sqrt{\Delta t}},$$

$$d_2 = d_1 - \sigma\sqrt{\Delta t}.$$

The first square bracket in Eq. (3.20) is a call option, which represents the present value of lost sales, and the second square bracket is the put option, which represents the present value of the opportunity cost.

Figure 3.3 shows a numerical example of Eq. (3.20), in which the dot-dashed line corresponds to the call option (the present value of lost sales), the dotted line corresponds to the put option, the present value of the opportunity cost, and the solid line is the total loss. Figure 3.3 is the continuous-time version of Figure 3.2. The loss of sales decreases with inventory, while the opportunity cost increases.

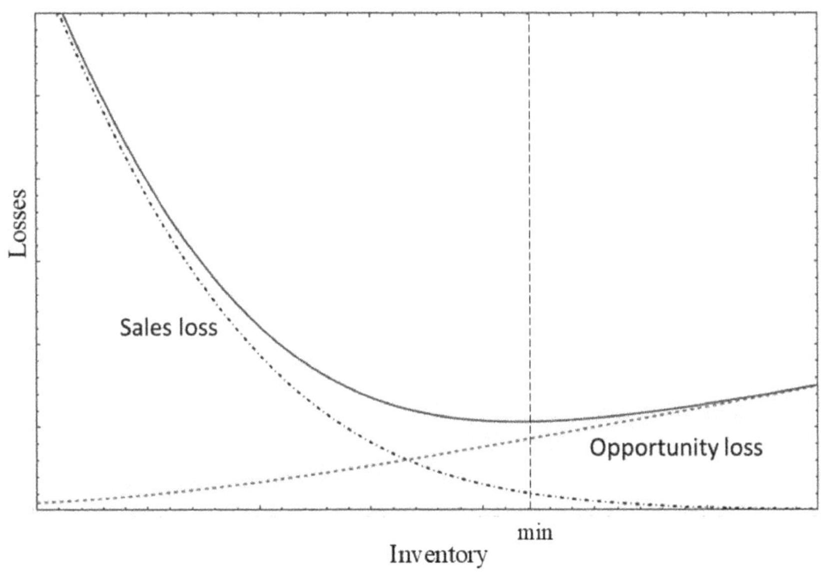

Fig. 3.3. Inventory losses: The Black–Scholes model.

It is easy to see that the two costs are asymmetric. When inventory levels are low, the marginal cost of lost sales exceeds the marginal opportunity cost, prompting firms to hold inventory.

3.2.2 *Inventory in macroeconomy*

In the context of the macroeconomy, inventory plays a stabilizing role. When one firm loses sales to a competitor, its inventory increases, while the competitor's inventory decreases. In a stable economy, these fluctuations cancel each other out, leaving the overall level of inventory relatively unchanged at the macroeconomic level.

In the U.S., the annual cost of inventory, which includes financial, storage, obsolescence, handling, and insurance costs, accounts for approximately 2% of GDP (Vandeput, 2020). With approximately $2.5 trillion in business inventory as of the second half of 2022, this number represents a significant portion of economic activity, particularly in relation to the U.S. GDP of $25.5 trillion that year.

Firms face two types of risks—idiosyncratic (firm-specific)[3] and systematic (economy-wide). While idiosyncratic risks such as equipment breakdowns or factory fires have minimal impact on the broader economy, systematic risks—such as wars or pandemics—can disrupt entire industries and create significant economic instability.

Excess inventory can contribute to a downturn in production and economic activity, becoming a systematic risk. Marx highlighted the dangers of overproduction, in which excessive inventory builds up due to a lack of demand, leading to an economic crisis (Marx, 1861):

> They cannot buy it because they have not the means, and they have not the means because they cannot continue to produce and they cannot continue to produce because too much calico has been produced ... In these crises there breaks out an epidemic that, in all earlier epochs, would have seemed an absurdity - the epidemic of over-production.... why? Because there is too much civilization, too much means of subsistence, too much industry, too much commerce.

During crises such as the COVID-19 pandemic, supply chain disruptions can lead to economic slowdowns. For example, inventory

[3]It is also known as diversifiable risk, or non-systematic risk.

turnover ratios among S&P 500 companies were lower than usual, reflecting overstocking and reduced demand.[4]

When inventory is in serious shortage, firms, governments, or organizations may release reserves to relieve the shortage. Inventory supports continuous sales, and reserves support continuous production. Both play crucial roles in stabilizing the economy during periods of uncertainty and can be included in a broader definition of inventory to include unfinished goods, raw materials, components, work in progress, and maintenance and repair supplies.

To fit inventory into a simple, manageable model, Eq. (3.19) has to be pared down even further. Using Eq. (3.17), Eq. (3.19) can be written as

$$\frac{Q_{\text{opt}}}{E_t S_{t+\Delta t}} = \frac{1}{1 - p_d\left(1 - \frac{S_L}{S_H}\right)} - 1 = p_d\left(1 - \frac{S_L}{S_H}\right),$$

which uses the approximation $1/(1-x) \approx 1 + x$. In the above expression, the inventory-to-demand ratio is determined by demand uncertainty. In principle, uncertainty increases with the time lag Δt. Assuming an average Δt across firms in the economy and treating it as constant, we linearize the expected demand as:

$$E_t S_{t+\Delta t} \approx S_t\left(1 + \frac{\Delta t}{S_t}\frac{\partial}{\partial t} S_t\right) = S_t(1 + B),$$

thereby bypassing the need for stochastic calculus by defining:

$$\eta = \frac{Q_{\text{opt}}}{E_t S_{t+\Delta t}} = \frac{Q_{\text{opt}}}{S_t(1+B)}, \tag{3.21}$$

where, after aggregating firms' inventories, η is treated as a constant under strong simplifying assumptions.

---

[4] *Slowing demand leaves US companies overstocked as turnover ratios decline* by P. Brennan and G. Dholakia, May 22, 2023, S&P Global website, accessed on December 10, 2023.

Firms produce output based on their expected demand; accordingly, we substitute output for demand in Eq. (3.21):

$$Q_{t,\,\text{opt}} = \eta Y_t = \eta f(K, L), \tag{3.22}$$

The economy-wide shortage or overstocking creates the gap Ω between the existing inventory and the optimal inventory:

$$\Omega = Q_{t,\text{opt}} - Q_t = \eta f(K, L) - Q_t. \tag{3.23}$$

As shown in Figure 3.3, when firms' inventories deviate from the optimal, their inventory losses increase. The first-order derivative of the cost function $h^*(\Omega_t)$ is:

$$h^{*\prime}(\Omega)\begin{cases} < 0 \ \Omega < 0 \\ > 0 \ \Omega = 0\,; \quad h^{*\prime\prime}(\Omega) \geq 0 \\ > 0 \,\Omega > 0. \end{cases} \tag{3.24}$$

Figure 3.3 shows that the inventory loss is convex—the second derivative $h^{*\prime\prime}(\Omega)$ in Eq. (3.21) is positive. At $\Omega = 0$, the inventory is optimal $Q_t = Q_{t,opt}$ but the inventory cost is not zero. To keep the model parsimonious, set

$$\begin{aligned} h(\Omega_t) &= h^*(\Omega_t) - h^*(0), \\ Y &= Y^* - h^*(0), \end{aligned} \tag{3.25}$$

where Y^* is the output without inventory losses and Y is the output net of the cost of the optimal inventory. Thus, the output (Y) takes the loss at the optimal inventory just like the scraps as a part of the routine production process. Then, the inventory loss function becomes:

$$h(\Omega)\begin{cases} > 0 \ \Omega < 0 \\ = 0 \ \Omega = 0 \ ; \quad h^{\prime\prime}(\Omega) \geq 0 \\ > 0 \,\Omega > 0. \end{cases} \tag{3.26}$$

Consistent with Eq. (3.21), the inventory loss decreases with inventory when in shortage $\Omega > 0$ and increases with inventory when overstocking $\Omega < 0$ (see Figure 3.3).

3.2.3 *Stabilizing effects of inventory*

Inventory is not a flow variable, but the inventory loss is. Whenever inventory loss occurs, firms will adjust inventory to minimize the loss. Hence, the macroeconomic identity incorporates both the inventory costs $h(\Omega)$ and the inventory adjustment $\dot{Q}$:

$$\dot{K} = f(K, L) - h(\Omega) - \dot{Q} - C - \delta K. \tag{3.27}$$

Another way to look at Eq. (3.27) is that the inventory adjustment $\dot{Q}$ competes with the investment in capital stock for the total amount of savings available:

$$\dot{K} + \dot{Q} = f(K, L) - h(\Omega) - C - \delta K. \tag{3.28}$$

When a firm maintains inventory at optimal levels, it replenishes the old inventory Q with the newly produced inventory. If consumption exceeds production output, the inventory decreases to offset the imbalance ($Q < \eta f(K, L)$), creating a positive inventory gap. Conversely, if consumption lags behind production, inventories ($Q > \eta f(K, L)$) produce a negative gap.

In the macroeconomic identity without inventory, Eq. (1.2), the demand $C + \dot{K}$ matches the supply $f(K, L) - \delta K$. After incorporating inventory, the demand in Eq. (3.28) is not equal to the supply because of inventory loss. The presence of inventory in the economy violates Condition C.2 of the classical dichotomy (see Section 2.1.2.3), meaning that money is no longer neutral. Instead, it has a direct impact on the real economy through inventory. However, once inventory is depleted, the injection of additional money into the economy no longer increases consumption or investment; it simply raises prices, and money becomes neutral again. In this way, inventory establishes the limit on how much money can directly affect the real economy.

In other words, the direct effect of money is only present when an economy holds inventory. Pumping money into the system can increase consumption or investment by reducing the inventory of either consumption goods, capital goods, or both. This is particularly important during economic recessions or crises, where increasing the money supply can stimulate demand and prevent a downward spiral.

However, if the economy has no accumulated inventory, increasing the money supply does not boost demand but instead harms the economy by creating adverse effects—not only inflation but also other long-term problems (see Chapter 4).

In a growing economy with increasing capital stock, firms expand their production capacity and build up inventory to meet rising demand. However, this additional inventory requires resources, which diverts savings away from investment in capital stock. As a result, the economy grows more slowly, as some of the potential investment in productive capital is instead allocated to maintaining or expanding inventory levels.

Conversely, in a declining economy where capital stock is decreasing, firms cut back on inventory and release inventory, which can boost investment and slow down the decline in capital stock. This process can help mitigate the effects of economic slowdown, potentially stabilizing the economy to some extent.

Inventory acts as a buffer between production and consumption, helping to smooth out fluctuations in economic activity, like a parking lot on the top of a hill in Figure 3.4. While inventory itself does not alter the type of stability of an economy, it can dampen the impact of sudden changes in production or consumption, as well as other shifts in economic conditions.[5]

Fig. 3.4. Neutral stability.

[5]The factors that affect inventory include supply chain disruptions, money supply conditions, liquidity risk, interest rates, inflation, fiscal policy, and trade balance.

3.3 Direct effects of money on the middle class

In modern economies, *finance* primarily revolves around the supply and demand for money and credit. Banks play a crucial role in this process by creating credit and facilitating the flow of funds between savers and borrowers. A broader definition of finance covers any matters regarding usage or reference of money, "broadly defined as anything that is used in exchange for goods and services and the settlement of debt" (Demetriades and Andrianova, 2004). The following model focuses on debt financing, as debt has become the primary form of money circulating within modern economies today.

Households in an economy often carry a certain level of debt, denoted as D. The debt payment is $\mu_{\text{out}}D$, where μ_{out} denotes the payment as a fraction of the principal (D). Households also take on new debt through bank loans $\mu_{\text{in}}D$, which increases their total debt over time at the rate of μ_{in}. Both μ_{in} (the rate of new borrowing) and μ_{out} (the rate of repayment) are dynamic and can change with economic conditions. The rate of change of households' debt $\dot{D}$ is the difference between the new loans and the debt payments:

$$\dot{D} = (\mu_{\text{in}} - \mu_{\text{out}} + R_D)D, \tag{3.29}$$

where R_D is the nominal interest rate on the loan. If households receive no new debt and pay R_D interest only, then principal D remains unchanged.

The payment schedule of a loan depends on the loan's structure. For example, mortgage payments typically consist of both interest and principal payments, which amortize the loan over time. Households pay the interest and also pay back a certain amount of principal each year.[6]

The amount of real goods that loans can purchase is the time derivative of D/P:

$$\dot{\left(\frac{D}{P}\right)} = \left(\frac{\dot{D}}{D} - \frac{\dot{P}}{P}\right)\frac{D}{P} = (\mu_{\text{in}} - \mu_{\text{out}} + R_D - \pi)\frac{D}{P}.$$

[6]The amortized loans typically require equal payments over the life of the loan; thus, the borrowers pay down the principal of the loan over time rather than pay a lump sum at the maturity of the loan.

To examine how debt affects the real economy in a straightforward way, we introduce the real loan growth rate Σ:

$$\Sigma = \dot{\left(\frac{D}{P}\right)} = (\mu_{\text{in}} - \mu_{\text{out}} + r_D)\frac{D}{P}, \tag{3.30}$$

where r_D is the real interest rate and

$$r_D = R_D - \pi, \tag{3.31}$$

which is the Fisher effect—the relation between nominal and real interest rates, and inflation. For example, a loan pays nominal interest rate R_D 3% and inflation π is 2%. Then, the real interest rate r_D =3%–2% is 1%, which means that the money lent will purchase about 1% more real goods a year later, raising the lender's real purchasing power by 1%.

The real growth rate Σ takes the inflation π into account so that the analysis does not need a separate equation for inflation and simplifies the analysis. However, the purchasing power of consumer loans depends on the inflation of consumption goods, while the purchasing power of business loans depends on the inflation of capital goods. Inflation rates vary with different goods and assets, so the specific inflation rate should be used for the particular loan and the specific products that the loan purchases.

Inflation does not manifest uniformly across sectors. Each category—food, technology, energy, housing—is shaped by both demand-side forces and supply-side conditions, including supply chain disruptions and external shocks like natural disasters or political crises. As a result, while the overall inflation rate is expressed as a single statistic, the inflation experienced in specific goods can vary substantially.

Food prices, for instance, are highly volatile and often subject to higher inflation due to weather conditions or crop failures. In recent years, wheat and corn prices have surged amid global supply chain disruptions and the Russian invasion of Ukraine. By contrast, technology products have experienced lower inflation or even deflation, as advances in manufacturing and continuous innovation—particularly in consumer electronics—expand supply. Smartphones, for example, have remained stable or declined in real terms despite improved features, while the cost per gigabyte of storage and laptop prices have also steadily fallen over the past decade due to progress in semiconductor production.

Macroeconomic models sometimes set the sum of all bank loans to be zero because, from an accounting perspective, the sum of all bank loans is treated as zero, meaning that every dollar of debt taken by a borrower is offset by a corresponding dollar of credit held by a lender.[7] However, while the zero-sum of debits and credits is true in accounting, it does not capture the dynamic effects of loans on the real economy.

When a borrower takes out a loan, the money is immediately injected into the economy and circulates within it. The repayment of the loan, however, occurs later, often over months or years. As repayments are made, money is effectively removed from circulation. In aggregate, unless new loans exactly match the closing of existing loans, the net effect is not neutral.[8]

It is clear that how consumer loans–additional money–affect the consumption patterns of the rich and the poor. The following model focuses on how a consumer loan changes the consumption of the middle class. By incorporating bank loans into Eq. (3.26), defining $\sigma = \Sigma/L$ and $q = Q/L$, and using per capita variables, the dynamics of the real economy are given by

$$\dot{k} + \dot{q} = f(k) - h(\omega) - (c + \sigma) - \delta k, \tag{3.32}$$

where

$$\omega = \eta \frac{Y}{L} - \frac{Q}{L} = \eta y - q = \eta f(k) - q. \tag{3.33}$$

The inventory loss function $h(\Omega)$ is convex (see Figure 3.3) and not homogeneous of degree one. For the function $f(x) = x^n$, which

---

[7]See Acemoglu (2008) and Blanchard and Fischer (1989) for further discussion.

[8]Economists attribute banking risk to the mismatch between short-term liabilities (deposits) and long-term assets (interest and loan payments), while banks also play a role in the process in maturity transformation (Diamond and Dybvig, 1983).

is homogeneous of degree n, the per capita function is given by:

$$\frac{f(x)}{L} = \frac{x^n}{L} = L^{n-1}\left(\frac{x}{L}\right)^n. \tag{3.34}$$

Equation (1.31) for the purpose of simplicity we define the per capita loss function as $h(\omega) = h(\Omega/L) = L^{n-1}\tilde{h}(\Omega/L)$, where L^{n-1} is absorbed in $h(\omega)$ as a constant because labor L is assumed to be fixed.[9]

When poor individuals receive a consumer loan, their consumption increases. In contrast, wealthy individuals have reached consumption saturation and do not increase their consumption with additional wealth. For middle-class individuals who receive a consumer loan, however, the funds may not be entirely allocated to consumption. Even though the loan can only be used for consumption goods, which becomes a mandatory component of consumption, it cannot prevent the loan recipients from investing more of their own income in capital stock, effectively splitting the loan between the voluntary part of consumption and investment.[10]

The economy maximizes consumption under the influence of loans:

$$\max_{c,q} \int_0^T e^{-\rho s} \ln(c_s + \sigma) ds, \tag{3.35}$$

where σ is a part of consumption because the consumer loans are restricted to spending on consumption goods. Introducing the new variable $v = V/L = k + q$, the state equation and the constraints for the maximization problem are

$$\dot{v} = f(v - q) - h(\omega) - (c + \sigma) - \delta(v - q), \tag{3.36}$$

$$v_0 = v_{IC}, \tag{3.37}$$

$$c_0 = c_{IC}, \tag{3.38}$$

[9]The inventory function is a nonlinear function and asymmetric between opportunity cost and the cost of lost sales (see Eq. (3.20)). Numerical computation can handle these issues.

[10]Some consumer loans allow borrowers to use the funds for various purposes, such as purchasing stocks or antiques, while others may impose use restrictions.

$$q_0 = q_{IC}, \tag{3.39}$$

$$\dot{c} < \infty, \tag{3.40}$$

$$\dot{q} < \infty, \tag{3.41}$$

where v_{IC} and q_{IC} are the initial values for v and q respectively at time 0, and c_{IC} is the consumption right before the new loans σ. The Hamiltonian for the maximization problem is:

$$\mathcal{H}(v, q, c, \theta, t) = \ln(c + \sigma) + \theta[f(v - q) - h(\omega) - (c + \sigma) - \delta(v - q)]. \tag{3.42}$$

Taking derivatives with respect to control variables to have the first-order conditions,

$$\frac{\partial \mathcal{H}(v, q, c, \theta, t)}{\partial c} = \frac{1}{c + \sigma} - \theta = 0, \tag{3.43}$$

which gives:

$$\theta = \frac{1}{c + \sigma} \tag{3.44}$$

and

$$\frac{\partial \mathcal{H}(v, q, c, \theta, t)}{\partial q} = \theta\{-f'(v - q) + h'(\omega)[\eta f'(v - q) + 1] + \delta\} = 0, \tag{3.45}$$

which gives the relationship between the marginal cost of inventory and the return on investment:

$$h'(\omega) = \frac{f'(v - q) - \delta}{1 + \eta f'(v - q)} = \frac{f'(k) - \delta}{1 + \eta f'(k)}. \tag{3.46}$$

Take the derivative of the Hamiltonian with respect to v to have:

$$\frac{\partial \mathcal{H}(v, q, c, \theta, t)}{\partial v} = \theta\{[1 - \eta h'(\omega)]f'(v - q) - \delta\} = \rho\theta - \dot{\theta}. \tag{3.47}$$

Equations (3.47) and (3.46) give:

$$\dot{\theta} = \left[\rho - \frac{f'(k) - \delta}{1 + \eta f'(k)}\right]\theta. \tag{3.48}$$

Replace θ with c in Eq. (3.43) yields:

$$\dot{c} = \left[\frac{f'(k) - \delta}{1 + \eta f'(k)} - \rho\right](c + \sigma). \tag{3.49}$$

When a firm experiences an inventory shortage, it faces a decision: how to allocate its resources between investing in capital stock and replenishing its inventory. The trade-off between these two types of investment depends on their respective marginal benefits. On the far right of Eq. (3.46) is the marginal benefit of investment in capital stock. On the left-hand side of the equation, $h'(\omega)$ represents the marginal benefit of increasing inventory. This benefit comes from reducing the costs associated with inventory loss, such as lost sales. Firms balance the marginal gains from inventory and capital stock investment.

Only when inventory is in shortage, $q < \eta f(k)$, the marginal benefit of increasing inventory is positive, which implies that firms do not aim to completely eliminate the inventory shortage (i.e., reduce the inventory gap to zero) but will tolerate a certain level of inventory shortage, as long as the marginal benefit from investing in inventory equals that of investing in capital stock. The model suggests that during periods of economic growth, firms naturally tend to maintain inventory shortages and create upward pressure on prices, thereby contributing to inflation because firms increase the prices to reduce demand when inventories are low.

In Eq. (3.46), the net return $f'(k) - \delta$ divided by the factor $1 + \eta f'(k)$ indicates that the presence of inventory shortages reduces the rate of return on capital stock. This modification reflects the fact that firms allocate resources to inventory, slowing down the increase in capital stock and the growth of the real economy.

Equation (3.46) defines an implicit relationship between q and k, and Eq. (3.32) provides the relationship between $\dot{k}$ and $\dot{q}$. Thus, either variable can be expressed in terms of the other:

$$q = \psi(k, \dot{k}), \quad \dot{q} = \varphi(\dot{k}, k). \tag{3.50}$$

Substituting Eq. (3.50) into Eq. (3.28), we eliminate q and have a state equation that incorporates the loan effect:

$$\dot{k} + \varphi(\dot{k}, k) = f(k) - h[\eta f(k) - \psi(k, \dot{k})] - c - \sigma - \delta k. \tag{3.51}$$

Figures 3.5 and 3.6 illustrate the dynamics of k and c, which can be compared with the case without consumption loans.

Figure 3.5 shows the paths during loan expansion, where σ is positive. In contrast to Figure 1.8, which depicts an economy with

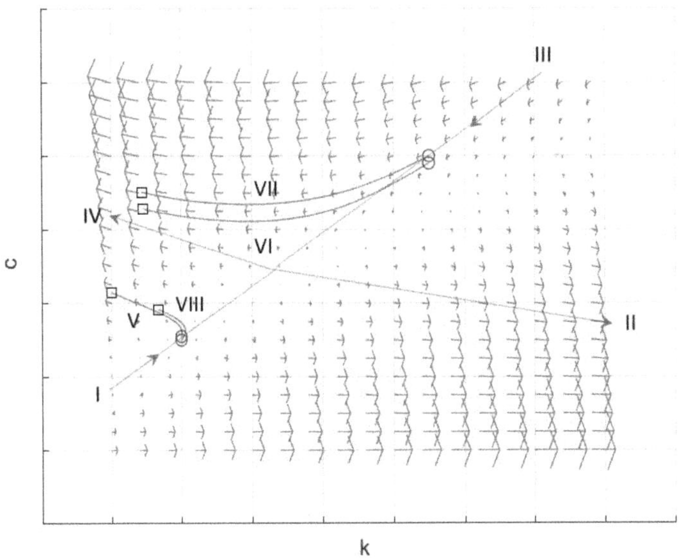

Fig. 3.5. Bank loan expansion.

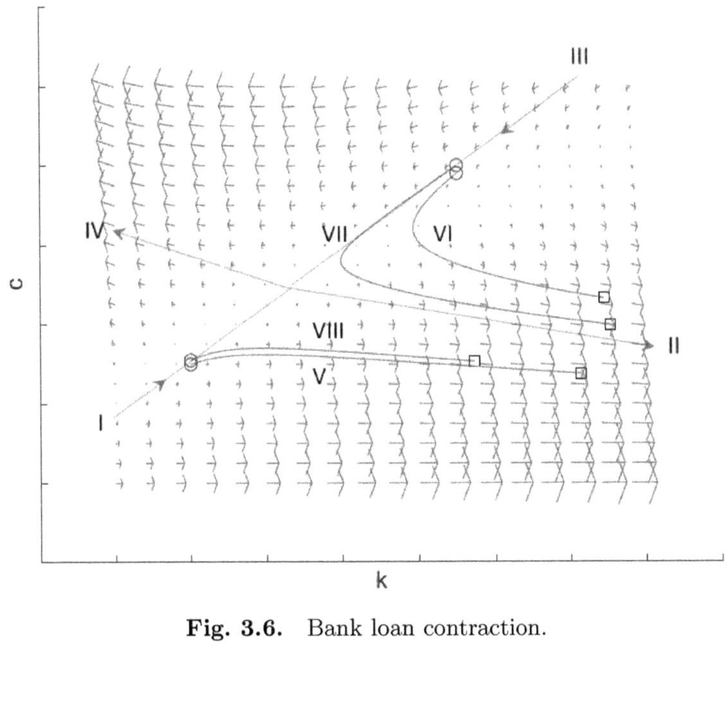

Fig. 3.6. Bank loan contraction.

zero bank loans, paths V and VI, below the stable paths I and III in Figure 3.5, turn leftward and reach the stable paths. If loan expansion continues, however, the economy moves away from the stable paths.

Economies below paths I and III are characterized as "expanding" economies, facing the challenge of overcapacity. Initially, consumer loans boost consumption, increasing demand and helping steer the economy back onto the stable path. However, if loan expansion persists, the economy drifts away from stability, becoming a "shrinking" economy, with declining capital stock and production capacity. Economies above paths I and III are characterized as "shrinking" economies, burdened by overconsumption. Consumer loans not only fail to help but also exacerbate the problem, driving these economies further from stability.

In the "lavish" economy on path V, characterized by overcapacity and rising consumption, the consumption loan reinforces demand. Initially, additional consumption reduces investment, halting capital accumulation. With persistence, the loan continues to stimulate consumption while triggering capital stock depletion. In contrast, the "frugal" economy on path VI, also burdened by overcapacity but facing declining consumption, the consumption loan slows down the decline of consumption. At first, additional consumption slows capital accumulation. However, prolonged reliance on consumption loans stimulates demand further, eventually initiating capital stock depletion.

Figure 3.6 illustrates the economy's response to loan contraction, with negative σ. Economies above paths I and III are classified as "shrinking" economies, challenged by overconsumption. First, loan contraction reduces consumption, increases investment, and helps restore stability. Yet if contraction persists, the economy drifts away from equilibrium, transforming into an "expanding" economy with accumulating capital stock and rising overcapacity. Economies below paths I and III are already "expanding" economies, burdened by excess capacity. Loan contraction worsens this condition by further reducing consumption and driving them farther from stability.

In the "frugal" economy on path VII, characterized by overconsumption and declining demand, loan contraction reinforces the downward trend. Initially, the further reduction in consumption increases investment, halting capital stock losses. With persistence, however, loan contraction continues to depress consumption while simultaneously generating overcapacity. In contrast, the "frugal" economy on path VIII, also burdened by overconsumption but experiencing rising demand, faces loan contraction that slows the pace of consumption growth. First, the savings from reduced consumption contribute to capital accumulation. Yet, prolonged contraction continues to suppress consumption while fostering overcapacity.

Inventory and capital stock share a symbiotic relationship, moving together as they draw from the same resources. Therefore, the dynamics of k and c resemble the dynamics of q and c, and similar figures to Figures 3.5 and 3.6 could be plotted for the q-c relationship. A key distinction is that the $q - c$ plot identifies the points at which inventory is exhausted; additional stimulus no longer boosts the economy but instead fuels inflation. At that point, the direct effect of money stops there, while indirect effects may arise.

Business loans can be analyzed similarly; however, for brevity, we leave that analysis to readers interested in exploring the effects of business loans. The common belief is that business loans increase the supply of goods, whereas consumer loans boost demand. This perception, however, is flawed. When firms utilize business loans for production, they purchase capital goods, which increases demand for those goods and reduces their inventory. Firms face the same tradeoff between investing in capital stock and replenishing capital goods inventory, making the short-term effects of business and consumer loans similar. Both types of loans deplete inventory, producing comparable short-term impacts on the economy. Over time, however, firms benefiting from business loans expand production and increase output, differentiating the supply-side effects of business loans from the demand-side effects of consumer loans.

Moreover, consumer goods and capital goods are not isolated categories. Money supply changes market demand and profitability, prompting firms with feasible technologies to shift products. For instance, companies producing food-processing machinery move into kitchen appliances, while automobile manufacturers shift between producing cars, heavy trucks, or even tanks.

Consider an economy that has a fixed amount of money in circulation. A new central planner aims to simulate the economy using additional money, such as private credit or government credit (e.g., food stamps or other programs). The overall effects of this new money depend on two key factors. The first is wealth distribution: The way wealth is distributed throughout the economy influences how new money impacts real economic activity. The second is the current inventory: The existing inventory of consumption and capital goods sets the limits on how much new money can increase real consumption or real investment.

The global economy is a closed system with a finite inventory. An open national economy can trade its surplus goods with the economies need them, easing domestic inventory accumulation. However, a net-importing economy—one that imports more than it exports—must finance this imbalance by selling national assets or borrowing from abroad. These net-trade flows significantly reshape the dynamics of both importing and exporting nations, as well as the global economy as a whole—a topic examined in Chapter 6.

Careful readers may observe that Figures 3.5 and 3.6 show more pronounced effects of consumer loans on capital stock than on consumption. Recall that saddle stability involves two eigenvalues with opposite signs. In the Ramsey model, the absolute value of the positive eigenvalue exceeds that of the negative one, implying that the economy diverges along the unstable arms (II and IV) more rapidly than it converges along the stable arms (I and III). In Figure 1.8, the arrows in the background move more strongly along capital stock than along consumption. From a system-control perspective, governments and central banks may exploit this characteristic to address problems of overproduction or underproduction.

3.3.1 *Keynes on "dig holes" and savings*

Keynes's central recommendation was active fiscal policy, whereby governments increase expenditure in recessions and reduce it during booms to mitigate inflationary pressures. The inventory-based model seems to align with this principle: credit should be expanded (whether through banks or governments) in periods of underconsumption associated with excess inventory and contracted in periods of overconsumption associated with inventory shortages. Nevertheless, unlike Irving Fisher, Keynes did not regard money as a primary cause of business cycle. In practice, however, money frequently plays an important—if not decisive—role in economic downturns. This issue forms the focus of the subsequent chapters.

The Great Depression left economies such as the U.S. and U.K. mired in stagnation, with soaring unemployment and collapsing demand. Keynesian economics represents Keynes's solutions to economic crises. The overriding priority was to boost aggregate demand and lift the economy out of recession. Keynes argued that the intrinsic value of a project was irrelevant—even seemingly wasteful undertakings, such as digging and refilling holes, were justified if they circulated money and created employment. What mattered was the generation of jobs and income, which in turn stimulated consumption and demand.

Keynes believed that paying workers to undertake such projects could generate a multiplier effect: initial spending would set off successive rounds of expenditure, as workers used their earnings to purchase goods and services, thereby creating further demand and employment. This process reinforced overall economic activity.

However, Keynes overestimated money's effects on economy, particularly on employment. This section shows that he incorrectly interpreted the macroeconomic identity, which grossly exaggerated the effect of money investment on economic output (employment).

Keynes's logic is as follows: monetary expansion reduces borrowing costs and lowers interest rates. When the interest rate falls below the expected return—what Keynes termed the Marginal Efficiency of Capital—firms invest. This investment amplifies aggregate demand through the Multiplier Effect. To meet the resulting increase in demand for goods and services, firms expand hiring, thereby raising employment. The indirect link between the money supply and employment, mediated through interest rates and investment, marks a major departure from classical economics.

President Nixon famously declared that "we are all Keynesians," reflecting a governmental tendency to adopt one aspect of Keynesian strategy—boosting employment through increased government spending. As Keynes asserted, "... the quantity theory of money can be enunciated as follows: 'So long as there is unemployment, employment will change in the same proportion as the quantity of money; and when there is full employment, prices will change in the same proportion as the quantity of money'" (Keynes, 1936). In Keynes's view, expanding the money supply was the primary mechanism to achieve full employment by stimulating investment.

While Keynes provided a mathematical framework for his ideas—defining *the marginal propensity to consume* as dC/dY, and the *investment multiplier* as $k_m = dY/dI$—his reasoning contains critical flaws. According to Keynes, the macroeconomic identity implies:

$$I = Y - C, \quad \frac{dI}{dY} = 1 - \frac{dC}{dY}. \tag{3.52}$$

He proposed the following:

> It follows, therefore, that, if the consumption psychology of the community is such that they will choose to consume, e.g., nine-tenths of an increment of income, then the multiplier k is 10; and the total employment caused by increased public works will be ten times the primary employment provided by the public works themselves, assuming no reduction of investment in other directions.—Keynes (1936)

In terms of an equation, he meant:

$$\frac{dI}{dY} = 1 - \frac{9}{10},$$

which implies $k_m = dY/dI = 10$, that is, if people consume 90% of an income increment, the multiplier k_m would be 10, implying that \$1 of investment leads to \$10 of output. Hazlitt critiqued this reasoning, remarking: "But if a community spends all of the additional income provided by the public works, then the multiplier is infinity" (Hazlitt, 1959).

Keynes's mistake lies in his misinterpretation of the macroeconomic identity. While Eq. (3.52) may appear to be a simple algebraic equation, it is, in fact, a differential equation, where $I = \dot{K} + \delta K$. Using a discrete AK model, where $Y = AK$ and $I = \Delta K$, we compare it with Keynes' framework of Eq. (3.52):

$$\Delta K_0 = (A - \delta)K_0 - C = \frac{1}{10}(A - \delta)K_0, \tag{3.53}$$

in which 1/10 of output is saved. Then the output in the next period is:

$$Y_1 = A(K_0 + \Delta K_0) = Y_0 \left(1 + \frac{A - \delta}{10}\right). \tag{3.54}$$

Here, capital stock and output increase only by a factor of $(A-\delta)/10$, where $A-\delta$ is the net return r in the AK model, making it impossible for output to grow by a factor of 10, as Keynes suggested.

Keynes insisted on money as the exclusive measure of aggregate real goods and the economy, believing it could miraculously increase output through the investment multiplier. Yet he overlooked Aristotle's insight that while money is unlimited, real goods remain finite.

Keynesian economics was challenged in the 1970s by the onset of stagflation—simultaneous high inflation and unemployment—which undermined confidence in Keynes's prescriptions. Consequently, monetarist and supply-side economics rose to prominence in the 1980s, advocating reduced government spending, tax cuts, and a focus on inflation control.

Chapter 4

Assets Markets

Voluminous books and articles—both old and new, theoretical, and practical—have been written on the stock market, particularly on profiting from it. Indeed, daily news about the stock market and making money rivals the popularity of sports news. While many believe that buying common stock is an "investment" in the economy, this notion often masks the true nature of the stock market.

Up to now, we have focused on the investment in capital stock, which produces real goods. Capital stock is a type of tangible asset, and there are many other assets that are not part of capital stock.

In financial accounting, an asset is any resource owned or controlled by a business or an economic entity. Asset owners can convert their assets into cash (although cash itself is also an asset) (O'sullivan *et al.*, 2008). The common economic definition of an asset is a resource, whether tangible, intangible, or financial, with the expectation of future monetary benefit.

Therefore, "investment" in assets differs from "investment" in the real economy. Putting it another way: a tailor purchases an antique sewing machine and waits for the price to go up. Another tailor buys a computer-programmed sewing machine to make clothes. Are both purchases "investments"? By the "official" definition, they are "investments," and most people may answer "yes."

The two "investments" follow different sequences of financial transactions. To use a crude analogy: The money invested in capital stock is "working" and capital stock itself represents "working assets." The tailor's new automatic sewing machine processes cloth inputs, produces clothes, and eventually wears out. Over time, the tailor replaces it, purchasing another new machine with the money earned from the clothes it produced. In this case, the tailor is investing money in "working assets."

The money invested in the antique sewing machine is "idle," simply waiting for its price to increase. Idle assets range from uncultivable land and antique cars to collectibles such as baseball cards or lunch boxes. The return of the money spent on such assets relies entirely on their price appreciation. In contrast to the popular expression "priceless" antiques, the return from an antique depends solely on rising prices. Without price appreciation, antique yields no return.

Taking gold as another example, the gold price was $20.67 per ounce in 1918 and is around $2,700 per ounce as of the end of 2024. If a family has been holding gold, the price appreciation represents a "return on investment" in financial terms, but this price increase is primarily driven by inflation.

Therefore, the money "invested" in the "working assets" and the money "invested" in the "idle assets" can be distinguished from one another, though the difference between the two is not always clear-cut. The "idle assets" can blend with the "working assets."

When the owner of a firm purchases capital goods in the goods market, the money turns into working assets, which contribute directly to the real economy. And yet, if someone pays a higher price to acquire the ownership of the assets from their existing owner in a secondary transaction, that money simply changes hands between owners; it does not directly inject new capital into the real economy. Now, we face the challenge of distinguishing natural diamonds from artificial diamonds. The separation of the real economy and money serves as the touchstone to tell the difference.

A common misconception is the conflation of real investment with financial investment. It is essential to distinguish between the two. Real investment refers to purchasing "working assets," such as machines, equipment, and production facilities, which directly increase the economy's production capacity. In contrast, purchasing "idle assets" has little to do with production.

Both economics and finance use the term "investment," which typically refers to any purchase of durable assets[1] including capital stock, jewelry, antiques, gold, or silver. However, this broad definition blurs the distinction between capital stock and idle assets. Ideally, we could differentiate between the two more clearly: *rinvestment* for investment that adds to capital stock and enhances production capacity, and *finvestment* that does not increase production capacity.

For example, *rinvestment* in a car manufacturer allows it to make more cars, while *finvestment* in an antique car merely anticipates price appreciation and has no impact on car manufacturing. However, to avoid awkward new words, this book will continue to use the term "investment" unless otherwise clarified.

4.1 Boons and Banes of Finance

The major players in the financial markets are the financial intermediaries, including institutions, such as banks, pension funds, mutual funds, stockbrokers, and exchangers. They serve as go-betweens in financial markets, connecting market participants. When households have money and firms that need it, without intermediaries, households would need to contact firms directly, and vice versa, which would involve high search costs. Financial intermediaries simplify this process by matching investors with firms efficiently. In addition, intermediaries, such as brokers, credit-rating agencies, and accounting firms, also provide information to market participants, assisting them in financial decisions.

Financial intermediaries facilitate trade between firms, particularly when trust is lacking. For example, a Chinese firm orders a product made by a German manufacturer for the first time. The German firm wants the Chinese firm to pay first and then ship the product, but the Chinese firm insists on paying after receiving the

[1]Durable assets are designed to last for an extended period, though there is no universal definition of how long. Consumer durables, a subset of durable goods, typically last at least three years. The Bureau of Economic Analysis defines durable goods as products purchased by households for nonbusiness use, with a life expectancy of at least three years. The EPA also defines durable goods as items with a lifespan of three years or more, though some exceptions apply.

product. Then, the potential business gets stuck. A bank can provide credit (Banker's Acceptances) and guarantee payment between a Chinese firm and a German manufacturer, enabling trade that might otherwise not occur.

Financial intermediaries go well beyond the aforementioned activities. During the 1980s and 1990s, the U.S. sought to boost economic growth through financial-sector liberalization. The Gramm–Leach–Bliley Act of 1999, signed by President Bill Clinton, repealed parts of the Glass–Steagall Act, allowing banks to own other financial companies. The deregulation expanded the influence of financial intermediaries.

While financial liberalization was intended to spur growth, it also led to increased volatility and contributed to the 2008 financial crisis. For instance, AIG, an insurance company, suffered massive losses due to its involvement in insuring Collateralized Debt Obligations (CDOs)[2] and selling Credit Default Swaps (CDSs)[3] against mortgage defaults (Kaminsky and Reinhart, 1999) (see Section 4.2.1). After the 2008 crisis, governments introduced regulations to promote financial stability. In the U.S., the Dodd–Frank Act of 2010 was enacted to reduce the risk of future financial instability. On a global scale, Basel III introduced stricter capital and liquidity requirements for banks.

The financial industry is formally a part of a country's GDP. Households and firms pay the financial intermediaries fees and commissions for information and financial transactions. The fees are part of the Gross Value Added (GVA). The System of National Accounts (SNA) of the United Nations provided the guidelines to estimate the monetary value of financial services and introduced in 1993 the measure of the value of financial services—Financial Intermediation Services Indirectly Measured (FISIM)—which estimates the value as the difference between the actual interest paid and interest received

[2]Banks used to hold the mortgages they issued. They later bundled them together and sold them to investors, thereby shifting mortgage risk to investors. CDOs use mortgage or debt repayments as collateral.

[3]The writer of CDS takes the default risk of the underlying asset, such as mortgages, and the buyer of CDS gets reimbursement if the mortgage defaults.

(Haldane *et al.*, 2010). The services include the following:

(1) taking, managing, and transferring deposits,
(2) providing flexible payment mechanisms such as debit cards,
(3) making loans or other investments, and
(4) offering financial advice or other business services.

The financial industry, despite its controversial role and mixed impact on the real economy, has grown significantly since financial liberalization. It grew from $122 billion in 2000 to $791 billion in 2022.[4] Its growth has outpaced the real economy. In 2020, finance and insurance represented 8.3% (or $1.7 trillion) of U.S. gross domestic product.[5] By comparison, America's farms contributed about 0.7% of U.S. GDP.[6] The financial industry does not produce real goods but is way larger than a key real-economy sector—agriculture.[7]

4.1.1 *Primary and secondary markets*

People buy and sell financial securities, including stocks, bonds, derivatives, and commodities, in financial markets. Like supermarkets that have physical markets (e.g., Walmart) and online markets (e.g., Amazon), the stock markets can have a physical building, such as the New York Stock Exchange, or a virtual network, such as NASDAQ, which evolved from the National Association of Securities Dealers Automated Quotations.

The stock market also has a primary market and a secondary market. The primary market is where private firms raise public funds by issuing shares or bonds, typically through an Initial Public Offering (IPO). The firm that intends to become a public company finds one or more investment banks that oversee the IPO process. After filing

[4]World Bank Data (data.worldbank.org), accessed on August 13, 2024.

[5]From Trade.gov, accessed on August 13, 2024.

[6]From ers.usda.gov, retrieved on August 13, 2024.

[7]Financial services are embedded in other services and activities, so official data provide only estimates. In 2023, the finance, insurance, real estate, rental, and leasing industry added $5.66 trillion, and accounted for 20.7% of the total U.S. GDP; within this total, real estate and rental and leasing contributed $3.67 trillion, finance and insurance added $1.99 trillion, and the professional, scientific, and technical services added $2.18 trillion (Statista; investopedia.com; accessed on April 17, 2024).

with the Securities and Exchange Commission (SEC), the firm and its banks gauge interest in the firm through face-to-face meetings with institutional investors (the road show) and determine the share prices and the number of shares to offer. The proceeds from these sales go directly to the firms which can use the funds for growth. That is, the investors invest money in the "working assets."

After the initial purchase of the IPO, the investors must hold the shares during the IPO lock-up period, typically 90–180 days. Subsequently, they can trade shares on the secondary market, which serves as a platform for the transfer of ownership. Unlike in the primary market, the money exchanged does not go to the issuing firms but rather changes hands between previous and new owners. Consequently, in the secondary market, the "working assets" and "idle assets" become intertwined.

Although firms do not directly benefit from secondary market trade, they can raise additional money by issuing new shares of common stock or bonds, which are then sold to investors in the secondary market. The distinction between productive investments ("rinvestment") and speculative investments ("finvestment") becomes blurred in this market.

The concepts of primary and secondary markets are not limited to stocks; they also apply to other markets, such as real estate and cars. In these markets, the "primary" market involves the sale of new houses or cars, with proceeds going to the builders or manufacturers. The "secondary" market involves the sale of existing houses or used cars, where gains or losses are borne by the sellers and buyers, not the original producers.

The extended definition of primary and secondary markets facilitates our discussions on the effects of money on the real economy. Firms raise funds from investors in the primary markets. The secondary markets facilitate the transfer of asset ownership from the old to the new owners without the involvement of firms.

Marx differentiated between real capital, which is tied to the means of production (e.g., factories and machines), and financial assets such as stocks and bonds, which he termed *fictitious capital* (see p. 127). These financial assets represent "tradeable paper claims to wealth," but the "money that is thrown into circulation as capital without any material basis in commodities or productive activity" (Marx, 1992). In Marx's dialectic language, capital goods (e.g., machinery and equipment) have a "double life," as both real capital (used in production) and as financial assets (such as common stock) that represent ownership in firms. While capital only truly exists in the form of physical goods, stocks represent a claim to the surplus value generated by those goods.

The double life of capital stock mystifies the secondary market. In the goods market, supply and demand determine prices. Thus, the secondary market is intended to serve the purpose of "price discovery" for capital stock. Proponents offer three main arguments for the secondary market:

(1) A buyer and a seller go through a price discovery process to find the fair price of the asset they want to trade. The trading prices in the secondary market facilitate price discovery.
(2) The movement of the secondary market indicates how a country's economy is doing.
(3) A buyer is willing to pay more for a liquid asset, which he can sell easily. The secondary market provides liquidity for common stocks.

The first argument, price discovery, involves discovering the "value" of firms. In 1964, Samuelson found in Paris Louis Bachelier's dissertation (1900), in which Bachelier presented the idea that financial market returns follow a random walk and are difficult to predict (Cootner, 1964). Nobel laureate Eugene Fama's *efficient-market hypothesis* (EMH) categorizes market efficiency into three forms: weak, semi-strong, and strong (Fama, 1970). According to Fama, the semi-strong form of efficiency holds that stock prices reflect all publicly available information. Without private information, no one can predict stock prices, as Bachelier's random walk model implied. However, critics such as Paul Samuelson suggest that the market may be "micro efficient" (efficient at the level of individual stocks) but not "macro efficient" (efficient in reflecting the overall economy) (Jung and Shiller, 2005).

The earlier chapters demonstrate the difference between "micro efficiency" and "macro efficiency." While prices balance supply and demand for a product with "micro efficiency," these prices and the associated "micro efficiency" do not reveal the dynamic processes of the real macroeconomy. The financial market does not move in tandem with the real economy, and after the suspension of the gold exchange standard, it resembles a bird freed from its cage, soaring higher and higher into open air.

History also challenges the argument of "price discovery." The infamous speculative bubble in the Dutch tulip market during the 1600s is highlighted as one of the earliest examples of market bubbles. Speculation drove the value of tulip bulbs to extremes during the early to mid-1600s. At one point, a buyer offered 5 hectares (12 acres) of land for a Semper Augustus' bulb (MacKay, 1852). A record showed 40 bulbs sold for 100,000 florins (also known as Dutch guilders), while a skilled craftsman made on average around 150 florins a year. The speculators believed that Semper Augustus was the holy grail of all tulip bulbs, which was the greatest achievement of horticulture. Ironically, it was the viral infection that made Semper Augustus extraordinary and beautiful by breaking the normal color and adding stunningly alternating white or yellow stripes, but it also destroyed the bulb's vigor and heredity. The example of the Semper Augustus bulb, whose beauty was due to a viral infection, serves as a metaphor for the fleeting and often irrational nature of market speculation.

The famous Semper Augustus bulb is an extinct species, but the financial bubbles are not. Financial market has thrived, alongside financial economics, for decades. Economists developed theories on an aggregate of stocks, a portfolio, in 1952 before the efficient-market hypothesis. Harry Markowitz, Nobel Memorial Prize winner, developed the modern portfolio theory that formalizes diversification, the practice of *The Merchant of Venice* (Shakespeare)—not putting all your eggs in one basket (Fabozzi *et al.*, 2008). In 1962, another Nobel Memorial Prize winner, William F. Sharpe, introduced the capital asset pricing model that relates the individual stock returns to the return of the market, the aggregate of all stocks (Sharpe, 1964).

These theories construct portfolios by minimizing risk for given portfolio returns. However, they primarily focus on minimizing the risks of *asset* portfolios rather than risks in the real economy. Despite these advancements, financial bubbles still occur.

The third argument for the secondary market is liquidity. A metaphor helps to explain liquidity: A billionaire invited his friends to a restaurant. After dinner, he realized he had left his wallet at home. At that moment, the billionaire had a liquidity problem: he did not have the money to pay the bill, despite having billions in assets. This example illustrates that despite wealth, the inability to access money can cause problems.

Banks are the most vulnerable institutions to liquidity problems. Banks make loans for the long term and do not hold large amounts of cash in their safes. If large numbers of customers seek cash from a bank at once, it creates a liquidity crisis, and a bank run can potentially bankrupt the bank.

While the secondary market provides liquidity, it also attracts speculators. This ease encourages speculators to engage in frequent trading, and as Keynes famously said, "the capital development of a country becomes a by-product of the activities of a casino" (see Section 4.2). Speculative activities contribute to market volatility and the formation of bubbles, which can disrupt the financial market and the broader economy.

The second argument—that the secondary market reflects the well-being of a nation's economy—has been adjudicated under the concept of "price discovery." The secondary market fails to reflect the real economy and, in fact, introduces instability. Economic historians have traced the economic crises and found that many economic crises had their roots in the financial sector, where they manifested themselves first through disruptions in the system of financial intermediation.

Periodic speculative bubbles in the secondary markets around the world followed the tulip mania. From 1920 to 1929, the U.S. economy grew by a massive 42%, spurred on by the widespread adoption of mass production and the introduction of electricity. The Great Depression followed the stock market crash, U.S. industrial production plummeted by 47%, and unemployment soared to 20%. A call for interventions led the U.S. government and the Federal Reserve to pump liquidity into the markets in later financial crises, the dot.com bubble in 2000, and the *financial* crisis of 2007–2008. Haldane (2010) showed that the net present value cost of a financial crisis lies anywhere between 1- and 3.5-times world GDP (Cetorelli *et al.*, 2012).

Understanding how the stock market is measured is key to comprehending its performance. Stock market performance is typically reported through indices, which are averages of representative stocks. The Dow Jones Industrial Average (DJIA), Dow Jones, or simply the

Dow, tracks 30 prominent companies listed on stock exchanges in the United States. The Standard and Poor's 500, or simply the S&P 500, is a stock market index tracking the stock performance of 500 of the largest companies listed on stock exchanges in the United States. The Wilshire Associates established the Wilshire 5000 Total Market Index in 1974, naming it for the approximate number of issues it included at the time. The Nasdaq Composite is a stock market index that includes all stocks listed on the Nasdaq stock exchange.[8]

Companies in these indices are weighted differently, leading to different interpretations of market performance. For example, the Dow Jones Index calculates a simple average, while the S&P 500 uses a market-value-weighted average, which considers the total market value of each stock. The use of different stock selections and weighting schemes illustrates how reported prices and returns depend on index construction.

Assume that one million shares of stock ABC are \$150 per share and 10 million shares of stock XYZ are \$10 each. The Dow Jones index calculates the equal-weighted average $(\$150 + \$10)/2 = \$80$. The S&P 500 index calculates the market-value-weighted average, which gives

$$\frac{\$150}{\$150 + 10 \times \$10}\$150 + \frac{10 \times \$10}{\$150 + 10 \times \$10} = \$94.$$

Accounting for the weighting methodology of stock indices, we observe that historical data shows a significant divergence between stock market growth and real GDP growth. For instance, in the period from 1929 to 2022, S&P 500 increased from 24.89 to 4,574, 184-fold increase.[9] In the same period, the U.S. real GDP increased from \$1191 billion to \$21,822 billion at constant 2017 market prices measured in US Dollars, 18.3-fold increase.[10]

This pattern of divergence between financial markets and real economies is observed globally. Financial markets have often outpaced the growth of real economies in other countries as well. The

[8]Wikipedia (wikipedia.org), accessed on April 21, 2024.

[9]*S&P 500 Historical Prices by Year*, multpl.com, accessed on July 13, 2024.

[10]*What Was the U.S. GDP Then?*, 1929–2022, measuringworth.com from the U.S. Bureau of Economic Analysis (1929–2022), BEA.gov. and Louis Johnson (1790–1929), accessed on July 13, 2024.

2022 world GDP was $100,562.01 billion, 2.88 times the 2002 GDP $34,925.12 billion.[11] The real GDP was $13.1 trillion in 2000 and $22.4 trillion in 2023, a 71% increase.[12,13]

Economists infer real GDP from the nominal GDP by adjusting for inflation. The method has multiple problems: what are counted in GDP, how it is counted, and how inflation is measured. In current U.S. inflation calculation, core inflation excludes food and energy, which may not reflect inflation for households' necessary consumption goods.

The relative numbers can be more reliable than the absolute numbers. The GDP per person in the U.S. economy has grown at a steady average rate of around 2% per year, starting at around $3,633 in 1870 and rising to more than $65,415 by 2022 at constant 2017 market prices—an 18-fold increase[14]—and the figures are consistent with Jones (2016).

Figure 4.1 compares the S&P 500 and the U.S. real GDP between 1929 and 2022 by normalizing both to be one in 1929. First, the period before the "Nixon shock"—1971—is in sharp contrast with the period after. Under the gold standard, the S&P 500 moved more closely with real GDP, but after the suspension of gold convertibility, the stock market began to soar independently of real economic growth. The decoupling after 1971 suggests that money creation may have driven financial markets since the end of the gold standard; financial markets have become more speculative.

Second, the random-walk theory of the stock market is popular, but it would be delusional to think the stock prices are random in light of Figure 4.1. The random walk theory of stock prices suggests that stock price movements are unpredictable and follow a random

---

[11] World GDP 1960–2023, MacroTrends.net, accessed July 5, 2024.

[12] Statista (statista.com), accessed on August 13, 2024.

[13] Other factors affect the calculations of the historical returns, and reported returns vary widely. Survivorship bias affects the returns of stock indices. Acheson *et al.* found that all of the return to stockholders came from dividends rather than capital gain for the British equity market in the period 1825–1870, after adjusting for survivorship bias (Acheson *et al.*, 2009).

[14] *What Was the U.S. GDP Then?* 1929–2022, measuringworth.com from the U.S. Bureau of Economic Analysis (1929–2022) and Louis Johnson (1790–1929), accessed on July 13, 2024.

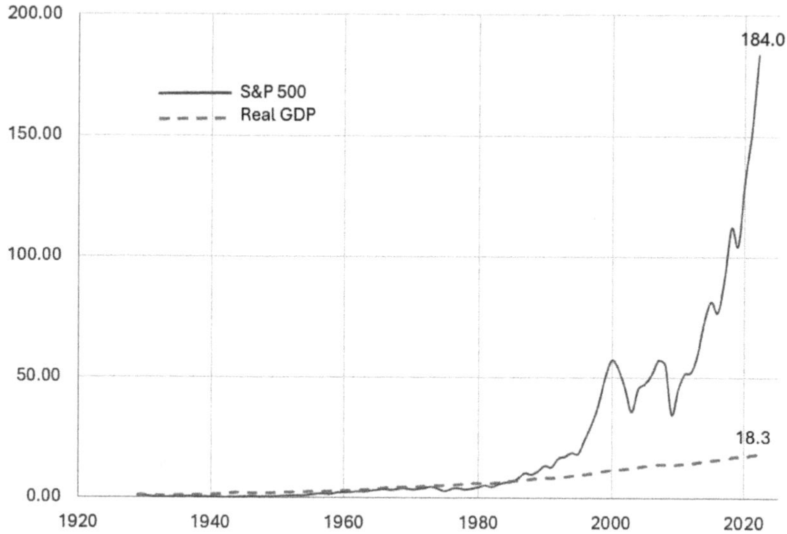

Fig. 4.1. Historical S&P 500 index and real GDP.

path. Stock prices, at the very least, need to be detrended before considering them as random-walk processes.

However, traditional finance labels high stock returns "the risk premium puzzle" and attributes the excess returns in stock markets to the risk investors take. A large body of literature has documented asset pricing, including real assets—land and real estate (Oikarinen, 2014; Smith *et al.*, 1988). Not just economics and finance literature, other disciplines that are traditionally unrelated to asset pricing have been publishing papers on the subject, which has become one of the hottest research topics. However, the "risk premium puzzle" may be posing the wrong question. Explanation of abnormal stock return by risk is insufficient; factors beyond risk, such as the role of money, play a significant part in driving stock returns. Money has much more to do with the stock return than risk does.

Despite the divergence between the financial market and the real economy, people often interpret a booming stock market as economic prosperity, and politicians love to claim a market boom as the result of their successful economic policies. Even the most brilliant economic minds, such as Irving Fisher and John Maynard Keynes, did not anticipate the stock market crash of 1929, despite their focus on the role of money in the economy, they failed to foresee how monetary factors could distort the stock market.

Irving Fisher was among the first economists to highlight the instability of the banking system, but he did not foresee stock-market instability. As noted earlier, he was unprepared for the collapse of the stock market bubble. Fisher's conviction in the self-correcting tendency of markets led him to dismiss evidence of overvaluation, maintaining that the market's strength was sustainable and that, in the long run, prices would converge to their true value. Although Keynes likened the stock market to a casino (see Section 4.2), he did not foresee the 1929 crash and incurred significant losses. He did not make financial-market dysfunction a key explanation, while interpreting the wider crisis mainly in terms of collapsing expectations, volatile private investment, and deficient aggregate demand.

Early in the COVID-19 pandemic, in February 2020, a headline in the news said, "Coronavirus wipes out $1.7 trillion in U.S. stock market value in two days."[15] The figure is not merely mind-boggling; it inevitably raises the question: "Where did the money go?"

4.1.1.1 *Capitalization*

The $1.7 trillion loss in the U.S. market is "fictitious," the loss of *capitalization.* In finance, capitalization primarily refers to the total dollar value of a company. The most common usage denotes the market capitalization (market cap) of a firm, the market price multiplied by its publicly traded shares, which serves as a primary measure of corporate size.

The concept also extends to idle assets. Gold capitalization is calculated by multiplying the total estimated above-ground stock of gold (all gold ever mined and available) by the current market price per unit, typically per troy ounce. Bitcoin market capitalization is determined by multiplying the current price per coin by the circulating supply of coins, which represents the number of coins mined to date, excluding those proven to be permanently lost. As of late November 2025, estimates place the total market value of gold

[15]Fitzgerald, Maggie (February 25, 2020), CNBC.com, accessed on November 26, 2023.

at approximately $29 trillion, while Bitcoin's market capitalization stands near $1.8 trillion.

Here, capitalization is fictitious for a different reason from Marx's "fictitious capital." A supermarket has 1,000 pounds of potatoes and a quarter per pound; thus, the total value of the potatoes is $250. Similarly, the total value, *the market capitalization*, of a firm's common stock is the price per share multiplied by the number of shares. Applied to other assets, for example, the latest price paid for a house becomes the value of other similar houses in the neighborhood. If the price goes up by $10,000, then the total value of 20 neighboring, similar houses increases by $200,000. In the U.S., recent sales of a property affect the appraisal value of similar houses. But, if all the neighbors put their houses on the market and ask for $10,000 more, they are unlikely to get the price they ask for. But the 1,000 pounds of potatoes will be sold at $0.25 per pound.

In the above examples, the market value does not differentiate between the real and the fictitious price. Capitalization is fictitious because a large proportion of it is based on a fictitious price. In the market $100,000 purchases 1,000 shares of a stock; each share is purchased for $100, which is the realized price. In contrast, if the company has 10,000 shares outstanding, then the capitalization is $1,000,000. This specific calculation determines the market value of a stock for its weight within the S&P 500 index (see Section 4.1.1). For stocks that are not traded, the price is not realized. That is one way to understand what is happening to money and prices.

Goods or assets change hands at real prices in transactions. The price tags in supermarkets and department stores show the real prices. In certain parts of the world, people bargain for prices. The latest sale price is real for the house buyer and seller, but a fictitious price for the neighboring, similar houses. The local government uses the fictitious price to determine the appraisal value, the basis for property tax.[16]

[16]Infrequent appraisals often lag the housing market and create a problem for price approvals in a booming real estate market, according to the National Association of Realtors Confidence Index Survey. Lenders typically do not approve a price for a house that appraises below the market price because the appraisal value, like the collateral value, is less than the price. In a downturn in the real

The stock market is much more liquid than the housing market. Stock prices change constantly, and the market capitalization calculated based on the latest price changes accordingly. For example, a company has one million shares outstanding, and each share sells at \$100. Then, the company's stock would have a market cap of \$100 million. If the latest trade is 100,000 shares at \$110, then the market capitalization goes up to \$110 million. That is, a \$1 increase in the stock price pushes the stock capitalization up by \$1 million. The *capitalization multiplier* m is the ratio of the total shares outstanding to the shares actively traded, $m = 10 = 1$ million/100,000. For the traded stocks, the price is real. The funds are transferred from buyers to sellers, and the corresponding gains and losses are thereby realized. Idle shares move up and down in value with the price of those actively traded. The value of those idle shares is fictitious because, if all shareholders wanted to realize the gain of \$10 per share by selling their shares on the market right after the latest price increase, they would not get \$10 gain but would more likely incur a loss.[17]

The Dow market capitalization as of December 7, 2023, is \$35.69 billion, and the average daily volume is 303 million. S&P 500 market capitalization is \$38.433 trillion as of December 2023,[18] and the daily average volume is 3.8 billion.[19] The number of Tesla stock (symbol TSLA) shares outstanding as of December 2023 is 3.176 billion, and its 65-day average trading volume is 121.06 million.[20] On average, people trade 4% of Tesla stock daily.

People put their savings in pension funds and mutual funds, with the fund managers making trading decisions. The fund turnover ratio, total transactions per year divided by total market value of a fund, tells how actively the manager trades a fund. The day traders buy and sell multiple times per day. On average, there were 450,000 individual day traders each year, of which about half (277,000) traded

---

estate market, homeowners face another problem: the difficulty of getting their property tax assessments adjusted.

[17]The literature on market micro-structure generally agrees that a large imbalance between sell and buy orders indicates private information. The market maker increases the bid-ask spread to compensate for the risk of market making.

[18]sliejeharts.com, accessed on December 10, 2023.

[19]yahoo.com, accessed on December 10, 2023.

[20]Barrons.com, accessed on December 12, 2023.

in amounts larger than $20,000 each day[21] and roughly $125 billion per day. Only a fraction of stockholders trades very actively for certain stocks, while other shareholders leave their retirement plans to financial institutions.

Index funds and the exchange-traded funds (ETFs)[22] are exceedingly popular, with people trading those funds much more than individual stocks. As a result, the market capitalization of the stocks in ETF fluctuates constantly due to ETF trading activities.

During COVID-19 pandemic, trading wiped out $1.7 trillion in the U.S. market. A large portion of this loss was fictitious money, which only disappeared from the financial statements. Fictitious prices and capitalization are not real; do they matter? For those people who have made money or lost money, they do matter psychologically. But whether they matter to the real economy is a separate question.

4.1.2 *Idle assets*

Figure 4.1 shows the index of common stock. The return on common stock implies a high opportunity cost for holding cash. The high returns on stocks create an incentive for people not to keep their money in cash, as the potential gains from holding assets significantly outweigh the benefits of liquidity. This stands in contrast to Keynes' emphasis on the liquidity preference theory, which stresses the safety and flexibility of holding cash (see p. 96).

As the money supply increases over time, the influx of new money into the markets can be likened to an overflowing reservoir. The stock market, being just one of many receptacles, experiences diminished returns when inundated with excessive capital. Consequently, this money flows into other areas, leading to an increase in "idle assets" as repositories for accumulated wealth. Money creation leads to a growing prevalence of non-productive assets as wealth accumulates within them.

The idle assets have a minimum *direct* effect on the real economy. Consider a wealthy collector who displays Pablo Picasso's paintings in his mansion. While the painting is immensely valuable, it does

[21]currentmarketvaluation.com, accessed on April 27, 2024.

[22]ETFs are like mutual funds but are traded in the same way as stocks.

not directly contribute to the production or consumption of goods in the economy. Toni Clayton, an art specialist, said, "Picasso is one of the top five selling artists in the West. His works have consistently proven to be worthwhile blue-chip investments, increasing on average 16% in value."[23]

Most idle assets are durable and in limited supply. When overall money supply increases, money flows into the market of idle assets, driving up prices. A rising tide lifts all boats. People who are interested in a specific idle asset speculate about the future demand of the asset. When money does not increase, a speculator must sell other assets to pay for the assets expected to have a higher return, which causes price fluctuations. These fluctuations occur without any change in the broader money supply of the economy.

In the following hypothetical example, we consider an economy with only an idle asset market—similar to one with a fixed number of existing houses with no place to build new houses. For such an economy, we replace the production output Y in Eq. (2.4) with the quantity of the idle asset Q, and limit M to the money circulating within the idle asset market. The generalized quantity theory of money can then be applied to this economy as shown by the equation:

$$MV = PQ. \tag{4.1}$$

The money M_s flowing into and out of a specific asset market has a direct impact only on the assets traded Q_s at time s. The quantity theory of money gives the relation between the money and trading price $M_sV = PQ_s$. The market capitalization PQ, where Q is the total number of the assets, which is a multiple time of the assets traded on the market. Thus, capitalization ratio is $m_s = Q/Q_s$, where m_s is the capitalization multiplier and $PQ = m_sPQ_s = m_sM_sV$. Capitalization amplifies the money's effect across all the assets, whether traded or not. A small sum of money can inflate market capitalization disproportionately. For simplicity, interpret M as the hypothetical amount of money that takes account of the multiplier, $M = m_sM_s$.

[23] *A Buyer's Guide to Pablo Picasso Prints*, myartbroker.com, retrieved on May 17, 2024.

Taking the derivative of Eq. (4.1) gives inflation π:

$$\pi = \frac{\dot{P}}{P} = \frac{\dot{M}}{M} - \frac{\dot{Q}}{Q}. \tag{4.2}$$

Inflation is the rate of price increase, $\dot{P}/P$, which increases with the percentage increase of the money $\dot{M}/M$ and decreases with the percentage increase of the idle asset $\dot{Q}/Q$. In a story, a group of struggling artists, desperate for recognition and financial stability, conspired to fake the death of one of their members. They knew that the death of an artist often leads to a surge in the value of his work, as the supply of new pieces ceases (represented by $\dot{Q} = 0$), which increases the money effect on the prices of the artist's earlier works. In general, the "idle assets," such as antiques, stamps, and paintings, have fixed supply $\dot{Q}/Q = 0$. Thus,

$$\pi = \frac{\dot{P}}{P} = \frac{\dot{M}}{M}. \tag{4.3}$$

More money goes to the goods market, driving the price up; people call it inflation. But when money goes to the asset market, people call the price increase "return on investment" or "price appreciation." Nevertheless, through the lens of the money identity, the "price appreciation" or "return on investment" is the same as inflation π for the "idle asset." This book consistently characterizes $\dot{P}/P > 0$ as inflation for any goods and assets. This is crucial to demystify the role of money in an economy.

Extend the definition of Σ in Chapter 3 to the money that comes into an idle-asset market and define:

$$\frac{\dot{M}}{M} = \Sigma \tag{4.4}$$

and

$$\pi = \frac{\dot{P}}{P} = \frac{\dot{M}}{M} = \Sigma, \tag{4.5}$$

in which the money expansion simply creates inflation of idle assets.

The holders of the "idle assets" maximize their consumption:

$$\max_{c} \int_0^T e^{-\rho t} \ln C dt, \tag{4.6}$$

where C is the consumption goods measured by money. The inflation of the idle asset does not affect the price of the consumption goods *directly*. Assume a stable price for the consumption goods, the real consumption increases with C, and the owners' budget constraint is:

$$\dot{\Phi} = \pi\Phi + wL - C, \tag{4.7}$$

where Φ is the total wealth of the owners of an idle asset, w is the average wage of the owners, and L is the total number of owners, and

$$\begin{aligned} &\Phi = \Phi_0 \; at \; t = 0, \\ &\dot{C} < \infty. \end{aligned} \tag{4.8}$$

Using the same method introduced in Chapter 1, the Hamiltonian for the consumption maximization of Eq. (4.6) is:

$$\mathcal{H}(\Phi, C, \theta, t) = \ln C + \theta(\pi\Phi + wL - C). \tag{4.9}$$

The first-order condition for the consumption requires:

$$\frac{\partial \mathcal{H}(\Phi, C, \theta, t)}{\partial C} = \frac{1}{C} - \theta = 0, \tag{4.10}$$

which gives θ:

$$\theta = \frac{1}{C}. \tag{4.11}$$

The first-order condition for the wealth Φ is:

$$\frac{\partial \mathcal{H}(\Phi, C, \theta, t)}{\partial \Phi} = \theta\pi = \rho\theta - \dot{\theta}. \tag{4.12}$$

Using Eq. (4.11), we have:

$$\dot{C} = (\pi - \rho)\, C. \tag{4.13}$$

Compared to the Ramsey rule Eq. (1.41), Eq. (4.13) replaces the real return $r = f'(k) - \delta k$ with the price appreciation π. Inflation drives consumption, and, thus, inflation—the return on idle assets—has a *wealth effect* on the economy.

This economy has a different stability from the Ramsey economy. Setting Eqs. (4.7) and (4.13) to be zero gives the equilibrium point (see Chapter 1),

$$\begin{aligned}\dot{C}^* &= F_1(\Phi^*, C^*) = (\pi - \rho)C^*,\\ \dot{\Phi}^* &= F_2(\Phi^*, C^*) = \pi\Phi^* + wL - C^*.\end{aligned} \tag{4.14}$$

Equation (4.14) suggests that inflation—the price appreciation—can keep an economy afloat without the real economy under two conditions. First, the inflation $\pi\Phi$ covers the difference between consumption and wage income $C - wL$, where the wage income comes from working for the idle asset market, such as the fees for managing other people's money. The wealth increase $\pi\Phi$ includes the gains of capitalization. The owners of the idle asset can sell the asset to buy consumption goods. For those who have a large holding of the idle asset, they can stay afloat without wage income if $\pi\Phi = C$.

Second, the inflation rate balances the discount factor. In an idle-asset market, equilibrium is achieved when the rate of price appreciation equals the discount factor, $\pi = \rho$. In contrast, in the real economy, equilibrium requires the real net return to equal the discount factor, $r = \rho$.

The difference between the idle asset economy and an economy based on production is that while price appreciation π in idle-asset markets might increase the wealth of asset holders, it does not contribute to the production of goods, creating a disconnect between financial gains and real economic activity. The price appreciation is often considered an "investment return" but crucially distinct from real returns, as it does not result from investment in capital stock or increases in output. Instead, this appreciation of idle assets leads to an indirect money effect, where the owners of these assets have growing wealth and spend the "return" on consumption accordingly.

Like the Ramsey model, it is convenient to collect the partial derivatives in a matrix $\mathcal{M}$, the Jacobian matrix that characterizes the system behavior near the equilibrium point:

$$\frac{d}{dt}\begin{bmatrix} C - C^* \\ k - k^* \end{bmatrix} = \mathcal{M}\begin{bmatrix} C - C^* \\ k - k^* \end{bmatrix}, \tag{4.15}$$

$$\mathcal{M} = \begin{bmatrix} \frac{\partial F_1}{\partial C^*} & \frac{\partial F_1}{\partial k^*} \\ \frac{\partial F_2}{\partial C^*} & \frac{\partial F_2}{\partial k^*} \end{bmatrix} = \begin{bmatrix} 0 & 0 \\ -1 & \pi \end{bmatrix}, \tag{4.16}$$

which has two eigenvalues 0 and π.

A zero eigenvalue implies that the equilibrium of this economy is not an isolated point but a line. This line is determined by

$$\pi\Phi^* = C^* - wL. \tag{4.17}$$

Any pair $\{C^*, \Phi^*\}$ that satisfies Eq. (4.17) is an equilibrium point, since C^* is independent of Φ^* in Eq. (4.14). The dynamics near the equilibrium point is given by:

$$\frac{d}{dt}(\Phi - \Phi^*) = \pi(\Phi - \Phi^*) \tag{4.18}$$

and wealth follows an explicit solution:

$$\Phi_t - \Phi^* = (\Phi_0 - \Phi^*)e^{\pi t}. \tag{4.19}$$

For a positive inflation rate ($\pi > 0$), the economy is unstable. At equilibrium, the "inflation income" $\pi\Phi^*$ bridges the gap between consumption and wages, $C^* - wL$. If the economy experiences a slight increase in wealth, such that $\Phi_0 > \Phi^*$, it receives more "inflation income." This compounding effect pushes the economy further away from equilibrium.

Conversely, if the economy loses a small amount of wealth, its "inflation income" decreases, and more wealth must be diverted to maintain consumption. This loss also compounds, as lower wealth generates even less "inflation income," pushing the economy further away from equilibrium.

Figure 4.2 shows a phase plot of an idle-assets economy with inflation. The dashed line represents the equilibrium condition, Eq. (4.17). Any point on this line is in equilibrium. Points off the line are unstable. The two small circles represent economies that are not in equilibrium, both drifting toward the small squares. The economy above the line, with wealth greater than equilibrium, moves upward, while the economy below the line, with less wealth, moves downward.

In contrast, under deflation ($\pi < 0$), the economy is stable. At equilibrium, the difference between wages and consumption, $wL - C^*$, must cover the deflation loss $\pi\Phi^*$. If wealth increases slightly, such that $\Phi_0 > \Phi^*$, the deflation loss rises, but the wage surplus does not, causing the economy to revert toward equilibrium. If the economy loses a small amount of wealth, the deflation loss decreases. The difference between wages and consumption, $wL - C^*$ exceeds the

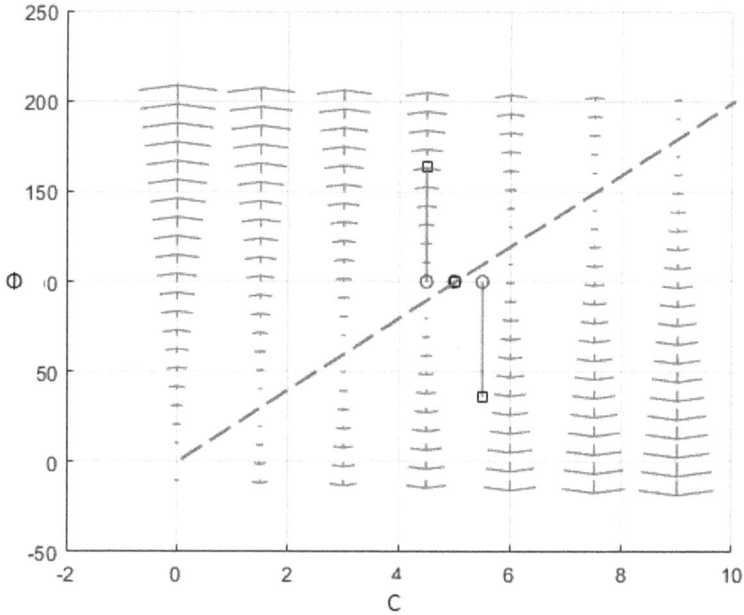

Fig. 4.2. An inflationary idle asset economy.

required amount to cover the loss, pulling the economy back toward equilibrium.

Figure 4.3 shows the phase plot of an idle-assets economy under deflation. The dashed line again represents equilibrium. The two small circles indicate economies that are out of equilibrium but are moving toward the small squares, converging toward equilibrium.

The idle asset economy is not merely theoretical. For instance, tax havens, which do not produce consumption goods, often manage large amounts of wealth—their own and other people's money. With the return π on their wealth and management fees, tax havens can buy consumption goods from elsewhere in the country or abroad.

Wealth represents an individual's claim on global resources. As Keynes noted: "Moreover, in order that an individual saver may attain his desired goal of the ownership of wealth, it is not necessary that a new capital asset should be produced wherewith to satisfy him. The mere act of saving by one individual, being two-sided as we have shown above, forces some other individual to transfer to him some article of wealth old or new" (Keynes, 1936).

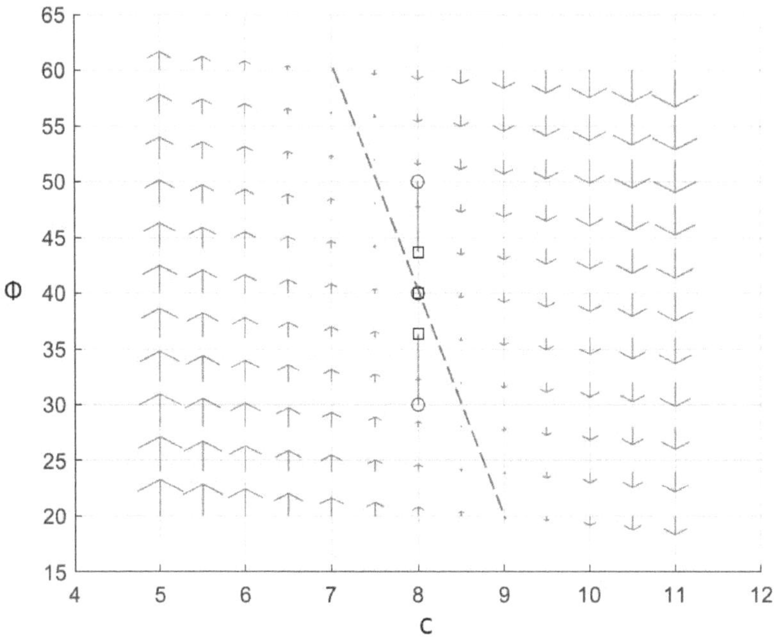

Fig. 4.3. A deflationary idle asset economy.

To visualize the relationship between wealth and ownership, consider Fig. 3.1 as a representation of global wealth distribution. The area under the curve represents total global wealth, which governs ownership of global production capacity. Wealth determines one's share of the pool. If some individuals or groups acquire more wealth—while "idle assets" continue to grow even as their owners sleep (see p. 275)—their share of global output rises, while others' shares must fall, given that the total output is fixed in the short run.

Although changes in ownership shares often unfold gradually and remain imperceptible in the short term, they become evident over time as the wealthy consistently accumulate assets—a process that has accelerated in recent centuries. This accumulated wealth is frequently converted into durable assets, including idle assets.

4.1.2.1 *Positive feedback*

The values of idle assets grow exponentially, if money supply Σ into the idle asset grows at a constant rate. The money supply rate determines the inflation of idle assets, driving the positive feedback described in Eq. (4.19). Positive feedback is encased in common things (see Appendix A.3.7 of Chapter 1). Compound interest rates are an example. In the language of a dynamic system, assume the input is \$100 and the output is \$110 at a 10% interest rate. Take a fixed fraction of the \$10 interest and feed it back to the input. The next output is more than \$10 and feeds back an even larger amount. "Compound interest is the eighth wonder of the world," while the wonder is just a consequence of positive feedback. Bond has built positive feedback in the system.

People's psychology can amplify the feedback effects. The tulip mania in Amsterdam in the early 1600s is a case where an idle asset exploded the whole market. When prices of assets rise, more participants are attracted, further driving up prices and generating momentum. This phenomenon is referred to as *herding* in behavioral finance, where people imitate others' actions, leading to self-reinforcing trends. In asset markets, herding can distort price correlations between assets that would otherwise be less connected (MacKenzie, 2003).

Behavioral economics calls the herding behavior *imitation*. Market stability arises when firms pursue diverse strategies and specialize in different niches. Yet imitation among firms can alter price dynamics, and when market participants follow one another's strategies, they can create price distortions and destabilize markets. When the effect of imitation runs deep, disastrous *crowding* occurs, causing extreme prices far more likely than under normal conditions (Lux and Marchesi, 1999; White, 2001).

Self-fulfilling prophecies are a classic example of a phenomenon driven by positive feedback loops. For instance, a group of traders, or "chartists," uses the so-called "technical analysis" as a guide of their trading decisions. Traders using technical analysis can collectively create the very price movements predicted by the analysis, thereby reinforcing the perceived accuracy of their trading strategies. Fortunately, technical analysis has various trading techniques, which are inconsistent with one another. The diversity of technical trading techniques helps prevent full synchronization of traders' actions, which mitigates the risk of extreme price movements.

As a counterbalance to positive feedback, a group of traders and fund managers—often known as contrarians or value investors—adopt a countercyclical strategy, actively buying during market downturns (the "dip") and selling during upswings (the "rally"). This behavior helps stabilize markets by moderating extreme price movements.

The banking sector is particularly vulnerable to the destructive power of positive feedback, as demonstrated by bank runs. Even a small rumor can trigger widespread panic, leading depositors to withdraw their money en masse, which depletes a bank's cash reserves and turns the rumor into reality. This chain reaction is a classic example of how small events can trigger system-wide consequences in a system governed by positive feedback (Ennis and Keister, 2010; Diamond and Dybvig, 1983).

The farming economy in Chapter 1 also illustrates positive feedback, which accelerates the growth or decline of the farms. If the seed supply exceeds the previous year's level, a higher crop yield generates more seeds for the following year. Without increasing consumption, the additional seeds feed back into crop production and accelerate the growth of the farming economy. Conversely, if the seed supply is lower than the previous year's, a reduced crop yield generates fewer seeds for the next year. Without reducing consumption, this feedback accelerates the decline in the farming economy.

Positive feedback serves as a wedge that widens the gap between the rich and the poor. Those who own assets capture an increasing portion of the world's resources, and those who do not have a decreasing share. The initial gap could be small, but the exponential growth creates an increasingly larger chasm between those who have and have not. In the old days, millionaires were rich people. Today, there are 2,781 billionaires in the world.[24] We will have trillionaires soon if money creation continues at today's pace.

4.1.3 *Working assets*

When people talk about the stock market, they generally mean the secondary market, where shares trade after their initial issuance. While firms can raise money in the secondary market, they prioritize other sources of financing for new projects or production

[24]Barrons.com, retrieved on April 3, 2024.

expansion. According to the pecking order theory (Myers and Majluf, 1984), internal financing—such as reinvesting profits—is preferred over external sources, with debt being favored over issuing new stock, which is considered a last resort. Another theory—the signaling theory (Spence, 1973)—suggests that firms only issue new shares when they perceive that their stock price is at a peak, which sends a negative signal to the market. Conversely, borrowing money is seen as a positive signal because it implies that firms have good investment opportunities and that their stock price is likely to rise. Eckbo *et al.* (2000) reported that common stock returns of industrial firms that made seasoned equity offerings (SEOs) underperformed control groups that did not conduct SEOs by 40–60% over the three-to-five years following the offering date.

Therefore, the secondary market does not serve as a major funding source for firms. Instead, its high liquidity and potential for stock price appreciation incentivize entrepreneurs to raise capital in the primary market. Without it, fewer entrepreneurs would pursue public financing, because the secondary market gives common stocks a "double life": they are both a representation of a company's real capital and a liquid, speculative financial asset.

As real capital goods, stocks are "working assets," while as financial assets, they represent "fictitious capital" and are "idle assets." As "working assets," stock values grow through capital accumulation, whereas as "idle assets," prices rise with the money supply. This dual role reveals the shadow side of stocks, reinforcing the arguments against "price discovery" in stock markets in Section 4.1.2. Therefore, the prices of individual stocks and indexes come from two sources: capital accumulation and monetary expansion. The inflation effect, as part of the price increase of a stock, mixes with the real growth of a firm's production capacity.

Public firms can have multiple classes of stock; each designed for different clientele needs. For example, Berkshire Hathaway has 1.45 million Class A shares and $611,244 per share, and 2.17 million Class B shares and $405.40 per share on April 19, 2024. The owners of Class A shares form the stable shareholder base of the company because transaction costs filter out the short-term stockholders. The low price of Class B shares makes the shares affordable to small shareholders and more liquid.

Most firms keep their stock prices per share not too expensive to buy. When a firm deems its stock price too high, the firm splits one share into multiple shares. Stock splits do not change the total value of a firm's stocks. For example, a firm splits one share into two, then one share at \$100 per share before the split becomes two shares at \$50 per share after the split. Similarly, when a firm deems its stock price too low after the price drop, it consolidates multiple shares into one.

To avoid complications in stock pricing, price P, can be simplified as the total capitalization Φ of firms divided by the underlying capital stock K, the amount of real production assets. Therefore, the relation is given by $\Phi = PK$.

Taking the derivative of $\Phi = PK$ with respect to time, we decompose the wealth change into two components[25]:

$$\dot{\Phi} = P\dot{K} + \dot{P}K = \frac{\dot{P}}{P}\Phi + P\dot{K} = \pi\Phi + P\dot{K} \tag{4.20}$$

or

$$\dot{\phi} = \phi + P\dot{k} = \pi\phi + P\dot{k}, \tag{4.21}$$

where $\phi = \Phi/L$.

If the Fed, banks, and the government could keep prices stable all the time, $\dot{P} = 0$, then we have the wealth ϕ as a good measure of the real economy, and the total value of common stock changes with the rate of change of capital stock $\dot{k}$. The other component is *pure* price appreciation (price inflation). When the real economy is in equilibrium, $\dot{k} = 0$, the wealth can still go up,

$$\dot{\phi} = \pi\phi,$$

where $\pi\phi$ is the inflation effect—the pure price appreciation.[26]

[25]Mahalanobis (1953) proposed a two-sector model, built upon Harrod and Domar's models (Domar, 1952). An economy is divided into a financial sector and a consumption goods sector. The control variable allocates resources between the two sectors. The result is a $\{0, 1\}$ control solution.

[26]The well-known *Tobin's q* in Macroeconomics provides the ratio between the market value and its corresponding book values (Kaldor, 1966). Equation (4.21) gives a different explanation of the ratio—the difference—between the market value and the book value or accounting value. Money creates the price appreciation, the inflation, of the price of capital stock. The market price inflated by money differs from the historical price—the book value—of capital stock.

Combining $\phi = Pk$ with the macroeconomic identity, $\dot{k}$ can be rewritten as

$$\frac{d}{dt}\left(\frac{\phi}{P}\right) = \left[f\left(\frac{\phi}{P}\right) - \frac{C}{P} - \delta\frac{\phi}{P}\right], \tag{4.22}$$

where C is the nominal consumption, i.e., consumption measured by money. Substituting Eq. (4.22) into Eq. (4.21), we have the wealth equation that incorporates capital stock:

$$\dot{\phi} = \pi\phi + Pf\left(\frac{\phi}{P}\right) - c - \delta\phi. \tag{4.23}$$

Equation (4.23) is a version of the macroeconomic identity modified by money, specifically by inflation. Households and firms have no control over the money supply. As a result, inflation is set exogenously.

From a household's perspective of a household, the wealth equation (4.23) takes the form of the budget constraint:

$$\dot{\phi} = (r + \pi)\phi + w - c. \tag{4.24}$$

Households own all common stock. Recalling $f(k) = f'(k)k + w/P$ where $f'(k) = r + \delta k$ in Table 1.3, Eq. (4.24) goes back to Eq. (4.23).

The stockholders maximize their consumption c:

$$\max_{c} \int_0^T e^{-\rho t} \ln c dt, \tag{4.25}$$

subject to Eq. (4.23) and

$$\phi = \phi_0,\ c = c_0,\ P = P_0,\ at\ t = 0,$$

$$\dot{c} < \infty, \tag{4.26}$$

$$\dot{\phi} < \infty. \tag{4.27}$$

The major difference between the current model and the Ramsey model is the replacement of capital stock with wealth as the state variable. In this new model, the economy can adjust its capital stock to an optimal level by using its wealth Φ, to purchase capital or vice versa in global markets.

Using the same method introduced in Chapter 1, we solve the utility maximization problem:

$$\mathcal{H}(\phi, c, P, \theta, t) = \ln c + \theta \left[Pf\left(\frac{\phi}{P}\right) - c - \delta\phi \right]. \tag{4.28}$$

Like the Ramsey model, taking the derivative of Eq. (4.28) with respect to c yields the first-order condition of consumption:

$$\frac{\partial \mathcal{H}(\phi, c, P, \theta, t)}{\partial c} = \frac{1}{c} - \theta = 0, \tag{4.29}$$

which gives:

$$\frac{1}{c} = \theta. \tag{4.30}$$

The dynamics of the co-state variable θ is given by:

$$\frac{\partial \mathcal{H}(\phi, c, P, \theta, t)}{\partial \phi} = \theta \left[\pi + f'\left(\frac{\phi}{P}\right) - \delta \right] = \rho\theta - \dot{\theta}, \tag{4.31}$$

which gives:

$$\dot{\theta} = \theta \left[\rho - \pi - f'\left(\frac{\phi}{P}\right) + \delta \right]. \tag{4.32}$$

Substituting Eq. (4.30), we have:

$$\dot{c} = \left[\pi + f'\left(\frac{\phi}{P}\right) - \delta - \rho \right] c. \tag{4.33}$$

At any time τ, the price is given by:

$$\dot{P} = \pi P, \text{ and } P_\tau = P_t e^{\int_0^\tau \pi_s ds}.$$

Remember that price P is a function of time. Since money supply is controlled and fixed, price and inflation satisfy the money identity Eq. (2.4); hence, price is not an additional state variable.

For a central authority seeking to control inflation, it must account for the rate of change in real economic output. In this simple model, capital stock is not treated as a state variable, since the asset owners can freely invest or divest to maximize their wealth. The implication is that if the combination—real return plus inflation—is lower than returns in other markets, including idle-asset markets, the asset owners will avoid investing in the capital stock in this market. Thus, price appreciation (inflation, π) becomes a key determinant of the competitiveness of a working asset market.

4.1.3.1 *Wealth effect*

In Eq. (4.33), inflation π has a *wealth effect* on the consumption of asset owners. In his 2013 bestseller *Capital in the Twenty-First Century*, Thomas Piketty demonstrates that capitalism is shifting away from a "meritocratic" society—where wealth is earned through labor—toward a form of patrimonial capitalism reminiscent of the 19th century, in which wealth is inherited. This dynamic rests on the condition that the rate of return on assets exceeds the rate of economic growth ($\pi > 0$). The poor, lacking assets, remain excluded; the middle class can reinvest only a fraction of their income; and the wealthy reinvest surplus wealth into assets, thereby fueling inflation.

The Fed pays close attention to the wealth effect and worries that a stock market downturn reduces households' consumption. The Federal Open Market Committee (FOMC) determines the monetary policy of the Fed. Each year, the FOMC schedules eight meetings, at which it reviews economic and financial conditions and decides on open market operations—purchasing and selling securities in the open market. Since Alan Greenspan highlighted the wealth effect, the Fed has been watching the financial markets closely and pumping up the markets. Cieslak and Vissing-Jorgensen examined the language of FOMC minutes and transcripts and found that the FOMC discussed the stock market conditions in its meetings and frequently emphasized the wealth effect on consumption as one of the main channels through which the stock market affects the economy (Cieslak and Vissing-Jorgensen, 2021).

Table 4.1. Balance sheet — the Federal Reserve Bank.

Assets		**Liabilities & Equity**	
Assets		Liabilities	
Treasuries	100	Reserves	100
			2
		Dividend	3
		Government Deposit	-3
			-2
		Equity	
		Interest	3
		Dividend	-3
Total	100	Total	100

The Fed's reports on open market operations generally do not conform to Generally Accepted Accounting Principles (GAAP) or government Cost Accounting Standards (CAS). Table 4.1 illustrates the changes in the balance sheet resulting from a central bank's market operations conducted through member banks' reserve accounts. For example, the Fed buys \$100 million short-term Treasuries from banks, which then pay \$5 million in interest to the Fed. Of that \$5 million, \$2 million is paid to the banks, and \$3 million is paid to the shareholders of the Fed, based on their holding ratios. The Fed then returns the \$100 million to the banks, injecting \$100 million in reserves into the financial system (Yamaguchi, 2021).

Under the current system, most central banks function as lenders of last resort to institutions that cannot obtain credit elsewhere and whose collapse could have serious implications for the economy. This role obligates central banks with a "duty to rescue."

However, central banks are prohibited from "printing" money or directly underwriting government borrowings. They must be creative in rescuing struggling institutions and have become more aggressive in responding to major crises. Their measures range from purchasing government securities in open market operations (OMO) to implementing quantitative easing (QE) to inject more liquidity into the financial system and support failing financial institutions.

The Bank of Japan introduced quantitative easing, or QE for short, after having negative interest rates in 1999 to avoid the meltdown of the real estate and financial markets. With interest rates at their Zero Lower Bound, the Bank of Japan shifted its focus toward targeting quantity variables—Quantitative Easing. Unlike the normal policy of a central bank, QE involved purchasing large quantities of government and other securities to increase liquidity in the banking system, encourage lending, and stimulate asset prices. The bank hoped that a high enough level of reserves eventually would spill over into the broader economy and drive asset prices up while removing deflationary forces (Joyce *et al.*, 2012).

The policy became widespread after the 2007–2008 financial crisis, with central banks, including the Fed, the central banks of the Euro area, and the UK, adopting similar strategies to avoid drastic asset price declines. The Fed injected money into financial markets at a much greater scale than the Bank of Japan did earlier (Murphey, 2008).

If governments and central banks have learned lessons from history, the first is that "Money saves the economy." Ben S. Bernanke set the record for money creation in his term as Chair of the Fed.[27] Then, Jerome Powell, Chair of the Federal Reserve, broke Bernanke's record in money creation. Unlike limited resources of production, governments and banks can create money without limit and keep money supply expanding.

Economists are debating the policy of quantitative easing. The Bank of Japan argued that the policy is ineffective (Fujiki *et al.*, 2001). Critics contend that it also leads to asset bubbles and inflation, which can harm the real economy. The Fed's focus on wealth effect has resulted in sustained asset price booms that diverge from the underlying fundamentals of the real economy. The larger the bubble becomes, the more money the Federal Reserve must inject to keep the wealth effect intact (Leonard, 2020).

Milton Friedman once famously said, "Inflation is always and everywhere a monetary phenomenon in the sense that it is and can be produced only by a more rapid increase in the quantity of money than in output." Friedrich August von Hayek held that the problem

[27]Ben S. Bernanke received the Nobel Prize for his research on financial crises.

lay with governments and made a strong statement about history: "I do not think it is an exaggeration to say history is largely a history of inflation, usually inflations engineered by governments for the gain of governments." Banks, governments, central banks, and asset markets are all elements in the inflation pump.

4.1.3.2 *Money effect on stability*

Inflation changes the equilibrium point of the economy:

$$\dot{c^*} = F_1(c^*, \phi^*) = \left[f'\left(\frac{\phi^*}{P}\right) - \delta + \pi - \rho\right] c^* = 0,$$

$$\dot{\phi^*} = F_2(c^*, \phi^*) = \pi\phi^* + Pf\left(\frac{\phi^*}{P}\right) - c^* - \delta\phi^*) - c^* = 0. \quad (4.34)$$

Similar to the previous stability analysis, collecting the partial derivatives in the Jacobian matrix gives:

$$\frac{d}{dt}\begin{bmatrix} c - c^* \\ \phi - \phi^* \end{bmatrix} = \mathcal{M}\begin{bmatrix} c - c^* \\ \phi - \phi^* \end{bmatrix}, \quad (4.35)$$

$$\mathcal{M} = \begin{bmatrix} \frac{\partial F_1}{\partial c^*} & \frac{\partial F_1}{\partial \phi^*} \\ \frac{\partial F_2}{\partial c^*} & \frac{\partial F_2}{\partial \phi^*} \end{bmatrix} = \begin{bmatrix} f'\left(\frac{\phi^*}{P}\right) - \delta + \pi - \rho & \frac{\partial}{\partial \phi^*} f'\left(\frac{\phi^*}{P}\right) c^* \\ -1 & f'\left(\frac{\phi^*}{P}\right) - \delta + \pi \end{bmatrix}.$$

Using Eq. (4.34) simplifies the matrix to

$$\mathcal{M} = \begin{bmatrix} 0 & \frac{\partial}{\partial \phi^*} f'\left(\frac{\phi^*}{P}\right) c^* \\ -1 & \rho \end{bmatrix}, \quad (4.36)$$

which has two eigenvalues:

$$2\left(\rho \pm \sqrt{\rho^2 - 4c^* \frac{\partial}{\partial \phi^*} f'\left(\frac{\phi^*}{P}\right)}\right), \quad (4.37)$$

which represents the saddle stability of the real economy.

The stock market exhibits a similar stability to the real economy. It can be compared to the Ramsey model, which also has four different types. The sign of the expression $\pi + f'(\frac{\varphi^*}{P}) - \delta - \rho$ determines whether an economy is "frugal" or "lavish." A negative sign indicates a "frugal" economy characterized by declining consumption, while a positive sign reflects a "lavish" economy with increasing consumption. However, unlike the Ramsey model, the sign of π (inflation rate) further influences whether an economy is "frugal" or "lavish." Deflation pulls wealth toward a "frugal" economy, while inflation pushes wealth toward a "lavish" economy.

By introducing four types of money economies based on the dynamics of wealth and inflation, we categorize them as follows: (1) frugal with wealth contraction, (2) frugal with wealth expansion, (3) lavish with wealth contraction, and (4) lavish with wealth expansion. The money supply plays a role in determining the type of economy, and inflation directly impacts the equilibrium and stability of the system.

However, equilibrium of the real economy does not guarantee equilibrium in the money economy. When π (inflation or deflation) is non-zero, Eq. (4.34) implies that the equilibrium in an economy with a stock market differs from that of the real economy. When idle-asset markets are taken into account, achieving overall economic equilibrium becomes even more unlikely. If the real economy reaches equilibrium, the asset markets can drive the economy away from it toward the equilibrium of the money economy. Conversely, even when the money economy reaches equilibrium, the underlying real economy may continue to change.

Thus, a necessary condition for achieving overall economic equilibrium is that inflation is zero ($\pi = 0$). As indicated in Eq. (2.11), stable prices ensure that the money economy coincides with the real economy.

Inflation and the wealth effect can drive extreme outcomes. The wealth effect supports consumption growth, leading to a "lavish, wealth expansion" economy. This effect creates positive feedback, potentially leading to asset bubbles. However, growth unsupported by the real economy is fragile and can quickly reverse. When the money supply contracts, the positive wealth effect becomes negative, consumption declines, and the economy transitions to a "wealth contraction" state. This feedback loop amplifies economic downturns, turning sharp growth into sharp decline.

In 1989, the money printed by the Bank of Japan created a stock price bubble. The Nikkei stock peaked a little shy of 39,000 points. The collapse of the stock market fell 60% in 9 months down to 14,000 by August 1990, which dragged the country into recession and helped trigger a "lost decade." (*The US won a trade war against Japan. But China is a whole new ball game* by James Griffiths, May 24, 2019, cnn.com, retrieved on January 11, 2024.)

The traditional stock valuation models discount the future profits to give the intrinsic value of a stock, and more sophisticated asset pricing models, such as the capital asset pricing model (Sharpe, 1964), adjust the risk of a stock to give the required return. People use intrinsic value to determine whether a stock is undervalued or overvalued. Those models try to quantify the "risk premium" but ignore the money effect (see p. 208). Had money not been created in the past, firms' profits would have been lower than realized. If no money had worked as the yeast, the rising asset markets would not have been like fermenting flour at the right temperature.

4.1.3.3 *Total assets markets*

Working assets compete head-to-head with idle assets (see p. 224), and this section analyzes the case. The representative households have total wealth:

$$\phi = \phi_i + \phi_w,$$

where ϕ_i is the wealth in the idle assets and ϕ_w is in the working assets. The dynamics of the working assets follow Eq. (4.23), and the idle assets follow the process:

$$\dot{\phi}_i = \pi_i \phi_i, \tag{4.38}$$

where the money flows into or out of the idle-asset market determines π_i. The household has a fraction α of its wealth in the working assets, $\phi_w = \alpha\phi$, and has the rest of its wealth in the idle assets, $\phi_i = (1 - \alpha)\phi$.

Combining the working assets of Eq. (4.23) and the idle assets of Eq. (4.38), we have the wealth equation that incorporates both types of assets:

$$\dot{\phi} = \pi_i(1 - \alpha)\phi + \pi_w \alpha\phi + Pf\left(\frac{\alpha\phi}{P}\right) - c - \delta\alpha\phi, \tag{4.39}$$

where c is the nominal consumption. The idle assets have inflation rate π_i, the working assets have inflation rate π_w (4.23), and the two rates differ because the money-flow patterns in the respective markets are distinct. Households and firms have no control over the money supply. As a result, inflation is set exogenously.

The household maximizes its consumption c:

$$\max_{c,\alpha} \int_0^T e^{-\rho t} \ln c dt, \tag{4.40}$$

subject to Eq. (4.39) and

$$\phi = \phi_0,\ c = c_0,\ P = P_0,\ \text{at } t = 0,$$
$$\dot{c} < \infty, \tag{4.41}$$
$$\dot{\phi} < \infty. \tag{4.42}$$

Here, α is another control variable.

Using Hamiltonian, we solve the utility maximization problem:

$$\begin{aligned}\mathcal{H}(\phi, c, \alpha, P, \theta, t) &= \ln c + \theta[\pi_i(1-\alpha)\phi + \pi_w \alpha\phi] \\ &\quad + \theta\left[Pf\left(\frac{\alpha\phi}{P}\right) - c - \delta\alpha\phi\right]. \end{aligned} \tag{4.43}$$

Take the derivative of Eq. (4.43) with respect to c yields the first-order condition of consumption:

$$\frac{\partial\mathcal{H}(\phi, c, \alpha, P, \theta, t)}{\partial c} = \frac{1}{c} - \theta = 0, \tag{4.44}$$

which gives:

$$\frac{1}{c} = \theta. \tag{4.45}$$

The dynamics of the co-state variable θ are given by:

$$\begin{aligned}\frac{\partial\mathcal{H}(\phi, c, \alpha, P, \theta, t)}{\partial\phi} &= \theta\left[(1-\alpha)\pi_i + \alpha\pi_w + \alpha f'\left(\frac{\alpha\phi}{P}\right) + \alpha\delta\right] \\ &= \rho\theta - \dot{\theta}, \end{aligned} \tag{4.46}$$

which yields the dynamics of θ:

$$\dot{\theta} = \theta \left\{ \rho - \left[(1-\alpha)\pi_i + \alpha(\pi_w - \delta) + \alpha f'\left(\frac{\alpha\phi}{P}\right) \right] \right\}. \tag{4.47}$$

Substituting Eq. (4.45) into Eq. (4.47) gives the dynamics of consumption:

$$\dot{c} = \left[(1-\alpha)\pi_i + \alpha(\pi_w - \delta) + \alpha f'\left(\frac{\phi}{P}\right) - \rho \right] c. \tag{4.48}$$

To optimize the asset allocation α, take the derivative of the Hamiltonian with respect to α:

$$\frac{\partial \mathcal{H}(\phi, c, \alpha, P, \theta, t)}{\partial \alpha} = \left[-\pi_i\phi + (\pi_w - \delta)\phi + f'\left(\frac{\alpha\phi}{P}\right)\phi \right], \tag{4.49}$$

where α is between zero and one, $\alpha \in \{0, 1\}$. We ignore short sales.

Using the definition $r_w = f'\left(\frac{\alpha\phi}{P}\right) - \delta$, Eq. (4.49) suggests

$$\alpha = \begin{cases} 0 & \pi_i > \pi_w + r_w \\ 1 & \pi_i < \pi_w + r_w. \end{cases} \tag{4.50}$$

The idle asset market and the working asset market compete for wealth—money. In this example the economy is large and cannot completely rely on other economies for consumption and capital goods, so it must maintain its own productive base. Therefore, the scenario where there is no production of real goods ($\alpha = 0$) is unrealistic. On the other hand, a situation where all wealth is allocated to working assets ($\alpha = 1$) is possible.

If the return in the idle asset market is lower than that in the working asset market, money will be withdrawn from the idle asset market and reallocated to working assets, represented by $1 - \alpha$ approaching zero.

Another realistic scenario occurs when $\pi_i = \pi_w + r_w$, meaning:

$$\pi_w + f'\left(\frac{\alpha\phi}{P}\right) - \delta = \pi_i, \tag{4.51}$$

in which the idle assets deliver comparable returns to the returns of working assets.

Some idle assets yield lower returns than working assets, yet they still compete with working assets for available funds. Why, then, isn't every dollar invested in working assets? The answer points to potential factors that are not included in our simple model.

The existing houses are not purely idle assets like paintings. Older houses also provide shelter for households or serve as rental properties that generate income. At lower levels of price appreciation, the real estate market can compete with the stock market. The current model, however, does not account for this additional utility value of idle assets. In the U.S., the S&P 500's historical 10% average annual return outpaces housing's typical 4%–8% gains.[28] According to most data, the real estate market is considerably larger than the total market capitalization of all publicly traded stocks worldwide; but most local real estate markets are segmented and can have substantially different returns.

Consider many "idle assets," such as antiques and fine art, which benefit from their scarcity and unique ownership. Because no new supply is available and they are only traded within a small circle of collectors, these assets are not highly liquid. Consequently, a price increase can be triggered by the willingness of just one buyer to pay a higher price.

Above all, money flowing into the idle asset market not only creates and sustains that market but also diverts money away from the working asset market. In the short term, when money flows from one market to the other, the return in the former can overtake the return in the latter market (Liu *et al.*, 1995).

As an economy accumulates a substantial amount of capital stock and the real return ($r = f'(k) - \delta$) of working assets declines, new money seeks opportunities for higher returns, thereby generating new idle assets.

Some idle assets arise from controlled scarcity and speculation, such as baseball cards and cryptos. Originally marketing tools in the late 1800s, baseball cards were overproduced in the 1980s, creating the low value "Junk Wax" era. To restore scarcity, companies introduced limited print runs, autographs, and memorabilia cards.

[28] *Has Real Estate or the Stock Market Performed Better Historically?* by Sean Ross, December 2, 2024, investopedia.com.

With eBay and major auction houses, cards evolved into a global secondary market, offering liquidity and information, similar to other assets.

4.2 Financial Games

The secondary market provides liquidity, making primary market investments more attractive. Beyond this benefit, the secondary market can resemble a "game table," where speculators engage in trading for quick gains and come and go at will:

> In one of the greatest investment markets in the world, namely, New York, the influence of speculation (in the above sense) is enormous. Even outside the field of finance, Americans are apt to be unduly interested in discovering what average opinion believes average opinion to be; and this national weakness finds its nemesis in the stock market. It is rare, one is told, for an American to invest, as many Englishmen still do, "for income"; and he will not readily purchase an investment except in the hope of capital appreciation. This is only another way of saying that, when he purchases an investment, the American is attaching his hopes, not so much to its prospective yield, as to a favorable change in the conventional basis of valuation, i.e., that he is, in the above sense, a speculator. Speculators may do no harm as bubbles on a steady stream of enterprise. But the position is serious when enterprise becomes the bubble in a whirlpool of speculation. When the capital development of a country becomes a by-product of the activities of a casino, the job is likely to be ill-done. The measure of success attained by Wall Street, regarded as an institution of which the proper social purpose is to direct new investment into the most profitable channels in terms of future yield, cannot be claimed as one of the outstanding triumphs of laissez-faire capitalism—which is not surprising, if I am right in thinking that the best brains of Wall Street have been in fact directed towards a different object.—Keynes (1936)

Keynes might talk about the New York Curb Exchange, New York's last outdoor stock market, also called "the gorge," a famous outdoor stock market where trading was chaotic and resembled a frenzy of activity. This chaotic environment highlights how financial markets can appear as mere gambling dens rather than structured systems for businesses to raise funds. The Curb Exchange eventually evolved into the American Stock Exchange, reflecting a move towards more formalized and regulated trading environments.[29,30]

Financial markets have been continuously adding more financial instruments to the markets. For speculators, a new instrument is a new game to play. Derivatives are a type of financial instrument that people have been using for thousands of years (Graeber, 2012). Derivatives, as the word suggests, derive their value from underlying assets—basic assets, such as stocks, bonds, or commodities. Historians trace the origins of options back to ancient Greece. The Greeks and Romans used them and spread them to other parts of the world.

Europeans have widely used *forward contracts* since the Middle Ages (Oosterlinck, 2017). A forward contract is a private agreement between parties to buy or sell a specified quantity of an asset at a predetermined price in the future. Before a harvest, a farmer and a miller can sign a private forward contract specifying the price and quantity of a crop delivered on a date after the harvest. With the forward contract, the farmer and miller know how much money to pay or receive for the specified amount of crop. The forward contract

[29]Journalist Edwin C. Hill wrote: "Hundreds of men on the street "writhed, leaped, swayed." " They communicated their orders by yelling or signaling out a window and anyone with lungs could trade, financial claimed in 1920, "some of those whirling dervishes down the street could borrow a million on their moral credit; for others the jail beckons." To Hill, it looked like hell. "Fingers in sets of two, three, and five at a time... shot up vertically or spanned horizontally sideways in mad play," while in the buildings overlooking the street, "windows were popping with grimacing faces—female, it seemed, as well as male—with grotesque and distorted features... with arms and hands that leaped from a mysterious interior to convey cryptic symbols to the upraised eyes of the leaping creatures in the gorge." If the visitor looked closely, Hill claimed, they could see the Curb for what it really was: a functioning stock market. On the street, the machinations of finance were visible to all. The Curb was "finance set to jazz music" and "money doing a shimmy."

[30]The exchange erected the original building in 1921, improving the stature of the New York Curb Exchange. The exchange enlarged the structure between 1929 and 1931 following an increase in trading volume and was renamed from the New York Curb Exchange to the American Stock Exchange in 1953. *"The New York Curb Market... Which Has No Organization Whatever": The Enclosure of New York's Last Outdoor Stock Market, 1900–1921*, Ann Daly, The Gotham Center for New York City History.

eliminates the price uncertainty of the crop after the harvest, but it does not eliminate all risks, particularly the counterparty risk that a party in the contract may not fulfill its part of the deal. If the crop price after the harvest is much higher than the price on the contract, the farmer might regret it and refuse to deliver the crop at the price specified in the contract. If the price after the harvest is much lower than the price on the contract, the miller might regret it and refuse to pay the price on the contract. Other things can happen and make it impossible for a party to follow through with the contract, such as the farmer not having enough crops because of a bad year for the crop, or the miller's business going under before the date of delivery.

Futures markets standardize forward contracts and make them public. From the 17th century, in Japan, the landlords collected rice as tax and transported the rice to major cities. The landowners and warlords sold the rice to the rice brokers through auctions. In addition, they also auctioned rice bills, the notes promising to be exchanged for rice. The owners of rice bills started to trade the bills actively, but the authority prohibited the trading for years because the authority regarded the bills as a form of gambling that caused rice prices to rise. The price of rice fell to record lows in the late 1720s; the samurai paid by rice grew worried (Moss and Kintgen, 2010). In 1730, the Tokugawa shogunate[31] officially authorized a market to trade rice bills and the world's first organized futures market to trade rice futures in Dojima Rice Exchange (Moss and Kintgen, 2010).[32]

In the futures market, a farmer (miller) does not have to find a miller (farmer) before a harvest to sell (buy) crops at a specified price after the harvest. They can either short (sell) or long (buy) the standard futures contract for the crop in the futures market. Today's futures exchangers reduce or eliminate the counterparty risk by requiring margin accounts from all traders and clearing all gains or losses daily. A dealer sets the amount of money that a trader must deposit in his margin account based on the price volatility and the size of his trading positions.[33] The dealers constantly credit the

---

[31] The shogunate was the hereditary military dictatorship of Japan, 1192–1867 (Britannica).

[32] *Dojima Rice Exchange*, jpcco.jp, retrieved on December 11, 2023.

[33] The volatility is the standard deviation of the asset price.

trader's gains into and debit the trader's losses out of the margin account, which is the practice of "marking to market."

For example, the corn contract size is 5,000 bushels. As the price is \$4.00 per bushel, one contract is \$20,000. At the beginning of the corn futures trading, a trader puts into his/her margin account the initial margin, typically 5–10% of contract sizes depending on the volatility of the corn price. In a volatile corn market, the trader needs to put \$2,000 per contract in his margin account. If the price goes up to \$4.10 per bushel and the seller (farmer) loses \$500 = \$0.10(5,000) and the seller's margin account drops down to \$1,500. The buyer gains \$500 and his margin account goes up to \$2,500. A brokerage firm also sets a maintenance margin, which is below the initial margin. Whenever a trader's margin account falls below the maintenance margin, the trader must add more money into his margin account.

Traders can exit futures contracts by entering offsetting positions, thus nullifying their obligations to deliver or receive the assets. A long (purchase) contract and a short (sell) contract cancel each other. At that point, the trader has already paid for all his losses or received all his gains, and his withdrawal from the contract does not affect the counterparty of the contract. Though futures reduce the counterparty risk of forward contracts, they also nullify the original intent of the delivery of the underlying assets. Futures contracts become the darling of the financial games. A speculator does not need to have an oil well to speculate oil prices in the future, does not need to raise cows to speculate beef prices, and does not need anything to speculate everything.

In addition, as the financial derivatives market became increasingly sophisticated, it gave birth to a new discipline "financial engineering."[34] Financial engineering has designed new financial products that are acclaimed as "financial innovations." Financial engineering also constructs specific cash flows to satisfy the needs of customers. Though it has been praised as "financial innovation,"

[34]A story recounted that Ohio Society of Professional Engineers protested that "financial engineering" misused the definition of engineering since finance had nothing resembling engineering.

a series of these innovations contributed to the financial crisis of 2007–2008.

4.2.1 *Financial innovations*

Advocates of financial innovations maintain that new instruments could distribute risk more effectively, making the system more stable. However, this belief was proven false during the financial crisis.

The regional housing markets do not normally rise and fall together. As researchers have noted, houses are traded among different house owners (Grebler, 1951) and different types of houses exist in the market (Wheaton, 1990). Housing is not a single market but a series of overlapping markets (Smith *et al.*, 1988), serving various needs in different regions (Grebler, 1951; Wheaton, 1990).[35] Although financial innovations were supposed to reduce the risks of local markets, they instead made the regional real estate markets in the U.S. highly correlated, leading to a nationwide collapse.

One of the key methods in *structured finance* is *securitization.* Banks pool mortgages together and sell them as Mortgage-Backed Securities (MBS) in financial markets. This securitization process was supposed to distribute the risks of mortgage defaults widely across the financial system, but it created a false sense of security. First, banks do not necessarily keep the mortgages in their own portfolio and, as a result, have limited concern for the repayment capacity of borrowers.

Second, banks sell the MBS at high prices by dividing the pool of mortgages into different risk levels. This slicing down into *tranches* allowed banks to produce high-quality securities from lower-quality mortgages, squeezing out juice from low-quality oranges. The people who buy A tranches receive interest and principal first and bear the lowest risk. Those who buy Z tranches receive interest and principal payments only after all the buyers of the other tranches have received the interest and principal; thus, the buyers of Z tranches take

[35]dwellsy.com calculated the total value of the residential rental real estate in the U.S. as \$383,760/unit $\times$ 44,000,000 units = \$16.9 trillion (retrieved on December 13, 2023).

the highest risk. Before 2008, banks squeezed 70–80% of AAA-rated securities from the lower-rated MBS.

A credit risk derivative, the *Credit Default Swap* (CDS), was introduced into the financial market in the 1990s. It is similar to an insurance contract, in which the seller will compensate the buyer in the event that the buyer's security holding defaults, and the buyer makes a series of payments just like insurance premiums. CDS were then used to create another financial innovation—synthetic collateralized debt obligation (synthetic CDO), which allows the holders to take exposure to credit risk without owning the underlying assets. When synthetics became the dominant form of CDOs in the U.S., their notional value reached $5 trillion by the end of 2006 (Zuckerman, 2010). CDOs bundled MBS with other debt instruments, producing more high-rated securities from the pool.

Though intended for risk management, derivatives have, through financial innovation, paradoxically become instruments of speculation that heighten market risks. During the financial crisis, the delinquency rate was much above 2.5% and reached a peak in 2010 at 11.5%. The delinquency rate for single-family residential mortgages reached about 11% in 2010.

4.2.1.1 *Managing risk with options*

As notably articulated by Warren Buffett in his 2002 Berkshire Hathaway chairman's letter, he termed derivatives "financial weapons of mass destruction." To understand the issues with derivatives, we must differentiate between arbitrage (hedging) and speculation.

Economics has *the law of one price*, which states that identical products should have the same price in efficient markets. If there are price discrepancies between markets, arbitrageurs can buy low in one market and sell high in another to make a risk-free profit. This process, known as *arbitrage*, is central to the market equilibrium[36] in economics and finance. Nathan Mayer Rothschild, a financier, was the most successful arbitrageur. One of Rothschild's big plays was buying gold at a lower price and selling it at a higher price—even smuggling it to get around Napoleon's blockades—to exploit price differences across Europe. His glittering arbitrage got the world's

[36]The real transaction involves shipping, taxes, or tariffs when crossing a country border. The market frictions give rise to merchants' business opportunities.

attention in the early 1800s. The British government turned to him to provide gold for its army and continental allies in their fight against Napoleon, asking him to violate Britain's own gold transfer restrictions. He funded the British national debt during the war. His wealth swelled by £578 million (about £36 billion in today's money) to over 200% of GDP by the end of the war (Ferguson, 2000).

The arbitrage opportunity makes it possible to make profits for sure. With today's technology, one just punches keys on the computer keyboard and makes money whenever an arbitrage opportunity arises. Technology also makes any arbitrage opportunity disappear faster, just like a $100 bill would not lie on a busy street for long. Arbitrageurs are watching and searching for the arbitrage opportunities in the financial market. Financial institutions are racing at millisecond speeds to find and execute arbitrage with algorithmic trading programs and automated trading.[37]

Besides low risk, arbitrage makes it possible to make money without money (MacKenzie, 2003). A penniless homeless person cannot arbitrage, but people with a brokerage account have different ways to get money, one of which is simply borrowing from their brokerage firms. Financial institutions can get substantial amounts of money. A well-known example is the hedge fund, Long-Term Capital Management, which borrowed $95 for every $5 it had. Before the downfall of Lehman Brothers in the 2008 financial crisis, it borrowed up to $44 for every $1 it had (MacKenzie, 2003; McDonald, 2016; *Lehman Brothers—The Bank That Bust the World*).

Another way to get money is short selling. Traders can borrow a security from their brokers and sell it on the spot-market for cash. If a trader borrows 100 shares of a stock from his broker and sells them on the market for $50 per share, he gets $5,000 cash. The trader owes 100 shares to the broker. If the stock drops to $45 per share, the trader buys 100 shares for $4,500 and gives 100 shares back to the broker. The trader makes $500 before the trading fee. If the stock price does not drop, the trader must buy 100 shares to pay back eventually, and he loses money. The derivative market provides other ways to get cash. Selling (writing) options, or credit default

[37]The movie *The Hummingbird Project* shows how a fiber-optic cable that is milliseconds faster becomes a high-stake game.

swap for payments is just like selling insurance for premiums. Those ways to raise cash are risky.

The law of one price implies that arbitrage opportunities should not exist in a competitive market, that is, prices satisfy *the arbitrage-free condition.* But in today's financial labyrinth, the games become much more complicated than the above example of gold arbitrage. Different financial instruments, such as certified deposits, Treasury bills, or various portfolios including derivatives,[38] can offer $50,000 a year later, which is an identical "product" after equalizing the risks. The risks can be eliminated or equalized using sophisticated financial products or financial engineering approaches. Arbitrage and speculation become kaleidoscopes of financial products.

One can identify an arbitrage opportunity by checking whether prices satisfy the arbitrage-free condition. A simple example is as follows: The current gold price is $2,000 per ounce. The interest rate is 5%. A bank offers $2,050 per ounce as a 1-year forward contract. An arbitrageur can borrow one ounce of gold from a broker, short-selling the gold to get $2,000, buy a 1-year bond with 5% interest, and enter the forward contract to buy one ounce of gold a year later. A year later, the arbitrageur withdraws the principal and interests $2,100 from the mature bond, pays $2,050 to receive one ounce of gold, and give the gold to the broker. This arbitrage process generates $50 profit ($2,100–$2,050). The arbitrage-free condition in this case is straightforward: The forward price must be $2,100 = $2,000(1+0.05), the same as the principal and the interest of the bond. Any forward price of more or less than $2,100 provides an arbitrage opportunity. Putting it into an equation, we have the formula for the forward price:

$$\text{Forward}\quad\text{price} = \text{Spot}\quad\text{price}(1+R)^T, \qquad (4.52)$$

where R is the nominal interest rate and T is the maturity of the forward contract.[39] Forward prices must meet arbitrage-free conditions—and so must all other derivatives.

Arbitrage-free pricing is the foundation of derivatives. Black and Scholes' option-pricing model (see p. 176) puts a stock and the option

[38]One can construct a portfolio that will pay a specific amount of money using forwards, futures, and options through the financial engineering approach.

[39]In this example, we ignore the risk involved, such as the bankruptcy risk of the bank offering the contract.

on the stock into a portfolio, then by imposing the arbitrage-free condition, Black and Scholes successfully solved the option pricing (Black and Scholes, 1973).[40] Financial engineering applies the theory of arbitrage pricing to construct sophisticated financial portfolios and financial products, wheels within wheels.

Businesses could use options to manage risk. The protective put is an example. A put option contract gives the buyer *the right* to sell the underlying asset at a specified price, the strike price, on or before a specified expiration date.[41]

Figure 4.4 shows how a put option protects the price that a farmer's lean hogs. The farmer expects to sell his lean hogs at a price of $100 in the coming June.[42] The horizontal axis is the possible lean hog prices in June, which are unknown. The vertical axis is the gain or loss from the $100 price. For instance, a June put option has a strike price of $100 per pound of lean hogs. If the price of lean hog is $90 in June, the put option has a profit of $10 (see the solid line in Figure 4.4). The lower the spot price of lean hogs at the expiration date, the higher the profit of the put option. If the price of lean hogs goes above $100, the farmer does not exercise his put option because he can sell his hogs at the market price that is higher than the strike price of the put option. The put option has no value when the market price is higher than the strike price of the option. The payoff of the put option has a kink point (see the solid line in Figure 4.4), which is the unique feature of options.

The farmer has protection if the price of lean hogs falls below $100. If lean hogs fall to $90 in June (see the dash line in Figure 4.4), the farmer sells her lean hogs in the cash (spot) market at $90—$10 below $100—while the farmer's put option profits $10. The profit exactly offsets the loss on the spot market. Putting the market price and the put option together, the farmer has a minimum price of $100

---

[40]Mathematicians developed the martingale theory of arbitrage pricing. A martingale is a sequence of random variable whose conditional expectation of the next value equals the current value. An equivalent martingale measure, or risk-neutral measure, is a probability measure such that the conditional expectation of the future value in the sequence is equal to the present value. A random walk is an example of a martingale.

[41]European options can be exercised only on the expiration day, while American options can be exercised at any time before the expiration day as well.

[42]A put option contract sets the minimum selling price.

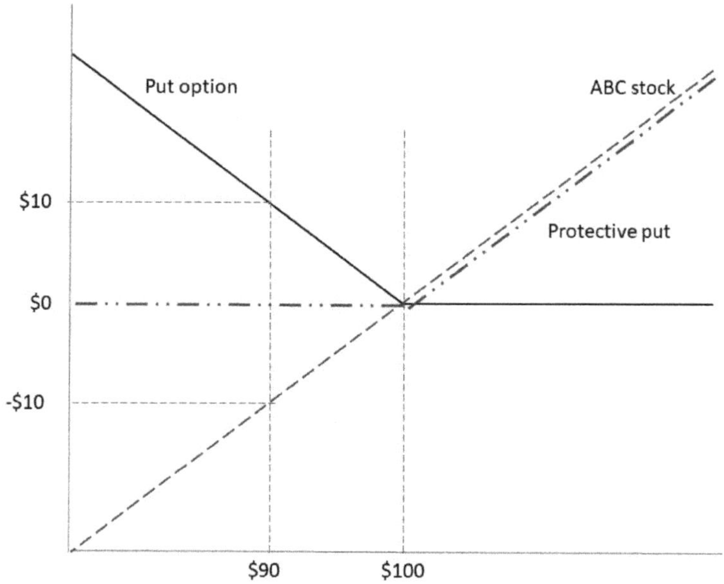

Fig. 4.4. Protective put.

and still has the upside potential. If the price of lean hogs goes above \$100, the farmer just sells her lean hogs at the market price (see the dash double-dot line in Figure 4.4). Protective puts can assist farmers in managing lean hog price risk, but unfortunately, options are also favored by speculators.

4.2.1.2 *Naked derivatives: Weapons of mass destruction*

Most derivatives contracts, such as futures, do not result in the physical delivery of the underlying assets. Instead, they are settled in cash, turning derivatives into speculative instruments rather than tools for managing the risk of actual commodities or assets. Less than 10% of futures contracts involve physical delivery (Hecht, 2021), and many traders are speculating on price movements rather than dealing with the actual underlying asset.

Moreover, derivatives allow traders to control large positions with relatively little money in their margin accounts. For example, a trader can speculate on \$50,000 worth of stock with only \$5,000 in margin in the futures market, effectively leveraging their position 10 times. This leverage can magnify both profits and losses, making derivatives a high-risk proposition.

While derivatives were originally used to manage risks (e.g., farmers hedging against crop price fluctuations), they have increasingly become tools for speculation. Like futures, traders can buy or sell options without holding the underlying asset, purely speculating on price movements. This type of trading, known as *naked options*, allows speculators to risk small sums to bet on significant future price movements for large gains.

Naked options involve high-risk due to their extreme leverage. For example, a put option on lean hog futures with a strike price of $0.80 per pound costs a premium of $0.02 per pound, implying 40:1 leverage ($0.80/$0.02). Since each contract covers 40,000 pounds, the notional value is $32,000, while the premium is $800. If the price of lean hogs falls by $0.02, the option breaks even; if it falls by $0.75, the option yields a 150% profit. However, if the price rises and remains above the strike until expiration, the option expires worthlessly and the $800 premium is lost.

Derivatives, like other financial innovations, are often claimed to optimize risk distribution among the market participants. Yet this argument conflates the risks inherent to financial markets with those faced by the broader economy. Options on financial assets, such as stocks or bonds, in contrast to commodity options (e.g., lean hogs, p. 241), exhibit only tenuous connections to the real economy. Naked options extend this detachment further, severing the link altogether and bearing no relation to underlying business risks. It is only when speculative positions of financial institutions unravel catastrophically—akin to a drowning individual grasping at anything within reach—that the broader economy is pulled down with them (see p. 244).

The 1688 book *Confusion of Confusions* describes the trading of "opsies" on the Amsterdam stock exchange (now Euronext), explaining that "there will be only limited risks to you, while the gain may surpass all your imaginings and hopes" (De La Vega, 2009). Today, people can trade on average over more than 11 million contracts a day on over 3,000 securities.[43] Another type of derivative that is the remote cousin of futures is a contract for difference (CFD),[44] which has no expiration date and, thus, has no delivery and is pure

[43] *Options Playbook*, The Options Clearing Corporation, 2023.

[44] The profit or loss of a CFD is determined by the difference between the opening and closing prices.

price speculation. Fortunately, CFDs are illegal in the United States but are traded outside the U.S. Forbes Advisor noted that IG.com offers CFD trading over 18,000 markets, including stocks, indices, commodities, currencies, and bonds.[45] Excluding CFDs, 11 million different contracts offer a staggering number of ways to speculate more than casinos could ever imagine.

In the financial markets, *open interest* is the total number of contracts. Multiplying the open interest by the amount specified in a contract gives the notional value. As of July 2023, the total market capitalization of domestic companies listed on stock exchanges worldwide is recorded as $112 trillion.[46] The notional value of outstanding over-the-counter (OTC) derivatives reached $715 trillion at the end of June 2023.[47] Over-the-counter securities are traded via the broker-dealer network and may not be listed on major exchanges in the United States. Compared to minimal upfront cash margin, derivatives can amplify both systemic returns and catastrophic losses during market shocks. In his 2002 Chairman's Letter for Berkshire Hathaway, Warren Buffett said, "We view them as time bombs, both for the parties that deal in them and the economic system." In 2016, at the annual Berkshire Hathaway company meeting, he warned again.

A bomb exploded before the downfall of the hedge fund Long-Term Capital Management (LTCM). The most prominent figures in economics and finance founded LTCM in 1994, including Myron Scholes and Robert C. Merton, and John Meriwether, the former vice-chairman, and head of bond trading at Salomon Brothers. Scholes and Merton shared the Nobel Memorial Prize in Economic Sciences for their contributions to the development of the option pricing model. No other team understood options better than the team of LTCM. Merton Miller asked Myron Scholes about the strategy of LTCM and recalled their conversation: "I asked him, what is it you guys are doing at LTCM, and Myron characterized it in that way of his. He said, well you know, one way is to think of us as a gigantic vacuum cleaner sucking up

[45]forbes.com, retrieved on December 13, 2023.
[46]statista.com, September 1, 2023, retrieved on December 13, 2023.
[47]bis.org, retrieved on December 13, 2023.

nickels from all over the world."[48] The strategy was successful with annualized returns of 21%, 43%, and 41% in the first three years, while LTCM had high leverage and took risks. Normally, the different prices for similar assets converge, but the prices that LTCM bet on their convergence kept diverging because of the 1997 Asian financial crisis and 1998 Russian financial crisis (Ferguson, 2008). To avoid a wider collapse in the financial markets, the Federal Reserve Bank of New York organized a bailout of $3.625 billion by the major creditors (Partnoy, 2010). LTCM left its investors and partners with only $400 million, a mere tenth of what they had not long ago. But the $3.625 billion did not overcome the fear of the financial market. On October 15, 1998, the Fed had an unscheduled emergency interest rate cut to calm down the markets (MacKenzie, 2003). The fund's collapse threatened the global financial system, necessitating a Federal Reserve-organized bailout.

4.2.1.3 *Greenspan put, Bernanke put, and Powell put*

Just as a farmer might use put options to set a floor on the price of commodities such as lean hogs, as illustrated in Figure 4.4, the Federal Reserve uses monetary policy to prop up the stock market during times of distress. The term "Greenspan put" originated with the Fed chair Alan Greenspan, who consistently intervened to prevent significant declines in financial markets.

Greenspan temporarily relieved the financial problem but created long-term economic distortions. In 2008, the fallout from the subprime mortgage crisis and the collapse in house prices forced Ben Bernanke, the Fed chair, to use QE as the Bernanke put to bail out banks and the two biggest mortgage companies. The Fed chair, Janet Yellen, and the chairman of the Fed, Jerome Powell, repeated the Greenspan put to boost falling asset prices. The Powell put exceeded all predecessors (Leonard, 2020). Other central banks followed the Fed's lead, which had impacts globally.

Central banks and governments can have large positions in put options and shuffle massive amounts of money in their bailouts. During the financial crisis of 2008, the U.S. government bailed out

[48] *A billion dollar bet*, NOVA, pbs.org.

nearly 1,000 companies through the $700 billion Troubled Assets Relief Program (TARP), including companies like General Motors and Chrysler.[49] In the United Kingdom, the National Audit Office reported the bank bailout of £1 trillion at its peak. As for Ireland, it cost €64 billion—more than twice total tax revenue in 2010—to rescue its banks. The bailout of firms and banks seems just corporate insurance, but government subsidization violates free competition, the capitalist principle. Governments criticize each other for subsidizing industries or companies, but they do the same thing. The market capitalism free of intervention has been transformed into protected capitalism, sustained by central banks' put options and government bailouts.

In the U.S., the players in the assets markets have the timeless wisdom of "Don't fight the Fed."[50] Financial markets understand well the effect of the Fed put. The Fed, as a lender of last resort, will come to rescue the failing financial institutions during the stock market distress. The Fed's new money makes the market participants optimistic about the financial markets in the future (Libich and Lenten, 2022; Hodula and Libich, 2023). The Fed chair, Jeromy Powell, set an inflation target of 2%. His inflation target is a promise of plenty of money to supply the economy.

Another competing motto for making money is "diversification, diversification, diversification," forgetting timing the market. It is an implication of the Markowitz portfolio theory and William F. Sharpe's Capital Asset Pricing Model. People should put money in the market portfolio, which includes all assets, both "working assets" and "idle assets," common stocks, bonds, real estate, commodities, foreign currencies, and many other financial assets. But many assets are not traded in the financial markets, and the true market portfolio does not exist. Hence, individuals should have those assets, like paintings, antiques, and others, in their portfolios.

While diversification addresses financial risks, it's important to note that these risks differ from the risks faced by the real economy.

---

[49] *What Is A Bank Bailout?* by Cassidy Horton, forbes.com, retrieved on April 6, 2024.

[50] Marty Zweig, investor and financial market forecaster, coined the phrase in 1970. *Mastering patience: The Timeless Wisdom of 'Don't Fight the Fed'* by Kevin Philip, May 3, 2024, investmentnews.com, retrieved on June 16, 2024.

More crucially, stock markets require money growth to generate returns. If the Fed continues its policies, asset prices are likely to keep rising. Thus, buy stocks when monetary policy eases and sell when it tightens: "Don't fight the Fed."

4.2.2 *The sure way to make money*

Academics ascribe the winners in the stock market to pure luck because the returns of stocks follow a random walk. The efficient-market hypothesis reinforces the random walk theory of the stock market. As Zvi Bodie, Professor Emeritus at Boston University, once imitated a winner in the stock market: "When some individual made a fortune in the stock market, we have a tendency to assume that that was because he knew something, and of course the individual himself is happy to reinforce that belief—yes, I was a genius, or I was very clever, or I always said Microsoft was going to make me rich. But what you don't see are the thousands, hundreds of thousands, perhaps millions of people who are going, I always said that ABC company was going to make me rich, and ABC company went bust."[51]

Take a step back and ignore the money's effect on stock returns. Suppose stock returns follow a random walk; then gamblers can win games surely with the Martingale betting system. Using a simple coin flip to simulate a random walk, the gambler who chooses heads doubles his bet after each tails until the coin comes up heads, then the gambler recovers all his earlier losses and secures a net gain. The gambler follows the Martingale betting system and makes money for sure.[52,53]

However, the money needed by the Martingale betting grows exponentially. The gambler starts with \$1 as a bet. If the first toss turns out to be tails, the gambler doubles his bet to \$2 ($= 2^{2-1} \times \$1$). If he wins after the \$1 loss, he makes \$1. If the toss turns out to

[51] *A billion dollar bet*, NOVA, pbs.org.

[52] It is an instance of the St. Petersburg paradox. Both gamblers of the game use the Martingale betting system, and both appear to win.

[53] Mathematicians developed the probability theory of *Martingales*, which models coin tossing as a random walk. The expected outcome of the next toss adds zero value: there is a, 50% chance to win and a 50% chance to lose.

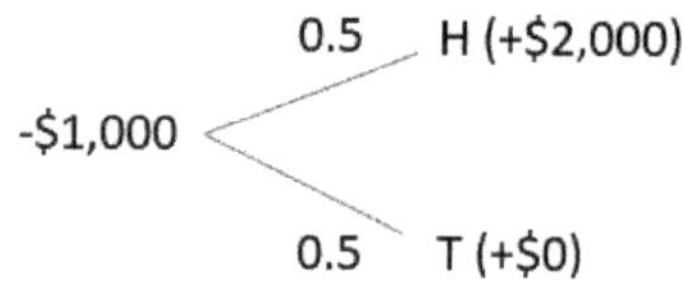

Fig. 4.5. Coin flip game: One toss.

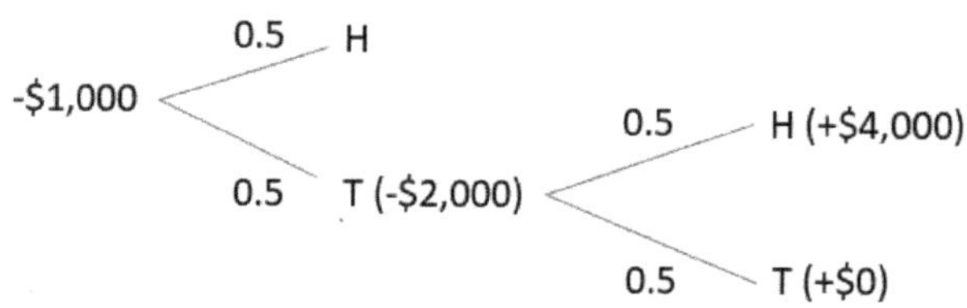

Fig. 4.6. Coin flip game: Two tosses.

be tails, his fourth bet is \$4 ($= 2^{3-1} \times \$1$). If he wins, after the \$3 loss, he makes \$1. If the toss turns out to be tails, his fourth bet is \$8 ($= 2^{3-1} \times \$1$). Following the same strategy, the nth bet needs $2^{n-1} \times \$1$. For those who know the story about an Indian king and the chess inventor, this illustrates how quickly the number doubling becomes astronomical. The chess inventor asked the king to give him wheat, starting with one grain on the first square and doubled the number of grains on each subsequent square (Macdonell, 1898; Tahan, 1993). With 64 squares, the total number of grains on the chessboard had been $2^{64-1} = 18.4 \times 10^{18}$, more than the world production of wheat. No gamblers have the money to bet 64 times. However, the game favors the gamblers who have more money.

Playing a coin flipping game that starts with \$1,000 and, a gambler with \$1,000 can play just once, while another with \$3,000 can do twice. The first player has 50% chance to win (see Fig. 4.5). For the second player, he has 50% to win in the first toss and, if unsuccessful, he doubles and has the second chance to win. The probability of losing both bets is 25% (see Fig. 4.6). The gambler with \$3,000 has a 75% chance of winning \$1,000. If a gambler has \$7,000, he can play three times and the chance to lose all is 12.5%. The probability is 0.5^n, where n is the number of times to play the game. The probability of losing decreases rapidly, vanishing exponentially with n. The more money a player has, the higher the probability of winning the coin flip game.

No players have more money than financial institutions, hedge funds, and banks. Banks have trading desks that engage in trading activities. Before Lehman Brothers went bankrupt, one trader who made more than $30 million received a bonus of more than $1 million, and some others who generated more than $100 million for the bank received bonuses of $10 million in a good year. In 2004, Lehman Brothers paid over $5 billion in bonuses to its staff, and the bonuses almost doubled by 2007.[54] Some well-known traders, such as Nick Leeson, a former derivatives trader at the bankrupted Barings Bank, and Jerome Kerviel at the French bank Société Générale, played billions of dollars in financial games. The reason we know the amount of dollars they played is that their banks either went bankrupt or reported huge losses. Other traders may play with even more money, but their banks do not want to reveal the gambling activities they engage in.

Accepting the efficient-market hypothesis, which assumes that all the public information is available in the secondary market, the market participants still do not have the same "information." In an interview, the legendary bond trader and the founder of LTCM, Meriwether, talked about the arbitrage activities in Japan. The head of Salomon's trading activities in Japan was the successful trader, Shigeru Miyojin. Meriwether said that someone who did not know Japanese would be at a disadvantage; in Japan, the tax and regulatory framework drove the price discrepancies that provided the arbitrage opportunities. An outsider would often find that framework hard to comprehend in sufficient depth (MacKenzie, 2003). Information asymmetry also makes it difficult for individual traders to compete with large institutions.

4.2.2.1 *Losers in the financial games*

If two players are involved in a coin-flip game, with one choosing "heads" and the other "tails," and both adopt the Martingale strategy, will both win? This scenario illustrates the St. Petersburg paradox. However, both players cannot simultaneously win; it's a

[54]*Lehman Brothers—The Bank That Bust the World*, TradingCoachUK Documentary.

zero-sum game where one's gain is the other's loss. Therefore, no player has infinite money, so one will eventually run out, ending the game.

While financial institutions possess superior resources, they often lack the patience for the small, gradual bets required for a successful Martingale approach, hindering their potential advantage. Gordon Gekko, played by Michael Douglas, in the movie *Wall Street* said, "Greed, in all of its forms; greed for life, for money, for love, knowledge has marked the upward surge of mankind." Echoing Gekko's words, "you got to take more risk risk risk risk risk and that risk leads more to the bottom line,"[55] Lehman Brothers CEO Richard Fuld once said. Lehman Brothers was lucky before the financial crisis. In 1994, one share of Lehman Brothers stock cost $4. By 2007, one share of Lehman Brothers stock had climbed to $82, a 20-fold increase. During the financial crisis, it used the borrowed money to play the property market. By 2007, it invested $60 billion in commercial property, hotels, shopping centers, and residential developments around the world before its bankruptcy. Greed brought about the downfall of Lehman Brothers.

Using the Martingale betting system, financial institutions have financial resources that put them in stronger positions in the financial games. However, if a financial institution puts all it has in one bet, it gives up its advantage. Financial institutions not only go all in on a bet but also borrow a lot more. They take even more risks in trading. A prudent financial institution should have started prudently with a new product—a new game—before it fully understands it. The New York Fed commented that LTCM ignored the risk of a lightning strike in a stormy field.

Nick Leeson, a derivatives trader, became notorious in 1995 for bankrupting Barings Bank, the United Kingdom's oldest merchant bank. After opening a Futures and Options office in Singapore, Leeson became a rogue trader, eventually losing over $1 billion of Barings' capital as its head of operations on the Singapore Exchange. On January 16, 1995, Leeson placed a short straddle on the Singapore and Tokyo stock exchanges.[56] The long position of

---

[55] *Bankruptcy of Lehman Brothers*, wikipedia.org, retrieved on April 28, 2024.
[56] *How Did Nick Leeson Contribute to the Fall of Barings Bank?* December 18, 2022, Investopedia, retrieved on December 22, 2023.

a straddle is an option trading strategy that involves purchasing both put and call options for the same underlying asset at the same time, speculating on a big price move either up or down. Leeson took the short position, speculating that the financial markets would remain calm and he could profit from the premiums paid by the traders who took the long position.

In a calm market, the short straddle would have made money for Leeson, but an unexpected event happened on January 17, 1995. An earthquake struck Kobe, Japan, and caused a sharp drop in the Asian financial markets. Leeson faced huge losses. To turn a loss into a gain, one must double the bet in the Martingale betting strategy. That is often what gamblers do. Leeson bet on the recovery of the Nikkei Stock Average on the Tokyo Stock Exchange with increasingly risky trades, but his losses piled up. In the end, his losses accounted for £827 million (or $1.4 billion), twice that of Barings' available trading capital.

Leeson held the record for the most trading losses until 2008. In 2008, the French bank Société Générale announced that a rogue trader named Jerome Kerviel had lost more than $7 billion by executing unauthorized trades. Financial institutions are the big winners in financial games, but ironically, the top losers are also financial institutions. The reason is simple: they gave up their advantage of strong financial resources and devoted substantial resources to a bet driven by greed. They might be lucky with consecutive heads in the financial game, but tails eventually showed up.

Chapter 5

Governments

5.1 Governments in Economy

5.1.1 *Government as a special consumer*

Economists define *Pareto efficiency* as a state where no one can be made better off without making someone else worse off. This is often used to judge the optimal allocation of resources in a market economy. In a *Walrasian equilibrium*, the market reaches a balance between supply and demand; the allocation of resources is considered Pareto efficient. However, taxation can disrupt this efficiency by redistributing wealth, reducing the utility of at least some individuals. Governments take wealth from some people and distribute it to others.

Economics often grapples with the tension between utilitarianism, which seeks to maximize happiness for the greatest number of people, and libertarianism, which emphasizes individuals' rights and freedom. Utilitarianism advocates that an economy should produce the greatest possible goods and allocate them in a way that maximizes utility for the majority—often summarized as the "greatest happiness for the greatest number." However, governments have often violated libertarian rights and also, have failed to maximize utility for the greatest number since ancient times.

Before the Industrial Revolution, land was the main capital stock and one of the primary means of production. A state could not accumulate land in the economy unless it conquered land by force.

Thus, setting aside land acquired by force, the macroeconomic identity simplifies to

$$Y - C - G = 0,$$

because of $I = 0$, where G is government consumption.

The division of consumption between the government and its people was a major issue in the real economy. Historically, governments collected taxes but often used the money for non-productive—or even self-destructive—programs, negatively affecting the real economy.

Clay tablets found at the site of the Sumerian city-state of Lagash, located between the Tigris and Euphrates rivers, first mention taxes. These early tablets, about 6,000 years old, contain information about taxes on transactions paid by farmers, cattle breeders, artisans, hunters, and merchants. Before the invention of money, taxes were paid in kind (e.g., crops and livestock), usually amounting to one-tenth of the income received. These early systems also included other forms of conscription, not limited to military service, such as the cultivation of temple lands or the construction of irrigation canals.[1] Without conscription, states had to collect taxes, so conscription reduced taxes and could be regarded as a different type of tax (Duindam, 2013). People could also pay to opt out of their civil conscription.

Hammurabi (see p. 125) was one of the early kings to collect taxes in silver, forcing farmers to sell part of their harvest on the market or borrow silver from usurers at high interest rates, often leading to the financial ruin of the farmers. Farmers who could not repay the money they borrowed became creditors' slaves or gave their children and other relatives as slaves. Farmers who did not pay taxes for three years lost the right to their land. The combination of land rules and the monetary taxes destroyed many farmers. Craftsmen and other occupations were slaves. Only farmers were free and motivated to produce more. Destroying farmers also meant destroying the economy.[2]

In ancient economies without active markets, collecting taxes in silver could lead to significant economic problems. With insufficient silver in circulation, farmers often had to borrow from moneylenders

[1] *Sumerians, Assyria, Babylonia: Tribute, Tithe, Tax Reform, Duty, Temple Fee*, Digital Tax Technologies, retrieved on April 3, 2024.

[2] *Code of Hammurabi*, history.com, retrieved on April 4, 2024.

at exorbitant interest rates. These high rates intensified demand for silver and further exacerbated the shortage, leading to a vicious cycle. As a result, many borrowers were at risk of being unable to repay their debts and facing insolvency.

In the feudal economy, feudal lords owned land. Land ownership and control over labor were central to the economy. Feudal lords granted the use of land in exchange for military and non-military services or *feods*, which were payments with real goods such as food, clothing, horses, or arms instead of money. The nobility consumed goods, most of which were luxury (Bloch and Koziol, 2014). States used taxes or physical labor to build palaces and mansions and conduct state "projects." The most renowned projects of ancient states are the world wonders like the Great Wall of China, the Egyptian Great Pyramids, and the Roman Colosseum.

William the Conqueror instituted the early tax system in England in 1066. The king controlled all the land in each territory and divided it among his lieutenants and supporters, who would pay him taxes, either in money or services, to keep their land. In return, the king protected the landholders. William decreed: "every man, no matter of whom he holds his land, is the king's man and owes allegiance to the king" (Maitland, 2001). Landholders were limited to renting property to others for a fee. In 1290, England passed the statute of Quia Emptores allowing tenants to sell their land to others but requiring the new owner to take on the same obligations to the lord as the previous owner. At the time, this system was called "free and common socage," a type of land ownership, and a person who held land was a "socman" who, in exchange, paid taxes or provided services related to farming instead of military service (Wallis *et al.*, 2006).

Citizens have basic needs and, without meeting them, a government cannot avoid collapse. However, governments have often failed to satisfy the poor with essential means of survival. In China, the First Emperor, Qin Shi Huang, started building the Great Wall in 221 B.C., which imposed heavy burdens on the peasants. Eventually, peasant uprisings ended the Qin dynasty, which lasted only 15 years.

In ancient China, equality was one of the guiding principles of governing a state. Taoist Laozi[3] said in his Tao Te Ching: "Universal

[3]Laozi, "Old Master" in Chinese, circa 4th century BC.

law is to curb superabundance to supplement deficiency." In the Song dynasty (960–1279 AD), peasant revolts used the slogan "even the rich and the poor."[4]

During the Qing dynasty, the state recognized that poverty problems could undermine the government. In the 1870s, Qing rulers and officials presented themselves as benevolent parents of the people and portrayed the famished as suffering children in need of the state's help. The government stored grain in granaries for the starving poor and emergencies. In response to the North China Famine of 1876–1879, the government opened the granaries to relieve the starvation of the people.[5] However, after the Western powers defeated China in the Opium Wars (1839–1842), the Qing government no longer had the resources it had before the war and distributed smaller amounts of grain to the starving population. For example, in Shanxi Province, where the famine was most severe, government relief offices dispensed a total of 10.7 million taels of relief silver, but only one million shi[6] of relief grain, during the disaster (Edgerton-Tarpley, 2004, 2016).

The state also relied on time-honored strategies such as selling state grain at below-market prices (pingtiao) in stricken areas to stabilize food prices, reducing or canceling taxes, investigating affected areas to classify households according to their degree of disaster, and collaborating with local elites to open soup kitchens and shelters. The customs official and historian of China, H.B. Morse, calculated that between 1876 and 1878 the Qing government granted over 18 million taels[7] of tax remissions, which equaled "more than one-fifth of one year's receipts of the imperial treasury," to drought-stricken Shanxi, Henan, Shaanxi, and Zhili. The central government also allocated over 5 million taels in direct aid for famine relief and ordered provinces outside the famine area to loan additional relief money to the drought-stricken provinces. The Qing government's

[4]In one of the earliest Chinese novels, the 14th-century *Water Margin* uses the phrase "kill the rich to help the poor."

[5]*North China famine, 1876–79*, DisasterHistory.org, retrieved on July 7, 2024.

[6]*Shi*, the basic unit of weight in ancient China. The first emperor of China in 221 B.C., Qin Shi Huang Di, unified basic units. He fixed the *shi* at about 60 kg. The modern *shi* is 71.68 kg (Britannica).

[7]*Tael*, a Chinese unit of weight that, when applied to silver, was long used as a unit of currency. Most taels were equivalent to 1.3 ounces of silver (Britannica).

practices served as economic insurance that private insurance could not afford.

Early history reveals an inherent tension between the state's use of economic resources and inequality. When government projects misallocated resources, they often deepened inequality and precipitated economic collapse. From Taoism to Marxism, various philosophies continue to shape debates about the role of the state in managing the economy and addressing inequality. The slogan "even the rich and the poor" has deep roots in Chinese culture. In a society dominated by peasants, this slogan was easily understood and had the power to persuade peasants to join revolts. The Communist revolution in China not only had the same appeal but also blended Taoism and Marxist ideology, forging a system rooted in both philosophy and economics. This synthesis resonated with intellectuals and gave such slogans a stronger allure among the masses. In comparison, capitalism does not have a slogan as simple and intuitive as "even the rich and the poor".

5.1.2 *Government as a special financial institution*

The Industrial Revolution transformed economies by introducing machines and fossil fuels, significantly enhancing productivity and changing the economic landscape. Capital investment $I = \dot{K}$ entered the macroeconomic equation. This shift allowed for vast capital accumulation, which in turn led to the concentration of capital in a few hands. As Keynes (2017) noted, "It was precisely the inequality of the distribution of wealth which made possible those vast accumulations of fixed wealth and of capital improvements which distinguished that age from all others," "...The immense accumulations of fixed capital which, to the great benefit of mankind, were built up during the half century before the war, could never have come about in a society where wealth was divided equitably. The railways of the world, which that age built as a monument to posterity, were, not less than the Pyramids of Egypt, the work of labor which was not free to consume in immediate enjoyment the full equivalent of its efforts." The massive capital accumulation came at the expense of growing inequality. As inequality deepened, debates arose over the role that governments should play in mitigating wealth disparities and safeguarding economic prosperity for all.

Economics normally includes governments in the macroeconomic identity:

$$I = Y - C - G, \tag{5.1}$$

Macroeconomic textbooks balance national income and spending in terms of *money*. Government spending G is considered government consumption. This book interprets macroeconomic identity as the *real goods* balance. In modern economies, governments are typically not the primary consumers, except in circumstances such as wartime or when corruption significantly distorts economic activity.

The example in Chapter 3 shows that bank loans to the poor have a direct effect on the real economy. Similarly, government intervention in the form of welfare programs can also have direct effects on the economy. If we replace bank loans with food stamps or other government assistance, the government program has the same effect on the real economy as bank loans.

The difference between banks and governments is who receives credit and who pays for it. For bank loans, the borrower pays the loan back. A government collects taxes from a group of households and firms and gives the money to different groups of households and firms. Governments redistribute money. Unlike producers in a capitalist economy, both banks and governments primarily handle money rather than real goods. In this sense, governments function similarly to banks; both create and distribute money. Governments are a special type of bank.

From a different viewpoint, a government functions as an insurance provider. Modern governments are uniquely positioned to provide large-scale insurance programs, including social security, healthcare, and national defense, due to their ability to mobilize financial resources at the national level.

The state credit theory views taxes as citizens' debts to repay the government for services provided. David Graeber referred to this concept as the *primordial debt* theory (see p. 125). Early governments or states primarily provided security "insurance" against foreign threats or invasions. As governments expanded, they added more insurance programs.

Like private insurance, government programs face *moral hazard* and *adverse selection* problems (Akerlof, 1970). For instance, those who have cellphone insurance are less careful with their phones because they know their insurance will cover any damage. Similarly, more generous unemployment benefits can create a *moral hazard* problem, disincentivizing recipients from seeking employment.

When a government promises expensive insurance benefits but cannot collect enough taxes to cover the claims, it faces a deficit problem. To avoid upsetting citizens by cutting benefits, governments often borrow money, shifting the financial burden to future generations.

Governments also have voluntary insurance programs, such as the Federal Long Term Care Insurance, which can face *adverse selection* issues. Insurance companies, unable to assess individual health conditions, charge an average premium. People with poor health are more likely to buy insurance, while those with good health opt out. This imbalance forces insurers to raise premiums, but higher premiums dissuade participation from those with lower risk, driving out healthier customers and potentially collapsing the insurance market.[8]

Socialism and communism can be viewed as forms of government insurance on a large scale. In these systems, individuals effectively pay "insurance premiums" to the government, which in turn provides insurance-like benefits to all. Individuals surrender their incomes to the government in exchange for these benefits. However, people naturally desire to contribute less by working less while still receiving the same level of benefits. What the government can provide depends on how much people produce. As output decreases, the benefits the government can offer diminish as well. This dynamic creates a self-reinforcing cycle where decreased benefits further demotivate workers. The vicious cycle in which moral hazard continually undermines economic performance culminates in the collapse of the system.

The Austrian school of economics theorizes that governments have no place in a pure capitalist, laissez-faire economy. In this view, the economy functions as a self-regulating system, requiring no external control or interference. In contrast, many economies that incorporate government intervention are referred to as *welfare economies*. These economies feature various degrees of government involvement

[8]George Akerlof illustrated adverse selection in his seminal paper on the "market for lemons" (Akerlof, 1970).

in providing social safety nets and redistributing wealth. Some welfare capitalist countries even identify themselves as socialist. The key distinction between capitalist and socialist economies lies in the ownership and control of enterprises. In a capitalist economy, private enterprises dominate the ownership of the means of production, whereas in a socialist economy, state-owned enterprises take the lead.

Socialist economies vary widely, ranging from Hitler's National Socialism to North Korea's model. Hitler's National Socialist economy was designed as a war machine, with the government not merely regulating but directing the economy (Gross, 2018). Historically, socialist experiments in the U.S. led by Robert Owen, Charles Fourier, and Saint–Simon collapsed under the weight of financial limitations and internal conflicts. Communist governments, on the other hand, claim that socialism is the first step toward achieving communism. In this framework, socialist governments assume control over private enterprises and manage the production and investment activities of state-owned enterprises.

Ironically, state-owned enterprises have been expanding within capitalist economies. According to an IMF study, state-owned enterprises have accounted for about half of global GDP over the past decade. These enterprises have become major players in the global economy, operating under different regulations and enjoying government support, which shields them from bankruptcy risk. State ownership continues to grow among the world's largest corporations.

In its infancy, the U.S. economy closely resembled a laissez-faire model (see the discussions in Chapters 1 and 4). Although the government played a minimal role in the real economy, the Federalists, led by Alexander Hamilton, the first Secretary of the Treasury under President George Washington, contended that the federal government needed strong financial powers—specifically, the ability to borrow money, collect taxes, and establish a central bank. As a result, the U.S. established the First Bank of the United States, chartered by Congress and signed into law by President George Washington in 1791. However, after 20 years, Congress declined to renew its charter. The Constitution of the United States divides the federal system into three branches: legislative, executive, and judicial. We loosely apply the term "U.S. government" to cover institutions ranging from Congress to the central bank.

The early laissez-faire economy of the U.S. was unstable. Following the expiration of the First Bank in 1811, the U.S. experienced a series of financial crises, including major bank panics in 1837, 1873, 1893, and 1907. In response, Congress passed the Federal Reserve Act in 1913, establishing the Federal Reserve System as a central bank aimed at addressing financial crises. However, despite these efforts, the U.S. soon faced its worst financial crisis: the Great Depression, which had devastating effects on both the U.S. and the global economies. The government's tax policies in the U.S. have undergone similar twists and turns, as the next section shows.

5.1.3 *The right to collect taxes*

The phrase "No taxation without representation" is often associated with the American Revolution, which drew inspiration from foundational principles of British law. The Magna Carta, signed by King John of England in 1215 to avoid civil war amid baronial unrest, established critical principles of governance, including limits on the king's authority to impose taxes. It required the king to seek the consent of the "common counsel" of the realm—comprising archbishops, bishops, abbots, earls, and barons—before levying certain taxes. While it did not express the later principle of "No taxation without representation," it marked an early step toward limiting absolute monarchical power and transferring some authority over taxation to a representative body. It also introduced important legal rights, such as the right of inheritance, for the first time in English law.

The French Revolution was largely fueled by fiscal and tax resentment. Before the Revolution, the First Estate (the clergy) had the power to collect the tithe, a 10% tax on agricultural produce. The Second Estate (nobility) did not pay taxes. Consequently, the burden of taxation fell on the Third Estate, which included everyone from peasants to businesspeople. The government imposed a direct tax called the taille (meaning "cut").

The French heavily relied on the taille to fund wars, which became a significant grievance for the Third Estate. The French Revolution ultimately abolished both the tithe and the taille and drew inspiration from the American Declaration of Independence for its own document: the Declaration of the Rights of Man. This document established that taxes should be based on the wealth a person possesses, reflecting the revolutionaries' pursuit of equality. The slogan of the Revolution—"Liberté, Egalité, Fraternité"—encapsulated the fight against the privileges of the upper classes. However, after the French Revolution, France introduced an income tax, while the property tax, called the taxe foncière, is still in use today. Besides income and property taxes, more taxes have been added to the list: corporate tax, sales tax, capital gain tax, and social purpose taxes.

The Founding Fathers of the U.S. fully understood the dangers of taxation without representation and sought to avoid imposing direct taxes on Americans without their consent. However, one of the Founding Fathers, Benjamin Franklin, famously acknowledged the inevitability of taxes, saying, "In this world, nothing is certain except death and taxes." During the American Revolutionary War (1775–1783), the U.S. imposed import taxes, such as tariffs of \$0.50 per ton on foreign vessels and \$0.06 per ton on American vessels, along with certain excise taxes.[9]

During the American Civil War (1861–1865), Abraham Lincoln signed the Revenue Act of 1861, which established the first progressive income tax. The tax schedule was initially a 3% tax on incomes between \$600 and \$10,000 and a 5% tax on higher incomes, later amended in 1864.[10] Lincoln promised that this income tax would be a temporary measure to help fund the war. Congress repealed the income tax in 1872, and the Commissioner of Internal Revenue, who oversaw tax collection, was disbanded.

The U.S. Constitution divides taxes into direct and indirect categories. A direct tax is one that the taxpayer pays directly to the government and cannot be shifted to another party, while an indirect tax can be passed on to others.[11] For example, property taxes are direct, while sales taxes are indirect. Article I of the Constitution grants Congress the authority to "lay and collect Taxes, Duties, Imports, and Excises" but requires direct taxes to be apportioned among the states based on population: "... direct Taxes shall be apportioned among the States ... according to their respective Numbers ... " This

[9]Excise taxes are taxes imposed on certain goods, services, and activities, such as cigarettes, alcoholic beverages, and gasoline (IRS.gov, retrieved on October 3, 2023).

[10]Congress later raised taxes and amended the schedule in 1864 to levy a tax of 5% on incomes between \$600 and \$5,000, a 7.5% tax on incomes in the \$5,000–\$10,000 range and a 10% tax on everything higher. *The First Income Tax*, battlefields.org, retrieved December 26, 2023.

[11]IRS.gov, retrieved December 27, 2023.

distinction has significant implications for how taxes are levied and collected in the U.S.

The Founding Fathers of the U.S. who wrote the Constitution had different ideas about the future United States. The Federalists led by Alexander Hamilton believed in a strong federal government and gave the government more power to make monetary policies and collect taxes. In contrast, the Republicans, led by Thomas Jefferson, guarded individual freedoms and the rights of states, opposing the federal government's power over states and people.[12] The Revenue Act of 1861 was short-lived. Since then, the power the federal government's power to tax Americans has undergone many changes, shaped by the alternating dominance of Federalists and Republicans. The debate between federalism and decentralization has continued not just in the U.S. but globally (Enikolopov and Zhuravskaya, 2007).

A key legal battle over taxation came in 1794, when Congress enacted a $16 tax on each carriage owned by an individual or business. Daniel Hylton challenged this tax, claiming it was a direct tax that should have been apportioned according to state populations. The Court concluded that the carriage tax was not a direct tax and thus did not violate the requirements for the apportioning of direct taxes. There were two major reasons for this conclusion. First, the U.S. Constitution did not clearly define direct and indirect taxes, leaving room for interpretation. The Court questioned whether Congress could reasonably apportion the taxes. Justice Chase stated, "the Constitution evidently contemplated no taxes as direct taxes but only such as Congress could lay in proportion to the census. The rule of apportionment is only to be adopted in such cases where it can reasonably apply."[13] Second, the court's interpretation of federal taxes on personal property as "indirect taxes" meant that direct taxes did not include any taxes on the possession of goods.[14]

In 1895, the case of Pollock v. Farmers' Loan & Trust Co. changed this interpretation when the court ruled that taxes on income from property were considered direct taxes. The Revenue

---

[12]The Federalist party and the Republican party of the early republic were not the ancestors of today's Democratic party and Republican party.

[13]*A Wealth Tax Is Constitutional* by Calvin H. Johnson and John T. Kipp, August 8, 2019, americanbar.org, retrieved on March 18, 2024.

[14]*Hylton v. United States*, ballotpedia.org, retrieved April 5, 2024.

Act or Wilson–Gorman Tariff of 1894[15] imposed a 2% tax on income over $4,000. In compliance with the Act, the New York-based Farmers' Loan & Trust Company announced the tax to its shareholders. Charles Pollock, a Massachusetts citizen who owned ten shares of stock in the Farmers' Loan & Trust Company, sued the company to prevent it from paying the tax. He lost in the lower courts but finally appealed to the U.S. Supreme Court. In 1895, the Supreme Court ruled in Pollock's favor, stating that the taxes levied by the Wilson–Gorman Act on income from property violated the U.S. Constitution because the tax on income from property is a "direct tax." This decision led to a significant change in the history of U.S. taxation.

To address this issue, the Sixteenth Amendment to the Constitution was ratified on February 3, 1913, giving Congress the power to levy income taxes without apportioning them among the states. This amendment effectively nullified the Supreme Court decision and marked a major shift in federal taxation. The Revenue Act of 1913 soon followed, establishing a federal income tax and transforming the federal government into a more powerful entity with increased financial resources.

The Sixteenth Amendment removed many of the constraints on taxation, allowing the government to impose income taxes more freely. During World War I (1914–1918), the highest income tax rate surged from 7% in 1913 to 77% in 1918. Similar tax increases occurred during World War II, with top rates rising from 79% in 1936 to 94% in 1945. In 1943, Congress passed the Current Tax Payment Act, requiring employers to withhold taxes from employees' wages and remit them to the government quarterly.[16]

Tax policy continued to evolve. The Revenue Act of 1964 under President John F. Kennedy cut taxes, reducing the top rate to 70% and corporate taxes from 52% to 48%. Reaganomics in the 1980s further slashed tax rates, including lowering the top rate to 50% and reducing capital gains taxes.[17]

[15]The 1890 McKinley tariff increased average duties across all imports. People called McKinley the "Napoleon of Protection" for his protectionism. *McKinley Tariff, Wikipedia*, retrieved December 26, 2023.

[16]*Constitutional Amendments - Amendment 16 - "Income Taxes,"* Ronald Reagan Presidential Library, retrieved March 18, 2024.

[17]*IRA for employees, The Untold History of Taxes & War in America*, Valuetainment, 2001, retrieved December 25, 2023.

In 2017, U.S. taxpayers paid a total of $1,587.12 billion in income tax, with corporations contributing $297.048 billion. Although corporate taxes represented a smaller share of federal revenues, they remained a significant source of funding.[18] Individuals paid income tax of 52% and payroll tax of 33%. A payroll tax is paid to the government social insurance programs like Social Security and Medicare.

Despite Americans' long-standing dislike for taxes, attitudes shifted over time. While federal income tax was once the most despised, surveys in the 1980s revealed that property taxes had become the most hated.[19] In 2022, U.S. government spending reached a significant 36.3% of GDP. While this is a substantial figure, it is still lower than in many other countries (see Table 5.1). Governments in these welfare states often act as major insurers, and their programs have a profound impact on their respective real economies.

Table 5.1. Government expenditure as percent of GDP.

Country	**2022**
France	58.33647
Italy	56.74398
Belgium	53.54714
Finland	53.04709
Austria	52.79795
Greece	52.49721
Germany	49.47735
Iceland	47.54084
Sweden	47.32258
Spain	47.1114
United Kingdom	44.30203
Japan	44.09254
Canada	41.43288
United States	36.25528

[18] *Above the Law*, December 23, 2019; *How Much Revenue from the Corporate Income Tax Does the Federal Government Collect?* statista.com, retrieved December 18, 2023.

[19] *National Conference of State Legislatures* website, retrieved on December 26, 2023.

5.2 Taxes and Governments' Programs

The legal publisher Commerce Clearing House compiled the Standard Federal Tax Reporter, a volume of 70,000 pages that represents the U.S. tax code.[20] As Einstein observed, "the most incomprehensible thing about the world is that it is comprehensible." Yet, he added, "The hardest thing in the world to understand is income tax." How could humans have created a system that even the brightest minds struggle to comprehend?[21]

Logic has enabled humans to comprehend the natural world, while the concept of "fairness" has shaped the tax system. The Internal Revenue Service emphasizes fairness by stating that individuals with different amounts of wealth or income should pay taxes at different rates.[22] However, there is no universally accepted definition of fairness. For socialists, it may be fair to redistribute wealth from the rich to the poor, whereas libertarians might disagree. The Founding Fathers themselves held conflicting views on what constituted a "fair" government. Today's tax code reflects these ongoing conflicts, as the various interpretations of fairness by legislators are embedded within it.

Analytic philosophy has largely avoided such ambiguous concepts as "fairness." In the context of the real economy, the ethical debate can be set aside to focus on whether a tax system enhances economic prosperity.

Given the complexity of the tax code, any tractable model must greatly simplify it (Diamond, 1980). Corporate tax is levied on earnings, which is different from the net return of capital stock (see Section 2.1.2.8). For simplicity, we approximate the corporate tax based on the net return. The U.S. government imposes a corporate tax rate $\tilde{T}_K$ on firms' profits. For losses, corporations—especially C corporations,[23] where shareholders are taxed separately from the corporation—can receive tax rebates. Typically, a corporation can

[20] *How Many Words are in the Tax Code?* by Joseph Bishop-Henchman, April 15, 2014, taxfoundation.org, retrieved on April 8, 2024.

[21] *Letters: February 22, 1963*, Time magazine online archive, retrieved November 19, 2023.

[22] *Lesson 1: How to Measure Fairness*, apps.irs.gov, retrieved on April 8, 2024.

[23] *What Is a C Corp?* by Andrew Ancheta, August 14, 2023, investopedia, retrieved December 29, 2023.

carry a net operating loss back two years to offset past profits or forward up to 20 years against future profits.

According to accounting rules, for a company without debt, corporate tax is levied on its revenue $(Pf(K,L))$ after deducting variable costs (wL) and fixed costs $(P\delta K)$. Using Eq. (2.7) gives

$$[Pf(K,L) - wL - P\delta K]\,\tilde{T}_K = PrK\tilde{T}_K. \tag{5.2}$$

Then for the shareholders, the net return on capital stock after the corporate tax is:

$$PrK(1-\tilde{T}_K). \tag{5.3}$$

The idea that a corporation pays taxes suggests that it operates like an individual, but no such entity exists as a single, cohesive person. The contractual theory of corporations views a corporation as a collection of agreements among various parties, particularly shareholders, bondholders, and managers. In the U.S., state laws govern corporations and define the legal rights and obligations of each party. The real question is who ultimately bears the burden of corporate taxes and how these taxes impact the various stakeholders. Households, specifically the middle class and the wealthy, ultimately own all firms and ultimately bear the burden of these taxes.

A capital gains tax is imposed on the increase in an asset's price relative to its purchase value. Chapter 4 distinguishes between the real return (r) on capital stock and the inflation (π) of stock prices. An ideal tax system would tax the real return and price inflation separately (see the later discussion on the asset gains tax). The current tax system does not distinguish between increases in stock prices driven by genuine growth in capital and those resulting from inflation. Both are subject to the capital gains tax $\tilde{T}_C$:

$$\tilde{T}_C[\pi\Phi + PrK(1-\tilde{T}_K)], \tag{5.4}$$

where $\pi\Phi$, the inflation of assets, is subject only to capital gains tax. Consequently, the stockholders pay tax twice on the real return, PrK. The combination of corporate tax and capital gains tax is widely known as *double taxation*.

In addition, households pay tax on their wages at the income tax rate $\tilde{T}_I$ and pay tax on consumption at the sales tax rate $\tilde{T}_S$. In the European Union, a value-added tax (VAT) applies to goods and services at each stage of production, from semi-finished products to final consumer goods. Japan introduced a national consumption tax of 3% in 1989. In the U.S., most states levy a sales tax on purchases of goods. After all taxes, households have the budget constraint:

$$\dot{\Phi} = (1 - \tilde{T}_C)[\pi\Phi + PrK(1 - \tilde{T}_K)] + wL(1 - \tilde{T}_I) - PC(1 + \tilde{T}_S). \tag{5.5}$$

According to the tax laws, the owners who hold a financial asset for more than a year pay the tax on the profit at the capital gains rate; otherwise, the profit is taxed at the ordinary income rate. Equation (5.5) assumes that households hold their assets for more than a year and pay the capital gains tax on the profits from the assets. At a constant price, $\pi = 0$, Eq. (5.5) goes back to the after-tax real economy:

$$\dot{K} = rK(1 - \tilde{T}_K)(1 - \tilde{T}_C) + \frac{wL}{P}(1 - \tilde{T}_I) - C(1 + \tilde{T}_S), \tag{5.6}$$

which reduces households' real income and increases consumption costs.

The U.S. government uses tax money in various programs, including food stamps, pensions, Medicare, and others. The government programs provide $\gamma_K r\Phi$ to firms and $\gamma_I wL$ to households. The benefits provided by the government programs are the payments to firms and households, and they are negative taxes. Putting taxes and benefits together, the government surplus or deficit S_{urp} is

$$\begin{aligned}\dot{S}_{urp} = {} & (\tilde{T}_K - \gamma_K + \tilde{T}_C)PrK + \tilde{T}_C\pi\Phi \\ & + (\tilde{T}_I - \gamma_I)wL + \tilde{T}_S PC + \Sigma,\end{aligned} \tag{5.7}$$

which uses the approximation,

$$(1 - \tilde{T}_K)(1 - \tilde{T}_C) \approx 1 - \tilde{T}_K - \tilde{T}_C,$$

because tax rates are lower than 100%, $\tilde{T}_K < 1$, and the capital gains tax is normally much less than 100%, $\tilde{T}_C \ll 1$, thus $\tilde{T}_C\tilde{T}_K$ is neglected for simplicity. The symbol Σ is the profits from the government money creation—the seigniorage. Economists consider seigniorage a form of inflation tax, which returns resources to the government. Issuing new currency instead of collecting taxes imposes an additional, hidden inflation tax on holders of existing currency (McIndoe-Calder, 2018; Snowdon and Vane, 2002). The following discussions ignore the inflation tax generated by seigniorage.

Incorporating the benefits from the government into Eq. (5.5) gives:

$$\dot{\Phi} = (1 - \tilde{T}_C)[\pi\Phi + PrK(1 - \tilde{T}_K + \gamma_K)] \\ + wL(1 - \tilde{T}_I + \gamma_I) - PC(1 + \tilde{T}_S). \tag{5.8}$$

Using a simpler notation $T_i = \tilde{T}_i - \gamma_i$, rewrite Eq. (5.8) using T_i to give:

$$\dot{\Phi} = (1 - T_C)\pi\Phi + I_m Pf(K, L) - P\delta K(1 - T_K)(1 - T_C) \\ - PC(1 + T_S). \tag{5.9}$$

where, using $wL = (1 - a)f(K, L)$, $I_m = a(1 - T_K)(1 - T_C) + (1 - a)(1 - T_1)$.

Note that governments normally do not give back capital gains tax or sales tax, and, thus, $\gamma_C = \gamma_S = 0$.

5.2.1 *Capital gains tax and asset gains tax*

The opponents of capital gains tax claim that *double taxation* is unfair to the shareholders. The former president, George W. Bush, had plans to phase out the capital gains tax gradually, but the Obama administration reversed it. Equation (5.5) supports the claim of double taxation by demonstrating that the current tax system taxes profits arising from the real economy twice, whereas profits attributable to inflation are taxed only once at the lower capital gains rate. However, phasing out the capital gains tax would render inflationary profits on idle assets tax-free, thereby encouraging speculation in idle assets (see Section 5.2.1).

Households allocate a fraction (b) of their wealth to stocks, represented as ($PK = b\Phi$), while the remaining ($(1 - b)\Phi$) is held in idle assets. The parameter (b) indicates the composition of assets in the real economy. A decline in (b) reflects a shift toward the "idle" economy (see Chapter 4). The current tax system imposes capital gains tax on both price appreciation $\pi\Phi$ – inflation – and the growth of capital stock $\dot{K}$. Ideally, the tax system separates the capital gains tax into two: Asset gains tax T_A is levied on idle assets, whereas capital gains tax T_C applies to working assets. The "idle assets" are not capital, so "capital gains tax" on "idle assets" is a mismatch. It is misleading people to think they are investing in "capital." Separating the asset price appreciation into its components—one on capital growth and one on inflation—Eq. (5.5) gives:

$$\dot{\Phi} = I_m P f\left(\frac{b\Phi}{P}, L\right) - \delta(b\Phi)(1 - T_K)(1 - T_C) + (1 - T_A)\pi\Phi - P_C C(1 + T_S). \tag{5.10}$$

Second, the inflation of assets and the inflation of consumption goods are not the same. Defining P_C as the price of consumption goods can differentiate the inflation of the two prices.

The economy must produce real goods, particularly for a large economy, thus b is not an option, and households maximize consumption:

$$\max_C \int_0^t e^{-\rho s} \ln C ds, \tag{5.11}$$

subject to the budget constraint Eq. (5.10) and

$$\begin{aligned} C &= C_0 \text{ at } t = 0, \\ \Phi &= \Phi_0 \text{ at } t = 0, \\ \dot{C} &< \infty, \end{aligned} \tag{5.12}$$

which gives the Hamiltonian:

$$\begin{aligned} \mathcal{H}(\Phi, C, \theta, t) = &\ln C + \theta(1 - T_A)\pi\Phi \\ &+ \theta\left[I_m P f\left(\frac{b\Phi}{P}, L\right) - \delta(b\Phi)\right. \\ &\left.\times (1 - T_K)(1 - T_C)\right] \\ &- \theta P_C C(1 + T_S). \end{aligned} \tag{5.13}$$

Taking partial derivative of Eq. (5.13) with respect to C, we have the first-order condition for C.

$$\frac{\partial \mathcal{H}(\Phi, C, \theta, t)}{\partial C} = \frac{1}{C} - \theta P_C(1 + T_S) = 0, \tag{5.14}$$

which gives:

$$\theta = \frac{1}{(1+T_S)P_C C} = \frac{1}{C_A}, \tag{5.15}$$

where $C_A = (1+T_S)P_C C$ is the nominal consumption including sales tax.

Taking the partial derivative of Hamiltonian Eq. (5.13) with respect to Φ gives:

$$\begin{aligned}\frac{\partial \mathcal{H}(\Phi, C, \theta, t)}{\partial \Phi} &= \theta\left[I_m P f_\Phi\left(\frac{b\Phi}{P}, L\right) - b\delta(1-T_K)(1-T_C)\right] \\ &\quad + \theta(1-T_A)\pi = \rho\theta - \dot{\theta},\end{aligned} \tag{5.16}$$

where

$$f_\Phi\left(\frac{b\Phi}{P}, L\right) = \frac{b}{P}\frac{\partial}{\partial(b\Phi/P)} f\left(\frac{b\Phi}{P}, L\right).$$

Substituting Eqs. (5.15) and (5.16) gives the consumption process:

$$\dot{C}_A = \left\{(1-T_A)\pi + I_m P f_\Phi\left(\frac{b\Phi}{P}, L\right) - b\delta(1-T_K)(1-T_C) - \rho\right\} C_A, \tag{5.17}$$

which assumes the price of consumption goods is stable, i.e., no inflation.

At the equilibrium point $\{C^*, \Phi^*\}$, both $\dot{C}^*$ and $\dot{\Phi}^*$ are zero:

$$\begin{aligned}\dot{C}_A^* = F_1 = \Bigg\{&(1-T_A)\pi + I_m P f_\Phi\left(\frac{b\Phi^*}{P}, L\right) - b\delta \\ &\times (1-T_K)(1-T_C) - \rho\Bigg\} C_A^* = 0,\end{aligned} \tag{5.18}$$

$$\begin{aligned}\dot{\Phi}^* = F_2 = (1-T_A)\pi\Phi^* &+ I_m P f\left(\frac{b\Phi^*}{P}, L\right) - b\delta\Phi^* \\ &\times (1-T_K)(1-T_C) - C_A^* = 0.\end{aligned} \tag{5.18a}$$

The same approach in Chapter 1 can be used to check the stability of the real economy by collecting partial derivatives in $\mathcal{M}$, the Jacobian matrix:

$$\frac{d}{dt}\begin{bmatrix} C_A - C_A^* \\ \Phi - \Phi^* \end{bmatrix} = \mathcal{M}\begin{bmatrix} C_A - C_A^* \\ \Phi - \Phi^* \end{bmatrix}$$

$$\mathcal{M} = \begin{bmatrix} \frac{\partial F_1}{\partial C_A^*} & \frac{\partial F_1}{\partial \Phi^*} \\ \frac{\partial F_2}{\partial C_A^*} & \frac{\partial F_2}{\partial \Phi^*} \end{bmatrix}$$

$$= \begin{bmatrix} (1-T_A)\pi + I_m P f_\Phi\left(\frac{b\Phi^*}{P}, L\right) - b\delta \\ \quad \times(1-T_K)(1-T_C) - \rho & I_m P \frac{\partial^2}{\partial \Phi^{*2}} f\left(\frac{b\Phi^*}{P}, L\right) C_A^* \\ & (1-T_A)\pi + \\ & I_m P f_{\Phi^*}\left(\frac{b\Phi^*}{P}, L\right) - b\delta \times \\ -1 & (1-T_K)(1-T_C) \end{bmatrix}. \tag{5.19}$$

Using Eq. (5.18) simplifies the matrix to

$$\mathcal{M} = \begin{bmatrix} 0 & I_m P \frac{\partial^2}{\partial \Phi^{*2}} f\left(\frac{b\Phi^*}{P}, L\right) C_A^* \\ -1 & \rho \end{bmatrix} \tag{5.20}$$

which has two eigenvalues:

$$\frac{1}{2}\left(\rho \pm \sqrt{\rho^2 - 4C_A^* I_m P \frac{\partial^2}{\partial \Phi^{*2}} f\left(\frac{b\Phi^*}{P}, L\right)}\right). \tag{5.21}$$

Equations (5.21) and (1.48) share similar dynamics, and taxes do not change the saddle instability of the economy. However, this equilibrium applies to the monetary economy rather than the real economy (see p. 228).

Equation (5.21) includes income tax, corporate tax, and capital gains tax in I_m, and sales tax in C_A^*. The influence of income-tax on after-tax consumption (C_A) is substantial, as it directly affects after-tax wages.

Substituting ρ in Eq. (5.21) using Eq. (5.18) gives

$$\rho = (1-T_A)\pi + I_m P f_\Phi\left(\frac{b\Phi}{P}, L\right) - b\delta \times (1-T_K)(1-T_C).$$

The effects of asset gains tax become evident. Additionally, since asset gains result from asset price inflation, a high asset gains tax can positively impact the economy by discouraging asset speculation and reducing the wealth effect.

Effective tax policy presupposes that the government evaluates the state of the real economy in relation to the stable path. Based on this assessment, the government can adjust tax collection and benefit programs to guide the real economy back toward stability. For a "shrinking, lavish" economy, the government might impose higher income and sales taxes while eliminate corporate taxes to curb consumption and encourage investment. Conversely, in an "expanding, frugal" economy, increasing corporate taxes and reducing income and sales taxes can help address overcapacity while boosting consumption.

5.2.1.1 *Asset gains tax*

A tax system should minimize its negative impact on the real economy. Equation (5.10) suggests that a system with a 100% asset gains tax and near-zero tax rates on other tax bases could achieve this, leaving the real economy unaffected. This concept aligns with the proposal by American economist Henry George in the 19th century.[24] George advocated for a single tax on land values rather than on labor and capital, arguing that such a system would create a more productive and just society.

Britain's modern tax system initially relied on taxing land, capturing what John Stuart Mill referred to as the "unearned increment":

> Landlords grow rich in their sleep without working, risking, or economizing. The increase in the value of land, arising as it does from the efforts of an entire community, should belong to the community and not to the individual who might hold title.—Mill (1998)

He believed that landowners should be taxed on these unearned gains, since rising land values stem from economic growth rather than mere ownership. Institutional economist Thorstein Veblen extended

[24]Henry George (September 2, 1839–October 29, 1897) was an American political economist and journalist.

George's ideas, noting that not only landowners, but also owners of financial assets, posed a similar threat to economic justice.[25] Veblen viewed unearned income from financial assets as an ideal source of taxation, which could discourage living off unearned income, promote efficient resource utilization, and encourage entrepreneurship and hard work.[26]

In Chapter 4, the concept of "unearned increment" is reframed as the price appreciation or inflation of assets, emphasizing that money itself can generate this unearned value.

Common stocks have two components: price appreciation (inflation) and the growth of capital stock (see Eq. (4.24)). The growth of capital stock is the engine of the real economy, not price inflation. The ultimate solution to eliminate inflation lies in controlling the money supply. Until inflation can be fully eradicated, an alternative approach is to distinguish real growth from price inflation: tax the latter heavily, while reducing or removing taxes on the former.

A heavy tax on idle assets drives speculators out of the market, reducing the supply of idle assets. Once such assets cease to be profitable, the need for a capital gains tax disappears. However, the asset gains tax merely addresses a symptom; eradicating the root cause of the problem requires curbing money creation.

Taxation can prioritize the needs of the real economy. Since industries are not equal, fiscal policy can support rather than penalize sectors that produce essential goods such as food and shelter. For instance, some U.S. states exempt food from sales tax. Extending similar tax relief to rent and corporate taxes on agriculture and housing construction could stimulate greater production of food and housing. Although U.S. agriculture already produces a surplus beyond domestic needs, global demand for food remains high, and policies that encourage exports or donations would be beneficial to the world.

Today's tax system does not resemble Henry George's proposal. The U.S. and the European Union tax based on Haig–Simons income, defined as consumption plus changes in net worth. Using the symbols

---

[25]Thorstein Bunde Veblen (July 30, 1857–August 3, 1929) was an American institutional economist and sociologist. Institutional economics views the economy as an evolutionary process, shaped by its interactions with institutions.
[26]*Four Horsemen - Feature Documentary*, Renegade Inc., 2013.

in this book, the Haig–Simons income is[27]:

$$\begin{aligned} PC + \dot{\Phi} &= PC + \pi\Phi + P\dot{K} \\ &= \pi\Phi + PrK + wL. \end{aligned} \tag{5.22}$$

All components of Haig-Simons income, as described in Eq. (5.22), are subject to taxation by governments.

In the current tax system, the average income tax rate ($\tilde{T_I}$) is higher than the capital gains tax rate ($\tilde{T_C}$). This disparity arises because price appreciation (inflation), unlike capital stock growth, which is subject to double taxation, is taxed only once at a low capital gains tax rate. Since the wealthy hold the majority of global assets, they benefit disproportionately from this preferential treatment, paying lower tax rates on asset gains. Meanwhile, income taxation burdens the middle-class households, reducing their disposable income and consumption. Moreover, wealth effect generated by price appreciation has little impact on households with few or no assets. Consequently, the current tax structure favors asset owners while penalizing non-owners, thereby widening the wealth gap between the haves and the have-nots.

The well-known Laffer curve illustrates a relationship between tax rates and government revenue. Laffer posits that no revenue is generated at both 0% and 100% tax rates, implying that there is an optimal tax rate between these extremes that maximizes revenue (Meyer, 2012). The Laffer curve concerns the average tax rate, whereas taxes on assets, firms, and consumption exert distinct—and at times opposing—effects on the real economy.

For instance, if the government were to impose an inflation tax close to 100% while reducing other taxes to a minimum, Eq. (5.10) after taxes becomes:

$$P\dot{K} \approx (1 - T_{\min})(PrK + wL - PC), \tag{5.23}$$

where $T_{\min}$ denotes the average tax rate after imposing a near-100% asset gains tax. The greater the revenue collected from taxing idle assets, the fewer other taxes are required, thereby reducing interference with the real economy. Most importantly, a nearly 100% tax rate

[27]Wikipedia, retrieved December 31, 2023.

renders idle assets unprofitable, causing them to eventually dwindle. While this would diminish asset gains tax as a revenue source, it would represent a tremendous success in curbing the wealth gap.

5.2.2 *Corporate tax*

Taxation has indirect consequences. Corporate taxation, for example, tends to lower employment levels and depress wages. A firm optimizes employment to maximize its after-tax profit:

$$\max_L [Pf(K, L) - PrKT_K]. \tag{5.24}$$

The wage that maximizes the after-tax profit of the firm is:

$$\frac{w}{P} = \frac{\partial}{\partial L}\{f(K, L) - [f_K(K, L) - \delta]KT_K\}. \tag{5.25}$$

The corporate tax reduces the workers' real wage by $f_{KL}(K, L)KT_K$. To get an explicit expression for the wage, we use the Cobb–Douglas production function, where corporate taxation reduces wages by:

$$a(1 - a)A\left(\frac{K}{L}\right)^a T_K. \tag{5.26}$$

The before-tax wage is:

$$\frac{w}{P} = (1 - a)A\left(\frac{K}{L}\right)^a, \tag{5.27}$$

and the rate of reduction is aT_K, where a is the output elasticity of capital stock:

$$\frac{K\partial f(K, L)}{f(K, L)\partial K} = a.$$

The larger the marginal product of capital stock, the less the marginal product of labor (see Eq. (1.17)), and the smaller the wage reduction.

5.2.2.1 *Tax and employment*

Corporate taxation tends to lower employment levels. When the corporate tax reduces the profitability of projects, firms cut back on both projects and staff, leading to declines in wages and employment. Equations (5.26) and (5.27) give the real wage after the corporate tax:

$$\begin{aligned}\frac{w}{P} &= (1-a)A\left(\frac{K}{L_T}\right)^a - a(1-a)A\left(\frac{K}{L_T}\right)^a T_K \\ &= (1-a)A\left(\frac{K}{L_T}\right)^a [(1-aT_K)], \qquad (5.28)\end{aligned}$$

and the number of workers L_T:

$$L_T = \left(\frac{(1-a)(1-aT_K)PA}{w}\right)^{1/a} K. \qquad (5.29)$$

With zero corporate tax, the number of workers is:

$$L = \left(\frac{(1-a)PA}{w}\right)^{1/a} K. \qquad (5.30)$$

Dividing L_T in Eq. (5.29) by L in Eq. (5.30) gives:

$$\frac{L_T}{L} = (1-aT_K)^{1/a}, \qquad (5.31)$$

which shows that corporate tax reduces employment and the reduction is a function of the output elasticity of capital stock, a, and the tax rate. The corporate tax has a double impact on households' consumption by lowering income through reduced wages and job losses.

5.2.2.2 *The value of tax shield and corporate borrowing*

A corporation deducts interest costs from revenue to calculate its pretax income (earnings before taxes). If the corporate tax rate is higher than the interest rate on the loan a corporation borrows, the combination of interest payment and tax payment is lower than the tax payment if the corporation does not borrow. The tax savings are the *value of the tax shield.* The value of the tax shield incentivizes corporations to borrow. Modigliani and Miller received the Nobel Prize in Economics for their theory on capital structure, the composition of equity and debt in a corporation's assets (Modigliani and Miller, 1963).

If a firm does not borrow, it pays corporate tax given in Eq. (5.2). However, if the firm borrows PK_b to repurchase its own stock, thereby reducing shareholders' ownership to K_e, which is the equity of the firm, the resulting debt lowers the firm's tax liability:

$$\begin{aligned}&[Pf(K_e + K_b, L) - wL - P\delta K - PR_bK_b]T_K\\&= P[rK - R_bK_b]T_K, \end{aligned} \tag{5.32}$$

where R_b is the interest rate on the debt and PR_bK_b is the value of the tax shield—a term introduced by Modigliani and Miller.

Interest payments on the debt reduce tax in Eq. (5.32). However, the firm's profit before tax—earnings before tax in accounting (EBT)—is reduced by the interest payment on PK_b:

$$EBT = P[rK - R_bK_b]. \tag{5.33}$$

Interest payments reduce pre-tax earnings by more than the tax savings provided by the debt's tax shield. Shareholders primarily care about profitability and are less concerned with the firm's ownership structure. When the firm's net return—measured as return on equity (ROE)—exceeds the interest rate on debt ($r > R_b$), shareholders benefit from leveraging debt.

When a firm issues debt, equity shares are reduced to K_e, meaning fewer shareholders divide the profits after interest payments to debtholders. If $r > R_b$, the difference accrues to the remaining shareholders, who then receive an increased return r^* compared to the pre-buyback return r:

$$\begin{aligned}Pr^*K_e(1 - T_K) &= [Pr(K_e + K_b) - PR_bK_b](1 - T_K)\\&= P[rK_e + (r - R_b)K_b](1 - T_K)\end{aligned} \tag{5.34}$$

and[28]

$$r^* = r + (r - R_b)\frac{K_b}{K_e}. \tag{5.35}$$

At a low interest rate (R_b) and higher (r), $r > R_b$, which is normally the case, the shareholders of the leveraged firm receive a higher return

[28]Modigniani and Miller Propositions.

r^*. Second, as K_b increases, the return r^* gets higher because fewer shares divide the larger excess return $(r - R_b)K_b$. This is one of the tricks of playing money—stock buyback. Yet, borrowing money carries the risk of being unable to pay interest and principal in the event of a business downturn. At a low interest rate, the trade-off between risk and return favors debt. The secondary market reacts to stock buybacks positively because of the higher return on the stocks.

After paying corporate tax and interest payments, shareholders pay personal taxes at the capital gains tax rate and bondholders pay taxes on interest payments received at the income tax rate:

$$P(rK - R_bK_b)(1 - T_K)(1 - T_C) + R_bK_b(1 - T_I). \qquad (5.36)$$

Shareholders pay fewer corporate taxes and personal taxes in total, while bondholders share the profits of leveraged firms and the tax liability by paying income taxes on the interest payments they receive. The tax treatment of corporate debt reduces the taxes collected by governments and encourages corporate borrowing, which contributes to the increase in global corporate debt.

Arbitrage-free conditions require that the returns after adjusting for risk should be the same. The taxes and interest rates set by governments and central banks, together with accounting rules, create tax-shield opportunities for corporations, thereby encouraging corporate borrowing. Tax laws and accounting rules often, intentionally or not, create loopholes for economic actors to use to their advantage.

5.3 War and Governments' Borrowing

Chapter 1 traces the origins of the word "economy" back to Socrates, who suggested that a ruler must manage both the economy and war. History has repeatedly shown how deeply intertwined these two are, and how wars place immense economic strain on nations. For example, the Seven Years' War (1756–1763), known as the French and Indian War in North America, nearly doubled Great Britain's national debt. In an effort to pay off this debt, Britain imposed new taxes on its American colonies, a move that contributed to the outbreak of the American Revolutionary War (1775–1783).

Similarly, the financial burden of the Seven Years' War exacerbated France's economic troubles. By 1785, the country faced a deep economic recession, worsened by poor harvests in 1787 and 1788.

These economic hardships, combined with political discontent, culminated in the French Revolution of 1789.[29] History demonstrates that war often necessitates higher taxes, and in turn, taxes can lead to revolts.

To avoid domestic revolts, governments often imposed taxes on colonies to raise revenues. David Graeber writes:

> This was already true in ancient Mesopotamia, where the inhabitants of independent cities did not usually have to pay direct taxes at all. Similarly, as Moses Finley[30] put it, "Classical Greeks looked upon direct taxes as tyrannical and avoided them whenever possible. Athenian citizens did not pay direct taxes of any sort; though the city did sometimes distribute money to its citizens, a kind of reverse taxation—sometimes directly, as with the proceeds of the Laurion silver mines, and sometimes indirectly, as through generous fees for jury duty or attending the assembly. Subject cities, however, did have to pay tribute. Even within the Persian Empire, Persians did not have to pay tribute to the Great King, but the inhabitants of conquered provinces did. The same was true in Rome, where for a long time, Roman citizens not only paid no taxes but had a right to a share of the tribute levied on others, in the form of the dole - the "bread" part of the famous "bread and circuses." In other words, Benjamin Franklin was wrong when he said that in this world nothing is certain except death and taxes.—Graeber (2012)

In 1765, the British Parliament passed the Stamp Act, which required colonists to pay taxes on every page of printed paper they used. This taxation without representation angered the American colonists, leading to the Stamp Act Congress in New York the same year. Representatives from nine colonies declared that the English Crown had no right to tax Americans who were not represented in the British Parliament. This growing sentiment of discontent ultimately culminated in the American Revolutionary War. In 1778, to quell the revolution, King George III ordered the British Parliament to declare that no further duties, taxes, or assessments would be imposed on the colonies for raising revenue.

---

[29] *French Revolution*, wikipedia.org, retrieved on March 30, 2024.

[30] Sir Moses Israel Finley, a Fellow of the British Academy, was an American-born British historian of the ancient world.

However, by then, it was too late—the colonies had already declared independence.[31]

During wars, the U.S. has faced the staggering costs of modern warfare. For example, the U.S. spent $27 billion on World War I, and the four years of involvement in World War II cost $4.1 trillion in 1913 dollars. In the final year of World War II, defense spending made up nearly 40% of GDP. Wars bring enormous economic losses globally. The cost to governments involved has been estimated at more than $1 trillion, not counting the human suffering, dislocation, or destruction of property.[32]

War, as Sun Tzu famously said, is "a matter of life and death, a road either to safety or to ruin."[33] In war, governments have no option but to fund war efforts. One of the most significant financial events in U.S. history—the abandonment of the gold standard—occurred during the Vietnam War. Although the U.S. government downplayed the war's impact on the economy, foreign governments did not and began to demand gold rather than U.S. dollars as inflation and deficits grew. This led President Nixon to take the U.S. off the gold standard, which transformed the international monetary system and had long-lasting effects on global economies. The Vietnam War cost the U.S. $738 billion in constant 2011 dollars from 1965 to 1975 (Daggett, 2008).

Beyond war, the U.S. maintains 750 military bases in 80 countries, costing taxpayers an estimated $55 billion annually. Constructing military infrastructure abroad costs between $70 billion and over $100 billion from 2000 to 2023, not including the costs of personnel stationed abroad, which could raise the total to over $80 billion (Vine *et al.*, 2021).[34]

The defense industry operates differently from other industries because its primary customer is the government, and it produces neither consumer goods nor capital goods. In wartime, the government becomes the largest consumer in the economy, purchasing weapons,

---

[31] *On This Day: The Stamp Act Plants the Seed of the Revolution*, National Constitution Center, retrieved on March 30, 2024.

[32] britannica.com, retrieved on April 10, 2024.

[33] *Art of War*, Sun Tzu, 5th century BCE.

[34] *750 Bases in 80 Countries Is Too Many for Any Nation: Time for the US to Bring Its Troops Home*, Cato Institute website, October 4, 2021, retrieved December 28, 2023.

aircraft, tanks, and ammunition. This shift exemplifies the power of governments in shaping economies during war. Since the Trojan War, governments have played dominant roles in mobilizing resources and directing economic efforts in times of conflict.

A war economy drastically reduces the production of consumer goods in favor of producing weaponry and ammunition. For example, Nazi Germany emphasized the enormous costs associated with producing a single tank, illustrating the collective sacrifice required for war production. Inside each Nazi tank, a manual informed the crew that "For every shell that you fire, your father has paid 100 Reichsmarks[35] in taxes, your mother has worked a week in the factory, and the trains have traveled 10,000 km. The tank's total cost was 800,000 Reichsmarks and 300,000 hours of work; 30,000 people will have given a week's salary, and 6,000 people will have worked a whole week so that you could have an armored combat vehicle. Everyone has been working for you, the tank crew. Think about what you have in your hands."[36]

In wartime, a government reallocates resources from non-defense industries to the defense industry, which leads to a significant restructuring of the economy. Production capacity is limited and cannot be increased overnight, so the defense industry must divert resources from other sectors.

Assume that, right before a war, a laissez-faire economy has only non-defense industries:

$$P\dot{K}_N = rPK_N + wL - PC, \tag{5.37}$$

where K_N is the capital stock of non-defense sectors of the economy. In peacetime, military activities are largely limited to routine maintenance, and the associated costs are relatively small compared to the overall economy. However, a war transforms the economies of the involved countries, shifting them into wartime economies. In such a scenario, governments direct resources and production to meet the demands of the war effort.

[35]Reichsmark was the monetary unit of the Third Reich, replaced in 1948 by the Deutsche Mark.

[36]*Blood Money Inside The Nazi Economy*, FreeDocumentaryHistory, retrieved March 3, 2024.

World War II, for example, transformed Great Britain from a free-market economy into a centrally managed economy, as the government assumed control over production, resource allocation, and labor to maximize war output (Broadberry and O'Rourke, 2010). Regardless of whether a government is capitalist or socialist, wartime production requires mobilizing all available resources, involving converting factories and industries that previously produced consumer goods into facilities that produce war goods, such as weapons, vehicles, and ammunition.

To reallocate resources to the defense sector, governments impose heavy taxes on the non-defense sectors, which stop growing:

$$0 = rPK_N(1 - T_K)(1 - T_C) + wL(1 - T_I) - P(1 - T_S)C_-, \quad (5.38)$$

where C_- is the consumption level before the war. Assuming the government keeps prices stable, it allocates all tax revenues to the defense industry:

$$P\dot{K}_D = P\dot{K}_N + rP\dot{K}_N(T_K + T_C) + wLT_I + T_C PC_-,$$

then, using (5.38), the amount of resources diverted to the defense sector is the production output before the war net of consumption and depreciation:

$$P\dot{K}_D = rPK_N + wL - PC_- = P[f(K_N, L) - C_- - \delta K_N]. \quad (5.39)$$

Once the government redirects resources to the defense industry, leaving only consumption goods C_- for civilians, the growth in the non-defense sector effectively halts. This stagnation diminishes corporate tax revenue from the non-defense industry, leading the government to rely on rising taxes to finance the war effort.

For instance, during World War I, the United States enacted the War Revenue Act of 1917 to raise funds for the war. This act significantly increased federal income tax rates while simultaneously lowering the thresholds for exemptions. Previously, the 2% tax bracket applied to incomes below \$20,000; the act lowered that threshold to \$2,000. Additionally, the top tax bracket, on incomes above \$2 million, was raised from 15% in 1916 to 67% in 1917 to 77% in 1918.[37] This drastic shift in tax policy exemplified how the government reallocated resources from individuals to the defense industry.

---

[37] *War Revenue Act of 1917*, wikipedia.org, retrieved April 3, 2024.

After the government allocates all tax revenue to the defense industry, the economy transforms to

$$\dot{K}_D = f(K_N, L) - C_- - \delta K_N - \frac{G}{P}, \tag{5.40}$$

where the government becomes the dominant consumer in the economy, in contrast to its peacetime role of merely reallocating money. A government in war faces the same trade-off between consumption and investment. Countries engaged in war attempt to expand their defense industries, but the limitations of growth are evident in Eq. (5.40). Wartime consumption—weaponry, ammunition, and other war expenses—diverts resources that could otherwise be invested in the defense sector. Yet, in a war economy, consumption—specifically weaponry and ammunition—is not optional and cannot be treated as a control variable. Unlike in a peacetime economy, where short-term reductions in consumption can enhance long-term production, in a war economy, the loss of key battles in the short term implies losing the war itself.

Within the context of the four types of economies described in Chapter 1, the "shrinking, lavish" economy faces the greatest difficulty shifting into a war economy. Such an economy already struggles with increasing household consumption alongside declining capital stock and production. Conversely, it is easier for an "expanding, frugal" economy to transition to a war economy. Before the war, it had excess production capacity and limited consumption. The shift to a war economy absorbs this excess capacity, turning its pre-war consumption problem into a wartime advantage. For instance, at the start of World War II, the U.S. had not fully recovered from the Great Depression, with weak consumption demand and idle production capacity. The war effort revitalized the U.S. economy, integrating two-thirds of it into the war effort by the end of 1943 (Henretta *et al.*, 2011). This transformation turned the U.S. into a wartime export powerhouse, an exceptional case in the history of war economies.

A comparison between capitalist and communist economies highlights the role of money in war. In a capitalist economy, the government raises taxes to finance the war. In a socialist or communist economy, the state confiscates goods and redirects production from consumer goods to weapons. Despite these different approaches, both systems reach the same endpoint: The strength of the real economy ultimately determines the outcome of prolonged conflicts.

During World War II, the U.S. economy could replace and even increase the production of airplanes, tanks, and warships, while Germany and Japan struggled to simply replace their losses. From mid-1943 onward, Germany shifted to a full war economy, significantly increasing military production. Yet, despite doubling or tripling production in categories like tanks and aircraft, Germany could not match the Allies' output. By late 1944, Allied bombings severely damaged German factories and cities, leading to the collapse of the German war economy in 1945. For example, synthetic fuel production dropped by 86%, explosive output by 42%, and tank output by 35% in just eight months.[38] Japan faced a similar fate. Its heavy industry was fully devoted to military production but suffered severe shortfalls due to its reliance on international trade and the loss of shipping capacity. By 1945, the war had effectively halted Japan's economy.[39]

The war machine is a monster with an insatiable appetite, consuming not only economies but also people and nations. Winning a war does not always translate into economic success. Despite being on the winning side of World War II, Great Britain lost its position as the world's dominant power and fell deep into debt. With few exports, Britain had no way to pay for imports, including food, and faced financial bankruptcy. To make matters worse, just weeks after Japan's surrender on September 2, 1945, U.S. President Harry S. Truman, as required by law, ended the Lend-Lease program.[40] Britain, which had relied on Lend-Lease for both necessities and arms, now faced a financial crisis. In a final act of service, John Maynard Keynes negotiated a $3.75 billion loan from the U.S. and a smaller one from Canada to keep Britain afloat (Broadberry and O'Rourke, 2010; *Britain since 1945*, Britannica). It took Britain more than 61 years to fully repay the U.S. loan, with the final payment made on December 31, 2006. After World War II, Britain faced severe economic constraints. Unlike the assertions of Modern Monetary Theory (see p. 144), it could not simply print pounds to acquire essential consumption and capital goods.

[38] *Economy of Nazi Germany*, wikipedia.org, April 11, 2024.

[39] *Economic History of Japan*, wikipedia.org, April 11, 2024.

[40] The Roosevelt Administration provided large-scale economic support to Britain through the Lend-Lease Act of 1941, supplying $31.4 billion in goods that did not require repayment.

The history of wars reveals the limits of monetary power and underscores the indispensability of the real economy. Even with the ability to create money, a nation cannot overcome economic challenges such as resource scarcity or production capacity constraints, demonstrating the principle that "money can't buy everything."[41] Winning a war relies on weapons and ammunition, and survival depends on food and shelter.

In the fairy tale of the Brothers Grimm, Princess Amelie—the salt princess—understood salt as an indispensable part of life, but the King did not. He banished Princess Amelie when she told the king she loved him as dear as salt. The King only learned to distinguish between necessities like salt and luxuries like jewelry or gold during the time of hardship.

During World War II, it was not the U.S. dollars but the production capacity of the U.S. that was the critical factor in defeating the Axis powers. The U.S. shared war goods with its allies. Under the 1941 Lend-Lease Act, the U.S. provided $50.1 billion worth of supplies (equivalent to $801 billion in 2023) to its allies, including $31.4 billion to the United Kingdom, $11.3 billion to the Soviet Union, $3.2 billion to France, and $1.6 billion to China.

Printed money requires the support of a strong real economy; otherwise, as in the case of the Venezuelan bolívar, its most practical use is making handicrafts to sell on the street (CNN News).

5.3.1 *Government borrowing*

Section 2.3.1 discusses government borrowing from the perspective of money creation, whereas this section considers it from the standpoint of the government deficit. When budget deficits occur—where expenses exceed tax revenue—the government needs additional money to cover the shortfall. If no surplus exists, the government faces a difficult choice: raising taxes, thereby reducing household consumption, or cutting spending to balance the budget, a measure often met with fierce public opposition. In those countries that are confronting the situation, "austerity" has become a dirty

[41]The origin of this phrase is unclear, though it is a variation of a sentiment expressed by Jean-Jacques Rousseau (1712–1778).

word due to the negative connotations of spending cuts.[42] Instead of facing the political fallout, governments often resort to borrowing, essentially "kicking the can down the road."

In the U.S., for example, the government issues Treasury securities to finance its deficits.[43] The Treasury Department determines the types and amounts of securities issued, as well as the auction schedule. The Federal Reserve conducts the auctions with the goal of minimizing the federal government's financing costs. The highest bidder secures them.

Modern Monetary Theory (MMT) challenges the conventional notion of government borrowing. According to MMT, government borrowing is a misnomer since the government essentially borrows from itself. A government with the power to issue its own currency does not need to borrow in the traditional sense; it can simply print more money to cover its spending. However, as discussed in Section 2.3.1.1, this practice—known as seigniorage—acts as an inflation tax. While MMT focuses on the availability of money, it overlooks the negative impact on the real economy.

Another financial maneuver governments may employ is issuing perpetual bonds, which have no maturity date. By paying only the interest, the government can indefinitely postpone the repayment of the principal. For example, in 1927, Chancellor Winston Churchill issued a "consol" bond as a war bond. Nearly a century later, in 2014, the UK Government announced its intention to redeem these perpetual bonds in full.[44] The U.S. government also issued consols from 1877 to 1930.[45] Those who lent money to the government may never see their principal repaid, and the real value of the principal can erode significantly over time due to inflation.

Supporters of government borrowing claim that it benefits an economy capable of generating a higher return than the interest on loans. This approach exploits arbitrage opportunities between different rates of return. The argument assumes, however, that the

[42] *What Is Austerity, and Why Is It a Dirty Word?*, thespinoff.com, retrieved March 23, 2024.

[43] Besides Treasuries, the U.S. government draws on several other sources to finance its deficit.

[44] *UK to repay part of perpetual WWI loans*, Financial Times, October 31, 2014.

[45] Wikipedia, retrieved April 11, 2024.

government invests the borrowed money in the real economy or purchases financial assets. In practice, governments often borrow to fund welfare programs they are unwilling to cut. This type of borrowing only exacerbates future problems. As interest and principal payments grow, the gap between government revenue and expenses widens, mirroring the dilemma faced by a "shrinking, lavish" economy. Addressing the gap is less painful when it is small, but if allowed to balloon, it becomes much harder to manage. Excessive debt accumulation can lead to higher interest payments, larger deficits, and the need for even more borrowing, which has contributed to the decline of ancient civilizations and modern states.

Clever governments avoid excessive borrowing and instead focus on financial investment when surplus funds are available. By investing in stocks, bonds, and other financial instruments through sovereign wealth funds, state-owned investment funds generated by government revenue or trade surpluses, these governments create additional revenue streams. This approach reduces the tax burden on citizens while allowing governments to provide more benefits. For example, Norway's sovereign wealth fund, the largest in the world, had a value of approximately $1.6 trillion in the first half of 2024 and achieved an 8.6% return, increasing the fund's total value by over $138 billion.[46] This type of financial management capitalizes on asset price appreciation fueled by decades of global money creation. Yet sovereign wealth funds raise critical questions about the government's right to pursue such strategies using tax revenues. Governments possess even greater financial capacity than private institutions. Their monetary expansion drives asset inflation, and when sovereign funds invest in these assets, they not only profit from money creation but also reinforce inflationary pressures by channeling capital directly into the market. As discussed above, the wealthy benefit most from asset inflation. In recent years, government interventions have propped up market downturns, becoming a force that sustains the rising market.

[46] *Norway's Sovereign Wealth Fund Gains $138 Bn In First Half*, barrons.com, retrieved on August 3, 2024.

5.4 Monetary Policies and Interest Rates

5.4.1 *Free market interest rates*

5.4.1.1 *Interests and returns*

The link between interest and investment is a key concept of Keynes's economics. As Keynes (1936) defined, "The rate of interest is the reward for parting with liquidity for a specified period" (see Section 2.1.2.2). The Loanable Funds Theory views the interest rate as the equilibrium price that balances the supply of savings (funds available to lend) with the demand for investment (funds to borrow). Yet, for Austrian and monetary-theory economists, calling the interest rate the price of money distorts its true meaning.

In Eq. (2.1), gold determines the prices of other commodities, but this raises the question: what is the price of gold itself? When demand for any commodity rises, its price increases until supply and demand reach a new equilibrium. By analogy, when money is in higher demand, the price of money—expressed as the gold price—rises. Yet this seems paradoxical: how can one ounce of gold be worth more than one ounce, i.e., 1 oz gold > 1 oz gold? An Austrian theory contended that interest is the price of time or credit. The interest rate resolves this contradiction by assigning greater value to one ounce of gold in the next period.

If all existing money is lent out without the creation of new money, borrowers must obtain funds to repay both principal and interest. Because the interest exceeds the existing money in circulation, some borrowers inevitably fail to secure the necessary funds and are pushed into bankruptcy. Higher interest rates require a larger new money supply, which exacerbates the money shortage and causes more bankruptcies.

This dynamic contradicts the expected relationship between interest rates and the required money supply: low interest rates, which are typically associated with greater money supply, and high interest rates, linked to reduced money supply. When monetary policy misaligns the supply and demand for money, it inherently produces cycles of boom-and-bust cycles.

In finance, assets that pay interest are classified as "fixed-income" securities, including certificates of deposit (CDs), government bonds, corporate bonds, preferred stock, Banker's Acceptances (see Section 4.1), MBS, and CDOs (see Section 4.2.1). These instruments provide investors with a predictable stream of interest payments until the principal is repaid at maturity.

However, the returns on fixed-income securities are not truly fixed. Floating-rate loans, such as adjustable-rate mortgages, tie the interest rate to prevailing market rates. Financial institutions often use the London Interbank Offered Rate (LIBOR) or the Secured Overnight Financing Rate (SOFR) as a benchmark for short-term rates. In addition, fixed-income instruments can be traded in financial markets, exposing them to price fluctuations.

In the bond market, active buying and selling create uncertainty in bond returns. A hypothetical example helps illustrate how "fixed-income" securities can lead to substantial losses or gains. A 30-year bond with an annual coupon payment of \$15 for a \$1,000 principal has a price of \$1,000 at an interest rate of 1.5%. If interest rates suddenly rise to 6.5%, new \$1,000 bonds issued at that rate must pay \$65 annually to market expectations for a 6.5% long-term interest rate. To make the old bond pay a 1.5% coupon yield 6.5%, its price must drop:

$$\text{Price} = \sum_{i=1}^{30} \frac{\$15}{(1+0.065)^i} = \$347.07,$$

resulting in a significant 65% loss in market value. Conversely, if interest rates fall from 6.5% to 1.5%, the situation reverses, leading to substantial gains for bond traders. In December 1980 and January 1981, the U.S. Prime Credit Rate (see p. 297) peaked at an unprecedented 21.5% before gradually declining. Following the 2008 Financial Crisis, interest rates in the United States remained close to zero.[47] Between these two periods, bond trading generated substantial returns.

5.4.1.2 *Tirole's model*

Banks lend money to businesses and set the loan requirements based on evaluations of their operations, while businesses search across

[47]Throughout 2009, the FOMC maintained the federal funds target range at its near-zero level of 0.0% to 0.25%, while the primary credit rate remained fixed at 0.50%.

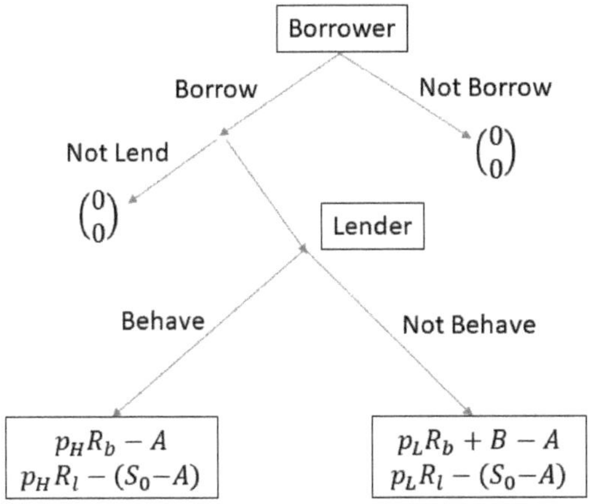

Fig. 5.1. Tirole's financing model.

lenders for favorable loan terms. Nobel laureate Jean Tirole developed a model in which interest rates are the outcome of a strategic game between lenders and borrowers (Tirole, 2010).

Figure 5.1 illustrates the game dynamics in Tirole's model. If neither the borrower nor the lender engages, both parties receive nothing. However, if the borrower has collateral A and seeks to borrow $S - A$ (where S is the total investment in the borrower's project), the lender faces moral hazard. The borrower might misuse the loan, deriving private benefits B, such as personal consumption, instead of working hard to ensure the project's success.

In Tirole's model, the borrower and lender share the project's outcome,

$$R = R_b + R_l, \tag{5.41}$$

with R_b going to the borrower and R_l to the lender. If the borrower misbehaves by seeking private benefits, the project has a lower probability of success, p_L. If the borrower works hard, the probability of success increases to p_H. The conditions for both parties to act in good faith are:

$$p_H R_b - A \geq p_L R_b + B - A, \tag{5.42}$$

$$p_H R_l - (S - A) \geq 0, \tag{5.43}$$

where Eq. (5.42) ensures that the borrower is incentivized to work hard, and Eq. (5.43) ensures that the lender at least breaks even.

Simplifying Eq. (5.42) gives:

$$R_b \geq \frac{B}{p_H - p_L}. \tag{5.44}$$

The borrower works hard only if the benefit of success exceeds the private benefit. The lender at least needs to break even:

$$p_H R_l - (S - A) = 0. \tag{5.45}$$

Setting Eq. (5.44) equal and using Eqs. (5.41) and (5.45) gives the minimum collateral $\tilde{A}$ that the borrower must pledge:

$$A \geq \tilde{A} = p_H \frac{B}{p_H - p_L} + S - p_H R. \tag{5.46}$$

The lender charges interest r on the loan $S - A$ and receives R_l at the end of the project. Thus,

$$R_l = (1 + r)(S - A).$$

For the lender to break even (Eq. (5.45)), the minimum interest rate is:

$$r = \frac{1 - p_H}{p_H}. \tag{5.47}$$

Tirole's model shows that a borrower must put up sufficient collateral for the loan and the lender must set loan terms, including interest rates, to mitigate moral hazard and align incentives between the parties.

In Tirole's model, the borrower is an entrepreneur, not a consumer. For consumer loans, collateral is also a key factor in determining borrowing costs. Banks promote mortgages and auto loans because houses and vehicles serve as collateral. The collateral can be worth more than the loans when purchasing houses or vehicles require down payments.

Historically, farmers pledged livestock, future crops, personal property, and even themselves or family members as collateral. Such practices had severe consequences under the usurious interest rates imposed by moneylenders and made interest a major concern for states. Accordingly, the notion of interest was contentious.

As the New King James Bible states: "You shall not charge interest to your brother—interest on money or food or anything that is lent out at interest." The Christian prohibition on usury was gradually redefined, beginning with the Protestant Reformation in the 16th century and formally lifted by the Catholic Church in the 19th century. Islam, however, continues to uphold this doctrine. In practice, the prohibition does not constrain lending with high returns since business contracts need not explicitly specify an "interest rate." As in Tirole's model, the effective rate is implicit, embedded in how profits and losses are shared between borrower and lender. In this sense, the concept of interest becomes even more elusive than the "price" of money.

5.4.1.3 *Historical perspectives on interest rates*

Throughout history, governments have attempted to regulate interest rates to address economic and social problems. In contrast to the Fed's approach of setting a minimum interest rate, ancient authorities focused on setting maximum rates or even canceling debts. For example, the Code of Hammurabi (circa 1800 B.C.) limited interest rates to 33.33% per annum for grain loans and 20% per annum for silver loans. Despite these measures, economic problems persisted. Although ancient Babylon was one of the most prosperous cities and became a center of trade, usury and high taxes turned free people into slaves, widening the wealth gap and dividing society.[48]

To tackle the slavery issue, Solon of Athens (635–558 B.C.) canceled all farmers' debts and abolished debt slavery but eliminated interest rate limits, introducing hypothecation (borrowing with collateral). Solon's laws lasted for centuries.

The Romans also regulated interest rates. The Twelve Tables (circa 450 B.C.) capped interest at 8.33% per annum and penalized higher rates with quadruple damages. Personal slavery for debt was also permitted, a practice that followed the Code of Hammurabi rather than Solon's reforms (Homer and Sylla, 1996).

In the feudal era, regulations aimed to control usury, as higher interest rates led to increased prices for goods, extracting more wealth from consumers and funneling it to moneylenders: "If the money-lender charged a high rate of interest to the merchant, the merchant must have charged a higher rate of profit on his goods.

[48] *Code of Hammurabi*, history.com, retrieved on April 4, 2024.

Hence, a large sum of money would be taken from the pockets of the purchasers to be put into the pockets of the money-lenders" (Gilbart, 1837).

Karl Marx criticized moneylenders as usurers, arguing that they bypass the capitalist formula of M-C-M' (money to commodity to more money) by directly turning money into more money (M-M'): "money which is worth more money, value which is greater than itself" (Marx, 2004). The people who had gold could lend their gold and charge interest. Gold was not a plant; it could not grow (Graeber, 2012). It was unnatural to ask for more without asking where it would come from.

Focusing solely on the quantity of money, one can differentiate the dynamics under and outside the gold standard. Under the gold standard, lenders issue loans at a fixed 5% interest rate. Yet because the supply of gold is limited, no additional 5% of gold exists to cover interest payments. Consequently, at least 5% of debt inevitably defaults.

By contrast, outside the constraint of the gold standard, banks can issue loans at lower rates (e.g., 2%) while expanding their lending portfolios at a 5% growth rate. Borrowers are able to roll over both principal and interest and draw further credit from the additional 3% of loans created. However, when banks later contract their lending back to 2%, the additional 3% of loans is no longer available to roll over existing loans. In this case, defaults arise not from a fixed monetary supply, but from flexible credit and contraction outside the gold standard.

5.4.1.4 *The own-rate of interest*

John Maynard Keynes introduced the concept of the "own-rate of interest," which refers to the return on an asset in its own terms. He noted that even in a world of inconvertible paper money, other assets, like gold, could influence domestic interest rates. Keynes posited that a competitive market would equalize the returns on different assets: "Our conclusion can be stated in the most general form (taking the propensity to consume as given) as follows. No further increase in the rate of investment is possible when the greatest amongst the own-rates of own-interest of all available assets is equal to the greatest amongst the marginal efficiencies of all assets, measured in terms of the asset whose own-rate of own-interest is greatest" (Keynes, 1936).

Keynes assumed that all rates are flexible, and the free market pushes up the price of assets in high demand and pushes down the price of assets in low demand to such levels that both assets have the same return.

Arbitrage facilitates the alignment of returns. When the borrowing rate is significantly lower than the potential returns on other assets, it creates an arbitrage opportunity. In a truly competitive free market, arbitrage opportunities would be quickly exploited, much like picking up dollar bills on a New York City street. Such opportunities would vanish almost instantly as market participants take advantage of price discrepancies. However, artificially low interest rates set by central banks' policy can create persistent arbitrage opportunities, like continuously dropping dollar bills on Wall Street from a helicopter. Market forces of arbitrage are insufficient to fully eliminate these opportunities due to central banks' persistent intervention to keep interest rates low, which disproportionately benefits those with access to cheap capital. For example, financial firms can borrow at very low rates to acquire high-return assets (see Section 5.4.1.5). Similarly, corporations exploit cheap credit to repurchase their own shares, thereby boosting stock prices (see Section 5.2.2.2).

Moreover, the Fed sets short-term interest rates but has limited control over long-term rates. For example, in mid-2004, the Fed raised short-term rates, yet long-term U.S. Treasury yields continued to decline. Former Fed Chair Alan Greenspan described this phenomenon as a "conundrum." To influence long-term rates, the Fed employed open market operations (OMO), buying and selling long-term Treasury securities.

Keynes was among the first to challenge classical economics, proposing that central banks could influence investment through interest rates and manage them across maturities by buying and selling bonds of different durations. This approach could link money supply to interest rates, enabling more precise monetary policy. The Fed has relied on similar strategies during crises—such as quantitative easing (QE)—following the example set by Japan. However, these interventions often have long-term side effects that become apparent only after significant economic disruptions.

Central banks' low-interest rate policies reduce borrowing costs, while simultaneously increasing the money supply, pushing up returns on assets. Their monetary policies drive wedges between borrowing costs and asset gains, and between different own-rates of interest.

5.4.1.5 *Easy money and negative externality*

In recent decades, central banks have adopted zero or negative interest rate policies. The Eurozone employs three key official interest rates, set by the European Central Bank (ECB), to conduct monetary policy. The Deposit Facility Rate (DFR) is the rate banks receive—or pay—for making overnight deposits with the ECB, typically establishing the floor for the money market. The Main Refinancing Operations (MRO) Rate is the rate at which banks can borrow funds from the ECB for one week against collateral. The Marginal Lending Facility Rate (MLFR) is the rate at which banks can borrow overnight from the ECB when they have run out of other options.

When the Eurozone implemented a negative DFR (from 2014 to 2022), the key dynamic was not that households or firms could borrow at negative rates. Rather, the negative rate functioned as a charge on commercial banks for holding excess reserves at the ECB. In some extreme cases—particularly in countries outside the Eurozone that also adopted negative interest rate policies, such as Denmark and Switzerland—highly creditworthy borrowers or large corporations with stable loan agreements saw their borrowing costs fall to near zero, or even slightly negative, effectively receiving a small payment from banks for taking out loans. Large financial players exploit the easy money environment.

A prime example is KKR, a New York-based private equity firm.[49] During a period of exceptionally low interest rates, KKR acquired Württembergische Metallwarenfabrik AG (WMF),[50] for approximately €660 million through a subsidiary located in a tax haven. KKR used €100 million of its own capital and borrowed €560 million from banks at extremely low rates. Four years later, KKR sold WMF to the French company Groupe SEB[51] for €1.6 billion,

---

[49] KKR & Co. Inc., also known as Kohlberg Kravis Roberts & Co., is an American global investment firm that manages multiple alternative asset classes.

[50] WMF is a German tableware and kitchenware manufacturer, founded in 1853 in Geislingen an der Steige.

[51] Société d'Emboutissage de Bourgogne (SEB) is a French consumer-goods company, known as the largest manufacturer of cookware in the world.

pocketing an additional €1 billion by leveraging artificially low borrowing costs and exploiting market inefficiencies.[52] This was not just KKR's "investment strategy" or good luck; an additional condition existed at the time: low interest rates and easy money to borrow. Firms, financial institutions, and wealthy individuals who could borrow large sums of money took advantage of these conditions.

Governments have a responsibility to curb negative externalities, which create indirect costs for uninvolved parties. For example, when a firm pollutes a river or lake that residents and fishers depend on, it imposes costs on those who are not involved in the polluting activity (Kaplow, 2012). In a broader sense, the fiscal and monetary policies of a government can also generate significant externalities that impact nearly everyone in the economy. When financial institutions or individuals accumulate wealth without contributing to the real economy—such as through speculative trading in financial markets—their gains reduce others' access to real goods and resources. Asset returns have increasingly become the dominant source of wealth accumulation, concentrating wealth more than ever before and generating externalities that threaten social stability beyond the economic sphere.

5.4.2 *Money rate and the rate of return*

5.4.2.1 *Rate of return, real return, and inflation*

In today's financial markets, borrowing extends beyond traditional loans. Traders can borrow through margin accounts, short-selling assets (borrowing an asset and selling it in the market), writing options, or borrowing in the repo market. Similarly, lending is just one way to earn returns, as traders constantly seek to maximize their gains by choosing from real assets, financial assets, and derivatives.

The Federal Funds Rate is the target interest rate established by the Fed for overnight lending of reserve balances between banks. In comparison, the Primary Credit Rate is the rate at which commercial banks can borrow funds directly from the Fed on

[52] *How the rich get richer – money in the world economy*, DW Documentary, 2017.

a short-term, typically overnight, basis. In addition to the federal funds rate and the prime rate, there are many other interest rates in the markets. Treasury rates are considered risk-free since the U.S. government has never defaulted on its debt. However, sovereign debt issued by other governments can default. For example, Asonuma (2016) studied 46 sovereign debt defaults of emerging market economies between 1985 and 2010. U.S. government agencies, like the Federal National Mortgage Association (FNMA), also issue bonds, but these are not risk-free. Municipal bonds, issued by states and local governments, are often tax-exempt. Corporate bonds vary in interest rates depending on their credit ratings. Additionally, the market includes payday loans and pawnshop loans, adding to the complexity of the interest rate landscape.

Keynes suggested that even if paper money could not be converted to gold, other assets could still influence domestic interest rates: "We could not get out of our difficulties...merely by decreeing that wheat or houses shall be the standard of value instead of gold or sterling. For...the same difficulties will ensue if there continues to exist any asset of which the own-rate of interest is reluctant to decline as output increases. It may be...that gold will continue to fill this role in a country which has gone over to an inconvertible paper standard" (Keynes, 1936). According to him, gold continued to influence domestic interest rates primarily through psychology and liquidity preference, while its price served as a psychological anchor of stability. Yet, gold no longer exerts such a strong influence on domestic interest rates today. Keynes's notion of the "own-rate of interest" reflects contemporary market realities, whereas the policy conception of the interest rate is inconsistent with the own-rate generated by competitive markets.

The interest rate plays a central coordinating role in the IS—LM model, functioning as the mechanism that links the goods market (IS curve) with the money market (LM curve) to determine the equilibrium levels of both output (Y) and the interest rate itself. Within the Investment–Saving (IS) curve, the interest rate (r) influences aggregate demand primarily through its effect on investment (I). As discussed in earlier chapters, the effects of money on real output and consumption can be direct, indirect, or purely inflationary. By comparison, the interest rate—a more elusive concept than money—exerts even more pervasive effects on the real economy.

Before the Industrial Revolution, there were few durable and liquid assets available, with gold and silver being the primary exceptions. Ignoring the borrowers' bankruptcy problem caused by a limited gold supply, if gold price increased by 3% (inflation) and the economic condition allowed lenders to charge a 5% nominal interest rate, the purchasing power of their gold—both principal and interest—would increase by 2%. This outcome follows directly from the Fisher effect (see Eq. (3.30)): the 2% represents the real interest rate—the real return for the lender.

In today's markets, beyond gold, a wide range of durable and liquid assets are readily available. We reconstruct the nominal interest rate from the components of the Fisher effect: inflation and the real interest rate. In aggregate, a 2% increase in real output—independent of the money supply—implies a 2% increase in the supply, thereby establishing the real interest rate at 2%. The nominal return, or nominal interest rate, corresponds to the rate of change in the money supply.

Chapter 4 decomposes asset returns based on the quantity theory of money:

$$R = \frac{\dot{M}}{M} = \frac{\dot{P}}{P} + \frac{\dot{Q}}{Q} = \pi + r_F, \tag{5.48}$$

which shows that inflation arises when the money supply exceeds the level required to maintain stable prices as real output grows. Adding the real return to inflation, the nominal interest rate (R) is the own-rate of assets.

The idle assets like antiques or paintings have no new supply ($\dot{Q} = 0$). Their own-rates of interest come from the money flowing into asset markets, driving up prices, and their own-rates of interest have only inflation.

Common stock is unique because it serves as both a financial and real asset. The own-rate of common stock, R_K, can be expressed as

$$\begin{aligned} R_K &= \frac{1}{PK}\frac{d}{dt}(PK) = \frac{\dot{K}}{K} + \frac{\dot{P}}{P} \\ &= r_K + \pi = \frac{\dot{M}}{M}, \end{aligned} \tag{5.49}$$

where r_K is proportional to the rate of change of capital stock, and the nominal return comes from two sources: the rate of change of capital stock and inflation.

Equation (5.49) can be applied to commodities like copper. In this case, the flow of money into the copper market determines copper's own-rate of interest, R: the rate of change in copper supply replaces r_K, and the difference yields the inflation rate of copper, π.

A stock's real rate is its real return, driven by production and consumption fundamentals:

$$r = f_K(K, L) - \delta = \frac{af(K, L) - \delta K}{K} = \frac{\dot{K} + C - \frac{wL}{P}}{K}, \tag{5.50}$$

which is consistent with r_K if the consumption is the same as the wages as in the Solow model, $C = wL/P$. Under this condition, real returns reflect the growth of capital stock.

By considering capital stock alongside other assets, inflation can be estimated as the difference between the rate of change in the money supply and the real return. The aggregate rate of inflation depends on the relative weights of these components in the economy. The greater the share of idle assets, the larger the inflationary component in the nominal return—the nominal interest rate.

Equating asset returns with the interest rate departs from the conventional definition of the interest rate. This book consistently decomposes asset returns—their own rates of interest—into real returns and inflation, a framework consistent with the components of the Fisher effect. By integrating asset returns into the own rates of interest, the otherwise elusive concept of the interest rate becomes more transparent and tractable.

To describe the interest rate as the "price of money" is misleading, for it begs the question: How many dollars is one dollar?—a rhetorical tautology akin to asking "How many meters is one meter?" Money, like other assets, can be converted into various assets to earn returns. As an asset, its capacity to generate returns constitutes its own rate of interest. In a free market, competition determines—explicitly or implicitly—the natural, own rate of interest, as in Tirole's model. By contrast, the "money rates" set by central banks are not true returns but instruments designed to influence the money supply and money creation.

Keynesian economics maintains that low-interest rate policies are expected to stimulate investment and raise output levels. Following Keynesian reasoning, central banks manipulate the "money rate," intending to control their economies. Putting aside the validity of this expectation, the low "money rates" are associated with money expansion, and high "money rates" with money contraction. The "money rate" is directly linked to the money supply. Thus, the contradiction of low "money rate" associated with high inflation disappears.

Keynes overlooked inflation as part of the own-rate of interest rate. Keynes's own-rate of interest consists of three components: the expected future yield Q_i, the carrying cost H_i, and the liquidity premium li. Thus, the own-rate of interest for a commodity i is defined as $Q_i - H_i + l_i$ (Keynes, 1936). This definition, however, is silent on the issue of inflation. The global economy is a closed system with finite inventory. Governments and central banks often fail to recognize that the limit of what money can do and the broader economic consequences it can create – driving up inflation and debt across every sector of the economy.

Critically, when central banks lower the "money rate," the resulting expansion of the money supply facilitates cheap lending, while simultaneously driving up asset returns—the own rates of interest—and opening arbitrage opportunities between the money rate and asset returns. Moreover, increased lending necessitates a greater money supply for borrowers to meet their repayment obligations. Yet, the inevitable reversal of monetary expansion by central banks eventually constrains liquidity, triggering defaults and perpetuating a debt cycle.

5.5 Fiscal Policies

Governments implement fiscal policies through money, and thus the limitations of money effects on economy apply to both fiscal and monetary policy. Monetary policy remains a blunt instrument, unable to channel money flows with precision—much like water escaping through a leaking pipe. Furthermore, the lag between policy implementation and economic response often produces overshooting, perpetuating cycles of boom and bust. By contrast, fiscal policy can exert a more direct and immediate influence on economy by targeting specific sectors or groups. Yet outcomes for many government fiscal policies remain discouraging: economic decline and mounting national debt.

Most governments tend to prioritize welfare programs over the productive economy. Taxation represents a direct intervention in the real economy. While higher taxes may enable greater government spending, their adverse effects on productive activity often outweigh the benefits. Moreover, governments frequently fail—or are unwilling—to eliminate existing programs, leaving their distortions permanently embedded in the system. Socialism and communism function as ultimate welfare societies, insuring all; if capitalism seeks to compete with them on welfare grounds, it has already conceded defeat.

Second, governments often leave the real economy on an unstable trajectory. Although they possess tools to steer their economies, they often fail to recognize the real economy as the foundation of welfare programs or lack the will and capacity to use those tools effectively. Providing welfare in the form of food or shelter requires food production and housing construction. No matter how well a welfare program for shelter is designed, without a robust construction industry it is akin to "drawing a house to satisfy the homeless." Tax policy, for example, can guide the real economy by increasing or decreasing consumption while simultaneously reducing or expanding production capacity, thereby steering the economy toward stability. Yet governments are often unwilling to reduce welfare by curbing consumption.

The above twofold problem is often shaped by political considerations. Governments may prioritize short-term political gains over long-term economic stability, resulting in policies that expand debt or resort to money creation—where political priorities override economic priorities. Sustainable prosperity requires farsighted governments and well-informed citizens who understand the consequences of shortsighted policies.

A central challenge to sustaining prosperity lies within the financial system. Over the centuries, financial institutions have expanded rapidly, becoming formidable forces in the modern economy. Efforts to reform the system—such as proposals for a 100% reserve requirement—encounter strong resistance. Yet without reform, capitalism itself risks losing its capacity to endure. In the United States, the growth of manufacturing, rising wages, and low living costs once supported a robust middle class. By the 1980s, however, these foundations had eroded: manufacturing jobs vanished, wages stagnated, and living costs soared. In their place, financial markets—fueled by money creation—emerged as dominant forces, enriching "lucky investors" even as the middle class declined. This bifurcated economy has failed to meet the needs of society at large, particularly younger generations.

At the same time, the global economy is experiencing profound transformation. Beyond the developed countries, capitalism itself faces growing challenges as socialist and communist systems gain renewed popularity. The West prevailed in the Cold War largely because of its superior economic performance relative to the Soviet Union. To remain viable today, capitalism must demonstrate its capacity to adapt to a changing world, maximize collective well-being, and safeguard individual freedom. The next two chapters will examine this evolving global economy and the ongoing economic transformation.

Chapter 6

Currencies and Global Economy

Section 1.2 of Chapter 1 introduced the concept of a *closed* economy. Chapter 4 implicitly *opens* it by allowing for the exchange of assets and capital across borders. Most economies do not function in isolation. Nations, such as tribes, often have neighboring economies. Even island nations, such as England and Japan, which might seem geographically isolated, have historically sought out interactions with other nations. Countries that share borders with multiple neighbors are naturally interconnected.

In the context of today's global markets, countries experiencing overproduction actively seek consumers to absorb their surplus, while those that consume more than they produce rely on imports to meet demands.

In some cases, nations turned to war to resolve economic challenges. Today, commerce weaves individual economies into a global network, with modern transportation making the world smaller and more interconnected.

In an open economic system, we modify the macroeconomic identity by incorporating imports and exports. An exporting country ships goods abroad, denoted by X (exports), so that:

$$I = Y - C - X > 0,$$

while an importing country brings in goods from abroad, which can be represented as negative exports ($X < 0$), leading to

$$I = Y - C + X < 0.$$

When all countries are considered together, the global economy forms a closed system, yielding:

$$\sum_i X_i = 0. \tag{6.1}$$

Although global imports and exports net to a net-zero, their impacts on individual countries and the global economy are profound. Just as industries specialize in products where they hold a competitive edge, complementing and competing with one another, so do countries. Nations complement each other by producing specialized products, while simultaneously competing for market share of common goods in global markets. This dynamic interplay of cooperation and competition forms a complex global economic pattern. Theories of complementary trade often portray a more harmonious multinational economy.

The capitalist economy evolved from the division of labor. Extending this principle to international trade, David Ricardo (1817) developed the theory of *comparative advantage*, which explains trade between countries. Ricardo's 200-year-old theory remains highly relevant in contemporary debates about free trade versus trade wars. Advocates of free trade often draw on comparative advantage to challenge protectionist measures. We now turn into a straightforward example to review Ricardo's theory.

Suppose the U.S. and China each have 200 units of resources. The U.S. can produce 200 desks or only 100 chairs with its 200 units. In other words, for the U.S., it takes one unit of resources to make a desk and two units to make a chair. China, on the other hand, can produce 200 chairs or only 100 desks with its 200 units of resources. For China, it takes one unit of resources to make a chair and two units of resources to make a desk. The U.S. is more efficient at producing desks, while China is more efficient at producing chairs. Therefore, the U.S. should specialize in producing desks, and China should specialize in producing chairs. Through specialization and trade, both countries can benefit from free trade.

If they do not trade and people in both countries prefer to match one desk with one chair as a set, we can calculate the number of sets, x, each country can produce. For the U.S., the number of sets is limited by its resources:

$$\frac{1 \text{ unit}}{\text{desk}} x \text{ (desks)} + \frac{2 \text{ units}}{\text{chair}} x \text{ chairs} = 200 \text{ (units)}, \tag{6.2}$$

and each set takes 3 units of resources,

$$x = \frac{200 \text{ unites}}{3 \text{ units}} \approx 67 \text{ sets.}$$

The U.S. can produce 67 sets. For China, it takes 1 unit to make a chair and 2 units to make a desk. China also makes a set with 3 units of resources and can produce 67 sets.

If the U.S. and China agree to trade one desk for one chair, and the U.S. produces 200 desks, and China produces 200 chairs, then after exchanging desks and chairs, each country ends up with 100 sets—50% more than they would have had without trade (see Fig. 6.1). Ricardo concluded that international trade benefits all parties when countries specialize according to their comparative advantages.

In Ricardo's theory, each country has a comparative advantage, producing something more efficiently than other countries. However, countries compete for market share in the same product in the international market rather than engaging in purely harmonious trade. Technology and money move easily across borders. The borderless nature of technology reduces the comparative advantages that depend on technological innovation. Intellectual property and technology protection have become critical issues in international trade. When countries have equal access to technology and capital, other

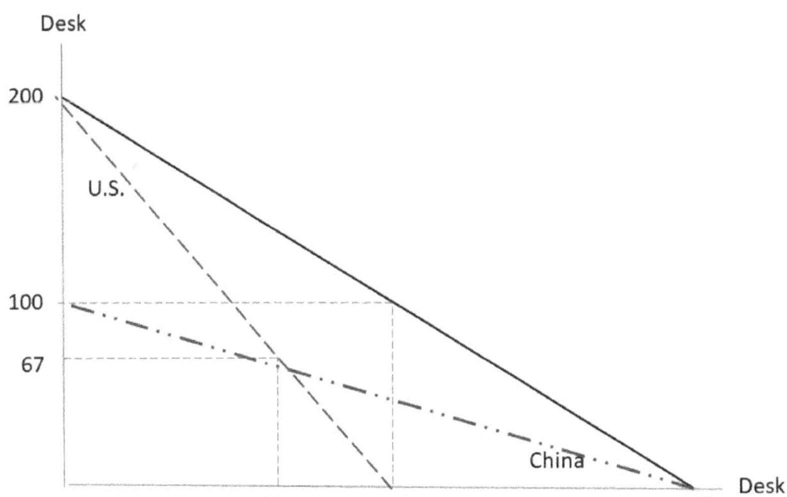

Fig. 6.1. Comparative advantage.

factors of production—such as labor, land, materials, and energy—become the sources of advantages for resource-rich countries, while others may be left at a disadvantage. Economic trading blocs, like the European Union, increasingly commit to greater mobility, exemplified by its "four freedoms": movement of goods, services, persons, and capital (James, 2024).

The importance of these production factors has changed over time. Take labor, for example: A low-wage country tends to consume less and invest more, while a high-wage country consumes more and invests less. If the two countries are isolated from each other, one will face overproduction problems, while the other will suffer from underinvestment. In an interconnected global economy, however, low labor costs give the low-wage country an advantage, while high labor costs put the high-wage country at a disadvantage.

The country with a surplus will export and receive payments, while the country with a shortage will import and pay for those goods. However, this arrangement cannot be stable in the long term. The importing country eventually exhausts its resources to finance imports or opts to reverse its trade deficit by reducing imports. In either case, the exporting country loses access to its market and is compelled to reform its economy.

The theory of comparative advantage presents a model of trade where countries specialize based on relative efficiencies, leading to mutually beneficial exchanges. However, it overlooks two critical realities of modern international economics. First, countries prioritize producing vital domestic goods and protecting their markets. Second, they pursue national wealth through direct competition in key sectors like electronics, autos, and pharmaceuticals. This competition creates market frictions, leading to protectionism and potential trade wars, as seen in U.S.–Japan and U.S.–China conflicts.

Countries strive to produce vital goods for their own economies. After World War II, for example, the U.S. produced the best weapons. According to the theory of comparative advantage, other countries should have given up weapon production and traded their specialized goods for U.S.-made weapons. However, the U.S. does not sell its most advanced weapons, and major countries are unlikely to abandon their defense industries. Free trade proponents may dismiss defense as an exception, but trade disputes can arise in other areas as well, such as agriculture. Even close allies of the U.S. have had trade disputes over agricultural exports. Most countries are unwilling to rely entirely on other nations for their food supply.

The pursuit of national wealth also fuels fierce competition within economic sectors. For instance, the U.S. was the world's largest steel producer in 1910, producing over 10 million tons annually. Steel production peaked at 111.4 million tons in 1973, but by 1984, it had collapsed to 70 million tons due to competition from the United Kingdom, Europe, and Asia, leading to overcapacity in the global market. The U.S. steel production reached another peak in 2000 but then fell again to 86 million tons by 2014. This illustrates the intense competition among countries in the international marketplace.[1]

Governments often intervene in international trade by subsidizing domestic industries, imposing tariffs, setting quotas, and creating regulations. Subsidies can take many forms, including those related to production, consumption, exports, imports, employment, taxes, or energy. Governments also help their domestic companies to gain market share or monopolies in international markets.[2] By far the largest estimate for any single sector is the global subsidy for fossil fuels. In 2022, the IMF reported that fossil fuel subsidies surged to a record \$7 trillion worldwide, equivalent to roughly 7.1% of global GDP that year. In other cases, governments collaborate to control the global supply of goods, such as through the Organization of the Petroleum Exporting Countries (OPEC).

As energy increases in value, those countries compete among themselves, but they have common interests in energy trading and share the desire to control energy prices in the global market. OPEC has been doing so since the Baghdad Conference attended by six major oil-producing nations—Iran, Iraq, Kuwait, Saudi Arabia, and Venezuela—in September 1960.[3]

Intense trade rivalries between nations can escalate into military conflict. For example, in the 18th and early 19th centuries, Chinese tea was a highly valued commodity in Britain, leading to a trade

[1]*A Brief History of the American Steel Industry*, nationalmaterial.com; *Steel crisis*, wikipedia.org; retrieved on March 21, 2024.

[2]Wikipedia, retrieved on April 17, 2024.

[3]*Memorandum From the Director of the Office of Near Eastern Affairs*, history.state.gov, retrieved on August 1, 2024.

imbalance in China's favor. To offset this, British merchants illegally sold Indian-grown opium in China, generating revenue for the British government and East India Company and paying for Chinese tea. When the Chinese government seized British-owned opium to curb the smuggling, Britain used this as a pretext to wage war, forcing China to open its markets to the opium trade. By the 1820s, the trade balance had shifted in Britain's favor (Melancon, 1999). Opium addiction became widespread in China, remaining a problem until the Communist government enforced a ban on opium use in 1949.

Competitive positions in international trade are constantly shifting. The U.S. has maintained a trade deficit with China for decades and relies on foreign capital, including Chinese investments, to finance its imports. Historian Niall Ferguson and economist Moritz Schularick coined the term "Chimerica" to describe the economic relationship between China and the U.S. The story of "Chimerica" underscores the competitive nature of international trade and the rise and fall of economic powers. Rather than specializing in Ricardo's theory, this chapter examines how nations producing identical goods position themselves in global competition.

6.1 Economic Union

The European Union (EU) is a political and economic union, but its economic integration is limited. Each member country manages its own government debt, trade deficits, long-term interest rates, and inflation rates. A fully integrated economic union should gradually converge toward uniform levels of productivity and per capita consumption. However, external forces—political, cultural, and otherwise—limit the extent of this convergence. In the short term, the union seeks to maximize collective utility by allocating consumption goods and capital stock across member states. Here, a simple case focuses on two countries of similar sizes, meaning they have the same population, L. The total combined capital stock is K, and the total combined consumption is C. Using per capita variables, we denote $c = C/L$ and $k = K/L$. The total population of the two countries is $2L$, so c and k represent per capita consumption and capital stock for two workers, one from each country. Country 1 has αc and βk per worker, while Country 2 has $(1-\alpha)c$ and $(1-\beta)k$ per worker.

The goal of the union is to maximize the combined consumption of both countries by optimally allocating capital stock between them:

$$\max_{\alpha,\beta,c} \int_0^t \{e^{-\rho_1 s}\ln(\ \alpha c) + e^{-\rho_2 s}\ln[(1-\alpha)c]\}ds, \tag{6.3}$$

subject to

$$\begin{aligned} \dot{k} &= f_1(\beta k) + f_2[(1-\beta)k] - c - \delta k, \qquad (6.4)\\ c_0 &= c_{\mathrm{IC}},\\ k_0 &= k_{\mathrm{IC}},\\ \dot{c} &< \infty. \end{aligned}$$

The standard formulation of the Hamiltonian (see Footnote 30, Chapter 1) for this example is:

$$\begin{aligned} \mathcal{H}(k,c,\theta,t) = e^{-\rho_1 t}\ln(\ \alpha c) + e^{-\rho_2 t}\ln[(1-\alpha)c] \qquad (6.5)\\ +\,\theta\{f_1(\beta k) + f_2[(1-\beta)k] - c - \delta k\}. \qquad (6.6) \end{aligned}$$

Taking partial derivatives of Eq. (6.6) with respect to c, we have the first-order condition for c:

$$\frac{\partial \mathcal{H}(k,c,\theta,t)}{\partial c} = [e^{-\rho_1 t} + e^{-\rho_2 t}]\frac{1}{c} - \theta = 0, \tag{6.7}$$

which gives θ. Taking partial derivatives of Eq. (6.6) with respect to k, we have the first-order condition for k:

$$\frac{\partial \mathcal{H}(k,c,\theta,t)}{\partial k} = \theta\frac{d}{dk}F(\beta,k) = -\dot{\theta}, \tag{6.8}$$

where

$$F(\beta,k) = f_1(\beta k) + f_2[(1-\beta)k - \delta k], \tag{6.9}$$

$$\frac{d}{dk}F(\beta,k) = [\beta f_1'(\beta k) + (1-\beta)f_2'[(1-\beta) - \delta]. \tag{6.10}$$

Taking the derivative of θ in Eq. (6.7) with respect to time, we have

$$\dot{\theta} = -\bar{\rho}\frac{1}{c} - \theta\frac{\dot{c}}{c}, \tag{6.11}$$

in which

$$\bar{\rho} = [\rho_1 e^{-\rho_1 t} + \rho_2 e^{-\rho_2 t}],$$

where $\bar{\rho}$ is just the weighted average of the discount factor. Substituting θ and $\dot{\theta}$ into Eq. (6.11),

$$\dot{\theta} = -\bar{\rho}\frac{1}{c} - \theta\frac{\dot{c}}{c} = -\theta\frac{d}{dk}F(\beta, k),$$

where θ is given by Eq. (6.7). Then,

$$\dot{c} = \left[\frac{d}{dk}F(\beta, k) - (e^{-\rho_1 t} + e^{-\rho_2 t})^{-1}\bar{\rho}\right]. \tag{6.12}$$

Next, we find the optimal allocations of consumption c and capital stock k:

$$\frac{\partial \mathcal{H}(k, c, \theta, t)}{\partial \alpha} = e^{-\rho_1 t}\frac{1}{\alpha} - e^{-\rho_2 t}\frac{1}{1-\alpha} = 0. \tag{6.13}$$

Solving for α, we have:

$$\alpha = \frac{e^{-\rho_1 t}}{e^{-\rho_1 t} + \alpha e^{-\rho_2 t}}, \tag{6.14}$$

which shows that the country where households have a smaller discount factor gets more consumption goods. The same amount of consumption carries larger total utility for *the country*. Solving for β yields:

$$\frac{\partial \mathcal{H}(k, c, \theta, t)}{\partial \beta} = k\{f_1'(\beta k) - f_2'[(1-\beta)k]\} = 0. \tag{6.15}$$

Figure 6.2 illustrates two production functions with the same technology but different output elasticities of capital stock, a_i. A firm that has accumulated less capital stock and relies on more labor has a smaller a_i. Equation (6.15) implies that the optimal allocation of capital stock requires the marginal product—the additional output from an additional unit of capital stock—to be equal in both countries. Graphically, this means the slopes of the two production

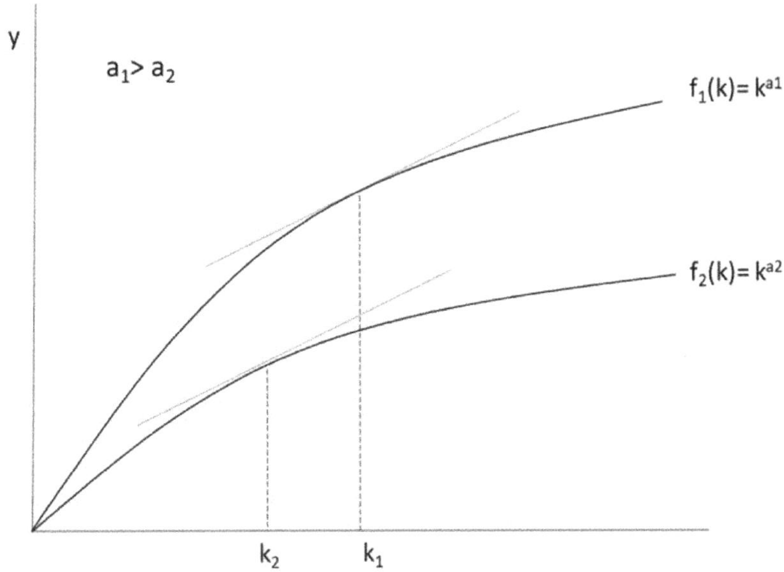

Fig. 6.2. Capital stocks allocation in an economic union.

functions must be equal at the point of optimal allocation. The production function with the higher output elasticity,[4] a_1, will have more capital stock, k_1, compared to the production function with the lower output elasticity, a_2, and less capital stock, k_2.

When considering an economic union of two countries, each can exhibit one of four types of economies: "expanding, frugal," "shrinking, frugal," "expanding, lavish," or "shrinking, lavish," as discussed in Chapter 1. However, the number of possible types of unions exceeds the straightforward mathematical combinations of these categories. When two countries of the same type form an economic union, the resulting type of union depends on the state of each economy before joining the union. For example, if one country's economy is very close to the stable paths—such as those at the starting points of paths V, VI, VII, or VIII in Figure 1.8—the reallocation of consumption and capital stock could cause the economy to move to the

[4]Output elasticity measures the responsiveness of output to changes in labor or capital input. Production function relates the output elasticity of capital stock or labor to the corresponding elasticity of output.

opposite side of the stable path, altering the type of either one or both economies.

There is an obvious scenario where economic stability could potentially improve: a union between a "shrinking" country and an "expanding" country — where one partner is "frugal" and the other "lavish." In these scenarios, the "expanding" country provides its surplus production capacity to the "shrinking" country. The economic union could move the overall economy closer to the stable path than if the two countries remained isolated.

However, this economic union resembles an international charity, where the "expanding" country unilaterally provides capital stock—as a gift—to the "shrinking" country, while the "frugal" country provides consumption goods to the "lavish" country as gifts—without receiving anything in return.

Lager countries have historically provided foreign aid to small countries, but these countries are not formally part of an economic union. This scenario is similar to when small countries or territories join larger countries, as was the case when Hawaii became the 50th state of the U.S. in August 1959. Although Hawaii's economy boomed after joining the U.S., lingering issues, such as land ownership disputes, remain, especially as land grows in value as a financial asset while its supply is limited.

For example, an economic union between a "shrinking, lavish" country and an "expanding, frugal" country could provide mutual benefits. The "shrinking, lavish" country is increasing consumption:

$$\dot{c}_{sl} = [f'_{sl}(k_{sl}) - \delta - \rho_{sl}]c_{sl} > 0,$$

where sl refers to "shrinking, lavish" country, which is losing capital stock:

$$\dot{k}_{sl} = [f(k_{sl}) - c_{sl}) - \delta k_{sl}] < 0.$$

The consumption of the "expanding, frugal" country is decreasing:

$$\dot{c}_{ef} = [f'_{ef}(k_{ef}) - \delta - \rho_{ef}]c_{ef} < 0,$$

where ef refers to "'expanding, frugal" country, which is accumulating capital stock:

$$\dot{k}_{ef} = [f(k_{ef}) - c_{ef}) - \delta k_{ef}] > 0.$$

By reallocating the overproduction capacity Δk from the "expanding, frugal" country to the "shrinking, lavish" country, the consumption of the "shrinking, lavish" country decreases compared to the consumption before forming the union because $f'(k)$ decreases with k—the diminishing return of capital stock. Thus,

$$\dot{c}_{sl}^{*} = [f_{sl}'(k_{sl} + \Delta k) - \delta - \rho_{sl}]c_{sl}^{*} < c_{sl},$$

where superscript * refers to the variables after joining the union. The "shrinking, lavish" country also has a different path of capital stock k_{pf}^{*}:

$$\dot{k}_{sl}^{*} = [f(k_{sl} + \Delta k) - c_{sl} - \delta k_{sl}] > \dot{k}_{pf}.$$

After joining the union, the "expanding, frugal" country increases its consumption to c_{rl}^{*}:

$$\dot{c}_{ef}^{*} = [f_{ef}'(k_{ef} - \Delta k) - \delta - \rho_{ef}]c_{ef}^{*} > \dot{c}_{rl},$$

and decreases its investment in capital stock k_{rl}^{*}:

$$\dot{k}_{ef}^{*} = [f(k_{ef} - \Delta k) - c_{ef}) - \delta k_{ef}] < \dot{k}_{rl}.$$

After exchanging consumption goods and capital stock, the two countries have the same gross return capital stock (Eq. (6.15)):

$$f_{ef}'(k_{ef} + \Delta k) = f_{sl}'(k_{sl} - \Delta k). \tag{6.16}$$

Using the Cobb–Douglas production function $f(k_i) = Ak_i^{a_i}$, in which the technology factor has no effect on the allocation of capital stock because the two countries share technology, and defining $\{i, j\} = \{ef, sl\}$, we have

$$\Delta k \approx \frac{k_i k_j \left[\ln a_j + (1 - a_j)\ln(k_j) - \ln a_i - (1 - a_i)\ln(k_i)\right]}{(1 - a_j)k_i + (1 - a_i)k_j}, \tag{6.17}$$

which uses the approximation $\ln(1 + \Delta k/k) \approx \Delta k/k$ for $\Delta k << k$. The terms in the square brackets of Eq. (6.17) represent the difference in the first derivatives of the two production functions. The larger this difference, the greater the capital stock adjustment, Δk.

The most prominent economic unions in the world are trade blocs. Notable examples include the Eurasian Economic Union (EEU), the CARICOM Single Market and Economy (CSME), and the Gulf Cooperation Council (GCC). The European Union (EU) has advanced beyond simply facilitating free trade in goods and capital; it has enabled the free movement of labor among member states, essentially creating a single labor market. While the EU has adopted a common currency, it lacks centralized fiscal authority. As a result, accountability for EU-level decisions often rests with "technocrats," who, as Jean-Claude Juncker, President of the European Commission, noted, "we all know what to do, but we just don't know how to get re-elected" (James, 2024).

Within the EU, surplus countries such as Germany, the Netherlands, Ireland, Belgium, Austria, and Sweden contrast with deficit countries like France, Italy, Spain, Portugal, and Greece. The Union is not charity—its members borrow funds to cover budget shortfalls. Unsurprisingly, southern European states carry far higher debt-to-GDP ratios, with Greece (180%), Italy (145%), Portugal (130%), and Spain (120%) in 2023. Although the Maastricht Criteria of 1992 set limits of 60% for public debt and 3% for budget deficits, many members have exceeded these thresholds for years. Without addressing the structural imbalances of individual economies, ECB loans only provide temporary stability while prolonging deeper problems. The EU's capacity to resolve these disparities will determine its future.

In 2009, Brazil, Russia, India, and China formed the BRICS group,[5] a geopolitical and economic bloc that meets annually to coordinate multilateral policies. Since its formation, additional countries have joined the bloc. In July 2014, during the sixth BRICS summit, the member countries signed an agreement to create the $100 billion BRICS Development Bank. As of now, BRICS represents 46% of the global population. China, which accounts for 70% of the bloc's total GDP, has ambitions to rival the United States as a global power, particularly in terms of currency and global influence.[6]

Economic blocs are reshaping global trade. OPEC remains a dominant force in energy markets, shaping oil prices and regulating supply. The EU, with its unified internal market, leverages economic

[5]The "S" in BRICS refers to South Africa, which joined in 2010.

[6]BRICS, wikipedia.org, retrieved January 8, 2025.

strength and trade agreements to influence global commerce. BRICS, a coalition of large emerging economies, is still pursuing deeper integration as a counterweight to Western-led institutions.

6.2 Assets and Trade

In an open economy where capital stock can be bought or sold between countries, we categorize economies into four types, depending on whether they are accumulating or depleting national wealth and increasing or decreasing consumption (see Section 4.1.3.2). Here, "wealth" is defined as a nation's total assets, contrasting with Adam Smith's definition of wealth as the economic output of land and labor. In general, wealth-expanding countries export goods and acquire foreign assets, increasing their wealth. Conversely, wealth-shrinking countries import goods and deplete their domestic assets, reducing their wealth.

Before precious metals, land and livestock were the primary stores of value, as most other early assets were subject to decay or high maintenance costs. In tribal and feudal systems, tribes or countries could conquer territories, but it was uncommon for them to engage in regular land trade. For example, if fishermen exchanged fish for crops, neither fishermen nor the crop farm could build up wealth because both fish and crops would eventually spoil. Additionally, trade could only occur if each farm had enough of its own products to meet its needs. If one farm was "lavish" and unable to produce enough to sustain itself, it would have little to offer in exchange. On the other hand, a "frugal" farm, with a surplus, could only give its excess to the "lavish" farm as a gift—if the frugal farm could not store its product as wealth.

As David Graeber (2012) describes, gift-giving was a common way to trade goods between tribes. Sometimes, labor was exchanged instead. A "lavish" economy might offer its labor in return for crops or meat from the "frugal" economy. However, the "frugal" economy could not accumulate wealth either, as it could not permanently retain labor to grow its workforce. While giving surplus goods as gifts could reduce economic instability in a gift-receiving economy, gift-giving was not a systematic form of economic assistance and could not solve the underlying issues of the "lavish" economy.

The introduction of money and durable assets profoundly changed trade dynamics, moving beyond traditional gift-giving (except for charity or foreign aid). Before the Industrial Revolution, nations primarily accumulated gold and silver as durable assets, enabling them to conduct trade across borders. After the Industrial Revolution, capital stock (or "working assets") joined the ranks of durable assets. This meant that land, buildings, and factories became readily tradable. Newly created money began to seek and create other durable assets as anchors, drastically transforming the global economy.

Creditor nations or individuals holding bonds and loans can use them to import goods. Conversely, borrowers can leverage debt to finance imports. However, for a "wealth-shrinking, lavish" economy, debt poses a significant challenge: it must repay loans with existing assets. Failure to meet these obligations can lead to a debt trap, eroding confidence and cutting off access to future borrowing.

The assets involved in international trade are highly diverse, ranging from currency, raw materials, and natural resources to financial instruments and transportation infrastructure such as shipping fleets, airlines, logistics networks, airports, and seaports. Intangible assets—including intellectual property, services, talent, and knowledge—also play a critical role. A country may borrow funds through sovereign debt or government bonds to finance imports, but such debt must ultimately be repaid with assets. The process resembles borrowing from a pawn shop: the borrower pledges assets as collateral, and if repayment fails, the lender takes possession of those assets.

A net importing country with a "wealth-shrinking, lavish" economy mirrors an individual overspending on credit. To reverse this, the nation must cease further borrowing and shift from import reliance to domestic production. Such a shift involves fostering a frugal lifestyle and channeling savings into the real economy to expand productive supply.

Oded Galor's research (Galor and Özak, 2016) highlights how geographical variations in land productivity and orientation toward investment and growth have long-term effects on economic growth. Governments have various tools to curb consumption, including taxation and welfare cuts, but these measures often meet resistance. Cultural norms also shape lifestyles, but these norms are often driven by the wealthy. Over centuries, the accumulation of wealth has enabled the rich not only to embrace luxury lifestyle but also to build entire industries that promote and sustain it. As a result, countries characterized by "wealth-shrinking lavishness" face a steep challenge in combating overconsumption.

In contrast, exporting nations more easily boost domestic consumption after export booms, as seen in the U.S., Japan, and China. The U.S. led the way in fostering a "consumer society," driven by a deliberate shift from fulfilling needs to cultivating desires, as articulated by Paul Mazur, a prominent Wall Street investment banker in the 1920s and 1930s: "We must shift America from a needs- to a desires-culture. People must be trained to desire, to want new things, ... Man's desires must overshadow his needs."

Japan, for instance, transitioned to greater domestic consumption in the late 1980s. While exports fueled its earlier growth, a new generation ("shinjinrui") embracing a Western consumer mentality and demanding a higher standard of living, coupled with advertising that linked consumption to happiness (Anderson and Wadkins, 1991), made domestic consumption an additional engine for growth.

6.2.1 *Currencies and exchange rates*

There are about 180 countries in the world today, most with their own official currency. The U.S. dollar, however, is widely used across Africa, Latin America, and Asia. The euro serves 19 countries in the Eurozone, while the CFA (Colonies Françaises d'Afrique) franc is used by 14 nations in West and Central Africa through two monetary unions (WAEMU and CEMAC). The Eastern Caribbean dollar circulates in 8 countries of the Eastern Caribbean Currency Union. Some regional currencies also exist.

Under the gold standard, the purchasing power of gold determined the value of a currency, and the exchange rate between two currencies reflected their equal purchasing power of gold. For example, before World War I, \$20.67 could buy one ounce of gold in the United States, while £4.2474 could buy one ounce of gold in Britain. Thus, the exchange rate between the U.S. dollar and the British pound was

$$\frac{\$20.67}{£4.2474} = \frac{\$4.8665}{£}.$$

The U.S. raised the price of gold to \$35 per ounce in 1934. In 1944, the Bretton Woods Agreement formalized this by pegging the U.S. dollar to gold at the same rate. However, the U.S. issued an excessive number of dollars without adjusting the gold price, leading to an international sell-off of dollars for gold. This pressure culminated in the suspension of the dollar's convertibility to gold in 1971.

After the collapse of the gold exchange standard, the global monetary system split into fixed and floating exchange-rate regimes. Countries in the fixed-rate regime maintain their currency's value relative to major currencies such as the U.S. dollar or the euro,[7] while other countries allow their currencies to float, with exchange rates determined by market forces. Most major economies have adopted floating exchange rates. Without the gold standard, the foreign exchange market has become a battleground between countries and a playground for speculators.

An exchange rate equal to the ratio of the price levels of two countries is known as the *absolute purchasing power parity*. For example, if a television in Japan costs ¥50,000 and a similar television in the U.S. costs \$500, then the fair exchange rate would be ¥100/USD (¥50,000/\$500). To compete in the U.S. television market, Japan might fix the exchange rate at ¥200/USD, making the television cost \$250 (¥50,000/¥200/USD).

How much Japanese goods a U.S. dollar can buy depends on the exchange rate, denoted as $\xi(\$/\yen)$, and the real exchange rate reflects the ratio of the purchasing powers of a pair of currencies. Let P_f be the foreign currency price of a unit of a product (or a basket of goods) and P_d be the domestic currency price of the same product (or the basket of goods). The exchange rate that satisfies the absolute purchasing power parity—i.e., where the real exchange rate equals one—is the ratio of the prices:

$$\xi = \frac{P_f}{P_d}. \tag{6.18}$$

If ¥50,000 buys a television, at the exchange rate ¥100/\$ and \$250 per television, then ¥50,000 exchanged to \$500 can buy two televisions. One can ship the two televisions back to Japan and make 100% arbitrage profit. Thus, at the exchange rate ¥100/\$, the dollar

[7]A country may also fix its currency against a basket of foreign currencies.

price of a television must be \$500 to maintain absolute purchasing power parity:

$$\xi = \frac{¥50{,}000}{\$500} = \frac{¥100}{\$}.$$

Likewise, at the exchange rate ¥200/\$, the dollar price of a television must be \$250:

$$\xi = \frac{¥50{,}000}{\$250} = \frac{¥200}{\$}.$$

The *law of one price* (see Chapter 4) implies that, after currency conversion, identical product should cost the same in different countries, which is the basis for absolute purchasing power parity. However, in reality, various factors, such as tariffs, import quotas, taxes, and transaction costs, prevent different currencies from having the same purchasing power for an identical product. Additionally, major economic powers have engaged in currency manipulation via exchange rate adjustments (Caprita, 2021).

A single currency typically has multiple exchange rates against various foreign currencies. In the floating exchange rate system, currency values are interconnected—affecting one currency influences the entire network. While a country may try to adjust all exchange rates relative to its domestic currency to favor its foreign trade, the ideal scenario is to sell its products at high prices while purchasing foreign goods at low prices. However, such attempts create arbitrage opportunities, and the arbitrage in the currency market undermines these efforts.

To illustrate, consider three countries with pseudonyms: Japan, the U.S., and Australia. Japan, as a major exporter, sold more goods to the U.S. than it imported coal and raw materials from Australia. Meanwhile, the U.S. imported goods from both Japan and Australia. Depending on trade flows, Australia could be either a net exporter or a net importer. In such scenarios, exporting countries often attempt to manipulate exchange rates to remain competitive with other countries' products.

Suppose the exchange rates are as follows: ¥100/\$, ¥100/AU\$, and \$1/AU\$1, where ¥ represents the Japanese yen and AU\$ represents the Australian dollar. At these rates, Japan struggled to export its excess production, so it intervened in the currency market by buying substantial amounts of U.S. dollars with yen, pushing the

Yen to ¥120/\$. Japan wanted to keep the exchange rate against the Australian Dollar unchanged, since it imported coal and materials from Australia. However, the currency market responded differently.

Arbitrageurs began selling Yen for Australian Dollars. They would first exchange ¥100 for AU\$1, then exchange AU\$1 for \$1, and finally use \$1 to buy ¥120. This arbitrage allowed them to profit by selling ¥120 for AU\$1.2 at the rate of ¥100/AU\$. The arbitragers made AU\$0.20 on every AU\$1 in the arbitrage. The arbitrage activity—selling large amounts of Yen for Australian Dollars—eventually pushed down the Yen's value and drove up the value of the Australian Dollar. The exchange rate between the Yen and the Australian Dollar ultimately settled at ¥120/AU\$. In such a system, any two exchange rates determine the third rate, known as the "cross-rate," which must satisfy the no-arbitrage condition.

A country attempting to manage its exchange rates must account for multiple bilateral rates, which can be a challenging task. Sometimes, several countries intervene jointly to influence their exchange rates against a single currency, as happened during the trade tensions with Japan in the 1980s. To simplify this issue, we consider the example of an exporting country and a representative importing country that reflects a broader group of nations reliant on its exports.

The exporting country receives foreign currency for its exports at price P_f, and the domestic price is P_d. The exchange rate P_f/P_d represents the foreign-currency value of one unit of domestic currency. This is known as the "indirect quote."[8] Ideally, a net exporting country wants to sell its products at high prices, which would result in a high P_f/P_d ratio. However, international competition often forces the country to do the opposite. The exporting country may need to lower its foreign exchange rate to create sufficient demand for its exports.[9]

The Bank of Japan (BOJ), Japan's central bank, is well known for its large currency interventions. Because Japan's economy is heavily dependent on exports, fluctuations in the yen's value have significant implications for economic performance. The BOJ has a long history

[8]A direct quote refers to the domestic currency price of a unit of foreign currency.

[9]Other factors affect the process. The income elasticity of demand also affects the demand of an importing country (Thirlwall, 2004).

of intervening in foreign exchange markets, particularly when excessive yen appreciation threatens export competitiveness. For instance, in 2011, following the earthquake and tsunami, Japan intervened aggressively to prevent a strong yen from undermining its recovery.

China has since surpassed Japan as the most active and consistent practitioner of currency intervention. The People's Bank of China (PBOC) manages the value of the Chinese yuan (CNY) by deploying vast foreign reserves to buy and sell currencies, especially U.S. dollars. This strategy is central to sustaining China's export competitiveness.

6.3 Exchange Rate and Exports

The foreign exchange market is the largest financial market in the world, with trillions of dollars trading daily. David Hume's *Price-Specie Flow Mechanism* (1752) explained that trade surpluses under the gold standard corrected themselves. Gold inflows expanded the money supply, raising domestic prices. As goods became costlier, exports fell and imports rose, bringing trade back into balance. Under a floating exchange-rate regime, an exporting country's currency appreciates, making exports more expensive and imports cheaper, thus reducing trade surpluses. The same adjustment mechanism applies symmetrically to importing countries (Yarbrough and Yarbrough, 2006). In practice, such self-adjusting mechanisms have not operated as theory predicted. Central banks of major countries possess the resources to influence exchange rates meaningfully. These countries, particularly those with widely traded currencies, periodically attempt to manipulate their exchange rates to benefit their domestic economies.

According to the Peterson Institute, four groups frequently engage in currency manipulation: longstanding advanced economies (e.g., Japan and Switzerland), newly industrialized economies (e.g., Singapore), developing Asian economies (e.g., China), and oil-exporting nations (e.g., Russia) (Gagnon *et al.*, 2012). Historical evidence shows that exporting countries often benefit from depreciating their currencies, with Japan and China being prime examples. China's currency intervention and accumulation of foreign exchange reserves have been particularly notable (Krugman, 2010).

Governments and central banks manipulate exchange rates not for profit but to support their domestic economies. These interventions can deter currency speculators who trade against the exchange rate that the government or central bank desires. Speculators are often highly leveraged, meaning they trade with borrowed money, magnifying their exposure. When governments or central banks intervene, the resulting exchange-rate shifts can inflict massive losses on speculators, potentially wiping out their margin accounts and driving them into bankruptcy. Consequently, interventions by major economies can significantly affect exchange rates.

Inflation erodes the purchasing power of a currency. The future of a foreign exchange rate is affected by the relative inflation levels of the two currencies. Taking the time derivative of the purchasing power parity equation (6.18) gives:

$$\frac{\dot{\xi}}{\xi} = \frac{\dot{P}_f}{P_f} - \frac{\dot{P}_d}{P_d} = \pi_f - \pi_d, \tag{6.19}$$

where π_f and π_d are the inflation rates of the foreign and domestic economies, respectively. This equation, known as the *relative purchasing power parity* or *the international Fisher effect*, suggests that exchange rate changes offset the difference in inflation rates between two currencies. The currency with higher inflation loses value relative to the currency with lower inflation because inflation erodes the purchasing power of a currency.

Equation (2.5) relates inflation to money supply. Substituting domestic inflation with domestic changes in money supply and output, Eq. (6.19) can be rewritten as follows:

$$\frac{\dot{\xi}}{\xi} = \pi_f - \frac{\dot{M}}{M} + \frac{\dot{Y}}{Y}.$$

Although money creation influences exchange rates, its effect on export economies is complex and tenuous.

Economics defines the price elasticity of demand, which measures the responsiveness of demand to price changes:

$$\gamma = -\frac{\frac{dX}{X}}{\frac{dP_f}{P_f}}. \tag{6.20}$$

Assuming $X = X_0$ when $P_d = P_f$. Integrating Eq. (6.20) gives the equation:

$$\frac{P_f}{P_d} = \left(\frac{X}{X_0}\right)^{-1/\gamma}. \tag{6.21}$$

This relationship shows that an exporting country can adjust its exchange rate to influence the importing country's demand X. However, two issues must be considered. First, the price elasticity γ varies by good. For typical goods, γ is positive, indicating that higher prices reduce demand. Veblen goods are luxury items, while Giffen goods are essential staples for low-income consumers. Both display negative demand elasticity (γ), meaning demand increases as price rises. For Veblen goods, higher prices enhance their desirability as symbols of status. In contrast, for Giffen goods, inflationary pressures push households to consume more of these necessities. If the food price rises, poorer consumers substitute toward bread, which is relatively cheaper, while reducing consumption of other, more expensive foods. However, for luxury goods, sellers cannot expect demand to keep increasing with rising prices indefinitely. At a certain high price for a Veblen good, even wealthy consumers will feel the pinch and reduce their purchases, causing γ to turn positive.

Second, empirical research has shown that in certain markets, such as oil, higher prices can actually increase demand. For instance, research based on data from the United States and Japan estimates the elasticity of demand for oil to be near -0.36, and other studies also indicate that higher oil prices often lead to increased demand. Similarly, in the real estate market, higher prices can stimulate demand. During the first half of 2019, real estate transactions showed a positive correlation between price and demand in many regions (Berkovec and Goodman Jr, 1996). These results contradict the price—demand relationship for normal goods in Walrasian equilibrium. Had the correlation been positive, exporters could have deliberately increased prices to generate demand.

Chapter 3 has demonstrated a positive price-demand correlation, in which new money generates additional demand, reduces inventory, and drives up prices. By contrast, Walrasian equilibrium assumes that households operate under a fixed budget constraint. When the price of a good increases, households reduce their purchases of that good and switch to less expensive alternatives.

As noted previously, many countries subsidized fossil fuels, and the U.S. expanded credit to encourage home ownership; in both cases, new money flowed into the markets. Barring such cases, importing countries are unlikely to create money solely to stimulate imports under normal circumstances.

Exporting goods with high-elasticity (with high γ) requires small price reduction to stimulate demand than exporting low-elasticity goods. By depreciating its currency, a country that exports high-elasticity goods and imports low-elasticity goods can exploit the differences in price elasticities between its exports and imports (Krugman and Obstfeld, 2009). This type of effect on the price elasticity of demand is secondary. A "frugal, expanding" economy has overcapacity and overproduced goods. Without exporting its production capacity and overproduced goods would be of no value. Although the economy could reduce production capacity by selling capital stock, cutting production is often not an option because it would reduce employment. Even when exporting overproduced goods at low prices, this is a gain for the exporting country.

6.3.1 *Net exports for assets*

The macroeconomic identity incorporating exports is commonly expressed as:

$$\dot{K} = f(K, L)–C - \delta K - X \tag{6.22}$$

which implies that exports have the effect of reducing investment $\dot{K}$.

To see what is missing from this expression, we return to the simple farming economy. Using simple numbers in the AK model of Eq. (1.5), $K = 1.2$ because of favorable weather in the previous year, and $C = 1.5$, the additional seed produced at the end of the year is given by:

$$\begin{aligned}\Delta K &= AK - C - \delta K,\\ &= 1.5(1.2) - 1.5 = 0.3.\end{aligned} \tag{6.23}$$

which is 0.3 million bushels above one million bushels at the equilibrium point. If the farming economy exports 0.3 million bushels, then:

$$\Delta K = AK - C - \delta K - X,$$
$$= 1.5(1.2) - 1.5 - 0.3 = 0, \tag{6.24}$$

and the farming economy returns to equilibrium. This result assumes that the farm gives 0.3 million bushels of seeds away for free. Exporting economies, however, sell their overproduced goods for money. If the farm has the domestic price P_d and sells seeds for the foreign price P_f, the money flows must account for the export proceeds:

$$P\Delta K = P_d(AK - C - \delta K - X) + P_f X,$$
$$= P_d(1.5K - C - X) + P_f X. \tag{6.25}$$

Equation (6.25) keeps both P_d and P_f, which makes it easy to identify the two currencies, but it also introduces inconsistency in the units; one way around it is to convert P_f into P_d units using the exchange rate ξ. In practice, an exporting country receives foreign currency for its exports and either holds the foreign currency as reserves or uses it to purchase foreign assets. Using general production function in continuous time, we rewrite Eq. (6.25) as:

$$P\dot{K} = P_d[f(K, L) - C - \delta K - X] + P_f X, \tag{6.26}$$

which suggests that the proceeds from exports $P_f X$ is like extra income.

Trade dumping occurs when a firm sells a product in a foreign market at a price lower than in its home market or below production costs. The rationale for selling at a loss is puzzling. A common explanation is that once a firm monopolizes the international market, it can raise prices. Yet, this argument is unconvincing, as many firms continue selling at low prices year after year without achieving market dominance. Another explanation points to government subsidies. WTO agreements seek to limit these subsidies, as they distort competition and harm other economies. The example provides a more plausible explanation: absent exports, overproduced goods would be wasted. Exporting thus transforms potential waste into income.

The total assets of the exporting country consist of domestic working assets, Φ_d, and global assets, Φ_f. Equation (6.26) holds only if the exporting country always uses the proceeds from exports, $P_f X$, to purchase capital stock for domestic uses, which is not always the case. We introduce the global assets Φ_f:

$$P_f X \in \Phi_f, \tag{6.27}$$

where Φ_f is a portfolio consisting of foreign assets and also the domestic idle assets. The domestic assets, Φ_d, consist of domestic capital stock:

$$\Phi_d = P_d K. \tag{6.28}$$

Equation (6.28) excludes domestic idle assets, which are part of the global portfolio. Since the real economy generates goods for export—the central concern of the maximization problem—classifying assets in this manner streamlines the model.

An exporting country earns foreign currency, $P_f X$, from its exports, which is then used to purchase foreign assets, including financial assets like stocks and bonds, as well as real assets like real estate. Combining domestic and global assets, the total assets Φ of the country are:

$$\Phi = \Phi_d + \Phi_f. \tag{6.29}$$

Global assets also have working assets and idle assets, and they have different returns. Introducing an average return, R, foreign assets follow the process:

$$\dot{\Phi}_f = R\Phi_f, \tag{6.30}$$

where R is assumed to be constant. Global assets vastly exceed any individual country's domestic assets, leaving the exporting country with little control over the return of global assets.

Moreover, investors tend to favor domestic assets over foreign ones, a phenomenon known in behavioral finance as *home bias* (French and Poterba, 1991). As a result, domestically created money has a greater impact on domestic asset prices than on foreign assets. While the money generated by an exporting country can affect the value of foreign assets, its impact varies and is, on average, far smaller than its effect on domestic assets.

Thus, the return on domestic working assets differs from the return of global assets. The domestic working assets, Φ_d, represent a fraction α of the total wealth, $\Phi_d = \alpha\Phi$, where α is a control variable that the exporting country seeks to maximize. Because money flows freely across borders, the exporting country can use foreign currency to purchase capital stock for domestic production and thereby optimize its exports. Accordingly, α is a function of exports, $\alpha = \alpha(X)$, and the remaining wealth is held in global assets, $\Phi_f = (1-\alpha)\Phi$.

The domestic assets follow the dynamics described by:

$$\dot{\Phi}_d = \pi_d \Phi_d + P_d \dot{K} = \pi_d \alpha \Phi + \left[P_d f\left(\frac{\alpha\Phi}{P_d}\right) - C - \delta\alpha\Phi - P_d X \right],$$

where C represents nominal consumption, measured in terms of money. Exporting countries intervene in currency markets to weaken their currency, creating and injecting domestic money that fuels inflation. As exports expand, interventions must become larger and more frequent, implying $\pi_d = \pi_d(X)$, which drives price dynamics P_d (see p. 223).

An exporting country uses its trade surpluses to purchase foreign assets, thereby increasing its wealth. In contrast, an importing country with trade deficits may sell off assets to cover its shortfall or accumulate debt, which represents negative wealth flow. Thus, the wealth equation for an exporting country reflects its income from exports, investment in capital stock, and returns from global assets:

$$\begin{aligned} \dot{\Phi} &= R(1-\alpha)\Phi + \pi_d \alpha \Phi \\ &\quad + \left[P_d f\left(\frac{\alpha\Phi}{P_d}\right) - C - \delta\alpha\Phi - P_d X \right] + P_f(X)X, \end{aligned} \tag{6.31}$$

where the foreign currency price is a function of export volume, $P_f(X)$. Higher export levels require a lower foreign price to stimulate demand.

The exporting country maximizes consumption:

$$\max_{C,\alpha,X} \int_t^T e^{-s\rho} \ln C_s ds, \tag{6.32}$$

subject to Eq. (6.31).

The Hamiltonian is given by:

$$\begin{aligned} \mathcal{H}(\Phi, C, \alpha, X, \theta, t) &= \ln C + \theta\{R(1-\alpha)\Phi + \pi_d \alpha \Phi + P_f(X)X\} \\ &\quad + \theta \left[P_d f\left(\frac{\alpha\Phi}{P_d}\right) - C - \alpha\delta\Phi - P_d X \right] \end{aligned} \tag{6.33}$$

in which α is assumed to be a control variable. The first-order condition with respect to C yields:

$$\frac{\partial}{\partial C}\mathcal{H}(\Phi, C, \alpha, X, \theta, t) = \frac{1}{C} - \theta = 0. \tag{6.34}$$

Thus,

$$\theta = \frac{1}{C}. \tag{6.35}$$

Taking the partial derivative with respect to Φ yields:

$$\begin{aligned}
&\frac{\partial}{\partial \Phi}\mathcal{H}(\Phi, C, \alpha, X, \theta, t) \\
&= \theta\left[R(1-\alpha) + \alpha f'\left(\frac{\alpha\Phi}{P_d}\right) + \alpha(\pi_d - \delta)\right] \\
&= \rho\theta - \dot{\theta},
\end{aligned} \tag{6.36}$$

which gives the dynamics of the co-state θ:

$$\dot{\theta} = \left[\rho - R(1-\alpha) - \alpha f'\left(\frac{\alpha\Phi}{P_d}\right) - \alpha(\pi_d - \delta)\right]\theta.$$

Using Eq. (6.7) gives consumption C:

$$\dot{C} = \left[R(1-\alpha) + \alpha f'\left(\frac{\alpha\Phi}{P_d}\right) + \alpha(\pi_d - \delta) - \rho\right]C. \tag{6.37}$$

Optimizing the asset allocation α by taking the derivative of the Hamiltonian with respect to α, we have:

$$\frac{\partial}{\partial \alpha}\mathcal{H}(\Phi, C, \alpha, X, \theta, t) = -R\Phi + \pi_d\Phi + f'\left(\frac{\alpha\Phi}{P_d}\right)\Phi - \delta\Phi, \tag{6.37a}$$

where α is between zero and one, i.e. $\alpha \in \{0, 1\}$.

The proceeds from exports are a part of the country's revenue but are missing in Eq. (6.37a). Without the marginal return on exports, we use an average return as approximation. Using the definition $r_d = f'\left(\frac{\alpha\Phi}{P_d}\right) - \delta$, α is given by:

$$\alpha = \begin{cases} 0 & R > \pi_d + r_d + P_f(X)\frac{X}{\Phi} \\ 1 & R < \pi_d + r_d + P_f(X)\frac{X}{\Phi}. \end{cases}$$

The global and domestic asset markets compete for an economy's wealth, as money flows freely in global asset markets. However, an exporting economy must produce real goods to support its exports. Therefore, the scenario where no real goods are produced ($\alpha = 0$) can be ruled out. On the other hand, a situation where all wealth is allocated to domestic assets ($\alpha = 1$) is conceivable. However, if export proceeds are fully reinvested in domestic capital stock, exports must absorb the continually growing surplus of goods. This outcome is therefore improbable.

First, as domestic production expands, surplus goods require growing export demand. Eventually, the export market reaches its saturation point. Once this happens, domestic production also hits its limit. At this stage, keeping the proceeds from exports in the domestic asset market leads to rising domestic inflation, π_d, a common phenomenon in exporting economies. When domestic working assets become more expensive than foreign assets, capital flows into global assets, possibly leading to the scenario where:

$$\pi_d + f'\left(\frac{\alpha\phi}{P_d}\right) - \delta + P_f(X)\frac{X}{\Phi} = R.$$

Using the Cobb–Douglas production function gives

$$\alpha = \frac{P_d}{\Phi}\left[\frac{R + \delta - \pi_d - P_f(X)X/\Phi}{aA}\right]^{1/(a-1)}. \tag{6.38}$$

The returns of domestic working assets and global assets become equal only for the specific exports in Eq. (6.38). If the exporting country is able to export more, the balance breaks, and the return on domestic working assets becomes higher than global assets. As α increases, the exporting country must lower the price of its goods to generate higher demand from importing countries, until it reaches the point where domestic and foreign asset returns become equal.

6.3.1.1 *Optimal exports?*

The above discussion suggests that an optimal level of exports may exist. If so, the question becomes: what is that level? The first-order condition with respect to the export X yields:

$$\begin{aligned}\frac{\partial}{\partial X}&\mathcal{H}(\Phi, C, X, \theta, t)\\ &= \theta[\alpha'(X)\Phi(\pi_d + r_d - R) + P_f'(X)X + P_f(X) - P_d] = 0,\end{aligned} \tag{6.39}$$

where α is not a control variable but a function of X, and the sufficient condition of maximization requires a negative second-order condition:

$$\alpha''(X)\Phi(\pi_d + r_d - R) + \alpha'(X)\frac{\Phi^2}{P_d}f''\left(\frac{\alpha\Phi}{P_d}\right) + P_f''(X)X + 2P_f'(X) < 0.$$

The first-order condition Eq. (6.39) is related to the price elasticity of demand, γ:

$$\alpha'(X)\Phi(\pi_d + r_d - R) + P_f(X)\left(\frac{XdP_f(X)}{P_f(X)dX} + 1\right) - P_d$$
$$= \alpha'(X)\Phi(\pi_d + r_d - R) + P_f(X)\left(-\frac{1}{\gamma} + 1\right) - P_d = 0, \quad (6.40)$$

where the price elasticity of demand γ is defined in Eq. (6.20). The price elasticity of demand measures the responsiveness of demand to price changes and imposes constraints on exports, playing a role in determining whether an exporting country can achieve export maximization.

For $0 < \gamma < 1$, the second and third terms in Eq. (6.40) are negative, which implies that exports lose revenue at the margin. Because exports require low foreign prices, higher export volumes require even lower foreign prices. Moreover, the percentage increase in demand is smaller than the percentage decrease in price, so the gain in demand does not compensate for the loss in price. To make this easier to see, using the definition of the price elasticity of demand γ from Eqs. (6.20), (6.21), and (6.40), can be rewritten as:

$$\alpha'(X)K(\pi_d + r_d - R) + \left(\frac{X}{X_0}\right)^{-1/\gamma}\left(1 - \frac{1}{\gamma}\right) - 1 = 0.$$

For most normal goods, $0 < \gamma < 1$, the second term is negative. Hence, the first term must be positive to satisfy the first-order condition. Taking the derivative with respect to X again gives the second-order condition:

$$\alpha''(X)\Phi(\pi_d + r_d - R) + \alpha'^2(X)\frac{\Phi^2}{P_d}f''\left(\frac{\alpha\Phi}{P_d}\right) + \frac{1-\gamma}{\gamma^2}\left(\frac{X}{X_0}\right)^{-(1+\gamma)/\gamma} < 0,$$

in which the third term is positive, while the second term is negative due to the diminishing returns of the production function. The sign of the first term depends on $\alpha''(\mathrm{X})$, which is expected to be negative. As exports increase, a lower price is required to generate sufficient demand, slowing the growth of export income and thereby reducing the expansion of the share of domestic assets.

The real economy clearly reveals its constraints: the diminishing returns of the production function, as the economy converges to an equilibrium point analogous to the dynamics of the Solow model. Nonetheless, a puzzling observation remains unexplained—the rapid accumulation of wealth and the sharp increase in asset values—which are embedded within π_d and certain global assets. Maintaining a low exchange rate to support larger exports requires greater intervention and expanded money creation, which becomes the primary driver of asset inflation. Financial markets, confident in an undervalued currency backed by a strong economy (see the following section), accept the newly issued money at face value. Accordingly, we explicitly incorporate money creation $M(X)$ into Eq. (6.31):

$$\dot{\Phi} = R(1-\alpha)\Phi + \pi_d \alpha\Phi + P_d\left[f\left(\frac{\alpha\Phi}{P_d}, L\right) - C - X\right] - \delta\alpha\Phi + P_f(X)X + M(X). \quad (6.41)$$

The first-order condition for maximizing exports X gives:

$$\alpha'(X)\Phi(\pi_d + r_d - R) + M'(X) + P_f'(X)X + P_f(X) - P_d = 0, \quad (6.42)$$

and the second-order condition requires:

$$\alpha''(X)\Phi(\pi_d + r_d - R) + \alpha'^2(X)\frac{\Phi^2}{P_d}f''\left(\frac{\alpha\Phi}{P_d}\right) + M''(X) + P_f''(X)X + 2P_f'(X) < 0. \quad (6.43)$$

A unit increase in X requires more money to lower the exchange rate, and the required amount grows faster as intervention intensifies to counter arbitrage. Yet an exporting country cannot increase money creation without limit, as the resulting distortions to international trade ultimately activate external pressures that constrain further expansion.

The effects of money creation in some exporting countries are complex, extending beyond domestic inflation and rising asset values. The trade war between the U.S. and Japan illustrates the instability of open economies and the delicate balance between exporting and importing countries. As wealth flows in one direction between these economies, the balance becomes increasingly fragile and eventually snaps. After the Plaza Accord, Japan's trade surplus began to decline, and the country faced a series of economic challenges that pushed it into recession. Today, the U.S.-China trade war appears to be a replay of this historical struggle, though the international relations backdrop has changed.

A similar analysis applies to importing countries, although space constraints prevent a detailed discussion here. In short, importing countries pay for imports with their assets and, with limited resources, often end up in debt, which further worsens the imbalance between importing and exporting countries.

Historical parallels can be drawn with the Roman Empire. During Tiberius' reign in 33 A.D., despite efforts to stabilize the economy, overconsumption and trade imbalances persisted. Gold and silver flowed out of the empire to pay for imports of luxury goods, draining domestic resources. In response, Tiberius and the Senate ordered lenders to invest two-thirds of their capital in Italian lands to prevent the flight of currency and falling land values. However, this policy backfired, leading to fire sales of real estate, widespread bankruptcies, and a financial crisis. Although the Roman government eventually bailed out the market, the underlying trade balance remained unresolved, resulting in a long-term decline in domestic currency circulation (Frank, 1935; Taylor, 2013; *Financial Crisis of 33*, wikipedia.org, retrieved on January 22, 2024).

Financial analysts view accounting statements as key indicators of firms' operations, while currency traders analyze the Balance of Payments (BOP) to gauge a country's economic health. However, the BOP does not provide a complete picture of a country's overall economy.[10] The following section reviews the BOP and further examines the puzzle of money creation in exporting countries.

[10]Thirlwall (2004) suggests that the equilibrium growth rate of the Balance of Payments equals the world growth rate weighted by the income elasticities of the demand for exports and imports (Caprita and Souza, 2021).

6.3.2 *Balance of payments*

During the interwar period, Keynes maintained that the Balance of Payments (BOP) played a primary role in determining the domestic interest rate and the domestic money supply:

> For in an economy subject to money contracts and customs more or less fixed over an appreciable period of time, where the quantity of the domestic circulation and the domestic rate of interest are primarily determined by the Balance of Payments, as they were in Great Britain before the war, there is no orthodox means open to the authorities for countering unemployment at home except by struggling for an export surplus and an import of the monetary metal at the expense of their neighbors.—Keynes (1936).

The Balance of Payments is an official record of all economic transactions between the households and firms of one country and those of foreign countries. Under the gold standard, the BOP played a key role in tracking a country's gold holdings.

Financial analysts use BOP to assess a country's financial health. The BOP serves as a financial statement for a country, similar to a company's accounting statement, which uses a double-entry bookkeeping system. A trade deficit (surplus) must be settled (earned) with gold in a country's reserve account; hence, the BOP must always balance. The BOP consists of several components: the Current Account, Capital Account, Financial Account, Net Errors and Omissions, and Official Reserve Account.

Net Errors and Omissions represent unrecorded international economic transactions, such as underground cross-border activities that governments cannot track. While missing data are often disregarded, black markets continue to exert considerable influence in some economies. For instance, black market activity once accounted for as much as 25% of Italy's economy, though it has decreased to an estimated 12% today.[11]

---

[11] *Something Terrible Is Happening in Italy*, YouTube, uploaded by Economics Explained, 14 Nov 2022, retrieved on March 4, 2024.

The most important accounts in the BOP are the Current Account and the Capital and Financial Accounts. Current Account has exports and imports of goods and services. The Capital and Financial Accounts measure international transactions involving financial and non-financial assets. The Capital Account records the acquisition and disposal of non-production, non-financial assets, such as real estate. The Financial Account includes Direct and Portfolio Investments. If foreign investors own 10% or more of voting shares in a domestic firm, the investment is classified as Direct Investment.[12] Investments with less than 10% ownership fall under Portfolio Investments. Since the Capital Account is typically smaller than the Financial Account, the two are often combined and referred to as the Financial/Capital Account.

The Official Reserve Account reflects the total currency reserves held by a central bank. We can summarize the BOP in a simplified equation:

$$\frac{1}{\xi}P_f(X)X - \Delta\Phi_f = \Delta B, \tag{6.44}$$

where $\frac{1}{\xi}P_dX$ is the Balance of Trade measured by domestic currency, $\Delta\Phi_f$ is the sum of the Financial/Capital Account, and ΔB represents the Official Reserves Account, which records the change of currency and securities held by a country's central bank.

The Current Account consists of the Balance of Trade and other minor accounts. The Balance of Trade is the dominant component of a country's Current Account for most countries. The Current Account and the Financial/Capital Account are the dominant components of the BOP, while the role of the reserve account depends on whether the country operates under a floating or fixed exchange-rate regime.

The exchange rate of a floating currency is determined by supply and demand in the foreign exchange market. Since there is no need to maintain currency reserves, a trade surplus enables the country to acquire foreign assets—represented as foreign currency outflows—to balance the BOP. Conversely, a trade deficit requires the country to liquidate domestic assets, including issuing bonds to borrow

[12]It's important to note that the term "Investment" in the context of the BOP refers specifically to *financial* investment—investment measured in money.

foreign currencies—represented as foreign currency inflows—to finance the deficit. Thus, the BOP of Eq. (6.44) becomes:

$$\frac{1}{\xi}P_f(X)X - \Delta\Phi_f \approx 0,$$

which carries an approximation sign since certain countries use relatively small reserves to manage exchange rates, such as through exchange rate intervention.

Under a fixed exchange-rate regime, a country must hold adequate foreign currency reserves. Intervention in the exchange rate market is necessary to maintain the fixed rate. When excessive selling of domestic currency occurs, pushing its value down and the foreign currency up, the country must counteract by selling foreign reserves and buying domestic currency. Conversely, when the domestic currency appreciates, the opposite intervention is required. Accordingly, Eq. (6.44) applies, and:

$$\frac{1}{\xi}P_f(X)X - \Delta\Phi_f = \Delta B.$$

For example, the U.S. has consistently run a trade deficit since the 1980s, often offset by positive inflows in its Financial/Capital Account. In 2013, the U.S. had a Current Account deficit of −\$400 billion and a Financial/Capital Account inflow of +\$368 billion, which means the U.S. exchanged assets for foreign currency to import goods. After adjusting for \$30 billion in Net Errors and Omissions, there was no change in the U.S.'s Official Reserves, $\Delta B \approx 0$.

In contrast, the Eurozone had a +\$305 billion Current Account surplus and −\$317 billion in Financial/Capital outflows in 2013. Despite these large numbers, the Eurozone's Official Reserves Account was negligible—only \$10 billion—and remained close to zero. The Eurozone achieved its account balance by converting its trade surplus into foreign assets holdings.

China, however, presents an exception. Since 2000, China has experienced both a Current Account surplus and positive inflows in its Financial/Capital Account. In 2013, China's BOP recorded a +\$183 billion Current Account surplus and +\$323 billion in foreign currency inflows in its Financial/Capital Account. This led to an increase of \$431 billion in China's Official Reserves Account after adjusting for Net Errors and Omissions—leaving the country with an exceptionally large stock of foreign currencies in its reserves. Reserve accumulation was not limited to 2013 but has persisted for decades. The anomaly of such extraordinary reserve growth suggests missing information regarding how these reserves have been used.

Linking the BOP and the real economy provides insight into the differences between the BOP and a country's economy. We use the difference operator, Δ, in place of d/dt to indicate the annual change in Eq. (6.41):

$$\begin{aligned}\Delta\Phi = R(1-\alpha)\Phi + \pi_d\alpha\Phi + P_d\left[f\left(\frac{\alpha\Phi}{P_d}, L\right) - C - X\right]\\ -\delta\alpha\Phi + P_f(X)X + M(X).\end{aligned} \tag{6.45}$$

Equation (6.45) does not specify how export proceeds are used to purchase foreign assets, which constitute part of the wealth change of an exporting country. If we approximate the wealth change, $\Delta\Phi$, as the foreign currency flow, then the terms corresponding to the Balance of Payments (BOP) are:

$$\Delta\Phi = P_f(X)X - \Delta B. \tag{6.46}$$

The terms in Eq. (6.45) corresponding to ΔB in Eq. (6.46) are:

$$\begin{aligned}R(1-\alpha)\Phi + \pi_d\alpha\Phi + P_d\left[f\left(\frac{\alpha\Phi}{P_d}, L\right) - C - X\right] - \delta\alpha\Phi + M(X)\\ = R(1-\alpha)\Phi + \pi_d\alpha\Phi + P_d\dot{K} + M(X).\end{aligned} \tag{6.47}$$

Equations (6.46) and (6.47) highlight limitations in the Balance of Payments (BOP) as a key indicator of a country's economy, omitting important information on the domestic economy and money creation. The domestic real economy forms the foundation of a nation. While exports are often interpreted as evidence of economic strength, they instead reflect overproduction and underconsumption—signs of an unstable trajectory. Thus, whether the domestic economy is stabilizing or continuing along an unstable path is the primary indicator of economic health. For exporting nations, domestic money creation is particularly significant as it facilitates both currency devaluation—thereby enhancing export competitiveness—and the acquisition of foreign assets. Furthermore, the inherent opaqueness of the Official Reserves Account can lead to misinterpretations of a nation's true financial position.

The Chinese Balance of Payments (BOP) data presents a compelling case for a more nuanced interpretation of official reserves. Rather than fully utilizing its substantial currency reserves to acquire foreign assets directly, China often reported a large annual increase in its Official Reserves Account. This pattern of year-over-year increases in official reserves raises a question: how were these foreign currencies actually held?

It is highly improbable that such vast sums were held as cash, given the significant opportunity cost associated with foregoing potential returns. Instead, China actively engaged in substantial foreign lending to developing countries and made significant purchases of foreign assets. In an ideal BOP framework, these activities would typically appear as negative flows in the Financial/Capital Account, thereby producing corresponding adjustments in the Official Reserves Account. However, the traditional BOP framework, as it stood, did not fully elucidate these complex financial flows, obscuring the true nature of China's foreign asset accumulation.

Currency analysts keep a close eye on a country's Official Reserves Account, as reserve accumulation often signals a currency's underlying strength. When a nation consistently runs a trade surplus and simultaneously builds up substantial official reserves, it naturally instills confidence in its currency among analysts and dealers.

An exporting country can strategically leverage this confidence by increasing its domestic currency supply, which allows it to achieve a dual objective: first, maintaining a low exchange rate for its currency, which in turn lowers the foreign prices of its exports, making them more competitive. Second, the newly created domestic currency can then be exchanged for foreign currencies, enabling the nation to purchase foreign assets. This approach not only supports an export-driven domestic economy but also facilitates the acquisition of foreign assets.

Japan serves as an important example of how trade surpluses and monetary policy can influence both domestic and global economies. Japan ended its chronic trade deficit in 1965 and became a surplus trading nation by the late 1960s. Japan had pegged the yen at ¥360 per dollar since 1949, a policy that rapidly expanded Japan's trade surplus while deepening the U.S. deficit. By 1971, Japan's trade surplus reached $4.3 billion, which led the U.S. to devalue the dollar and pressure Japan to revalue the yen. The short-lived *Smithsonian Agreement* of 1971—an international accord aimed at preserving the fixed exchange-rate system by revaluing several major currencies—re-pegged the yen at ¥308 per U.S. dollar. Nevertheless, Japan's trade surplus continued to expand, reaching $5.1 billion in 1972.[13]

In the 1980s, Japan emerged as an economic power, largely through the expansion of its money supply. The Bank of Japan significantly increased *window guidance* loan quotas, a credit allocation system controlled by the central authority. Under window guidance, the Bank of Japan directed domestic banks on the amount of loans they should lend in the upcoming quarter or year, and specified which sectors of the economy should receive those loans. The central bank decided which projects to support, while individual banks issued loans, with large borrowers needing to be on the central bank's approved list.

During the late 1980s, loan quotas grew at an average rate of 15% per year in Japan. This money flooded the domestic market, leading to an extraordinary real estate bubble. The scale of this bubble was astonishing compared to real estate in the U.S. and Canada. At its peak, the garden surrounding the Imperial Palace in central Tokyo was valued at roughly the same as the entire state of California. Japanese land was worth four times that of the U.S., a country 26 times larger than Japan. The total estimated market value of the land in Tokyo's Chiyoda Ward, one of Tokyo's 23 districts, exceeded the value of all the land in Canada.[14] In 1985, the yen's exchange rate peaked at ¥260 per U.S. dollar.[15] Japan's trade surplus reached a high of $82.7 billion in 1986. The money created by the Bank of Japan ignited a surge in the Japanese stock market, with the Nikkei stock average jumping from 6,868 in 1980 to 34,051 in 1989, a fivefold increase in just nine years.[16]

When a country creates excessive money, that money often spills over into foreign assets. Japanese capital flows multiplied from a net inflow of more than $2 billion in 1980 to an outflow of $132 billion in 1986. Japanese buyers targeted assets worldwide, including art objects and other valuables. High-profile purchases included the Rockefeller Center, Columbia Pictures, and Pebble Beach Golf

[13] *Trade policy of Japan*, wikipedia.org, retrieved on March 4, 2024.
[14] *Princes of the Yen*, Documentary Film, 2014.
[15] macrotrends.net, retrieved on January 11, 2024.
[16] google.com, retrieved on July 14, 2024.

Course. In 1986, Japanese investors bought 75% of all U.S. Treasury bonds auctioned off.

The Plaza Accord was signed by G5 nations—the U.S., Japan, West Germany, France, and the U.K.—on September 22, 1985. The Accord dramatically changed the exchange rate of yen/$: the U.S. dollar fell sharply, and the yen nearly doubled in value against the dollar between 1985 and 1987. After the Plaza Accord, Japan's trade surplus began to decline, and the country faced a series of economic challenges that pushed it into recession.

China has pursued a strategy similar to Japan's, generating persistent trade surpluses and accumulating foreign assets. The People's Bank of China adopted window guidance in the early 1990s to allocate credit, boosting the economy, particularly exports and government projects. Window guidance expanded credit and contributed to the Chinese property bubble and the 2015–2016 Chinese stock market bubble. The People's Bank of China also used window guidance to ensure the profitability of commercial banks within the Chinese financial system and as a tool to control the overheated real estate sector. The central bank adjusted credit policies during the 2015–2016 Chinese stock market bubble and the more recent real estate bubble from 2020 to 2022, which led to the creation of ghost megacities.[17]

One notable example of the fallout from these bubbles is China Evergrande Group, once the largest residential real estate developer in China. After the property bubble burst, Evergrande incurred massive losses, leading to its bankruptcy in August 2023. The company was unable to restructure its $300 billion debt owed to investors. In January 2024, a Hong Kong court ordered Evergrande to liquidate. *The Wall Street Journal* reported that of the company's 1.2 million pre-sold units, about 800,000 remained unfinished.[18] The downward trajectory of China's real estate market persisted in 2025.

6.4 Stability of the global economy

The global economy can be conceptualized as a closed system where each nation operates its economy akin to a large household.

[17] Window guidance, wikipedia.org, retrieved on February 4, 2024.

[18] *The Story Behind the Many Ghost Towns of Abandoned Mansions Across China*, by Katherine McLaughlin, architecturaldigest.com, retrieved on February 24, 2024.

The inherent disparity among countries contributes to economic instability; some nations generate exportable surpluses, while others rely on imports for goods they cannot produce (see Chapter 1). The interdependence between exporting and importing countries is unstable, even as global markets appear to provide solutions for nations confronting either overproduction or overconsumption. Yet these solutions deliver only superficial stability, concealing deeper vulnerabilities within the real economy. Moreover, unlike domestic economies, the global economy lacks centralized authority with the power to enforce comprehensive regulations and oversight, thereby exacerbating these fragilities. Nevertheless, exceptions exist in the form of economic unions and partnerships, often bolstered by initiatives akin to "economic charities," which strive to promote international cooperation and stability.

In the aftermath of World War II, the United States was instrumental in the economic reconstruction of Japan and Germany. Following their post-war recovery, developed nations generally accepted tariffs that favored developing countries. However, these arrangements were primarily motivated by political considerations rather than pure economic mechanisms. As global circumstances continue to evolve, these dynamics are shifting, with heightened competition increasingly overshadowing "charity" in the international economic landscape.

The stability of the global economy depends on individual nations, given their decentralized nature. If every nation could successfully steer its economy toward a stable trajectory and achieve self-sufficiency, net importing and exporting economies no longer exist. Instead, countries would engage in trade based purely on utility enhancement rather than necessity, fostering stable international trade.

However, just as individuals possess diverse abilities, nations are endowed with different resources and unique comparative advantages and disadvantages. In the fierce global competition, countries frequently resort to currency manipulation and trade barriers to gain an edge. This brings us back to the critical questions raised in Chapter 1: How can we measure the economic value that serves as the basis for aggregates of real goods and the real economy? Furthermore, how can nations with disparate resource endowments compete fairly in the global market? These topics will be explored in the next chapter.

Chapter 7

Work Theory of Value

Since the dawn of human history, economies have tended to expand, reinforcing assumptions of perpetual growth and rising consumption, and fostering the illusion—among most people but not economists—that growth can continue indefinitely. Coupled with that historical economic growth, an ever-growing money supply creates the impression that nations can become "richer" without any limits. However, an increase in the money supply does not automatically translate into goods or assets. Instead, money continually converts perishable goods into enduring assets.

To illustrate this point, let us revisit the debt-driven economy (as discussed in Section 2.4), but with a twist: imagine a banker who fully automates all transactions through robots. The banker's interest income is spent on jewelry and sculptures crafted by artisans, thereby fostering a new profession dedicated to converting money wealth into lasting assets. These craftsmen, in turn, spend their earnings on food. Over time, this cycle leads to a growing accumulation of assets. As asset accumulation and money creation by the bank unfold concurrently (see Chapter 4), the proportion of wealth derived from the annual salaries of farmers and craftsmen declines. Under normal economic circumstances, asset creation and accumulation may appear inconsequential. However, when certain farm products become scarce, the market mechanism always prioritizes access for the banker's family, leaving some farmers and craftsmen excluded from obtaining those goods.

Technology has indeed advanced and accelerated productivity, further fueling the perception of a perpetually growing economy.

However, technology cannot achieve economic scale without sufficient natural resources. For instance, the steam engine's feasibility arose not by chance but from the advent of large-scale coal mining. Similarly, it was not until liquid fossil fuels became widely available that Leonardo da Vinci's helicopter vision could be realized. Throughout history, economic transformations have mirrored energy revolutions.

Despite these advancements, as the economy expands, a growing amount of working assets—including production facilities, machines, equipment, and infrastructure—decay over time. Sustained maintenance, repair, and eventual replacement of assets become indispensable, steadily drawing on greater resources. The growth of the real economy eventually converges to a limit set by natural resource constraints, at which point the system reaches an equilibrium at which the gross rate of return equals the depreciation rate, expressed as $f_K(K, L) = \delta$. When these forces achieve equilibrium, economic progress stagnates or begins to decline.[1] To understand what drives economic growth and what could halt it, we can turn to history for valuable insights.

The "Neolithic Revolution" of 12,000 years ago marked humanity's first major energy revolution. Before the Neolithic Revolution, the Younger Dryas cooling period is believed to have begun approximately 12,900 years ago, following a hypothesized comet impact. This event was followed by a rapid warming trend that brought temperatures close to those of today. Some researchers suggest that the impact may have significantly contributed to the extinction of large animals during that period, as well as the decline of the Clovis culture, which is characterized by its mobile bands of hunter-gatherers who utilized distinctive Clovis points for hunting large game, including mammoths and mastodons. Following the extinction of megafauna, societies underwent a significant shift from hunting to farming, marking a transformative change in their regional economies.

During this period, farmers harnessed energy through crops, which acted like "bio-solar panels," converting solar energy into chemical energy to meet human needs. By expanding farmland and

[1] Lionel Robbins rejects the "materialist" definition of economics and proposes an alternative definition of economics which has come to be known as the "scarcity definition of economics" (Robbins, 2007).

improving irrigation systems, humans increased their ability to capture solar energy. The energy revolution allowed humans to control their food supply, differentiating themselves from apex predators that were dependent on nature's bounty without control over it. The shift to agriculture transformed civilization. Cities grew with farming, and the global population rocketed—from five million people 10,000 years ago to eight billion today. The Neolithic Revolution can be seen as the dawn of the solar energy civilization, where agriculture relied on the Sun's short-wave radiation.[2]

The energy captured in crops, along with hydraulic, wind, and biomass energy, all originate from the Sun. For instance, solar radiation vaporizes water, which later falls as rain and can be harnessed as hydraulic energy. As long as the sun burns, the Earth receives a continuous influx of energy, making it an open system in terms of energy. The term "renewable energy" is therefore a misnomer—energy simply transforms from one form to another; it does not disappear, and it cannot be "renewed." To avoid the misconception associated with the term "renewable," this book refers to "direct energy" sources—such as solar, wind, biomass, and hydropower—which are continuously replenished by the energy from the Sun. The use of the "direct" energy increased from 0.602 quadrillion BTU in 1950 to 1.096 quadrillion BTU in 2022.

Stored energy, on the other hand, refers to energy that has been accumulated over millions of years within the Earth's crust. This category includes fossil fuels, nuclear energy, and geothermal energy. The Industrial Revolution marked the second energy revolution, where humans began tapping into stored energy, primarily in the form of fossil fuels. The combination of stored energy and machinery fueled the rapid growth of industrialized economies. However, accelerated depreciation of capital and infrastructure, together with declining fossil fuel supplies, drives the economy toward equilibrium unless nuclear fission is adopted or new energy sources are discovered.

Equilibrium in economics differs from its thermodynamic counterpart; in economics, it refers to a "steady state." To avoid confusion, this chapter calls the thermodynamic equilibrium *t-equilibrium*. In thermodynamics, *t-equilibrium* refers to a state where no energy or

---

[2] *The Development of Agriculture*, education.nationalgeographic.org, retrieved on July 16, 2024.

materials flow into or out of a system—a state of complete isolation.[3] Lord Kelvin referred to this as "heat death," in which all physical processes come to rest. At this point, all properties within a system, like temperature and pressure, become uniform, and the system remains unchanged indefinitely.

7.1 Entropy: The Drift Toward Disorder

Life itself is a constant battle against the natural drift toward equilibrium. Without energy inflow, all life ceases, systems lose functionality, and both living and non-living matter eventually break down into simpler forms. This process applies even to "durable" materials like gold. For instance, the French have preserved standard meter bars made of platinum–iridium—more durable than gold—in airtight containers to prevent oxidation and corrosion. Even the most resilient objects are subject to the thermodynamic process. Beneath all human constructs, including the economy, lies the inexorable pull of thermodynamics.

Daily experience provides simple examples of this process. Without electricity or gas, food spoils in refrigerators within days or weeks, and in abandoned houses, wood decays and metal rusts. These examples illustrate objects moving from an ordered to disordered state. Physics measures this degree of disorder with the concept of *entropy*—the higher the entropy, the greater the disorder.

To quantify disorder, consider a simple example with four balls and four boxes. Two of the four balls are blue and the other two are red. If there are no restrictions on which ball can go into which box, we can arrange them in 24 different ways. Any of the four balls can go to box 1 and there are 4 possibilities. After we put the first ball into box 1, there are 3 balls left. Then, any one of the three balls can go to box 2, so there are 3 choices. After we put the second ball into box 2, there are 2 balls left. Next, one of the two balls can go

[3]Thermodynamics, a branch of physical science, deals with laws governing energy flow—the first and second laws of thermodynamics. The first law of thermodynamics, the law of conservation of energy, for example, explains how heat energy transforms into work, such as how steam drives a piston in an engine, and vice versa (Haddad, 2019).

to box 3 and there are 2 possibilities. After we put the third ball into box 3, there is one ball and one box left. Finally, there is only 1 possibility: putting the last ball in the last box—box 4. Therefore, the total number of arrangements is:

$$4 \times 3 \times 2 \times 1 = 24.$$

The second case imposes restrictions: the two blue balls can only go to boxes 1 and 2, and the two red balls can only go to boxes 3 and 4. For the two blue balls, we can put one of the two blue balls in box 1, and there are 2 choices. The remaining blue ball must go into box 2, resulting in only 1 possibility. There are 2 arrangements. The same number of arrangements exists for the two red balls and boxes 3 and 4. The total number of arrangements in the second case is

$$2 \times 2 = 4.$$

Comparing the two cases, we observe that the unrestricted setup (24 arrangements) offers more possible configurations than the restricted one (4 arrangements). Consequently, the former exhibits higher entropy than the latter.

The natural inclination of systems is toward higher entropy, given that these states are statistically more probable due to their greater number of microscopic arrangements. A common example is smoke injected into a room; it invariably expands to fill the entire volume instead of staying localized. For any isolated system, an increase in entropy is irreversible without an external influence.

Irreversibility is a key principle of the second law of thermodynamics, whereas Newtonian mechanics operates under reversible processes. Lifting a weight by a pulley consumes energy, which can then be recovered by releasing the weight. However, in thermodynamics, processes involving heat are not fully reversible. For example, while a refrigerator uses electrical energy to cool its contents, that energy cannot be fully recovered. A steam engine admits hot, high-pressure steam that expands against a piston, delivering work while its temperature and pressure fall. The piston then returns as the exhaust steam is discharged into a heat sink at temperature (T_e), thereby completing the Carnot cycle. This release of steam, carrying an amount of heat (e_h), causes an unavoidable loss of heat energy and a corresponding increase in entropy. Macroscopically, this entropy change is represented as e_h/T_e.

In another example, when people lift weights, their bodies sweat to dissipate excess heat, helping maintain core body temperature. This lost heat is an irreversible energy transfer that increases entropy.

Any complex system—biological, mechanical, or economic—require negative entropy flows to keep them from falling into disorder. This universal principle is grounded in thermodynamics, wherein energy functions as the source of negative entropy flows. Romanian economist Nicholas Georgescu-Roegen recognized that the economic system is an entropic flow constrained by energy resource depletion (Georgescu-Roegen, 1986; Michaelian, 2005; Raine *et al.*, 2006). Fossil fuels are not only essential for industrial operations but also for sustaining the real economy—providing food, shelter, and transportation. Without this vital energy input, the economic system will inevitably succumb to increasing entropy and disorder.[4]

7.2 Energy Creates Complex Systems

Energy inflows not only prevent a system from decaying but also drive the emergence of complex patterns from simple systems, pushing them toward more advanced states. Nobel Prize winner Ilya Prigogine, who received the award in 1977, termed this phenomenon *self-organization*: the spontaneous rise of complex order from simple structures (Prigogine and Stengers, 2018). One example is the emergence of hexagonal Bénard cells when heating a liquid in a flat pan. Similarly, under a microscope, snowflakes reveal intricate patterns formed by water droplets and air particles moving through cold clouds under specific temperature and humidity conditions.

A dynamic system can include feedback loops, where outputs are fed back into the system as inputs. In economics, for instance, a portion of economic output is saved and reinvested into the economy. While feedback can also create stability problems for systems, positive feedback loops underpin many chemical and biological processes that sustain life. For example, termites build their nests through a simple feedback mechanism: Termites deposit lumps of earth, and

[4]Henri Poincaré pioneered the work of non-equilibrium thermodynamics from the perspective of dynamical systems theory (Gaspard *et al.*, 2007).

areas with slightly higher concentrations of lumps attract more termites due to increased hormone levels, leading to the construction of a nest through positive feedback.

Prigogine also illustrated how cities emerge in a logistic model of migration and urbanization (Allen and Sanglier, 1978). People tend to migrate to areas with higher populations, which generate more economic activity, provide more job opportunities, and consume more goods. This two-way feedback loop, known as the urban multiplier, accelerates local economic activities and builds the infrastructure necessary to support them. Economic development emerges spontaneously, from the division of labor to trade, and eventually leads to the formation of markets and cities (Burley and Foster, 2013). Population concentration and economic activity have been evolving since (Rossi-Hansberg, 2019).

The growth of cities is a product of positive feedback and intensified activity fueled by energy inflows. Artificially created towns that eventually become ghost towns stand as counterexamples, violating these core principles.

In general, energy flows in nature are uncontrolled: they generate and sustain landscapes of great beauty—from flowers to the Grand Canyon—but also generate destructive forces such as hurricanes and tsunamis. Humans, however, depend on controlled energy flows.

The role of energy, specifically fire, may clarify the enigma of human knowledge accumulation and our dominance over other apex animals. The utilization of fire marked a pivotal "primitive energy revolution" for humans, assuming they share a common ancestor with other apex species. Homo erectus (or Homo ergaster) was the earliest known hominin to control fire, starting around two million years ago and using it regularly by 400,000 years ago (Anton, 2003). Fire provided humans with crucial environmental control, offering warmth and expanding food options through the advent of cooking. Humans experimented with cooking nearly everything—plants, animals, and even stones. This not only diversified food sources and vastly improved the edibility and digestibility of various plants and animal products, thereby increasing food supplies and boosting nutritional intake, but also laid the groundwork for what effectively became our first empirical science: alchemy.

The nutritional benefits of cooked foods likely fueled significant increase in human physical size and brain capacity. Notably, brain volume nearly tripled during the transition from Homo erectus to Homo sapiens, expanding cognitive abilities. This evolutionary leap in brain capacity, akin to computers gaining intelligence with increased memory, allowed humans to separate from and dominate other apex species. The human brain accounts for about 2% of body weight but consumes about 30% of the body's energy.

At the peak of the last ice age, approximately 20,000 years ago, hunters began settling, growing crops, and raising animals. Hunting required vast tracts of land—around 600 acres to support one person—whereas the modern American diet requires 2.67 acres of arable land per person.[5] Villages formed, followed by towns and cities. Over time, people built temples, and elites emerged to administer increasingly complex communities. Civilization was born.[6] Each step toward civilization—migration, farming, and building infrastructure—required energy.

The Industrial Revolution marked a significant leap in energy use, reshaping the economy and revolutionizing production. The fossil fuels that had lain dormant for millions of years suddenly unleashed immense power during the Industrial Revolution. Thomas Savery's first steam engine, patented in 1698, generated one horsepower, equivalent to the work of ten strong manual laborers.[7] Early inventions like the Aeolipile, a rudimentary steam engine invented by a Greek in the first century A.D., had no significant application due to the lack of large-scale energy sources. However, coal mining operations, such as Sir George Bruce's 1575 pit under the sea in Scotland, eventually fed the hungry steam engine with fossil fuel, giving rise to industrialization.[8]

Electricity then provided a more economical way to transfer and distribute energy over distances. The power harnessed from fossil fuels enabled economic and social systems to grow faster than ever before, propelling the initial accumulation of capital stock—tools,

---

[5] *Which diet makes best use of Farmland? You might be surprised*, ensia.com, retrieved on July 15, 2024.

[6] *The Birth of Civilization—The First Farmers (20000 BC to 8800 BC)*, September 7, 2020, thehistocrat, retrieved on January 21, 2024.

[7] artsandculture.google.com, retrieved on January 19, 2024.

[8] *History of coal mining*, wilipedia.org, retrieved on January 19, 2024.

equipment, and machinery—and shifting production to rely increasingly on energy inputs.

Fossil fuels significantly increased the economy's energy input, fostering the division of labor and a leap in productivity. Both military technology and economic growth depend on energy. The 19th-century dominance of European nations exemplifies history as primarily an energy narrative, rather than simply the tales of kings, generals, or influential figures.

An average person consumes 2,500 calories a day, with a manual laborer burning up to 1,600 calories during an 8-hour shift. A gallon of gasoline contains about 31,000 calories of energy, which is equivalent to 20 days of human labor (Burley and Foster, 2013; Jenkins, 2005). The energy consumption of an average person is stable. Taking more energy than needed does not improve but hurts a human's health. The overweight problem is the energy problem—people take in too much energy. Furthermore, the 2,500 calories that a person takes in are only the energy in the food, while other consumption besides food—at minimum, clothing, shelter, and transportation—requires far more energy than the food alone. The world's actual labor force was 3.4 billion people in 2023,[9] while the global liquid fuel consumption alone reached 100 million barrels per day, equating to the labor of 8.4 billion workers, far exceeding the world's actual labor force. These substantial energy inputs are crucial for sustaining today's economy.

7.3 Work Produces Economic Value

The concept of "value" in economics and finance is often narrowly understood as exchange value (monetary price) rather than *economic value.* This distinction remains elusive, largely due to the complexities of non-homogeneous goods as discussed in Chapter 1. Economists tried to measure exchange value using labor hours, a concept that reached its zenith in Karl Marx's *Capital.* However, even Marx acknowledged that labor is not the only source of value; capital stock and materials also contribute. Economists abandoned the

[9]World Bank website, retrieved on January 17, 2024.

labor theory of value but still conflated the two concepts, exchange value and economic value, mistakenly using the former to explain the latter.

In addition, since the Industrial Revolution, the industrial production process has masked the underlying forces of production. Historically, the primary bottlenecks in economic production have been labor and capital stock—conduits for energy delivery from sources like the Sun and fossil fuels—since the Industrial Revolution, masked the underlying driving force of energy. Abundant energy enabled limited labor and equipment to multiply productivity. Yet even with plentiful energy, economic production remained constrained by limited capital stock and low-intensity labor, which explains why traditional production functions focus on capital stock K and labor L.

If breakthroughs such as nuclear fusion occur or global consensus on nuclear fission is reached, with abundant energy sources, the capacity of the energy conduit would still be a practical constraint, and the overall energy supply itself would cease to be a concern. However, as economies amass substantial capital stock, the conduit's size would no longer constrain the limited energy supply. Instead, without abundant alternative energy resources, fossil fuels will inevitably become the limiting factor for economic growth.

Thermodynamics suggests that energy might be a measure of value, but energy itself is conserved and cannot be created or destroyed. The Sun radiates energy to Earth, and an equal amount of energy must eventually leave the planet; otherwise, Earth's temperature would continuously rise, making it uninhabitable. If energy were the sole measure of value, then manufacturing would add no value since it consumes energy but does not produce it. Therefore, energy alone cannot fully measure economic value.

Not all forms of energy are equal. Humans digest natural products—food—which contain specific chemical energy that the body can absorb. Through labor, humans convert this chemical energy into *work*, a specialized form of energy in thermodynamics. Work involves applying force to an object and moving it over a distance.

For example, an engine transforms chemical energy from gasoline into work by pushing pistons back and forth, while human muscles function as biological pistons to perform work. The human body converts chemical energy from food to sustain life. About 75% of this energy maintains basic functions at rest, while approximately 25% is converted into work—representing only a fraction of the 1,600 calories consumed during eight hours of labor.[10]

Energy conversion to work always occurs at an efficiency $b < 1$. For fossil fuels, this conversion—such as gasoline to mechanical work—inherently incurs losses as waste heat. Even multi-step conversions, like fossil fuel to electricity via a generator and then to work via an electric motor (which can reach 78% peak efficiency), still result in significant overall energy loss; b is the ratio of initial fossil fuel energy to final work output. For an electric motor, electrical energy is transformed into work, with peak efficiency at $b = 0.78$.

The inverse of this efficiency, $1/b > 1$, varies by product type. For example, an electric heater converts electrical energy to heat with an efficiency near 1, yet a heat pump can achieve an efficiency greater than 1 by transferring more heat than the work it consumes. In effect, it "pumps" heat from a colder environment into a warmer room.

Putting blue and red balls into specific boxes requires work, whether performed by a human or a robot. Heat energy cannot accomplish this unless it is transformed into work. It is work not energy that creates economic value.

The economy's work input is currently fossil-fuel dependent. Should these fuels deplete without viable alternatives, the resulting limited energy supply would severely hinder workflows, moving the production bottleneck from labor and capital stock to energy, and the conventional production function must incorporate work inputs.

A production function can be constructed based on work inputs, enhancing the traditional framework to explicitly include work delivered by capital stock (ν_K) and labor (ν_L), represented as $f(\nu_K, \nu_L)$. For capital stock,

$$\nu_K = \nu_{K,opt}\left[\min\left(\frac{\nu}{\nu_{K,opt}}, 1\right)\right],$$

in which the function (*min*) selects the smaller of the two terms in the brackets. Accordingly, if work input (ν) falls below the optimal ($\nu_{K,opt}$), capital utilization is incomplete and some capacity lies idle.

---

[10] *Work, Energy, and Power in Humans*, Chemistry LibreTexts, LibreTexts, Sept. 21, 2023, chem.libretexts.org, retrieved on July 31, 2024.

If, instead, work input surpasses $\nu_{K,opt}$, the excess is wasted because it generates no additional output.

Here, $\nu_{K,opt}$ is the optimal work capital stock K can deliver. When work supply is abundant, capital stock always operates at $\nu_{K,opt}$, fully realizing its productive potential. Thus, with unconstrained work, production output is primarily determined by capital stock capacity, justifying the exclusion of work input in traditional production functions.

Despite variation across producers, the work required to produce identical goods is defined by the socially necessary work for their production—an average across producers, akin to Marx's "socially necessary labor-hours." In competitive markets, firms' pursuit of work efficiency drives out less efficient producers.

Analogous to capital stock, work input by labor is defined as

$$\nu_L = \nu_{L,\text{opt}} \left[\min \left(\frac{\nu}{\nu_{L,\text{opt}}}, 1 \right) \right].$$

If labor input (ν) is below the optimal level ($\nu_{L,\text{opt}}$), insufficient labor is available to deliver optimal work. Conversely, when labor input exceeds ($\nu_{L,\text{opt}}$), the surplus is wasted, as it cannot be productively converted into additional output.

The production process can be modeled as a workflow network: capital and labor supply workflows to intermediate stages, and the finished product embodies economic value equal to the sum of these flows. However, human consumption—such as food or heating—is measured in energy units (e.g., daily calories, BTUs) rather than in work. Although energy and work can be translated interchangeably through a conversion factor (b), consistency requires choosing one as the primary unit. In the following analysis, energy will serve as the primary unit, and products derived from work input will be expressed in energy terms. Accordingly, we interpret macroeconomic identity in terms of energy:

$$\dot{K} = f(\nu_K, \nu_L) - C - \delta K. \tag{7.1}$$

Economies are divided into energy producers and consumers; globally, energy exporters meet the demands of importers. If work creates economic value, a paradox emerges: how do sectors or countries that procure or import energy manage to generate economic value? This intriguing problem will be examined in the following sections.

7.3.1 *Hunting economy*

In a hunting economy, hunters hunted animals for food utilizing primitive hunting tools, which required minimal craftsmanship and held little value ($K = 0$). Assuming that tribes did not domesticate animals, they could not accumulate wealth because animal meat does not last. Thus, $\dot{K} = 0$, and Eq. (7.1) reduces to

$$f(0, \nu_L) - C = 0. \tag{7.2}$$

Hunters consume animal meat that contains the amount of energy Ln_c, where L is the number of hunters and each hunter on average consumes the amount of energy n_c.

A hunter used his muscles to hunt, and only a fraction of his energy consumption was effectively transformed into work that supported his hunting activities. The total work input of L hunters is

$$\nu_L = bLn_c.$$

Hunters have such skill A_H that they can hunt a number of animals that contain more energy than the energy they consume. The AK framework gives the production function:

$$f(0, \nu_L) = \frac{A_H}{b}\nu_L = A_H L n_c,$$

in which the factor $1/b$ converts the output measured by work to the output measured by energy.

Hunters annually expend energy (Ln_c), converting it into work (bLn_c) during hunting. The hunted animals, once processed, yield a total energy of $A_H L n_c$, in which A_H serves as an energy (work) multiplier, representing the ratio of energy obtained from the hunted animals to the energy expended by the hunters.

Hunters and their families shared food, resulting in a total energy consumption of $(L + L_e)n_c$, where L_e represents the number of non-hunting community members. Consequently, Eq. (7.2) becomes:

$$A_H L n_c - (L + L_e)n_c = 0,$$

which gives the work multiplier A_H:

$$A_H = 1 + \frac{L_e}{L}, \tag{7.3}$$

The energy of the hunting economy comes from the animals at the bottom of food chain up to apex predators at the top. Herbivores eat grass and plants, which get energy from the Sun. Carnivores eat other animals and obtain solar energy indirectly. Omnivores get solar energy too. In a hunting economy, all energy $A_H L n_c$ comes from the Sun. Solar energy is free, but the animals hunted by hunters have economic value, which is measured by the hunters' work input bLn_c. The hunting economy described in Eq. (7.3) remains in equilibrium because the surplus energy captured, $(A_H - 1)Ln_c$, sustains non-hunting community members. Thus, Eq. (7.3) presents the necessary condition for the hunting economy's sustainability.

7.3.2 *Farming economy*

In the early farming economy, the means of production, such as spades, grape hoe, rake, and sickle, were no comparison with the modern capital stock. The farming economy also relied on draft animals, such as oxen, horses, mules, or donkeys, which performed physically demanding work—cultivating land, sowing, and transporting.

Draft animals consume crops and provide work in production. For this reason, draft animals' consumption and work input are equivalent to the number L_a of farmers. As discussed in Chapter 1, seeds (K_A) are a unique capital stock. In the early farming economy, assuming land and labor did not constrain output, seeds K_A were the determining factor and required work input to grow them into crops. The macroeconomic identity for the farming economy is then expressed as

$$\dot{K}_A = f^A(\nu_K, \nu_L) - C - \delta K_A, \tag{7.4}$$

where K_A, the seeds, are measured by energy, and ν_L is the combined work inputs from farmers and draft animals—the only work inputs needed to grow seeds:

$$\nu_L = b(L + L_a)n_c.$$

The optimal amount of work to grow the seeks K_A is $\nu_{K,A}$:

$$\nu_{K,A} = bL_{K,A}n_c,$$

where $L_{K,A}$ is the optimal equivalent number of workers, including draft animals, to deliver the optimal amount of work to grow the seeds. The work input is $(L + L_a)bn_c$, and, interpreting AK production function as "AE" model, where "E" denotes energy, we have:

$$f^A(\nu_K, \nu_L) = f^A\left[\nu_{K,A}\min\left(\frac{\nu}{\nu_{K,A}}, 1\right)\right] = \frac{A_A}{b}\nu_{K,A}\min\left(\frac{L + L_a}{L_{K,A}}, 1\right).$$

Accounting for nonproductive individuals and draft animals (L_e), the total energy consumption in the farming economy is $(L+L_e+L_a)n_c$. The macroeconomic identity then becomes:

$$\dot{K_A} = \frac{A_A}{b}\nu_{K,A}\min\left(\frac{L + L_a}{L_{K,A}}, 1\right) - (L + L_e + L_a)n_c - \delta K_A, \tag{7.5}$$

where the term δK_A represents the energy in the seeds depreciated at a rate δ, which is one for the seeds of annual crops.

In the optimal scenario, work input from labor and draft animals match the work needed to grow seeds, i.e., $L + L_a = L_{K,A}$. Assume that the farming economy had no technology to store crops, then $\dot{K}_A = 0$, Eq. (7.6) simplifies to

$$\frac{A_A}{b}\nu_{K,A} = A_A(L + L_a)n_c = (L + L_e + L_a)n_c + \delta K_A,$$

yielding the energy multiplier A_A:

$$A_A = 1 + \left(\frac{1}{L + L_a}\right)\left(L_e + \frac{\delta K_A}{n_c}\right). \tag{7.6}$$

Equation (7.6) provides the necessary condition for the agricultural economy's sustainability: the work multiplier A_A must exceed the consumption, $(L + L_a)n_c$ by farmers and draft animals, who convert this consumed energy into work, $b(L+L_a)n_c$, to cultivate seeds. The crop production process utilizes free solar energy, yields crop output, $(L + L_a + L_e)n_c$, whose economic value corresponds to the required work, $\nu_{K,A} = b(L + L_a)n_c$.

Economic value is the key metric for producers—*the firms in the modern economy*—to manage resources efficiently. On average, a farmer produces 50 bushels of crops annually, and a hunter hunts down 2000 pounds of wild animal meat a year. One bushel of crops equals 40 pounds of meat, which aligns with Marx's labor theory of value, but economic value does not determine exchange value, which mirrors consumer preferences, market sentiment (see Section 7.3.3).

In addition, labor is only one medium through which work is delivered, and work is the ultimate measure of economic value. The work is required for agricultural production—such as plowing, sowing, and harvesting. In a similar vein, the work exerted by hunters to track and capture wild animals contributes to the value of the meat.

Although the work theory of value may resemble the labor theory of value, the two theories rest on distinct foundations. The work theory of value is rooted in thermodynamics—work reduces the entropy of a system. For example, when farmers use draft animals in farming, the work done by draft animals adds value the same as the work done by farmers; the same principle applies to AI-powered robots. However, the labor theory of value cannot explain the value of products without labor, but the work theory of value takes account of the work done by draft animals or robots.

The farming economy discussed here refers to ancient agriculture. Equation (7.5) does not account for modern farming equipment and machines, which significantly boost productivity. The next section considers the impact of equipment and machines on the agricultural economy.

7.3.2.1 *From primitive roots to modern agricultural economy*

Agricultural practices improved over time. Advancements like the 14th-century three-field crop rotation system in the Low Countries boosted the yield ratio to 1:14 from 1:2.5 during the 9th century. Consequently, seeds lost their importance as the primary constraint on crop output. Following the Industrial Revolution, two new economic sectors emerged: energy and industry. The *industry* discussed in this chapter excludes the energy sector, including activities such as mining and refining. Farming benefited from both energy and industrial production. The advent of farming machinery powered by fossil fuels delivered far more work than human labor could ever provide. As a result, these machines gradually replaced human labor and draft animals in farming. Consequently, capital stock became an integral component of the production function:

$$f^A(\nu_{K,opt}, \nu_L) = \frac{A}{b}\nu_{K,opt}^a \nu_L^{1-a},$$

where $\nu_{K,opt}$ denotes the optimal work input for the machinery. As capital stock continued to accumulate, it increasingly substituted for human labor, leading to a gradual rise in the output elasticity of capital stock a over time.[11]

The contribution of human labor and draft animals has been steadily diminishing. Once it became negligible compared to the input from fossil fuels, the Cobb–Douglas production function simplifies to the AK model:

$$f^A(\nu_{K,opt}, \nu_L) = \frac{A}{b}\nu_{K,opt}.$$

At this stage, machines had replaced human labor as the primary source of work, and humans served mainly as mental laborers—such as managers and engineers. A smaller select group of manual workers is assigned to more complex tasks that are beyond the scope of machine and automation, including the operation and maintenance of machinery. As agriculture develops and human labor becomes less essential, the supply of labor becomes more available and no longer constrains production capacity.

With the emergence of energy and industrial economies, the second consequence is that modern agriculture produces agricultural products, referred to as F, not only to meet its own needs but also to supply agricultural commodities to both the energy and industrial economies:

$$f^A(\nu_K, \nu_L) = F = F_A + F_E + F_I, \quad (7.7)$$

where F_A, F_E, and F_I are the agricultural products for itself, the energy economy, and the industrial economy, respectively. The modern agricultural economy exchanges F_E for energy E_A produced by

[11]The estimates of the output elasticity of capital stock a vary widely. Some more recent results even reported $a > 1$.

the energy economy and exchanges F_I for industrial products Γ_A produced by the industrial economy. The industrial output, denoted as Γ_A, comprises both consumption goods, represented as $\Gamma_{A,c}$, and capital goods that contribute to the creation of new capital stock and cover the depreciation, $\dot{K}_A + \delta K_A$, in the agricultural economy:

$$\Gamma_A = \Gamma_{A,c} + \dot{K}_A + \delta K_A, \tag{7.8}$$

where K_A is primarily composed of farming machinery and equipment measured by energy, as seeds represent a negligible portion in comparison. Substituting Eq. (7.8) into Eq. (7.7) gives the dynamics of the modern agricultural economy:

$$\dot{K}_A = f^A(\nu_{K_A}, \nu_L) - F_A - E_E - \Gamma_{Ac} - \delta K_A, \tag{7.9}$$

where K_A represents farming machines and equipment.

The work input into a series of production processes generates a product, but natural processes subsequently degrade that product, effectively reversing the work that was invested in its creation. The work expended in production is equivalent to the work lost during the natural degradation process. This equivalence enables us to assess the economic value of both a machine and a piece of land.

For example, a machine is denoted as $K_{A,i}$, where the subscript i refers to the specific machine in question. The economic value of the machine is then the total work dissipated in depreciation,

$$\int_1^n e^{\rho t} b \delta K_{A,i} dt,$$

where n represents the lifespan of the machine. It is the same amount of work required for the industrial economy to produce the machine. Specifically, the work input involves organizing raw materials to create the machine, while natural processes tend to disorganize and degrade that structure over time.

In monetary terms, accounting substitutes the initial investment in a machine with its accumulated depreciation:

$$P_0 \dot{K} = \sum_{i=1}^{n} P_i \delta K. \tag{7.10}$$

By applying this approach to all investments, accounting effectively smooths out the initial lump-sum expenditure, resulting in a more consistent appearance of net income over time. It posits that the monetary value of capital stock corresponds to the total accumulation of its monetary depreciation throughout its lifespan. If the discount factor is ignored and the price, P, is constant,[12] the accounting depreciation seems to be consistent with the economic value depreciation: The amount of work needed to produce a piece of capital stock is the cumulative depreciation, which reflects the work that has been lost during its life.

However, accounting is based on exchange values, which can be influenced by factors beyond actual work and may even be speculative. Wasteland has no economic value but may still carry an exchange value. Accounting depreciation is not only sensitive to prices (see Section 2.1.2.8); it also permits firms to keep two sets of books using different depreciation methods for tax filings and earnings reports. By contrast, the physical process that takes an asset from its initial state to full depreciation is independent of monetary considerations.

The environmental impact of materials used in construction can extend well beyond their complete monetary depreciation. While many abandoned houses, buildings, and even entire cities may lose their monetary worth, the physical depreciation of these structures back to dust can take centuries, if not millennia. This prolonged decay often results in significant ecological consequences that are frequently overlooked during the initial development, design, and planning processes. Through physical depreciation, an economic product eventually reverts to its natural constituents, embodying the essence of sustainability. However, it is crucial to acknowledge that many modern economic developments are irreversible within a human lifespan, resulting in a permanent loss of certain aspects of nature.

For example, a single-use plastic container loses its monetary value the moment it is used, but the physical breakdown of the plastic can take hundreds of years. The environmental consequences of such materials can persist long after their financial worth has dissipated, leading to significant and lasting negative externalities and ecological impacts.

This perspective on depreciation is relevant when examining land value. Early farmers often sought land near rivers, where natural

[12]See Tobin's q in Footnote 27.

irrigation provided fertile conditions for cultivation. In contrast, when such prime land was unavailable, work was required to convert non-arable land into productive farmland. As a result, the economic value of the land can be articulated as the following integral:

$$\int_0^n b\delta\mathcal{L}e^{-\rho t}dt,$$

where $b\delta\mathcal{L}$ is the physical depreciation of the land $\mathcal{L}$ and n denotes the time required for farmland to revert to its natural state as wild land. It is conceivable that this period is not indefinite, and the same amount of work is needed to cultivate wild land into farmland. Specifically, the work input consists of labor to render wild land arable, while natural processes gradually disorganize and degrade the land over time. Although accounting conventions treat farmland as having an infinite life, its true economic life is defined not by the age of the Earth but by the labor required to transform non-arable land into arable land.

Land, much like capital stock, is a vital asset in agricultural production and demands continuous care to preserve its productive capacity. While arable land serves as a "bio-solar panel," yet it contrasts sharply with industrial solar panels, whose life cycle—from manufacturing to disposal—generates environmental pollution. Land is a natural resource created by nature and remains part of the ecosystem, vulnerable to pollution.

Vertical farming aims to transcend the natural constraints of arable land by growing crops in vertically stacked layers, yielding higher production than traditional farming methods. While this approach reduces the need for land, it does demand specialized equipment and more work to maintain optimal productivity. Furthermore, vertical farming relies significantly on artificial lighting, which poses a challenge compared to traditional farming, where crops can harness free solar energy for growth.

7.3.3 *Economic value versus exchange value*

David Ricardo and Karl Marx both aimed to uncover the determinants of exchange value, yet they overlooked a critical distinction between exchange value and the value of labor. The value articulated in labor theory is not the determinant of exchange value; instead, it is the *economic value*—the economic resources necessary for the production of a commodity in an economy that heavily relies on human labor. Exchange value links two opposing forces: supply and demand. The preferences and utility functions of households, coupled with their budget constraints, shape the demand for that commodity.

Beneath the surface of fluctuating market prices—the exchange values—lies the economic value, which is more stable and serves as an indicator how effectively the economic resource—work—is used to produce individual goods and whether it is allocated optimally. For instance, the exchange value relation in Section 2.1.2 gives the following: 10 bushels of wheat = 100 lbs of beef. However, the economic values of 10 bushels of wheat and 100 lbs of beef need not be identical. This relationship captures consumers' preferences and budget constraints, which vary with psychological factors and broader economic conditions. In a Walrasian equilibrium, the exchange value reflects monetary balance rather than the balance of economic value.

For the sake of simplicity, let us set aside the complexities of modern agriculture and consider a scenario where farmers depend solely on labor for their production processes. Farmers who cultivate wheat and raise cattle understand that producing 10 bushels of wheat and 100 pounds of beef requires an equivalent number of labor-hours. However, if consumer preferences shift toward increased beef consumption before supply can adjust, the exchange rate may temporarily change to 15 bushels of wheat for 100 pounds of beef. This ratio signifies a disparity where the amount of wheat that requires 1.5 labor-hours to grow exchanges for the amount of beef that takes 1 labor-hour to produce. Consequently, this altered exchange value incentivizes wheat farmers to pivot from cultivating wheat to raising cattle. This transition will likely reduce wheat supply while simultaneously increasing beef production. As these supply dynamics evolve, the exchange value will gradually adjust to reflect the original labor-hour balance of 10 bushels of wheat for 100 pounds of beef.

The tension between exchange value and economic value serves as a crucial dynamic within the capitalist economy. Exchange values represent the relative demand for various commodities, influenced by consumer preferences and their budgets. Producers, in turn, aim to optimize the allocation of economic resources—work—to meet that demand effectively. Through their monetary "votes," consumers signal their choices to the market, revealing preferences and utilities influenced by changes in economic conditions, wealth distribution, and other factors, such as new products and technological change. In contrast, economic values are physical and objective measures, independent of human psychology.

This distinction can be illustrated also in international trade. Globally, the production of a commodity requires "socially necessary work." Thus, a chair or a desk embodies economic value. If a chair has an economic value equivalent to one unit of work but an economy expends two units to produce it, then one unit of work is wasted in terms of economic value. Ricardo's theory of comparative advantage (see Chapter 6) concerns maximizing global economic value by efficiently allocating resources across nations. Conversely, if a country artificially lowers its exchange rate to export overproduced goods, it may misallocate economic resources and, in doing so, ultimately squander global resources. More broadly, it is not uncommon in the global economy for products to be produced in ways that are less than fully efficient.

The book title, *Money and the Real Economy*, stresses that money represents the preferences of individuals regarding various goods, while the real economy is constrained by the work inputs into the physical production. Ideally, if each person wielded an equal vote, the goods produced would align with the broader preferences of the population. However, the number of votes a person holds is proportional to their wealth. Moreover, these votes—wealth—can multiply and grow over time, and the votes—money—can also be artificially created.

As a result, the types of goods produced, and the overall structure of the economy cater to the preferences of affluent voters. High-end products and upscale businesses, while serving a small segment of the population, can be just as profitable as those serving a larger demographic. Amid housing shortages, the construction pipeline for luxury coastal and beachfront hotels and golf resorts has been booming, with many projects scheduled to open between 2024 and 2027.

Following the Russian Revolution of 1917, a debate emerged among socialists and communists regarding the potential abolition of money (along with private property). Notably, Leichter (Leichter, 1923) posited that money could be replaced with a system based on labor-hours to determine prices. Vladimir Lenin once illustrated this idea by stating, “When we are victorious on a world scale, I think we shall use gold for the purpose of building public lavatories in the streets of some of the largest cities in the world. This would be the most just and most educational way of utilizing gold for the benefit of these generations...” (Lenin, 1921).[13]

Economists such as Keynes and Mises also overlooked that economic value measures the resources used, while prices—as expressions of exchange value—measure the will of economic agents. Mises asserted, “Without a pricing mechanism, there is no economic calculation” (Mises, 1990). Yet economic value and exchange value function in opposite ways: economic calculation is independent of money, whereas people’s preferences are expressed through money via prices.

Abolishing money would undermine the “democracy” of the marketplace that allows consumers to express their preferences for different products. Without consumer “votes,” producers remain in the dark about whether their goods truly meet public needs. Contrary to Mises’s belief that a socialist economy might assess “the will of the economic subjects,” socialism and communism falter because the government acts as a blind guide, steering the economy off course without knowing the direction people wish to go.

A capitalist economy stands in sharp contrast to a socialist one. At the micro level, firms continually search for gaps between economic value and exchange value, reallocating resources to produce the goods consumers want, while consumers maximize utility across an expanding range of choices. In socialism, state-owned enterprises lack both the motivation and information to pursue this gap, so they fail to deliver the products that consumers genuinely desire. At the macro level, the capitalist economy not only satisfies household needs through efficient resource allocation; it also fosters innovation, advancing technology and productivity and leaving socialist economies behind.

[13]Inspired by Vladimir Lenin’s vision of the ultimate capitalist waste, a jeweler has built two solid gold toilets in a gem-encrusted bathroom gilded with 24-carat gold.

Since the Industrial Revolution, numerous products have been produced through complex and intricate processes, making it challenging to trace the work inputs involved. Traditionally, market prices have functioned as the chief indicator of "values" among products and a gauge of overall economic performance. However, with the rise of the information age, we now possess the capability to collect detailed data on the work inputs used in these production processes. This advancement enables us to evaluate real-economy performance and optimize the use of economic resources based on economic value.

7.3.4 *Energy economy*

The advent of fossil fuels ignited the Industrial Revolution, creating a new energy sector (a new energy economy). A pure energy economy produces energy (E) for itself, the agricultural economy, and the industrial economy:

$$f^E(\nu_K, \nu_L) = E = E_E + E_A + E_I, \tag{7.11}$$

where the energy economy consumes energy E_E in the process of producing the total energy output E, and E_A and E_I are the energy exported to the agricultural economy and the industrial economy, respectively. The energy economy trades energy (E_A) for agricultural products F_E and energy (E_I) for industrial products Γ_E:

$$\Gamma_E = \dot{K}_E + \Gamma_{E,c} + \delta K_E, \tag{7.12}$$

where $\Gamma_{E,c}$ denotes industrial consumption goods and $\dot{K}_E + \delta K_E$ represents the capital goods. Substituting Eq. (7.12) into Eq. (7.11) gives the macroeconomic identity for the energy economy:

$$\dot{K}_E = f(\nu_K, \nu_L) - E_E - F_E - \Gamma_{E,c} - \delta K_E. \tag{7.13}$$

The capital stock K_E requires a specific amount of work input, $\nu_{K,E}$, to produce the optimal output:

$$\nu_K = \nu_{K,E} \min\left(\frac{\nu}{\nu_{K,E}}, 1\right), \tag{7.14}$$

where ν_K represents the work input to the production process and $\nu_{K,E}$ denotes the amount of work required for capital stock K to operate at maximum capacity. In the early days of coal mining, human labor was the primary source of work in production. The relationship between labor input and the operational capacity of the mining process can be represented mathematically as follows:

$$\nu_L = \nu_{L,E} \min\left(\frac{\nu_L}{\nu_{I,E}}, 1\right) = \nu_{L,E} \min\left(\frac{L}{L_E}, 1\right), \tag{7.15}$$

where the total work input is $\nu_L = bLn_c$ and the optimal work input is $\nu_{L,E} = bL_E n_c$, where L_E represents the number of workers needed to provide the optimal work input.

When the energy economy started using machines, capital stock entered the production process. By combining Eq. (7.14) and Eq. (7.15), the production function of the energy economy can be expressed as follows:

$$f^E(\nu_K, \nu_L) = f^E\left[\nu_{K,E} \min\left(\frac{\nu_K}{\nu_{K,E}}, 1\right), \nu_{L,E} \min\left(\frac{L}{L_{K,E}}, 1\right)\right]. \tag{7.16}$$

Equation (7.16) extends the traditional production function by incorporating the principle that work generates value. The formulation is tailored to the context of the energy economy, but it is general and applicable across different economies.

Modern energy production is capital-intensive, relying heavily on advanced machinery and equipment, such as both land and offshore oil rigs, which extract oil from deep underground reserves. The contribution of human labor has diminished significantly in comparison to the output derived from fossil fuels; many of the remaining human employees no longer perform manual tasks. When fossil fuels were abundant and inexpensive, the work input ν_K—sourced from these fuels—was also plentiful and cost-effective relative to the work from human labor. With labor's work input becoming negligible, the production function simplifies to the AK model:

$$f^E(\nu_{K,E}, \nu_{L,E}) = f^E(\nu_{K,E}) = \frac{A_E}{b}\nu_{K,E}. \tag{7.17}$$

By substituting Eq. (7.17) into Eq. (7.13), the dynamics of the energy economy become:

$$\dot{K_E} = \frac{A_E}{b}\nu_{K,E} - E_E - F_E - \Gamma_{Ec} - \delta K_E. \tag{7.18}$$

At equilibrium, the energy balance is represented as:

$$\frac{A_E}{b}\nu_{K,E} = E_E + F_E + \Gamma_{E,c} + \delta K_E = E_E + F_E + \Gamma_E. \qquad (7.19)$$

Equation (7.19) also indicates that both the agricultural and industrial economies depend on the fossil fuels supplied by the energy economy:

$$\frac{A_E \nu_{K,E}}{b} - E_E = F_E + \Gamma_E,$$

where the energy economy consumes energy to produce energy. Oil rigs convert the energy, E_E, into work $\nu_{K,E}$ at its maximum capacity:

$$bE_E = \nu_{K,E}.$$

As an energy provider, a drilling rig's energy input ($E_E = \nu_{K,E}/b$) must be less than the energy output ($A_E\nu_{K,E}/b$) in order to generate a surplus that can be exported to other economies:

$$\frac{A_E - 1}{b}\nu_{K,E} = F_A + \Gamma_I. \qquad (7.20)$$

In Eq. (7.20), the right-hand side of the equation is the energy that is exported to both the agricultural and industrial sectors. The factor A_E is critical, as it affects the surplus energy available to agricultural and industrial economies.

The AK model's zero second-order derivative violates the principle of diminishing returns, which is necessary for maximization. To satisfy the second-order condition, for example, define a multiplier A_E^* as the energy output corresponding to the work input $\nu_{K,E}$; the net energy output becomes:

$$A_E^* \nu_{K,E} - \nu_{K,E}/b = (A_E^* - 1/b)\nu_{K,E}.$$

As the energy-conversion efficiency b declines with high-quality fossil-fuel depletion, producing the same amount of energy requires more energy input, and the multiplier $(A_E^* - 1/b)$ correspondingly decreases.

A mine produces $A_E^*\nu_{K,E}$ units of coal using work input $\nu_{K,E}$ from a gasoline-powered machine. As gasoline becomes more energy-costly to produce, the mine's net energy output declines. Likewise, as oil resources deplete and drilling rigs must operate at greater depths, the productivity parameter A_E^* is no longer constant. Because an oil well also relies on oil as its energy source, both A_E^* and b decline. As discussed in Section 1.2.2.3, current production functions are constructs rather than scientific formulations. Linking workflows to physical processes grounds production in reality and enables the design of principle-based production functions.

7.3.5 *Industrial economy*

The energy revolution fueled the Industrial Revolution, enabling energy-intensive industrial production. A pure manufacturing economy that lacks agricultural resources and depends on the energy economy for fossil fuels produces industrial goods, not only for itself but also for the energy economy and agricultural economy:

$$f^I(\nu_K, \nu_L) = \Gamma = \Gamma_A + \Gamma_E + \Gamma_I, \tag{7.21}$$

The subscripts A, E, and I denote the agricultural economy, energy economy, and industrial economy, respectively, and Γ_I covers industrial consumption goods and new capital goods, and depreciation of the existing capital stock:

$$\Gamma_I = \Gamma_{I,c} + \dot{K}_I + \delta K_I. \tag{7.22}$$

The industrial economy exchanges Γ_A for food F_I and Γ_E for energy E_I. Putting Eq. (7.21) and Eq. (7.22) together gives:

$$\dot{K}_I = f(\nu_K, \nu_L) - E_I - F_I - \Gamma_{I,c} - \delta K_I. \tag{7.23}$$

In mass production, labor operates machines, making sure that machines run efficiently. In this case, the production function can be expressed as:

$$f^I(\nu_K, \nu_L) = f^I\left[\nu_{K,I} \min\left(\frac{\nu_K}{\nu_{K,I}}, 1\right), \nu_{L,I}(K) \min\left(\frac{L}{L_{K,I}}, 1\right)\right]. \tag{7.24}$$

Similar to the energy industry in Eq. (7.17), as machines increasingly replace human labor, the work contributed by labor becomes negligible compared to the work input of machines. When labor no longer constrains the economy, Eq. (7.24) simplifies to the AK production function:

$$f^I(\nu_K, \nu_L) = f^I(\nu_{K,I}) = \frac{A_I}{b}\nu_{K,I}. \tag{7.25}$$

Substituting Eq. (7.25) into Eq. (7.23), we obtain:

$$\dot{K}_I = \frac{A_I}{b}\nu_{K,I} - E_I - F_I - \Gamma_{Ic} - \delta K_I. \tag{7.26}$$

At equilibrium, the balance of production output is given by

$$\frac{A_I}{b}\nu_{K,I} = E_I + F_I + \Gamma_{I,c} + \delta K_I \tag{7.27}$$

Although Eq. (7.27) resembles Eq. (7.19), their underlying work dynamics are distinctly different. Unlike the energy economy, which *produces* energy—fossil fuels—the industrial economy primarily *consumes* it. While some industrial products, such as those made from wood or plastic, can release energy when burned, they are not designed as primary energy sources.

The industrial economy can improve the efficiency of its machinery, yet it remains constrained by the laws of thermodynamics. It cannot exceed 100% efficiency and must also consider capital stock depreciation—an aspect that necessitates additional energy for maintenance or replacement. This situation poses a crucial question: How does the pure industrial economy create economic value despite its dependence on energy imports? Moreover, how have industrialized nations like Japan, which lack energy resources, managed to achieve prosperity?

To simplify the discussion, we assume that the agricultural economy does not use fossil fuels, and the energy economy exports all its energy output to the industrial economy. The energy imported by the industrial economy is given by

$$E_I = \frac{A_E - 1}{b}\nu_{K,E}. \tag{7.28}$$

The industrial economy converts this imported energy into work. Assuming that both the energy economy and the industrial economy share the same energy-to-work conversion efficiency, b, the work input

($\nu_{K,I}$)—representing the economic value of industrial products—must at least be the economic value of the energy it imports from the energy economy:

$$\nu_{K,I} = bE_I = (A_E - 1)\nu_{K,E}.$$

The economic value associated with this imported energy is the work required for its production, denoted as $\nu_{K,E}$ (see Eq. 7.17), which represents the fair value the industrial economy must pay. Consequently, the industrial economy must extract at least $\nu_{K,E}$ units of economic value from the import. Hence, the output of the energy economy must both cover the work expended and provide an equivalent amount in its exports. In energy terms, the output must not only offset the energy used in production but also generate a surplus—the export of equal magnitude. Thus, the energy output must be at least twice the energy expended.

To illustrate the concept of *doubling economic value*, consider an analogy with wild blackberries. John forages for blackberries in the wild and trades them with Mary for tools and containers. Blackberries serve as the sole energy source for both agents. John consumes part of his harvest to sustain his labor and exchanges the remainder. Mary, in turn, produces tools and containers, receiving berries in exchange. For equilibrium to be maintained, John's harvest must satisfy the condition:

$$E_j \geq 2C_j,$$

where C_j denotes John's energy cost of collection and E_j the energy yield of harvested berries—one unit required for John's sustenance and one unit for Mary's.

Energy output must have at least twice the economic value, since the industrial economy must generate more economic value than the economic value of the imports:

$$\begin{aligned} \nu_{K,I} - \nu_{K,E} &= bE_I - \nu_{K,E} \\ &= (A_E - 1)\nu_{K,E} - \nu_{K,E} \\ &= (A_E - 2)\nu_{K,E} \geq 0. \end{aligned} \tag{7.29}$$

This represents the critical condition for the sustainability of the industrial economy, emphasizing two key points. First, the industrial economy is entirely dependent on the energy economy for its survival, with its ability to create value crucially relying on the energy economy's energy multiplier (A_E). Second, the energy multiplier in the energy economy must equal or exceed two times to maintain viability.

To further clarify the intuition behind Eq. (7.29), we can turn to Daniel Defoe's classic narrative (Defoe, 2020) featuring Robinson Crusoe and Friday. On their isolated island, Robinson acts as the fisher while Friday crafts fishing equipment. After his meal, Robinson barters his leftover fish with Friday in exchange for the gear Friday constructed.

Since Friday produces no food himself, his survival depends on Robinson's fishing effectiveness, which requires Robinson to catch enough fish to feed both of them—that is, about twice his own consumption. Conversely, Robinson's fishing ability is enhanced by Friday's craftsmanship. This reciprocal relationship underscores the mutual dependence of their roles.

In conditions of cheap energy, the industrial economy produces economic value in excess of its energy costs. As the energy multiplier declines, however, the economic value of energy rises, while the economic value the industrial economy creates per unit of energy import falls. These dynamics transfer wealth from the industrial economy to the energy economy. At the point where energy production reaches "double economic value," the industrial economy reaches breakeven: the economic value of energy imports equals the economic value of industrial output. As more work is required to produce energy, the industrial economy obtains less work per unit of imported energy. If market prices align with economic value, the industrial economy operates at a loss. Certain niche sectors may endure due to demand, but the industrial economy in its broader form becomes unsustainable.

The work theory of value addresses another question: Raw materials are indispensable to industrial production, but they are products of nature, created neither by human labor nor machines. If so, they would have no economic value. The work theory of value links the economic value of raw materials to the amount of work required to extract them. For instance, the economic value of sea salt is derived from the work needed to separate it from seawater.

From the perspective of the work theory of value, raw materials are equivalent to other industrial products.

Industrial production transforms raw materials into finished products through multiple stages, including mining, intermediate processing, and the final assembly. Each stage adds value by refining inputs through additional work, resulting in a final product that embodies the cumulative work input across the entire production chain. Broadly speaking, energy, crops, and animals all represent forms of natural materials that rely on work to unlock their economic value.

By analyzing data on the work inputs to the agricultural, energy, and industrial sectors, one can estimate the economic value of an economy or the global economy. While energy serves as the foundation for work, total energy production or consumption does not accurately reflect the complete amount of work contributing to production. This discrepancy arises primarily from two factors: (1) a considerable portion of energy is consumed by households and other non-production-related activities; and (2) there is significant variability in the efficiency of converting energy into work. Consequently, by taking into account the diverse applications of energy and the variability in energy-to-work conversion efficiency, an adjusted conversion factor must be used to estimate the economic value of a real economy based on total energy consumption.

Former Chinese Premier Li Keqiang distrusted the GDP figures reported by provincial or local governments and instead checked local energy consumption against reported GDP. His intuition was correct: energy consumption is a more accurate measure of real economic activity. Similarly, Professor Luis Martinez from the University of Chicago conducted a study that examined night-time satellite imagery of 173 countries (Martinez, 2022). He found that regions with increased nighttime lighting corresponded with GDP growth. However, local energy consumption varies with industries and non-productive uses, and nighttime lighting is only an indirect measure of production. Moreover, the energy contained in crops and livestock is not typically included in energy consumption metrics, even though they provide energy to humans.

The U.S. industrial sector's energy use increased from 7.489 quadrillion BTU in 1950 to 19.934 quadrillion BTU in 2022, a

2.66-fold increase.[14] During the same period, U.S. real GDP grew from 2,458.5 billion to 21,822 billion at constant 2017 prices, an 8.88-fold increase. As discussed earlier, real GDP is derived from nominal GDP and adjusted for inflation, but money can distort both nominal GDP and inflation. Industrial energy use provides a more realistic estimate of the real economy's output.

7.4 Energy and AI's Hold on Growth

Energy (work) is the economy's lifeblood, much like nourishment for an organism. Energy inputs must cover both consumption and the inevitable depreciation of machinery and infrastructure. If energy inflows are insufficient, equipment will be neglected, and essential infrastructure will deteriorate. Just as young individuals need to consume more energy than they expend to grow, genuine economic growth occurs only when energy (work) inflows exceed the combined demands of consumption and depreciation.

In the past, energy was abundant, and its supply was not a concern for manufacturing economies. Alfred Marshall, in his *Principles of Economics*, stated, "If hydrocarbon fuels are infinite, then society is sustainable." Today, however, we realize that in a short span of history, humans have consumed much of the fossil fuels that took millions of years to accumulate. British Petroleum estimated that by the end of 2018, 1.7297 trillion barrels of crude oil remained globally, which would last another 50 years.[15] The energy future has two potential outcomes: fossil fuel depletion without alternative, or abundant alternative energy.

The dwindling supply of fossil fuels forces society to confront the consequences of pervasive energy scarcity, presenting humanity with a critical choice: transition to a plentiful energy resource—either nuclear fission, potentially nuclear fusion if the technology succeeds,

[14] *What Was the U.S. GDP Then?, 1929–2022*, measuringworth.com from the U.S. Bureau of Economic Analysis (1929–2022), BEA.gov. and Louis Johnson (1790–1929), retrieved on July 13, 2024.

[15] *BP Statistical Review of World Energy*, 68th edition, 2019, retrieved on January 14, 2024.

or something entirely new. Failure to achieve such a transition would force society into a downsized economy that relies more on manual labor and adopts frugal lifestyles, accepting pre-Industrial Revolution conditions.

7.4.1 *The impacts of energy scarcity on economic sectors*

The total value created by the agricultural, energy, and industrial economies is the sum of the work each economy contributes:

$$\sum_{i=1}^{3} \nu_i = \nu_A + \nu_E + \nu_I. \tag{7.30}$$

Energy depletion's direct consequence is economic contraction, but its impact will vary across sectors. This variance will lead to significant shifts in economic dynamics, influencing the distribution of assets and wealth. In terms of energy dynamics, the energy sector is a source, while the industrial sector acts as an energy sink. Agriculture occupies a middle ground, using solar energy for food production while still relying on fossil fuels for various farming operations.

During energy depletion, the industrial sector faces the worst position. For the same amount of energy exports, the energy economy gains economic value. In contrast, for the same amount of energy imports, the industrial economy extracts less economic value.

While the agricultural economy may seem less vulnerable to fossil fuel supply constraints than the industrial economy, this is only partially true. Crops collect solar energy, but modern agricultural production relies heavily on machines and equipment for sowing, harvesting, and processing agricultural products. Therefore, a decline in fossil fuel supply inevitably affects the agricultural economy.

Modern agriculture's heavy reliance on fertilizers, particularly nitrogen, makes it highly dependent on fossil fuels. Natural gas provides the methane for 72% of global nitrogen fertilizer production, with coal contributing another 22%.[16] Fertilizers account for 40–60% of crop yields in temperate regions like the U.S. and England, and

[16]gardenmyths.com, retrieved on January 21, 2024.

even more in tropical areas, according to Stewart and Roberts (2012). In this sense, fossil fuels not only power industries but also "feed" people.

U.S. farmers now use over 40 times the amount of nitrogen fertilizer compared to the 1960s.[17] Without fertilizers, feeding the growing global population would be nearly impossible. While genetically modified (GM) seeds have boosted agricultural efficiency, some countries still ban GM foods. Despite these advances, the Food and Agriculture Organization reports that 925 million people worldwide remain undernourished, even as obesity rates paradoxically rise in wealthier nations (Stewart and Roberts, 2012).

Although scientists report that Earth still holds vast energy reserves—including coal equivalent to at least 10,000 billion tons of oil—accessing these reserves is challenging. The world's proven gas reserves are equivalent to 52.3 times its current annual consumption, meaning there are about 52 years of gas left at current consumption rates.[18] However, extracting these resources requires increasing amounts of energy, which speeds depletion as more work is needed to extract each unit of output. Energy-intensive industries may reduce their demand first, leading to a gradual economic contraction. Energy shortages exacerbate inflation in essentials like food and housing, worsening conditions for vulnerable populations. For example, the energy crisis in 2022 pushed 11 million more Europeans into poverty.

Solar energy represents the ultimate source of power. On average, approximately 342 watts of solar energy fall on every square meter of Earth's surface, amounting to a tremendous total of 6.94×10^{17} watts.[19] The global economy currently harnesses only a small fraction of this energy. Advances in photovoltaic technology are promising; for instance, a solar panel developed by the U.S. Department of Energy's National Renewable Energy Laboratory (NREL) recently achieved 47% efficiency in lab settings and 40% in real-world

[17]Grist.org, retrieved on January 20, 2024.

[18]worldometers.info, retrieved January 21, 2024.

[19] *The Balance of Power in the Earth-Sun System*, nasa.gov, retrieved on February 3, 2024.

conditions.[20] Scientists are racing to improve efficiency and explore new solar-synthetic technology.

Meanwhile, energy scarcity reshapes international wealth distribution, reallocating economic power across nations. As energy becomes more valuable, energy-producing economies grow wealthier, while other economies face stagnation or decline. For example, in 2021, the world had an estimated $520 trillion in real assets, including machinery, equipment, real estate, and natural resources, and $510 trillion in financial assets; these assets are increasingly moving toward energy-rich regions. Energy-producing economies accumulate more assets, while energy-dependent economies may have to liquidate assets to sustain their standard of living. Financial assets, such as bonds, stocks, pension funds, and cash—representing ownership of both current and future income—also shift toward energy-rich economies.[21] In international trade, energy-exporting countries gain a significant advantage. For instance, Qatar, with a population of just 313,000 in 2017 and one of the world's largest reserves of natural gas and oil, has one of the highest GDPs per capita (Hammond and Winnett, 2009).[22]

Industry classification systems like the North American Industry Classification System (NAICS) and the Global Industry Classification Standard (GICS) organize economic sectors hierarchically, with different levels of detail. The impacts of energy supply differ across these sectors, with further variations at more granular levels.

Table 7.1 summarizes U.S. energy consumption by various sectors.[23] Although agriculture and construction together account for less than 4% (11% × 35%) of total energy use, safeguarding their energy supply is crucial for ensuring food and shelter. An energy shortage that leads to food scarcity and severe housing shortages could trigger chaos and a potential collapse of both the real economy and broader society.

[20] *Commercial Solar Panel Efficiency: What You Need to Know*, velosolar.com, retrieved on February 3, 2024.

[21] *The rise and rise of the global balance sheet: How productively are we using our wealth?*, mckinsey.com, retrieved on August 5, 2024.

[22] Wikipedia, retrieved on January 14, 2024.

[23] U.S. Energy Information Administration, retrieved on January 20, 2024.

Table 7.1. U.S. energy consumption.

Industry	Sub Industry	Sub Industry (%)	Industry (%)
Transportation			36
Industry			35
	Manufacturing	76	
	Mining	12	
	Construction	7	
	Agriculture	4	
Residential			16
Commercial			13

According to a report from KTH Royal Institute of Technology in Sweden, the Internet's global electricity consumption has risen from 8% in 2012 to approximately 10% today, with projections indicating it will reach 20% by 2025. Should an impending energy shortage necessitate economic downsizing, sectors not directly contributing to the real economy would likely be the first to experience cutbacks.

Crops, as natural "solar panels," efficiently capture solar energy through arable land. In Spain, the Almería region has established the "plastic sea" of greenhouses, covering over 150 square miles. Countries heavily reliant on fossil fuel exports must transition to alternative economic models, as the depletion of these resources is inevitable in the foreseeable future. Saudi Arabia has been converting desert into farmland, an initiative that represents forward-thinking economic policy. However, Saudi Arabia's ambitious projects like NEOM—an ultra-modern 170-kilometer city designed to house up to nine million people in two parallel skyscrapers[24]—deviate from focusing on essential economic needs. Meanwhile, Qatar invested heavily in tourism and transportation. Energy-intensive sectors will be among the earliest to experience scarcity if fossil fuel availability diminishes and alternative sources either remain unimplemented or prove inadequate replacements.

[24] *NEON*, YouTube, www.youtube.com/@NEOM, retrieved on January 20, 2024.

7.4.2 *Service economy*

Throughout history, the role of human labor has undergone significant transformations. It has evolved from the era of hunting and gathering to farming, and subsequently diversified to include miners and factory workers, driven by advancements in energy utilization and technological innovation. Computers, automation, AI, and robots have been displacing not only manual laborers but also cognitive workers. This trend is expected to accelerate, ushering in an era where AI performs knowledge-based work and replaces humans across diverse economic activities. In an extreme scenario, the AI-driven economy could operate with minimal human labor, relying solely on AI technology and automation. The AI era in which robots replace humans raises a question: if machines and robots produce all goods, where will people find jobs?

Agriculture offers a historical example. In the past, agriculture was the dominant sector, employing 80–90% of the global population. The percentage of U.S. farmers has declined from 90% in 1790 to less than 2% in 2023.

In certain agricultural activities, labor and draft animals were interchangeable. For example, a group of workers or donkeys could pull a wheat mill. However, fossil-fuel energy has transformed the relationship between labor and capital stock. Machines powered by fossil fuels have largely replaced manual labor, making human labor less substitutable for capital stock.

Furthermore, as living standards rose, the cost of manual labor became significantly higher than the cost of fossil fuels that provide equivalent amounts of work. Manual workers are no longer an economically viable alternative to machines powered by fossil fuels.

Increasingly sophisticated machines—robots—take even more jobs from humans. Unlike past transformative periods such as the Neolithic Revolution (which ushered in farming jobs) and the Industrial Revolution (which created industrial employment), the current AI revolution stands apart. It differs sharply because it does not appear to be generating a new category of mass employment. To date, no new sector has emerged to produce real goods or generate large-scale employment to offset the job displacement caused by the AI "revolution." Consequently, the service sector has taken on the role of a "sponge," absorbing many of these displaced workers.

While GDP treats the service sector and goods-producing sector similarly, using GDP to compare their economic value can be misleading. Service work, unlike the production of tangible goods, does not directly contribute to the output of physical products. Historically, essential tasks such as cooking, childcare, elder care, and education were often performed within families by members like wives and the elderly. Though seemingly domestic, these roles were crucial for the continuation of human society, knowledge, and traditions. As economies grew more complex and services became socialized, a distinct service sector emerged, encompassing restaurants, schools, hospitals, and financial institutions.

The service sector relies on the real economy to provide consumption goods. As a result, only relatively small economies can sustain themselves exclusively through services. The tax havens are an example: It relies on providing financial services to import consumption goods. In Hong Kong, the financial services industry serves as the cornerstone of the economy, contributing significantly to the city's GDP. Additionally, sectors such as logistics, tourism, and professional services play important supporting roles. Historically, Hong Kong has acted as the sole overseas financial gateway to mainland China, benefiting greatly from its real economy. However, as China opens its economy and cultivates alternative financial centers, Hong Kong now faces heightened competition that challenges its long-established status as a leading global financial hub.

Some services rely on the real economy not only for essential consumption but also for capital goods. For instance, healthcare depends on medicines, medical equipment, and facilities—all products of the real economy. The extent to which healthcare can be adequately supported is inherently constrained by production capacity. Growth in services like healthcare increases the demand for medical equipment and pharmaceuticals. However, producing these supplies requires economic resources, which may divert capacity from other sectors. Countries facing limited production capacity must navigate difficult trade-offs between prioritizing health services and supporting other vital sectors and infrastructure.

The increasing automation of tasks by AI is impacting virtually all sectors, including services. For instance, emerging trends highlight the "metaverse" as the next frontier in technology: a spatial computing platform offering immersive digital experiences that serve as alternatives to real-world interactions. The metaverse holds potential across various sectors, including entertainment, social interaction, and business operations, especially through its integration with AI and robotics. While this innovation can enhance operational efficiency, it also contributes to job displacement, impacting professionals in communication, the internet, social media, and even healthcare—including medical practitioners and healthcare workers.

However, automation is not a new phenomenon. Technology has long advanced, making machines smarter and more capable of handling increasingly complex tasks. Computers and computerized machinery have already been replacing workers who once performed sophisticated jobs.

AI, although often seen as a recent development, has roots in technological advances from the 1950s marked by innovations in automation, computing, and control theory, which collectively laid the groundwork for modern AI.

During the 1950s, industries began implementing automated control systems to enhance efficiency and productivity, influenced by the concept of cybernetics introduced by mathematician Norbert Wiener in his 1948 book *Cybernetics: Or Control and Communication in the Animal and the Machine* (Wiener, 2019). Early numerical control machines used feedback mechanisms to self-regulate and perform tasks autonomously. Instructions were encoded on punch cards to automate complex manufacturing tasks.

In his landmark 1950 paper, *Computing Machinery and Intelligence* (Turing, 1980), Alan Turing laid the theoretical groundwork for computers and AI. Turing posed the question, "Can machines think?" He proposed what would later become known as the Turing Test: a measure of a machine's ability to exhibit intelligent behavior indistinguishable from that of a human.

The summer of 1956 saw the Dartmouth Conference, where the term *Artificial Intelligence* was coined. The synergy between the development of automated machinery for industrial production and theoretical advancements in computer science created fertile ground for AI research. This not only set the stage for modern AI but also transformed industrial production, leading to automated systems that are now integral to our world.

Recent AI advancements are driven by two key factors: speed and information. The smartphone in your pocket, for instance, has more computing power than the computer in the spacecraft that put men on the moon in 1969.[25] The convergence of deep neural networks and optimal control theory forms the core framework for sequential decision-making in robotics and AI. These models require fast computing power and vast amounts of data to train the networks effectively. Modern internet infrastructure and information technology provide the "big data" necessary for AI development.

Despite these advances, AI does not change the core role of the real economy in producing food, clothing, shelter, and transportation. AI will not alter the way crops grow or how people sow, tend, and harvest them. Instead, energy and technology have already replaced more than 70% of the American labor force in agriculture. Any productivity gains from AI will further benefit the real economy. For example, AI-powered robots streamline assembly, painting, welding, and material handling, reducing manual labor in repetitive or risky tasks. AI accelerates this process by substituting technical workers, and even experts with robots. Consequently, the economy requires fewer people to produce goods, pushing those who do not work in production into the service sector.

To illustrate the service economy, consider the farming economy as a starting point. Agriculture employs just 2% of the population but provides enough food for everyone. Now, imagine AI replaces those 2% of workers with robots; agriculture would have entered the AI era.

In this scenario, the traditional production function of the economy would consist solely of capital—robots and machines—with the macroeconomic identity represented as

$$\dot{K} = f(\nu_K) - C - \delta K, \tag{7.31}$$

where firms produce without the obligation of remunerating labor, and the consumption term C in Eq. (7.31) becomes entirely disconnected from production. For Marxists, such an economy validates the vision of a society in which goods produced by robots are directly allocated to the people. Some capitalists likewise consider that state distribution of goods or income to households could serve as a solution. Yet a society that neglects and fails to reward creativity risks losing vitality. While manual labor has become negligible in the

[25] *Fast-forward—comparing a 1980s supercomputer to the modern smartphone*, adobe.com, retrieved on February 16, 2024.

production of tangible goods, human creativity remains indispensable and cannot be replicated by AI. From production to services, improvements and inventions have always been—and will continue to be—human achievements. Historical progress underscores this point: the Neolithic Revolution depended on innovations such as crop rotation and irrigation to secure productivity gains, while the Industrial Revolution was driven by the invention of the steam engine and its subsequent expansion through electricity.

In this economy wages are derived primarily from the service sector. The Households' wealth or budget equation that includes the service sector becomes:

$$\dot{\Phi} = \pi\Phi + P_s r_s L + PrK + w_s L - (P + P_s)C, \tag{7.31a}$$

where r_s is the net return of service sector, P denotes the price of real goods excluding service charges, and P_s represents the service charges. For example, new housing service charges (P_s) consist of insurance and HOA fees. In education, service charges cover all expenses remaining after factoring in facilities, computers, and teaching equipment. Likewise, the price of restaurant French fries includes both the cost of potatoes and a service charge. Once basic physiological needs are satisfied, services target psychological needs, directly boosting consumer utility.

Assuming equilibrium in both the real and service sectors, and a zero discount factor (see Page 63), we have:

$$\dot{K} = \dot{\Phi} = \pi = r_s = r = 0, \tag{7.31b}$$

and Eq. (7.31a) reduces to:

$$w_s L = (P + P_s)C, \tag{7.31c}$$

that is, service sector wages must cover both physical goods and service fees. In the real economy, production provides income and drives product demand while supplying essential goods. Conversely, the service economy provides income but does not guarantee internal demand. Because services are discretionary luxuries rather than necessities like food and housing, the sector faces a structural risk: if service workers cannot afford these services, the economy cannot sustain itself. Falling demand directly erodes service jobs and wages. For the service economy to thrive, its offerings must be affordable for

Table 7.2. Large sectors by number of jobs (2025).

Sector	Number of jobs (million)	%
Private education & health services	27.2	17.1
Professional & business services	22.6	14.2
Leisure & hospitality	17.0	10.7
Retail trade	15.6	9.8
Local government	15.1	9.5
Manufacturing	12.8	8.0
Financial activities	9.3	5.8
Construction	8.3	5.2
Transportation & warehousing	6.8	4.3
Wholesale trade	6.2	3.9
Other services	6.0	3.8

its own workforce. Exorbitant pricing that targets only the wealthy excludes ordinary service workers, a structural issue that disproportionately affects the younger generation.

Over the past several decades, employment declines in traditional U.S. industries—most notably manufacturing and mining—have been largely offset by growth in the service sector. This evolution reflects a gradual structural transformation of the U.S. economy toward service-based activities, particularly in health care, information, and specialized services.

In the 1950s, largest sectors in the U.S. are: manufacturing (30%), agriculture (10–15%), construction (growing), and services (20–25%). By 2025, according to Table 7.2, private education and health services accounted for 17.1% of total employment, professional and business services 14.2%, leisure and hospitality 10.7%, and retail trade 9.8%. Employment in health care and elder assistance is immune to offshore outsourcing and must be performed locally. Highly skilled healthcare roles—such as nurses and technicians—offer stable, high wages, whereas entry-level positions often provide lower pay and fewer benefits. Professional and business services represent high-wage occupations, including management consulting, legal services, accounting, computer systems design, and IT support. Leisure and hospitality, by contrast, tends to offer jobs at the lower end of the wage scale, such as restaurant staff, hotel and motel workers, and employees in amusement parks and entertainment venues.

Traditional brick-and-mortar retail has undergone a significant employment shift, moving from sales-floor positions to logistics-focused roles, including warehouse and storage workers, logistics managers, last-mile delivery drivers, and specialized maintenance and sorting machine operators. Between 1850 and 2015, the trade sector's share of total U.S. employment rose by 12.8%, making it one of the largest growth areas in the modern era of the workforce. Since the 1990s, both physical and virtual supermarkets have reshaped employment within the sector, with the share of the retail workforce fluctuating between 9% and 12% in recent decades.

Consider a hypothetical economy consisting of two distinct sectors: an automated agricultural farm requiring no human labor, and a service sector of restaurants preparing and selling meals. Because farming is automated, all workers are employed in restaurants, making the service sector the sole source of income. In this economy, each worker specializes in crafting a unique dish while consuming the diverse culinary outputs of other restaurants.

In the hypothetical scenario where all individuals are employed in restaurants—a symbol of the service economy—large cities have undergone a long-standing evolution toward service-oriented activity. Urban populations now provide a diverse range of services, including hospitality, transportation, banking, education, healthcare, and public administration (see Table 7.2).

As automation and AI continue to displace jobs in the real economy. John Maynard Keynes predicted in 1930 that the productivity gains from automation would reduce the workweek to just 15 hours (Keynes, 1930). However, the length of the workweek has not declined as he predicted; instead, new types of jobs have emerged. David Graeber referred to some of these positions as "bullshit jobs" (Graeber, 2018), framing them within a system he termed managerial feudalism. He observed that a substantial share of the workforce in Europe and North America spends entire careers engaged in tasks they privately regard as unnecessary. "Flunkies" whose sole service is to make someone else feel important or look prestigious fall into this category. He called service job "shit jobs" that are frequently perceived as lacking prestige or glamour.

Across much futuristic fiction and film, the economy of the future is envisioned as a realm of technological abundance and glamorous living. This vision echoes Iain M. Banks's Culture series, which depicts a post-scarcity society governed by advanced artificial intelligence—known as Minds—that manage all resources and infrastructure. In this society, individuals enjoy unrestricted access to everything they need or desire, enabling them to pursue their passions and interests freely (Banks, 1994).

Modern cities, as service hubs that free the younger generations from the brutal manual labor of previous generations, boast glamorous shopping malls. Yet, behind this shiny facade, the actual service jobs are drab, and some cities struggle with homelessness and deteriorating neighborhoods. Other cities have adapted more effectively, anchoring their development in affordability and striving to mitigate socio-economic polarization. This divergence illustrates the trajectory of the service economy.

In many cities, street vendors shape the urban landscape—selling goods at traffic lights, performing music in public spaces, and operating small shops along streets and highways. Platforms such as Uber and Airbnb have become integral components of this ecosystem, alongside digital nomads and behind-the-scenes programmers and technicians. Municipal governments play a crucial role in safeguarding the livelihoods of small vendors, family-owned shops, and local businesses from displacement by large corporations. In such environments, individuals compete based on merit and hard work rather than formal credentials, and they retain the freedom to choose, including choices about education and health care. The protections of economic democracy are indispensable to the functioning and resilience of a capitalist economy.

The real economy produces goods that fulfill basic human physiological needs, while services often cater to higher levels of human needs, aligning with Maslow's hierarchy. Services are inherently optional and demand for services is less stable than for food and housing. Ensuring that the service market remains competitive and free of monopoly is critical. All "willing" products must be given the opportunity to present themselves as candidates for consumers' "votes." Family-owned and small businesses play a particularly important role: though they lack large capital reserves, they are able to explore local markets and discern differences between exchange value and economic value. Street vendors, for example, meet the specific demands of neighborhoods, while local markets supply crafts and farm goods, often relying on surplus products sold in spot markets. By contrast, large supermarkets secure supply through forward contracts.

In response to this challenge, many service industries have repositioned their offerings—banking, telecommunications, the internet, insurance, and higher education—as indispensable elements of modern living. Combined with limited job availability in the real economy and low wages in the service sector, mandatory services intensify the burden as the economy shifts toward services.

In the United States and many other countries, primary and secondary education is compulsory, and an increasing number of professions now require college or university degrees. Since the Middle Ages, guild apprenticeships laid the groundwork for the modern German *Ausbildung*, while Plato's Academy and medieval universities (evolved from cathedral schools and monastic centers for devoted philosophers and scholars), focused on academic and scientific education. For example, in Germany, nearly half of all school leavers opt for vocational training instead of university. This choice highlights the enduring value placed on craftsmanship and skills gained through direct, hands-on experience, which are often more effective than abstract instruction (Solga *et al.*, 2014).

In 1950, during a speech at Columbia University, President Dwight Eisenhower referred to faculty as "employees of the university." Isidore Rabi, a faculty member, responded: "Mr. President, we are not employees of the university. We are the university." Fast forward to today, and the dynamics have shifted; faculty are now regarded as employees by university administrations. In particular, for-profit universities epitomize the trend of positioning education within the service sector. As governments continue to cut funding for education, universities have increasingly focused on attracting tuition dollars and building endowments. This shift in priorities is reflected in the organizational structures and practices, as universities emphasize job training as a core component of their mission.

Let us briefly diverge. The widespread availability of the Internet has made information—once limited to books and confined to libraries—accessible to everyone at the click of a button. A plethora of teaching materials and videos, including recordings of university lectures, have been made available online. As a result, self-directed learning has become more achievable than ever, empowering young people to explore a wide range of subjects independently.

The concept of free online university education is now a reality, albeit without a formal degree. Universities could transition into test centers that validate the knowledge of self-taught learners, offering credentials and career services that make college education nearly free. This model would not only alleviate the financial burden on families but also liberate universities from the current constraints of routine instruction. Instead, they could refocus on their core mission: generating new knowledge and nurturing talents that will drive future advancements in various fields.

Isaac Newton formulated the principles of gravitation in 1666, at the tender age of 23. Similarly, Albert Einstein unveiled his theory of special relativity around the age of 26. Tragically, Frank Ramsey's life was cut short at 26, following his significant contributions to multiple fields. However, extensive academic pursuit, including advanced degrees such as master's and Ph.D., and postdoctoral study, may paradoxically diminish scientific creativity. This phenomenon seems to trade the innovative spirit of youth for the accreditation of diplomas, potentially stifling the boundless creativity often associated with young people.

Moreover, when services become compulsory or quasi-compulsory—education being a prime example—they diminish household utility while intensifying financial strain. While mandatory services may provide a sense of job stability in certain sectors, the costs associated with these services reduce household consumption of other goods, ultimately straining family budgets and causing significant economic and social problems. For example, the total average student loan debt (including private loan debt) may be as high as $40,681 in 2024.[26]

The transition toward a service economy in the United States has been gradual. In principle, all households could enjoy goods increasingly produced through automation and artificial intelligence, because—under neoclassical economics—the supply of goods balances with demand, represented by total household income, regardless of the absolute amount of money in circulation, as

[26] *Student loan debt statistics in 2024* – USA Today, usatoday.com, retrieved on November 11, 2025.

discussed earlier. Beyond real economic growth, however, this outcome also requires that the wealth gap not widen. A pressing concern is whether younger generations can sustain the standard of living that older cohorts have enjoyed. On the demand side, total household income determines prices, and household purchasing power, independent of the absolute measure of income. Yet younger generations face a disadvantage due to the bifurcation between asset holders and non-holders. The former accumulate income passively, even while they sleep, by benefiting from processes of money creation. On the supply side, the decline of the real economy in the U.S. and many developed nations further exacerbates the challenge for younger generations.

Joseph Stiglitz, a Nobel laureate in economics, contends that government intervention may be essential to facilitate the reallocation of labor and capital from sunset sectors to sunrise sectors:

> The political institutions created in the nineteenth century gave undue weight to the rural agrarian communities, and the mindset of these communities is often at odds with that of today's dominant urban communities. While this disparity between politics and the underlying economic realities is stark, the disparity is even greater when it comes to the movement now underway into the postindustrial societies, to the service and knowledge based economies of the 21st centuries.—(Stiglitz, 2017)

Sustaining this economic transition dictates that service outputs remain accessible to the service workforce (see p. 385). Under a simplified equilibrium framework, the average service wage implied by Eq. (7.31c) is given by:

$$w_s = \frac{(P + P_s)C}{L}.$$

Affordability is characterized not by elevated nominal wages, but by minimized wage disparity. As established by the quantity theory of money (see Section 2.1.2.2), the equilibrium volume of circulating money dictates the aggregate price level $(P + P_s)$, which is expressed as:

$$P + P_s = \frac{MV}{C},$$

Assuming the real economy utilizes a total capital work input of v_K, and the service sector employs a total labor work input of v_L, the service component of the aggregate price level—evaluated at prices that yield optimal resource allocation—is given by:

$$\frac{P_s}{P + P_s} = \frac{v_L}{v_k + v_L}.$$

In terms of energy (work), fossil fuels provide the work input required to produce capital stock. Human labor, however, contributes far more than merely replacing the calories expended in leisure or physical activity. Human creativity remains indispensable to the functioning of the economy and cannot be replicated by AI. Human consciousness remains an enigma. In the marketplace, human demand cannot be replaced by that of robots, artificial intelligence, or a central planner.

Therefore, a structural transition of human labor—from industrial production to service provision—and a corresponding shift in household income sources are necessary. Economic management plays a critical role in guiding and stabilizing this transition (see Section 7.5.2).

A final point about the limitations of robots is worth noting. Science fiction often portrays either a robotic utopia or a terrifying future where robots dominate the world. Like nuclear technology, robots can elevate or destroy human civilization. Because no computer programming is bug-free, AI faces far greater risks than traditional software. Therefore, robots must always operate under human supervision and will not entirely replace knowledge workers like managers and engineers.

While AI and automation aggressively challenge human labor in terms of economic efficiency—forcing the workforce to continuously generate novel, complex services to preserve full employment—the technologies themselves face a critical constraint: exponential algorithmic complexity is inherently energy-intensive. For example, an average industrial robot consumes 21,915 kWh per year (based on 20 hours of work per day at an average power draw of 3 kW). A cleaning robot consumes 102 kWh per year (based on 2 hours of work per day at 0.14 kW). A mobile platform, an intelligent machine that can recognize, move, and interact with the environment, and respond to unforeseen events, consumes 21,586 kWh per year (based on 3 hours of work per day at 19.7 kW).[27] In contrast, an average human

[27] robodk.com, retrieved on January 21, 2024.

consumes approximately 1,058.5 kWh per year, derived from food energy equivalent to 2,500 calories per day.

As capitalism fractures under existing wealth disparity, the transition to a service economy further destabilizes the system. This book concludes by examining the challenges of managing this transition, a core issue in debates over the future of economic systems.

7.5 Economic Transition

7.5.1 *Resources and population*

Thomas Robert Malthus emphasized that Earth's resources, particularly food, could only support a limited population (Malthus and Winch, 1992). In his view, food supply grows linearly, while population grows geometrically. This would lead to a global population outstripping food supply, resulting in widespread famine and poverty.[28] Marx criticized Malthus's theory as a "libel on the human race," contending that resource shortages and mass poverty were not natural laws but rather the failures of the capitalist system to provide adequate employment.[29,30]

Lenin criticized the "moribund" capitalist system for exploiting both domestic resources and those of colonies, using force to protect the private interests of capitalists (Lenin, 2015). Marx envisioned a post-capitalist society where resources would be managed collectively, allowing for the elimination of poverty and more equitable distribution.

Communism challenges capitalism due to inequality and poverty. Capitalism's protection of private property stands in tension with the principle of equal distribution, as wealth determines access to resources and output.

---

[28]For Marx, the post-capitalist society will make it possible to organize production of the necessity of life, eliminate poverty and manage population.

[29]Malthus advocated using the cost of labor—that is, wages—as the standard for measuring the values of other commodities. We can see the link between Malthus's wage theory of value and Marx's labor theory of value. But David Recardo rejected Malthus's theory and the debate between the two lasted decades (Dorfman, 1989).

[30]Marx viewed Malthus's theory as unhistorical, directly opposing Marx's historical materialism. Nonetheless, resource constraints have played a significant role in human history.

The ultimate form of private property and ownership is money. Money enables the purchase of property and the conversion of assets—including the means of production and natural resources—into ownership. In contemporary markets, property and ownership can likewise be reconverted into money. Both property and ownership are measured in monetary terms, with a given sum representing a fraction of global assets. Thus, to abolish private property and ownership, a communist economy must eliminate money.

In a pond, if one species grows much faster than the others, it will eventually deplete their nutrients, causing the weaker species to dwindle. Likewise, if the capitalist economy fails to correct its current trajectory, it faces the risk of systemic collapse.

The real economy grows gradually because, first, expanding production or starting new factories takes time, second, the real physical resources available for expansion are limited (Chapter 3). In contrast, the financial markets are driven by money creation, which has no physical constraints, even under the gold standard (Chapter 2). Consequently, the monetary values of assets rise with money (Chapter 4). Figure 4.1 shows that S&P 500 increased 184 times, while, based on unreliable inflation numbers, the real economy increased 18 times. Had wages and corporate valuations tracked the growth of the real economy, the gap between workers and owners in the U.S. would be significantly narrower. Instead, shareholders amassed wealth at a rate 184 times greater, leaving wage earners trailing far behind.

Financial markets are the soil that grows not only flower but also weeds, which can overrun the flowers without weeding. As money floods into the markets, idle assets take root and flourish. These idle assets require little to no management, yet—echoing John Stuart Mill's words—they grow "while the owners sleep," alongside productive assets (see Section 5.2.1.1). Accounting for this idle asset growth, owners' wealth expands far beyond 184 times. Nominal figures show today's financial markets are about 450 times larger than in the 1920s.[31]

To curb the widening wealth gap, such idle assets must be weeded out. Much like a lottery, where larger payoffs entice more participants despite lower odds, financial markets create the illusion of

[31]The ratio is based on $1 trillion in 1929 and $450 trillion in 2024 (gemini.google.com).

overnight riches, drawing in less informed speculators. If money creation were restrained and only truly informed participants invested, these market sensations would also be weeded out. Businesses could then expand more gradually, reflecting the natural pace of the real economy, and prudent growth might prevent crises such as the dot-com bubble or even the Great Depression.

The relationship between money and population goes beyond wealth inequality. While monetary forces often disadvantage the poor, they also produce more nuanced effects on demographic outcomes.

The debate surrounding wealth and population dynamics presents an intriguing paradox: many developed countries are grappling with the issue of population decline. For instance, South Korea currently has the lowest fertility rate among developed nations, with the average woman having fewer than one child in her lifetime—far below the replacement rate of 2.1 required to sustain a stable population. European countries are facing comparable challenges, as their birth rates also fall short of what is needed for population stability.

China, which once prioritized the control of overpopulation through restrictive birth policies, now finds itself in a similar predicament. Despite relaxing these policies after an economic boom, the anticipated increase in birth rates has not materialized; instead, the birth rates continue to decline.

Chinese history may provide some insight. In China, there is an old saying: "Raise sons for old age"[32] and "The more sons, the more happiness." In earlier times, Chinese families did not have modern means of accumulating assets for retirement, nor was there a social retirement system. Raising sons was the traditional way to ensure support in old age. Parents shared what they earned with their children, and later, when parents grew old, their adult children supported them in return. The more children the parents had, the more support they could expect in old age.

Today, saving for retirement through pension systems or social security is standard practice in developed countries. Yet such insurance arrangements create "moral" hazard (see Chapter 5) and generate unintended consequences. Individuals save money—tokens

[32]In China, historically, when a daughter married, she would leave her family to join her husband's household.

reflecting their economic contributions—and lend it to others to consume. In turn, borrowers repay these loans by sharing their future income with the original lenders. The saying "money is wealth across time" reflects this intergenerational sharing arrangement.[33]

The saying "The more sons, the more happiness" has, in modern contexts, been transformed into "the more retirement savings, the more happiness." The direct consequence is that raising children is no longer necessary to secure support in old age, as individuals in developed countries can rely on accumulated savings to cover retirement expenses. In this way, retirement systems do not encourage child-rearing. Yet the original saying also reflects the idea that population growth benefits the older generation by providing a larger pool of younger individuals to support them. However, those who enjoy robust retirement systems and have profited from booming stock markets are disincentivized to have children. The declining population creates challenges, as fewer young people are available to assist an aging demographic.

Worsening the situation, the younger generation earns less income than the older generation. Consequently, when goods are shared between age groups, the younger generation commands a reduced share of total consumption.

Younger generations face a financial dilemma when saving for retirement competes with the expenses of raising children. This tension can discourage people from forming families, a trend that is becoming increasingly pronounced in many nations. In these contexts, rising inflation-driven living costs are compounded by the rapidly escalating expenses associated with child-rearing expenses, especially in service sectors such as healthcare and education (see Section 7.4.2).

If current demographic trends persist without corrective economic policies that support families, the population may shrink to a point where a country's long-term viability is threatened. Should this become a global trend, it would threaten humanity's status as the

[33]In the "overlapping generations (OLG) model," each generation partially overlaps with the next, allowing for interactions between young and old individuals in the economy (Aliprantis *et al.*, 1990).

most successful apex species, become a self-destructing example of evolutionary theory.

7.5.2 *Managing resources*

Socrates interpreted economics as management. As the book's title suggests, this management rests on two principles: managing *money* and managing the *real economy*. Money represents "money democracy," whereby individuals in a capitalist system express their economic preferences through monetary "votes." The real economy, by contrast, represents the optimal allocation of resources to satisfy those preferences.

Some capitalist economies have failed on both fronts. Successfully steering an economy requires a government's ability to balance state control with "money democracy," as the two are not always aligned. Effective policy guides the economy in a chosen direction while still preserving household choice. For example, when firms cannot compete with foreign rivals due to lower wages abroad, workers may face the choice of accepting lower pay or losing their jobs. Monetary votes cannot be substituted by other mechanisms, since genuine choices—whether between chicken and beef or renting versus buying a home—are expressed as prices, i.e., monetary votes. Just as the political system requires careful regulation, so too does the monetary voting system.

The second principle is the management of the real economy, which requires balancing production, consumption, and growth. Managing real investment drives authentic, long-term growth of the real economy. Without effective management the real economy is unstable. In a capitalist economy, it is a failure for a government to operate primarily as a bank or an insurance company. Governments bear responsibility to steer the economy toward stability through fiscal, tax, and other policy measures grounded in the resources at hand.

Capitalist economies have historically delivered superior performance because money functioned both as a form of "votes" that guide firms and as a reward mechanism for individual creativity and hard work. Firms are motivated to exploit the gap between exchange value and economic values, thereby driving efficient resource allocation.

Money democracy demands a meaningful reduction of the wealth disparities rooted in capitalism's early era, when economies of scale were secured through the concentration of capital among a privileged few. Yet, since the abandonment of the gold standard, money itself has become "sick," as the voting system has broken down. The money supply created by banks and governments has widened inequality, producing a new class division between asset owners and non-owners. Idle assets, in particular, allow owners to accumulate wealth passively, without contributing to the real economy. Wealth distribution now disproportionately empowers the wealthy in economic decision-making, while the rise of asset owners and the decline of the middle class continue to widen the gap.

For example, while average households might pay $200,000 for a home, wealthy buyers bid prices up to $400,000, thereby setting market values near that level. In such cases, the monetary votes of average households carry little weight. Consequently, the housing market favors high-end luxury real estate, while lower-end housing remains neglected. Innovations such as Elon Musk's vision of convertible homes and the rising demand for Boxabl reflect genuine interest in affordable solutions. However, attempts to revolutionize housing by shifting from "stick-built" to "mass-produced" construction are constrained by slow-moving regulations, leaving the industry unable to secure the capital investment needed to scale.

In addition, speculative activity layered on top of money creation undermines financial markets and creates financial and economic crises. The 2007–2008 housing bubble illustrates how such distortions can escalate into a full-scale financial and economic crisis. More importantly, as monetary dysfunction contributes to crises and then deepens as those crises unfold, thereby widening wealth gaps.

Wealth gaps have long provided fertile ground for socialist and communist ideologies in poorer countries. In some wealthy nations, however, the wealth gap and uncertain employment prospects facing younger generations have reignited debates over socialism and communism as alternatives to capitalism, with advocates calling for government control of economic resources and equitable wealth distribution. Contrary to Marx's expectation that communist revolutions would erupt in industrialized nations, the Leninist and Maoist branches of Marxism succeeded instead in agrarian societies such as

Russia and China. In these cases, it was not capitalism but pervasive poverty and stark wealth disparities that fueled the demand for radical change.

A communist economy violates both principles: money democracy and efficient management of the real economy. The means of production are socially owned, eliminating commodity exchange between private owners. It removes the need for money and the monetary "voting" system. Moreover, state-owned enterprises lack both information about consumer preferences and incentives to allocate resources efficiently. They cannot exploit discrepancies between exchange value and economic value in the way millions of private businesses—from corporations to street vendors—do under capitalism. Without money and private enterprises, communism simply cannot compete economically with capitalism.

Furthermore, communism functions as a vast insurance scheme. It is inherently vulnerable to moral hazard and thus structurally predisposed to failure. A capitalist economy that attempts to compete with socialist or communist systems by expanding welfare has already undermined its own foundations.

The founding fathers of the United States were deeply cautious about granting government the power to impose economic burdens on its citizens, whether through taxation or money creation. As government expanded, it often forgot—or ignored—the historical lessons they emphasized: taxation and mandatory programs were not to be exercised without the consent of the governed. Economically, governments cannot replicate the efficiency of market pricing and resource allocation. State-sponsored insurance programs inevitably generate moral hazards, and their consequences are long-lasting and difficult to reverse—challenges that welfare states continue to struggle with today.

Since the time of Marx, socialism and communism have persisted across the globe. Economically disadvantaged nations continue to grapple with the competing systems of socialism, communism, and capitalism. Yet the allure of a communist utopia endures, ensuring that some nations will pursue it despite its flawed logical framework (see Chapter 2) and its historical record of failure.

While capitalism may lack a simple, "inspiring" slogan such as "from each according to his ability, to each according to his needs," it has historically offered a tangible and realistic promise—the American Dream. Yet fewer members of the younger generation now believe this dream is attainable, and the capitalist system faces unprecedented challenges. Its ability to sustain this vision depends on whether it can return to core economic principles while skillfully navigating the complex obstacles that lie ahead.

Bibliography

Abdujalilov, H. and Sheraliev, O. (2024). Inflation through the ages: Understanding its dynamics and global impacts, *American Journal of Modern World Sciences* **1**(3), 39–54.

Acemoglu, D. (2008). *Introduction to Modern Economic Growth* (Princeton: Princeton University Press).

Acheson, G. G., Hickson, C. R., Turner, J. D., and Ye, Q. (2009). Rule britannia! British stock market returns, 1825–1870, *The Journal of Economic History* **69**(4), 1107–1137.

Adams, C. F. and Adams, J. Q. (1871). *The Life of John Adams*, Vol. 1 (Philadelphia, NJ: J. B. Lippincott).

Akerlof, G. A. (1970). The market for "lemons": Quality uncertainty and the market mechanism, *Quarterly Journal of Economics* 488–500.

Aliprantis, C. D., Brown, D. J., Burkinshaw, O., Aliprantis, C. D., Brown, D. J., and Burkinshaw, O. (1990). The overlapping generations model, Existence and optimality of competitive equilibria, In *Existence and Optimality of Competitive Equilibria* (Berlin/Heidelberg: Springer-Verlag), pp. 229–271.

Allen, P. M. and Sanglier, M. (1978). Dynamic models of urban growth, *Journal of Social and Biological Structures* **1**(3), 265–280.

Alogoskoufis, G. (2019). *Dynamic Macroeconomics* (Cambridge, MA: MIT Press).

Anderson, L. and Wadkins, M. (1991). Japan-a culture of consumption? *Advances in Consumer Research* **18**(1).

Antón, S. C. (2003). Natural history of homo erectus, *American Journal of Physical Anthropology* **122**(37), 126–170.

Aristotle (2006). *Politics* (ReadHowYouWant.com).

Aristotle, A. (1986). *De anima (On the soul)* (London: Penguin).

Atanelishvili, T. and Silagadze, A. (2018). Xenophon: Economy finds the name, *Bulletin of the Georgian National Academy of Sciences* **12**(4), 163–166.

Atkinson, A. B. (1971). Capital taxes, the redistribution of wealth and individual savings, *The Review of Economic Studies* **38**(2), 209–227.

Bacon, F. (2021). *The New Organon* (Canada: Phoenix Classics Journal).

Bagliano, F.-C. and Bertola, G. (2004). *Models for Dynamic Macroeconomics* (OUP, Oxford).

Banks, I. M. (1994). *A few notes on the culture, Culture Shock 10*, (Amherst, MA: The Media Education Foundation).

Barro, R. J. and Sala-I-Martin, X. I. (2003). *Economic Growth* (Cambridge, MA: MIT Press).

Baskin, J. B. and Miranti Jr., P. J. (1999). *A History of Corporate Finance* (Cambridge, MA: Cambridge University Press).

Baxendale, T. (2010). Public attitudes to banking, *proyecto de asesoría de un estudiante del centro ESCP Europe for the Cobden Centre.*

Beenstock, M. and Ilek, A. (2010). Wicksell's classical dichotomy: Is the natural rate of interest independent of the money rate of interest? *Journal of Macroeconomics* **32**(1), 366–377.

Bénassy, J.-P. (2011). *Macroeconomic Theory* (Oxford, UK: Oxford University Press).

Berkovec, J. A. and Goodman Jr, J. L. (1996). Turnover as a measure of demand for existing homes, *Real Estate Economics* **24**(4), 421–440.

Bjerg, O., McCann, D., Macfarlane, L., Nielsen, R. H., and Ryan-Collins, J. (2017). Seigniorage in the 21st century: A study of the profits from money creation in the United Kingdom and Denmark, Available at *SSRN* 2921225.

Black, F. and Scholes, M. (1973). The pricing of options and corporate liabilities, *Journal of Political Economy* **81**(2), 637–654.

Blanchard, O. and Fischer, S. (1989). *Lectures on macroeconomics* (Cambridge, MA: MIT Press).

Bloch, M. and Koziol, G. (2014). *Feudal Society* (London and New York: Routledge).

Bornewasser, J. A. (1977). *Winkler Prins geschiedenis der Nederlanden (Winkler Prince History of the Netherlands)* (Amsterdam: Elsevier).

Bridgman, P. (1953). Reflections on thermodynamics, in *Proceedings of the American Academy of Arts and Sciences* **82**, 301–309.

Bridgman, P. W., Bridgman, P. W., Bridgman, P. W., and Bridgman, P. W. (1927). *The Logic of Modern Physics*, Vol. 3 (New York: Macmillan).

Broadberry, S. and O'Rourke, K. H. (2010). *The Cambridge Economic History of Modern Europe: Volume 2, 1870 to the Present* (Cambridge: Cambridge University Press).

Brown, E. (2007). Dollar deception: How banks secretly create money, July. webofdebt.com/articles.

Burley, P. and Foster, J. (2013). *Economics and Thermodynamics: New Perspectives on Economic Analysis*, Vol. 38 (Berlin: Springer Science & Business Media).

Caprita, W. and Souza, L. F. d. (2021). The exchange rate in orthodox, keynesian and new developmentalism theoretical models: A literature review, *Brazilian Journal of Political Economy* **41**, 220–235.

Cass, D. (1965). Optimum growth in an aggregative model of capital accumulation, *The Review of Economic Studies* **32**(3), 233–240.

Cetorelli, N., Mandel, B. H., Mollineaux, L., *et al.* (2012). The evolution of banks and financial intermediation: Framing the analysis, *Federal Reserve Bank of New York Economic Policy Review* **18**(2), 1–12.

Chang, W. W. (2016). A concise guide to dynamic optimization, Available at SSRN 1944607.

Chomsky, N. (2006). *Language and Mind* (Cambridge: Cambridge University Press).

Cieslak, A. and Vissing-Jorgensen, A. (2021). The economics of the fed put, *The Review of Financial Studies* **34**(9), 4045–4089.

Click, R. W. (1998). Seigniorage in a cross-section of countries, *Journal of Money, Credit and Banking*, 154–171.

Cobb, B. R., Rumí, R., and Salmerón, A. (2013). Inventory management with log-normal demand per unit time, *Computers & Operations Research* **40**(7), 1842–1851.

Coleman, D. (2007). *Hume: Dialogues Concerning Natural Religion: And Other Writings* (Cambridge: Cambridge University Press).

Collins, D. (2009). *Portfolios of the Poor: How the World's Poor Live on $2 a Day* (Princeton: Princeton University Press).

Cooper, R. N., Dornbusch, R., and Hall, R. E. (1982). The gold standard: Historical facts and future prospects, *Brookings Papers on Economic Activity* **1982**(1), 1–56.

Cootner, P. H. (1964). *The Random Character of Stock Market Prices* (Cambridge, MA: MIT Press).

Daggett, S. (2008). Costs of major us wars, in *Congressional Research Service Report for Congress* (Washington, DC: Congressional Research Service, Library of Congress).

Daly, G. (2007). Napoleon and the 'city of smugglers', 1810–1814, *The Historical Journal* **50**(2), 333–352.

Das, C. (1985). On the solution of some approximate continuous review inventory models, *Naval Research Logistics Quarterly* **32**(2), 301–313.

Dawkins, R. (2016a). *The Extended Selfish Gene* (Oxford: Oxford University Press).

Dawkins, R. (2016b). *The Selfish Gene* (Oxford: Oxford university press).

De La Vega, J. (2009). *Confusión de confusiones: diálogos curiosos entre un philosopho agudo, un mercader discreto, y un accionista erudito descriviendo el negocio de las acciones, su origen, su ethimología, su realidad, su juego y su enredo* (Editorial Maxtor).

Defoe, D. (2020). *The Life and Strange Surprizing Adventures of Robinson Crusoe: The Stoke Newington Edition* (New Brunswick, New Jersey: Rutgers University Press).

Demetriades, P. and Andrianova, S. (2004). Finance and growth: What we know and what we need to know, in *Financial Development and Economic Growth: Explaining the Links* (London, UK: Palgrave, Macmillan), pp. 38–65.

Deng, F. F. (2007). A comparative study on landownership between China and England, Available at *SSRN* 965170.

Descartes, R. (2013). *Meditations on First Philosophy* (Milton Park, Abingdon, Oxfordshire: Routledge).

Diamond, D. W. and Dybvig, P. H. (1983). Bank runs, deposit insurance, and liquidity, *Journal of Political Economy* **91**(3), 401–419.

Dimand, R. W. (2008). Monetary economics, history of, in *Monetary Economics* (Berlin: Springer), pp. 189–204.

Domar, E. (1989). *Capitalism, Socialism, and Serfdom: Essays by Evsey D. Domar* (Cambridge, UK: Cambridge University Press).

Domar, E. D. (1952). Economic growth: An econometric approach, *The American Economic Review* **42**(2), 479–495.

Dorfman, R. (1969). An economic interpretation of optimal control theory, *The American Economic Review* **59**(5), 817–831.

Dorfman, R. (1989). Thomas Robert Malthus and David Ricardo, *Journal of Economic Perspectives* **3**(3), 153–164.

Duarte, P. G. (2009). The growing of Ramsey's growth model, *History of Political Economy* **41**(Suppl_1), 161–181.

Duindam, S. (2013). *Military Conscription: An Economic Analysis of the Labour Component in the Armed Forces* (Berlin: Springer Science & Business Media).

Duncan, G. M. (1980). Formulation and statistical analysis of the mixed, continuous/discrete dependent variable model in classical production theory, *Econometrica: Journal of the Econometric Society*, 839–852.

Eckbo, B. E., Masulis, R. W., and Norli, Ø. (2000). Seasoned public offerings: Resolution of the "new issues puzzle," *Journal of Financial Economics* **56**(2), 251–291.

Edgerton-Tarpley, K. (2004). Family and gender in famine: Cultural responses to disaster in north China, 1876–1879, *Journal of Women's History* **16**(4), 119–147.

Edgerton-Tarpley, K. (2015). North China Famine, 1876–79. DisasterHistory.org, (Manchester, UK: University of Manchester).

Eisenberg, E. (1961). Aggregation of utility functions, *Management Science* **7**(4), 337–350.

Ellis, M. and Christofides, P. D. (2015). Economic model predictive control of nonlinear time-delay systems: Closed-loop stability and delay compensation, *AIChE Journal* **61**(12), 4152–4165.

Engels, F. (1959). *Anti-Dühring: Herr Dühring's Revolution in Science* (Beijing: Foreign Languages Publishing House).

Engels, F. (1960). *Dialectics of Nature* (London: Wellred Books).

Engels, F. (2020). *Principles of Communism*, Vol. 27 (Beijing: Foreign Languages Press).

Engels, F. and Untermann, E. (2021). The origin of the family, private property and the state, in *Politics and Kinship* (Milton Park, Abingdon, Oxfordshire: Routledge), pp. 217–223.

Enikolopov, R. and Zhuravskaya, E. (2007). Federalism and political centralization, in *Political Institutions and Development: Failed Expectations and Renewed Hopes*, pp. 101–139 (Cheltenham and Camberley, UK: Edward Elgar Publishing, Incorporated).

Ennis, H. M. and Keister, T. (2010). On the fundamental reasons for bank fragility, *FRB Richmond Economic Quarterly* **96**(1), 33–58.

Epper, T., Fehr, E., Fehr-Duda, H., Kreiner, C. T., Lassen, D. D., Leth-Petersen, S., and Rasmussen, G. N. (2020). Time discounting and wealth inequality, *American Economic Review* **110**(4), 1177–1205.

Esfeld, M. (2015). Atomism and holism: Philosophical aspects, *International Encyclopedia of the Social & Behavioral Sciences*, pp. 131–135 (Amsterdam: Elsevier).

Evelyn-White, Gerard, H., *et al.* (1914). *Hesiod, the Homeric Hymns, and Homerica*, Vol. 57 (Cambridge, MA: Harvard University Press).

Fabozzi, F. J., Markowitz, H. M., and Gupta, F. (2008). Portfolio selection, in *Handbook of Finance*, Vol. 2 (Hoboken, NJ: John Wiley & Sons).

Fama, E. F. (1970). Efficient capital markets: A review of theory and empirical work, *The Journal of Finance* **25**(2), 383–417.

Feige, E. L. *et al.* (1996). Overseas holdings of us currency and the underground economy, in *Exploring the Underground Economy*, pp. 5–62 (Germany: University Library of Munich).

Ferguson, N. (2000). *The House of Rothschild: Volume 2: The World's Banker: 1849–1999*, Vol. 2 (New York, USA: Penguin).

Ferguson, N. (2008). *The Ascent of Money: A Financial History of the World* (Penguin).

Fisher, H. H. (1955). *The Communist Revolution: An Outline of Strategy and Tac Tics*, 2 (Stanford, CA: Stanford University Press).

Fisher, I. (1936). *100% Money (1935)* (New York: Adelphi).

Fisher, I. (2006). *The Purchasing Power of Money: Its' Determination and Relation to Credit Interest and Crises* (New York: Cosimo, Inc.).

Fischer, S. (1979). Capital accumulation on the transition path in a monetary optimizing model, *Econometrica: Journal of the Econometric Society*, 1433–1439.

Flaschel, P., Franke, R., Semmler, W., Day, R. H., *et al.* (1997). *Dynamic Macroeconomics: Instability, Fluctuation, and Growth in Monetary Economies* (Cambridge, MA: MIT Press).

Frank, T. (1935). Thc financial crisis of 33 AD, *Thc Amcrican Journal of Philology* **56**(4), 336–341.

Frederick, S., Loewenstein, G., and Ódonoghue, T. (2002). Time discounting and time preference: A critical review, *Journal of Economic Literature* **40**(2), 351–401.

French, K. R. and Poterba, J. (1991). Investor diversification and international equity markets, NBER Working Paper Series, Cambridge, MA.

Friedman, M. (1953). The methodology of positive economics, *Essays in Positive Economics* **3**(3), 145–178.

Fujiki, H., Okina, K., and Shiratsuka, S. (2001). Monetary policy under zero interest rate: Viewpoints of central bank economists, *Monetary and Economic Studies* **19**(1), 89–130.

Gagnon, J. E. *et al.* (2012). Combating widespread currency manipulation, *Policy Brief in International Economics*, 12–19.

Galor, O. and Özak, Ö. (2016). The agricultural origins of time preference, *American Economic Review* **106**(10), 3064–3103.

Gandolfo, G. (1997). *Economic Dynamics: Study Edition* (Berlin: Springer Science & Business Media).

Gaspard, P., Henneaux, M., and Lambert, F. (2007). From dynamical systems theory to nonequilibrium thermodynamics, in *Symposium Henri Poincaré: Proceedings*, Vol. 1 (Brussels: International Solvay Institute for Physics and Chemistry), pp. 97–119.

Georgescu-Roegen, N. (1986). The entropy law and the economic process in retrospect, *Eastern Economic Journal* **12**(1), 3–25.

Getz, W. M. and Martin, D. H. (1980). Optimal control systems with state variable jump discontinuities, *Journal of Optimization Theory and Applications* **31**, 195–205.

Gilbart, J. W. (1837). *The History and Principles of Banking* (London: Longman, Rees, Orme, Brown, and Green).

Gong, G. and Semmler, W. (2006). *Stochastic Dynamic Macroeconomics: Theory and Empirical Evidence* (Oxford: Oxford University Press).

Graeber, D. (2012). *Debt: The First 5000 Years* (London: Penguin).

Granger, C. W. and Lee, T.-H. (1989). Investigation of production, sales and inventory relationships using multicointegration and non-symmetric error correction models, *Journal of Applied Econometrics* **4**(S1), S145–S159.

Grant, R. M. (1996). Prospering in dynamically-competitive environments: Organizational capability as knowledge integration, *Organization Science* **7**(4), 375–387.

Grebler, L. (1951). The housing inventory: Analytic concept and quantitative change, *The American Economic Review* **41**(2), 555–568.

Greiner, A. and Semmler, W. (1996). Saddle path stability, fluctuations, and indeterminacy in economic growth, *Studies in Nonlinear Dynamics & Econometrics* **1**(2).

Griffin, R. C., Montgomery, J. M., and Rister, M. E. (1987). Selecting functional form in production function analysis, *Western Journal of Agricultural Economics* 216–227.

Gross, S. G. (2018). The Nazi economy, in *A Companion to Nazi Germany*, pp. 263–279 (Cambridge: Cambridge University Press).

Guyer, P. and Wood, A. W. (1998). *Critique of Pure Reason*.

Haddad, W. M. (2019). A dynamical systems theory of thermodynamics, in *A Dynamical Systems Theory of Thermodynamics* (Princeton: Princeton University Press).

Haldane, A., Brennan, S., and Madouros, V. (2010). What is the contribution of the financial sector: Miracle or mirage, *The Future of Finance* **87**.

Haldane, A. G. (2010). The $100 billion question, *Revista de Economía Institucional* **12**(22), 83–110.

Hammond, G. P. and Winnett, A. B. (2009). The influence of thermodynamic ideas on ecological economics: An interdisciplinary critique, *Sustainability* **1**(4), 1195–1225.

Hanushek, E. A. and Quigley, J. M. (1979). The dynamics of the housing market: A stock adjustment model of housing consumption, *Journal of Urban Economics* **6**(1), 90–111.

Hausman, D. M. (1989). Economic methodology in a nutshell, *Journal of Economic Perspectives* **3**(2), 115–127.

Hawking, S. (2009). *A Stubbornly Persistent Illusion: The Essential Scientific Works of Albert Einstein* (Philadelphia, PA: Running Press).

Hazlitt, H. (1959). *The Failure of the "New Economics"* (Auburn AL: Ludwig von Mises Institute).

Hecht, A. (2021). Taking delivery of commodities via the futures market, *The Balance*. thebalancemoney.com.

Hegel, G. W. F. (2014). *Science of Logic* (Berlin: Routledge).

Hegel, G. W. F. (2018). *Hegel: The Phenomenology of Spirit* (Oxford: Oxford University Press).

Hegel, G. W. F. and Wallace, W. (1975). *Hegel's Logic* (Oxford: Oxford University Press, Oxford).

Hemmo, M. and Shenker, O. R. (2012). *The Road to Maxwell's Demon: Conceptual Foundations of Statistical Mechanics* (Cambridge: Cambridge University Press).

Henretta, J. A., Edwards, R., and Self, R. O. (2011). *America's History, Combined Volume* (New York: Macmillan).

Herder, J. G. (2005). *Against Pure Reason: Writings on Religion, Language, and History* (Eugene, OR: Wipf and Stock Publishers).

Historical origins of food preservation, by Nummer, B. A. and Brian, A. (2002), National Center for Home Food Preservation, University of Illinois Extension, paperzz.com, retrieved on November 25, 2025.

Hobbes, T. (1983). De cive: the English version entitled, in *The First Edition, Philosophicall Rudiments Concerning Government and Society*, (Oxfordshire: Clarendon Press).

Hodula, M. and Libich, J. (2023). Has monetary policy fueled the rise in shadow banking? *Economic Modelling* **123**, 106278.

Homer, S. and Sylla, R. E. (1996). *A History of Interest Rates* (Brunswick, NJ: Rutgers University Press).

Hueng, C. J. (1999). Money demand in an open economy shopping-time model: An out-of-sample-prediction application to Canada, *Journal of Economics and Business* **51**(6), 489–503.

Hume, D. (2000). *A Treatise of Human Nature* (Oxford: Oxford University Press).

Humphrey, L. (2012). *First National Bank of Montgomery vs Jerome Daly* (Chisinau, Moldova: Claud Press).

James, W. (1975). *The Meaning of Truth*, Vol. 2 (Cambridge, MA: Harvard University Press).

James, H. (2024). *The IMF and the European Debt Crisis* (Washington, D.C., USA: International Monetary Fund).

Jenkins, A. D. (2005). Thermodynamics and economics, *arXiv preprint* cond-mat/0503308.

Jones, C. I. (2016). The facts of economic growth, in *Handbook of Macroeconomics*, Vol. 2 (Amsterdam: Elsevier), pp. 3–69.

Joyce, M., Miles, D., Scott, A., and Vayanos, D. (2012). Quantitative easing and unconventional monetary policy–an introduction, *The Economic Journal* **122**(564), F271–F288.

Jung, J. and Shiller, R. J. (2005). Samuelson's dictum and the stock market, *Economic Inquiry* **43**(2), 221–228.

Kaldor, N. (1966). Marginal productivity and the macro-economic theories of distribution: Comment on Samuelson and Modigliani, *The Review of Economic Studies* **33**(4), 309–319.

Kaminsky, G. L. and Reinhart, C. M. (1999). The twin crises: The causes of banking and balance-of-payments problems, *American Economic Review* **89**(3), 473–500.

Kant, I. (2016). Foundations of the metaphysics of morals, in *Seven Masterpieces of Philosophy*, pp. 277–328 (Berlin: Routledge).

Kaplow, B. L. (2012). Optimal control of externalities in the presence of income taxation, *International Economic Review* **53**(2), 487–509.

Keefe, J. R. (2009). Stalin and the drive to industrialize the Soviet Union, *Inquiries Journal* **1**(10).

Keller, A. A. (2010). Generalized delay differential equations to economic dynamics and control, *American-Math* **10**, 278–286.

Keynes, J. M. (1923). *A Tract on Monetary Reform* (New York, USA: Cosimo Classics).

Keynes, J. M. (1930). *Treatise on Money: Pure Theory of Money Vol. I* (London: Macmillan and Company).

Keynes, J. M. (1936). *The General Theory of Employment, Interest, and Money* (London: MacMillian).

Keynes, J. M. (2017). *The Economic Consequences of the Peace* (New York: Harcourt, Brace and Howe).

Khan, M. S. (1990). The macroeconomic effects of fund-supported adjustment programs, *Staff Papers* **37**(2), 195–231.

King, L. W. *et al.* (2023). *Codex Hammurabi* (Cleveland, OH: DigiCat).

Koopmans, T. (1965). On the concept of optimal growth, in *The Econometric Approach to Development Planning*.

Krugman, P. (2010). Chinese rumbles, *The New York Times*, 1–4.

Kuhn, T. S. (1970). *The Structure of Scientific Revolutions*, Vol. 111 (Chicago, IL: University of Chicago Press).

Laurent, A. and Sghari, J. (2009). Money supply in a simple economic growth model and multiple steady states equilibria, *Frontiers in Finance and Economics* **6**(2), 67–95.

Leichter, O. (1923). Die Wirtschaftsrechnung in der sozialistischen Gesellschaft, Vol. 5 (Vienna, Austria: Verlag der Wiener Volksbuchhandlung).

Lenin, V. I. (1921). The importance of gold now and after the complete victory of socialism, in *Collected Works*, Vol. 33 (New York: International Publishers).

Lenin, V. I. (2015). Imperialism, the highest stage of capitalism, in *Conflict after the Cold War* (Paris: Foreign Languages Press), pp. 319–326.

Leonard, C. (2020). How jay Powell's coronavirus response is changing the fed forever, *Time*. Retrieved time.com/5851870/federal-reservecoronavirus/.

Lester, R. A. (1946). Shortcomings of marginal analysis for wage-employment problems, *The American Economic Review* **36**(1), 63–82.

Lester, R. A. (1947). Marginalism, minimum wages, and labor markets, *The American Economic Review* **37**(1), 135–148.

Libich, J. and Lenten, L. (2022). Hero or villain? the financial system in the 21st century, *Journal of Economic Surveys* **36**(1), 3–40.

Lindsay, R. B. (1937). A critique of operationalism in physics, *Philosophy of Science* **4**(4), 456–470.

Liu, M. and Liu, X. S. (1998). Chomsky and knowledge of language, in *The Paideia Archive: Twentieth World Congress of Philosophy*, **32**, 76–82.

Locke, J. (2016). *Second Treatise of Government and a Letter Concerning Toleration* (Oxford: Oxford University Press).

Lukács, G. (1971). *History and class consciousness*: Studies in Marxist dialectics (R. Livingstone, Trans.) (Cambridge, MA: The MIT Press).

Lucas Jr, R. E. (1976). Econometric policy evaluation: A critique, in *Carnegie-Rochester Conference Series on Public Policy*, **1**, 19–46.

Lux, T. and Marchesi, M. (1999). Scaling and criticality in a stochastic multi-agent model of a financial market, *Nature* **397**(6719), 498–500.

Macdonell, A. A. (1898). Art. XIII. - The origin and early history of chess, *Journal of the Royal Asiatic Society* **30**(1), 117–141.

Machlup, F. (1956). Rejoinder to a reluctant ultra-empiricist, *Southern Economic Journal* 483–493.

MacKay, C. (1852). *Extraordinary Popular Delusions and the Madness of Crowds* (Mansfield Center, CT: Martino Fine Books, reprint).

MacKenzie, D. (2003). Long-term capital management and the sociology of arbitrage, *Economy and Society* **32**(3), 349–380.

Macpherson, C. B. and Cunningham, F. (1962). *The Political Theory of Possessive Individualism: Hobbes to Locke* (Oxford UK: Clarendon Press).

Mahalanobis, P. C. (1953). Some observations on the process of growth of national income, *Sankhyā: The Indian Journal of Statistics (1933–1960)* **12**(4), 307–312.

Maitland, F. W. (2001). *The Constitutional History of England: A Course of Lccturcs Dclivcrcd* (Clark, NJ: The Lawbook Exchange, Ltd.).

Malinvaud, E. (1953). Capital accumulation and efficient allocation of resources, *Econometrica, Journal of the Econometric Society*, 233–268.

Malthus, T. R. and Winch, D. (1992). *An Essay on the Principle of Population* (Cambridge: Cambridge University Press).

Marshall, A. (2009). *Principles of Economics: Unabridged Eighth Edition* (New York: Cosimo, Inc.).

Martin, K. D. and Hill, R. P. (2015). Saving and well-being at the base of the pyramid: Implications for transformative financial services delivery, *Journal of Service Research* **18**(3), 405–421.

Martinez, L. R. (2022). How much should we trust the dictator's GDP growth estimates? *Journal of Political Economy* **130**(10), 2731–2769.

Marx, K. (1861). Chapter six. Results of the direct production process, in *Economic Manuscripts of Karl Marx 1861-1864*, Vol. 64 (Philadelphia, PA: Patter Books).

Marx, K. (1933). Rukopisi, matematicheskie, *Pod Znamenem Marksizma* **1** (London and New York: Routledge).

Marx, K. (1972). *Critique of the Gotha Programme (1875)* (Saint Louis, MO: Good Press).

Marx, K. (1992). *Capital: Volume III*, Vol. 3 (London: Penguin).

Marx, K. (2004). *Capital: Volume I*, Vol. 1 (London: Penguin).

Marx, K. (2005). *Grundrisse: Foundations of the Critique of Political Economy* (London: Penguin).

Marx, K. (2008). *Theses on Feuerbach* (Cheyenne, WY: Newcomb Livraria Press).

Marx, K. and Engels, F. (1970). *The German Ideology*, Vol. 1 (New York: International Publishers Co.).

Marx, K., Engels, F., Kuhn, R., Moore, S., and Draper, H. (2012). Manifesto of the communist party, 1848, in *Social Theory Re-Wired*, pp. 128–135, (London: Routledge).

McDonald, O. (2016). *Lehman Brothers* (Manchester: Manchester University Press).

McGlynn, C. (2015). Aristotle's economic defense of private property. *The Student Economic Review*, **29**, 1–16.

McIndoe-Calder, T. (2018). Hyperinflation in Zimbabwe: Money demand, seigniorage and aid shocks, *Applied Economics* **50**(15), 1659–1675.

Melancon, G. (1999). Honour in opium? the British declaration of war on China, 1839–1840, *The International History Review* **21**(4), 855–874.

Meltzer, A. and Robinson, S. (1989). Stability under the gold standard in practice, in *Money, History, and International Finance: Essays in Honor of Anna J. Schwartz*, pp. 163–202 (Chicago, IL: University of Chicago Press).

Merton, R. C. and Samuelson, P. A. (1992). *Continuous-Time Finance*, (Hoboken, NJ: Wiley-Blackwell).

Meyer, L. H. (2012). *The Supply-Side Effects of Economic Policy*, Vol. 1 (Boston/The Hague/London: Kluwer Nijhoff Publishing).

Michaelian, K. (2005). Thermodynamic stability of ecosystems, *Journal of Theoretical Biology* **237**(3), 323–335.

Mill, J. S. (1836). On the definition of political economy; and on the method of investigation proper to it, *London and Westminster Review* **4**(October), 120–164.

Mill, J. S. (1998). *Principles of Political Economy: And, Chapters on Socialism* (Oxford, USA: Oxford University Press).

Mill, J. S. (2012). A system of logic, in *Arguing About Science* (New York: Harper & Brothers, Publishers), pp. 243–267.

Mirowski, P. (1991). *More Heat Than Light: Economics as Social Physics, Physics as Nature's Economics* (Cambridge: Cambridge University Press).

Misak, C. (2020). *Frank Ramsey: A Sheer Excess of Powers* (Oxford: Oxford University Press).

Mishra, S. K. (2007). A brief history of production functions, Available at *SSRN* 1020577, (Amsterdam: Elsevier).

Modigliani, F. and Miller, M. H. (1963). Corporate income taxes and the cost of capital: A correction, *The American Economic Review* **53**(3), 433–443.

Morgenstern, O. *et al.* (1935). Perfect foresight and economic equilibrium, in *Selected Economic Writings of Oskar Morgenstern*, pp. 169–183 (Abingdon and New York: Routledge).

Morrissey, T. W., Cha, Y., Wolf, S., and Khan, M. (2020). Household economic instability: Constructs, measurement, and implications, *Children and Youth Services Review* **118**, 105502.

Moss, D. A. and Kintgen, E. (2010). *The Dojima Rice Market and the Origins of Futures Trading* (Cambridge, MA: Harvard Business School).

Murphey, D. D. (2008). Greenspan's bubbles: The age of ignorance at the federal reserve, *The Journal of Social, Political, and Economic Studies* **33**(4), 521.

Myers, S. C. and Majluf, N. S. (1984). Corporate financing and investment decisions when firms have information that investors do not have, *Journal of Financial Economics* **13**(2), 187–221.

Nichols, D. and Gonczy, A. M. L. (1992). *Modern Money Mechanics: A Workbook on Bank Reserves and Deposit Expansion* (Chicago: Federal Reserve Bank of Chicago).

Nietzsche, F. (1908). *Human, All too Human: A Book for Free Spirits* (Cheyenne, WY: Newcomb Livraria Press).

Noether, E. (1983). Invariante variations probleme, in Gesammelte Abhandlungen, Collected Papers (Berlin: Springer), pp. 231–239.

Nymoen, R. (2005). *Introductory Dynamic Macroeconomics* (Paper) (Oslo: Department of Economics, University of Oslo).

Obstfeld, M. (1992). *Dynamic Optimization in Continuous-Time Economic Models (A Guide for the Perplexed)* (Manuscript) (Berkeley, CA: University of California).

Oikarinen, E. (2014). *Studies on Housing Price Dynamics* (Turku, Finland: Turku School of Economics).

Oosterlinck, K. (2017). *History of Forward Contracts (Historical Evidence for Forward Contracts)*, pp. 1–3 (London, UK: Palgrave, Macmillan).

O'sullivan, A., Sheffrin, S. M., and Perez, S. J. (2008). *Economics: Principles, Applications, and Tools* (Edingbur, Scotland: Pearson Education).

Partnoy, F. (2010). *Infectious Greed: How Deceit and Risk Corrupted the Financial Markets* (London: Profile Books).

Pearl, J. and Mackenzie, D. (2018). *The Book of Why: The New Science of Cause and Effect* (New York: Basic Books).

Pfeiffer, R. H. (1922). On babylonian-assyrian feudalism (ilku), *The American Journal of Semitic Languages and Literatures* **39**(1), 66–68.

Prasso, S. T. (2001). The Riel value of money: How the world's only attempt to abolish money has hindered Cambodia's economic development, *Asia-Pacific Issues*, January (49), 1–8.

Prigogine, I. and Stengers, I. (2018). *Order Out of Chaos: Man's New Dialogue with Nature* (New York: Verso Books).

Quine, W. V. O. (1951). Two dogmas of empiricism, *The Philosophical Review*, **60**(1), 20–43.

Radford, R. A. (1945). The economic organisation of a pow camp, *Economica* **12**(48), 189–201.

Raine, A., Foster, J., and Potts, J. (2006). The new entropy law and the economic process, *Ecological Complexity* **3**(4), 354–360.

Ramsey, F. P. (1928). A mathematical theory of saving, *The Economic Journal* **38**(152), 543–559.

Richardson, T. (2015). Banking panics of the gilded age, *Federal Reserve History* (December).

Robbins, L. (2007). *An Essay on the Nature and Significance of Economic Science* (Auburm, AL: Ludwig von Mises Institute).

Robinson, J. and Dow, S. (2021). *Economic Philosophy* (Oxfordshire, UK: Routledge Classic).

Ross, W. D. *et al.* (1928). *Metaphysica*, Vol. 8 (Oxford, UK: Clarendon Press).

Rossi-Hansberg, E. (2019). Geography of growth and development, in *Oxford Research Encyclopedia of Economics and Finance* (USA: Oxford University Press).

Russell, B. (1914). *Scientific Method in Philosophy* (Oxford, UK: Clarendon Press).

Russell, B. (2009). *The Philosophy of Logical Atomism* (London and New York: Routledge).

Sargent, T. J. (2009). *Dynamic Macroeconomic Theory* (Cambridge, MA: Harvard University Press).

Sayers, S. (2011). *Private Property and Communism* (London, UK: Palgrave, Macmillan), pp. 101–132.

Schopenhauer, A. (1901). *The Wisdom of Life, and Other Essays*, Vol. 19 (Washington and New York: Dunne).

Schopenhauer, A. (1966). *The World as Will and Representation*, Vol. 2 (New York: Routledge).

Schwartenbeck, P., FitzGerald, T. H., Mathys, C., Dolan, R., Kronbichler, M., and Friston, K. (2015). Evidence for surprise minimization over value maximization in choice behavior, *Scientific Reports* **5**(1), 16575.

Seierstad, A. and Sydsæter, K. (2009). Conditions implying the vanishing of the Hamiltonian at infinity in optimal control problems, *Optimization Letters* **3**(4), 507–512.

Sharpe, W. F. (1964). Capital asset prices: A theory of market equilibrium under conditions of risk, *The Journal of Finance* **19**(3), 425–442.

Shephard, R. W. (2015). *Theory of Cost and Production Functions* (Princeton: Princeton University Press).

Sinha, A. (2010). A note on Ricardo's 'invariable measure of value', *Cahiers d'économie politique/Papers in Political Economy* **1**, 133–144.

Skidelsky, R. (2010). The crisis of capitalism: Keynes versus Marx, *Indian Journal of Industrial Relations*, 321–335.

Smith, A. (1822). *The Theory of Moral Sentiments*, Vol. 1 (London: Penguin).

Smith, A. (2010). *The Wealth of Nations: An Inquiry into the Nature and Causes of the Wealth of Nations* (Oxford: Clarendon).

Smith, L. B., Rosen, K. T., and Fallis, G. (1988). Recent developments in economic models of housing markets, *Journal of Economic Literature* **26**(1), 29–64.

Snowdon, B. and Vane, H. R. (2002). *An Encyclopedia of Macroeconomics* (Northampton, MA and Cheltenham Glos: Edward Elgar Publishing).

Snyder, L. V. and Shen, Z.-J. M. (2019). *Fundamentals of Supply Chain Theory* (John Wiley & Sons).

Solow, R. M. (1956). A contribution to the theory of economic growth, *The Quarterly Journal of Economics* **70**(1), 65–94.

Solow, R. M. (1985). Economic history and economics, *The American Economic Review* **75**(2), 328–331.

Solow, R. M. and Diamond, P. A. (1990). *Growth, Productivity, Unemployment: Essays to Celebrate Bob Solow's Birthday* (Cambridge, MA: MIT Press).

Sornette, D. (2014). Physics and financial economics (1776–2014): Puzzles, ising and agent-based models, *Reports on Progress in Physics* **77**(6), 062001.

Spear, S. E. and Young, W. (2014). Optimum savings and optimal growth: The Cass–Malinvaud–Koopmans nexus, *Macroeconomic Dynamics* **18**(1), 215–243.

Spence, M. (1973). Job market signaling, *Quarterly Journal of Economics* **87**(3), 355–374.

Sraffa, P. and Dobb, M. H. (1951). *The Works and Correspondence of David Ricardo*, Vol. 1 (Cambridge: Cambridge University Press).

Stearns, P. N. (2020). *The Industrial Revolution in World History* (New York and London: Routledge).

Stellinga, B., de Hoog, J., van Riel, A., and de Vries, C. (2021). How does the sovereign money system work? in *Money and Debt: The Public Role of Banks* (Cham, Switzerland: Springer), pp. 117–137.

Stewart, I. M. (1979). *Reasoning and Method in Economics: An Introduction to Economic Methodology* (London: McGraw-Hill Book Company).

Stewart, M. (2009). *The Management Myth: Why the Experts Keep Getting It Wrong* (Ashland, OR: Blackstone Audio, Incorporated).

Stewart, W. and Roberts, T. (2012). Food security and the role of fertilizer in supporting it, *Procedia Engineering* **46**, 76–82.

Sydsæter, K., Seierstad, A., and Strom, A. (2008). *Further Mathematics for Economic Analysis* (Harlow, England: Pearson Education).

Tahan, M. (1993). *The Man Who Counted: A Collection of Mathematical Adventures* (London: W. W. Norton & Company).

Taylor, B. (2013). Tiberius used quantitative easing to solve the financial crisis of 33 AD, SyesWildeShut, https://syesworldview.wordpress.com/.

Thirlwall, A. (2004). The balance of payments constraint as an explanation of international growth rate differences, in *Essays on Balance of Payments Constrained Growth* (Routledge), pp. 39–45.

Tirole, J. (2010). *The Theory of Corporate Finance* (Princeton: Princeton University Press).

Trever, A. A. (1924). The age of Hesiod: A study in economic history, *Classical Philology* **19**(2), 157–168.

Turing, A. M. (1980). Computing machinery and intelligence. *Creative Computing* **6**(1), 44–53.

Van Fraassen, B. C. (1980). *The Scientific Image* (Oxford: Oxford University Press).

Van Fraassen, B. C. (2000). The false hopes of traditional epistemology, *Philosophical and Phenomenological Research*, 253–280.

Vandeput, N. (2020). *Inventory Optimization: Models and Simulations* (Berlin and Bostan: Walter de Gruyter GmbH & Co KG).

Vine, D., Deppen, P., and Bolger, L. (2021). Drawdown: Improving us and global security through military base closures abroad, *Quincy Institute* **20**.

Von Hayek, F. A. (1989). The pretence of knowledge, *The American Economic Review* **79**(6), 3–7.

Von Mises, L. (1990). *Economic Calculation in the Socialist Commonwealth* (Auburn, Alabama: Ludwig von Mises Institute).

Wallis, J. J., Weingast, B. R., and North, D. C. (2006). The corporate origins of individual rights, in *Economic History Association Meeting* https://econweb.umd.edu/~wallis/MyPapers/Wallis_Weingast_North_COIR_EHA.pdf.

Weber, T. A. (2011). *Optimal Control Theory with Applications in Economics* (Cambridge, MA: MIT Press).

Werner, R. (2015). *Princes of the Yen: Japan's Central Bankers and the Transformation of the Economy* (London and New York: Routledge).

Werner, R. A. (2014). Can banks individually create money out of nothing? The theories and the empirical evidence, *International Review of Financial Analysis* **36**, 1–19.

Wheaton, W. C. (1990). Vacancy, search, and prices in a housing market matching model, *Journal of Political Economy* **98**(6), 1270–1292.

Whitaker, A. C. (1904). *History and Criticism of the Labor Theory of Value in English Political Economy*, Vol. 19 (New York: Columbia University Press).

White, H. C. (2001). *Markets From Networks: Socioeconomic Models of Production* (Princeton: Princeton University Press).

Wiener, N. (2019). *Cybernetics or Control and Communication in the Animal and the Machine* (Cambridge, MA: MIT press).

Wittgenstein, L. (2009). *Philosophical Investigations.* (Hoboken, NJ: John Wiley & Sons).

Wittgenstein, L. (2013). *Tractatus logico-philosophicus* (New York and London: Routledge).

Xenophon (1890). *The Economist*, Vol. 1 (London: Macmillan and Company), translated by Dakyns, Henry Graham and others.

Yamaguchi, K. and Yamaguchi, Y. (2021). Accounting system dynamics modeling of money stock as debts: Theory and case analysis of Japan, in *Feedback Economics: Economic Modeling with System Dynamics* (Cham, Switzerland: Springer), pp. 69–95.

Yarbrough, B. V. and Yarbrough, R. M. (2006). *The World Economy: Open-Economy Macroeconomics and Finance*, 7th edn. (Mason, Ohio: Thomson South-Western).

Zedong, M. (1987). On contradiction, *Chinese Studies in Philosophy* **19**(2), 20–82.

Zuckerman, G. (2010). *The Greatest Trade Ever: The Behind-the-Scenes Story of How John Paulson Defied Wall Street and Made Financial History* (New York: Crown Currency).

Index

www.ingramcontent.com/pod-product-compliance
Lightning Source LLC
LaVergne TN
LVHW051053210926
848486LV00002B/99
9789819814992